STUDIA POST-BIBLICA
VOLUMEN DUODEVICESIMUM

STUDIA POST-BIBLICA

INSTITUTA A P. A. H. DE BOER

ADIUVANTIBUS

T. JANSMA ET J. SMIT SIBINGA

EDIDIT

J. C. H. LEBRAM

VOLUMEN DUODEVICESIMUM

LEIDEN
E. J. BRILL
1971

THE TRIAL OF JESUS

A STUDY IN THE GOSPELS AND JEWISH
HISTORIOGRAPHY FROM 1770 TO THE PRESENT DAY

BY

DAVID R. CATCHPOLE

LEIDEN
E. J. BRILL
1971

75 - 864216

To

ANN

CONTENTS

INTRODUCTION

This book is an attempt to survey and analyse the distinctive views of Jewish scholars who have written about the Trial of Jesus during the last two hundred years. It also represents an effort to examine some of the many historical problems surrounding that trial.

The scope of the work is dictated in time by the change in the situation of the Jews around the end of the 18th century, in which movements towards external emancipation, together with parallel internal religious tendencies, enabled the Jews to treat more and more openly the problem of Jesus. This problem of Jesus has, however, been for the Jews intensely and painfully focussed in the problem of his trial. For Jesus' own via dolorosa had tragically and shamefully become a blood-stained path for his fellow-countrymen of later generations. Indeed, the trial of Jesus had, in a way which Christians can now only recall with heartfelt and agoinzed sympathy, led to a reversal of roles which placed the Jew in the dock. While at one and the same time one who tries to investigate objectively the course of historical events must not allow conclusions to be prejudged and dictated by subjective considerations, he cannot fail to understand why the very occurrence of a trial of Jesus before Jewish authorities should often have been denied by Jews, partly no doubt in self-defence, and similarly by many Christians, partly no doubt in the interests of better and more cordial relationships between Christians and Jews. Whereas this book sets out the case for a different conclusion from the evidence, viz., that the Sanhedrin did examine and condemn Jesus, I wish to state categorically at the outset that I abhor anti-Semitism and totally disown and repudiate any logic by any one who has used the view that Jewish leaders tried Jesus as an excuse, pretext or rationalization for persecuting in any form any Jews of any time. Anti-Semitism, whatever its alleged reasoning, is sickening and sub-human.

Whereas the present historical study begins with Mendelssohn in 1770, this was of course not the beginning of Jewish attempts to wrestle with the problem. The classic texts recording these efforts are the Talmudic ones, and for this reason the first section of this work begins with their influence. Within the overall tendency to castigate the credentials and obliterate the influence of these texts it can be seen that an unconscious predilection for their orientation on Jesus remains as well as at other times a plain and open espousal of their ideas. The story of this mole-like influence, working silently underground but every so often appearing bluntly on the surface, is the first to be told.

In the Talmudic sources a common theme transcends all variations and qualifications: Jesus was a dangerous teacher who led Israel astray. But how and why? The answer can only be found by examining the charge laid against him—in other words, issues of christology and law, of Jesus' consciousness and theological environment. In particular this involves complex discussions of the titles Messiah and Son of God, joined in parallel in Mk 14.61 and Mt 26.63 but separate in Lk 22.67-70. A second main topic therefore follows logically, containing within itself questions which need to be set in their Jewish context and also examined for their own sake. Within an overall trend toward an evaluation of Jesus' downfall in political terms, Jewish writers have wrestled with theological issues too. Accordingly while scrutinizing their approaches, this second chapter includes a discussion of such pressing questions as messianic transcendence (pp. 92-94), Jesus' alleged Pharisaism and conservative position vis-à-vis the law (pp. 107-112), Jesus and the Zealots (pp. 118-126), the possible crimes committed by Jesus (pp. 126-148), and the identity of the arrest party (pp. 148-152).

It is at this point that attention to an urgent source-critical problem can no longer be delayed, in spite of the fairly restricted reference to it by Jewish scholars until recent times: the origin and historical value of Luke 22.54-71. Other sections of the Lukan Passion narrative have been examined by Jeremias, Schürmann and Rehkopf, but a detailed analysis of the sections immediately bearing on the Sanhedrin hearing has still needed to be undertaken. If the results here proposed are agreed, then a new approach to the historical problems of Jesus' trial can fairly be claimed as necessary.

The final chapter investigates two problems of related character and recurring influence: the relation of Jesus' trial to Mishnaic legal procedure, and the question of Jewish freedom not only to pass but also to execute death sentences. While the role of the first may be said to have gradually diminished, that of the latter has risen to something of a crescendo in recent years. On both these questions I have attempted a survey of Jewish argumentation and of what can now be proposed as a tentative conclusion.

This material was presented in an earlier form as a Ph. D. dissertation at the University of Cambridge in 1968. I owe a very great debt to Dr. Ernst Bammel who supervised my work and not only suggested the Jewish historiographical framework for this study but also continually gave me stimulus and guidance. I am also most grateful to Professor C. F. D. Moule for many kindnesses and encouragements, and also for the friendly interest of the late Professor Josef Blinzler. I also recall with gratitude my former colleagues and students at Clifton Theological College, Bristol, among whom much of the writing of this material took place, and whose friendship and kindness I shall always prize. My friends Jennifer Draffan, Michael Freeman, William Horbury and Alan Millard generously helped at various stages in the preparation of the manuscript and I would like to take this opportunity of thanking them. I would also like to express my appreciation of Dr. J. C. H. Lebram's assistance with the publication of this book. Finally, my wife's persistent encouragement and unselfish help during the production of this volume have been an unfaltering support for which I cannot be too thankful.

Lancaster, September 1970.

ABBREVIATIONS

ASTI	=	Annual of the Swedish Theological Institute
Bib	=	Biblica
BibZ	=	Biblische Zeitschrift
BJRL	=	Bulletin of the John Rylands Library
CBQ	=	Catholic Biblical Quarterly
CJT	=	Canadian Journal of Theology
CommViat	=	Communio Viatorum
EJ	=	Encyclopaedia Judaica
EvTh	=	Evangelische Theologie
HJ	=	Hibbert Journal
HTR	=	Harvard Theological Review
HUCA	=	Hebrew Union College Annual
JBL	=	Journal of Biblical Literature
JE	=	Jewish Encyclopaedia
JJGL	=	Jahrbuch für Jüdische Geschichte und Literatur
JJS	=	Journal of Jewish Studies
JJSoc	=	Jewish Journal of Sociology
JQ	=	Jewish Quarterly
JQR	=	Jewish Quarterly Review
JR	=	Journal of Religion
JTS	=	Journal of Theological Studies
JZ	=	Jüdische Zeitschrift
LJ	=	Die Lehren des Judentums
LQHR	=	London Quarterly and Holborn Review
MGWJ	=	Monatsschrift für Geschichte und Wissenschaft des Judentums
NovT	=	Novum Testamentum
NTS	=	New Testament Studies
RB	=	Revue Biblique
REJ	=	Revue des Études Juives
Rev Hist	=	Revue Historique
RHPR	=	Revue d'Histoire et de Philosophie Réligieuse
RHR	=	Revue de l'Histoire des Religions
RSR	=	Recherches de Science Réligieuse
StTh	=	Studia Theologica
TDNT	=	Theological Dictionary of the New Testament
ThLZ	=	Theologische Literaturzeitung
ThZ	=	Theologishe Zeitschrift
TU	=	Texte und Untersuchungen
TWNT	=	Theologisches Wörterbuch zum Neuen Testament
VC	=	Vigiliae Christianae
ZNW	=	Zeitschrift für die Neutestamentliche Wissenschaft
ZRGG	=	Zeitschrift für Religion und Geistesgeschichte

CHAPTER ONE

THE INFLUENCE OF RABBINIC SOURCES

A. Survey of the Sources

Rabbinic literature contains a number of texts referring to Jesus of Nazareth, and the first major task of this work is to examine the influence of these texts on Jewish writers during our period.

There are a number of reasons for beginning with b. Sanh. 107b (cf. the parallel versions in b.Sota 47a and j.Hag. 2.2), part of the Gemara on Sanh. 10.2. Firstly, as M. Guttmann has pointed out, it is the main source from which the conclusion has been drawn that the ancient Jewish tradition knew about someone called Jesus.[1] Correspondingly, objections to this text have often been made the reason for dismissing with it all the Jesus-passages in Rabbinic literature.[2] Secondly, this passage stands on its own as a partial exception to the rule stated by G. Lindeskog, viz., that to the oldest Rabbinic witnesses Jesus stands as a heretic.[3] The text runs as follows:

> Our Rabbis taught: Let the left hand repulse but the right hand always invite back: not as Elisha, who thrust Gehazi away with both hands, and not like R. Joshua b. Perahjah, who repulsed Jesus (the Nazarene) with both hands . . . . . What of R. Joshua b. Perahjah?— When King Jannai slew our Rabbis, R. Joshua b. Perahjah (and Jesus) fled to Alexandria of Egypt. On the resumption of peace, Simeon b. Shetach sent to him: 'From me, (Jerusalem) the holy city, to thee, Alexandria of Egypt (my sister). My husband dwelleth within thee and I am desolate.' He arose, went, and found himself in a certain inn, where great honour was shown him. 'How beautiful is this Acsania!'[4] Thereupon (Jesus) observed, 'Rabbi, her eyes are narrow.' 'Wretch', he

---

[1] MGWJ 75 (1931), 252.

[2] Thus, the non-Jew and former Christian, G. B. English, all of whose arguments are learnt from Jews, in his book written in 1813: The Grounds of Christianity, London 1852. Cf. also S. Hirsch, Die Religionsphilosophie der Juden, Leipzig 1842, 622; L. Philippson, Haben wirklich die Juden Jesum gekreuzigt?, 2nd ed., Leipzig 1901, 23; E. Schreiber, Die Prinzipien des Judenthums, Leipzig 1877, 108.

[3] 'Es steht fest, daß Jesus schon in den ältesten rabbinischen Zeugnissen als Ketzer hingestellt wird.' Die Jesusfrage im neuzeitlichen Judentum, Uppsala 1938, 16.

[4] The word denotes both inn and innkeeper.

rebuked him, 'dost thou thus engage thyself?' He sounded four hundred trumpets and excommunicated him. He (Jesus) came before him many times pleading, 'Receive me.' But he would pay no heed to him. One day he (R. Joshua) was reciting the Shema when Jesus came before him. He intended to receive him and made a sign to him. He (Jesus) thinking that it was to repel him, went, put up a brick and worshipped it. 'Repent', said he (R. Joshua) to him. He replied, 'I have thus learned from thee: He who sins and causes others to sin is not afforded the means of repentance.' And a Master has said, 'Jesus the Nazarene practised magic and led Israel astray'. [1]

With this must be compared the parallel version in b.Sota. 47a where, in some manuscripts, the disciple is anonymous. Also of importance is the text of j.Hag. 2.2:

> The inhabitants of Jerusalem wanted to confer on Juda b. Tabai the functions of Nasi, but he had taken flight and gone to Alexandria. So the Jerusalemites wrote: 'Jerusalem the great to Alexandria the little! For how long will my husband continue to stay with you while I for my part remain abandoned?' Juda, in order to comply, left the town by ship. 'What was there lacking in Deborah the hostess who gave us lodging?' One of his disciples replied: 'Master, she was one-eyed.' 'You offend there on two counts,' said Juda. 'First, you surprise me in having regarded her as beautiful; then, it is a proof that you looked at her with desire. In fact I did not say it was a matter of a beautiful woman, and I only spoke about her in passing.' [2]

Clearly there is a common pattern reproduced in both these versions, and this has led scholars to the conclusion that b.Sanh. 107b is secondary as compared with either the anonymous b.Sota. 47a version or j.Hag. 2.2 [3] or both. [4] It is likely, however, that in the evolution of the tradition the mention of Jesus is original and has been altered to 'one of his disciples' (a) in line with the tendency away from explicitly mentioning Jesus' name, a tendency manifest in e.g. the 'such a one' reference in Yeb. 4.13, and (b) as a solution to the chronological problem. [5] As to the relationship between the two texts quoted above,

---

[1] Translation from I. Epstein ed., The Babylonian Talmud, London 1935.

[2] Text in M. Schwab, Le Talmud de Jérusalem, Paris 1960.

[3] R. T. Herford, Christianity in Talmud and Midrash, London 1903, 52. On the Jewish side, see the authors mentioned on p. 61.

[4] J. Blinzler, Der Prozeß Jesu, 4th ed., Regensburg 1969, 41f.

[5] J. Jeremias, The Eucharistic Words of Jesus, 3rd ed., London 1966, 19, regards the text as referring to a totally different Jesus who lived c. 100 B.C. The reason suggested by R. T. Herford, op.cit. 53, for the alleged insertion of the name Jesus, i.e. a desire to explain the connexion of Jesus with Egypt, would simply mean the solution of one problem by the creation of a worse one.

the combination of common features and divergent elements suggests that we have to do not with straight dependence but with parallel schemes. The tradition, clearly a Tannaitic one, in b.Sanh. 107b must therefore be examined in its own right.[1]

As to the content of the text, certain details like the worship of the brick are notoriously difficult to interpret.[2] But other features are clear and particularly important: (a) Jesus is dated c. 100 B.C.[3] This means that he is linked with an event bringing tragedy to Judaism. (b) Jesus was not wrong from the beginning, but only went astray at a second stage. Originally he had been the disciple of a very distinguished Rabbi,[4] had moved in Pharisaic circles and had been one of the righteous victims of Sadducean persecution. In passing, it is worth noting that there is here a point of agreement with the view of Josephus that Jesus was a σοφὸς ἀνήρ (= hakam) and διδάσκαλος.[5] (c) Jesus receives sympathetic treatment [6] to the extent that a large share of the blame lies on the other side. Thus the tragedy resulted from what on Jesus' side were only misunderstandings, firstly of R. Joshua's remark about the inn, and secondly of the gesture welcoming him back. On the Rabbi's side we have an unfortunate intransigence and, finally, a clumsiness which the tradition deprecates. (d) Although the reproving and ultimately the exclusion of Jesus were unfortunate, the latter was in the end unavoidable. It could have been wished otherwise, hence R. Joshua's urging of repentance even after Jesus had worshipped the brick—but sadly the halakah had been laid down: 'He who sins and causes others to sin is not afforded the means of repentance.'

It is clear that we have here a significantly different attitude from

---

[1] For the interpretation of the Talmudic Jesus-passages I am in many respects indebted to the exposition by E. Bammel in a seminar in Cambridge in 1964-65. Cf. E. Bammel, Christian Origins in Jewish Tradition, NTS 13 (1967), 317-335.

[2] For two recent attempts, cf. H. J. Zimmels, Jesus and putting up a Brick, JQR 43 (1953), 225-228, who amends the text to replace 'brick' by 'fish', and S. B. Lachs, A Jesus Passage in the Talmud re-examined, JQR 59 (1969), 244-247, who takes as basis the apocryphal gospels' story of Jesus constructing twelve sparrows out of clay, and also amends the text so that it reads at the end 'the people worshipped him'. Lachs appeals to the association of idolatry and a brick in b.A.Z. 46a,53b.

[3] For the persistence of this Jewish tradition dating Jesus somewhere in the 2nd century B.C., see Nachmanides' scheme placing him 30 weeks, i.e. 210 years, before A.D.70; cited in O. S. Rankin, Jewish Religious Polemic, Edinburgh 1956, 195. For the theological basis of this dating, E. Bammel, Christian Origins, 321.

[4] E. Bammel, Christian Origins, 321.

[5] Cf. the version reconstructed by T. Reinach, Josèphe sur Jésus. REJ 35 (1897), 1-18.

[6] Noted already by H. Laible, Jesus Christus im Thalmud, Berlin 1891, 44.

that underlying, for instance, b.Sanh. 43a or 67a.[1] The positive characteristics allowed to Jesus are numerous: he is not in the story itself a
magician, his personal background is Pharisaic, he goes to Egypt for
the best of reasons, far from being allied to the 'malkuth' [2] he is persecuted by it, and Judaism has even been harmed by the sad break with
him. All of this suggests so unhardened and flexible an approach to
Jesus that one suspects that the tradition may have arisen quite early in
the Tannaitic period.[3]

The next important text is b.Sanh. 43a, a Tannaitic tradition included in the Gemara to Sanh. 6.1:

> It was taught: On the eve of the Passover Yeshu (ms.M: the Naza
> rean) was hanged. For forty days before the execution took place, a
> herald went forth and cried, 'He is going forth to be stoned because he
> has practised sorcery and enticed Israel to apostasy. Anyone who can
> say anything in his favour, let him come forward and plead on his
> behalf.' But since nothing was brought forward in his favour he was
> hanged on the eve of the Passover (Florentine ms.: and the eve of
> Sabbath)!—Ulla retorted: Do you suppose that he was one for whom
> a defence could be made? Was he not a mesith, concerning whom
> Scripture says, Neither shalt thou spare neither shalt thou conceal
> him? With Yeshu however it was different, for he was connected with
> the government.

This is a remarkable passage, both for detailed content and apologetic stance. The latter feature is specially important for the development of a trend in later Jewish historiography. As the Jewish scholar
T. Reinach noted with some exasperation,[4] the Jews fully accept
responsibility for the trial and execution of Jesus. In spite of the undeniably historical Roman execution, Jesus is here tried and executed
according to the Sanh. 6.4 method of stoning and hanging. Here then
we have a passage which is early in date, which makes a defence against
Christian allegations (the 40 days appeal almost certainly seeks to
repel some kind of accusation), which stems from circles well aware
of the anti-Jewish polemic in the gospels—and yet does not find that

---

[1] See below, pp. 6,9-11.
[2] b.Sanh. 43a.
[3] The more flexible attitude to Jesus in the Tannaitic period is noted by Lindeskog, op.cit. 15.
[4] Art.cit. 17: 'Les Juifs eux-mêmes, à trois ou quatre siècles de l'événement ont
eu l'imprudence d'accepter la responsabilité de ce prétendu forfait et presque de
s'en vanter.'

defence in a denial of Jewish involvement.[1] At the extreme point of Jewish participation indeed, there can be no question of dependence on the gospels. In a nutshell, the Jews' defence is found in a statement of the reasons for and the justice of their involvement, rather than, as has been the modern pattern, a denial of that involvement or reduction of it to the handing over of Jesus to Pilate. This primitive approach finds confirmation in the repeated acceptance of Jewish involvement by Celsus' Jew in Contra Celsum II. 4, 5, 9:

> His Jew then says to believers from the Jewish people: Quite recent-
> ly, when we punished this fellow who cheated you, you abandoned the
> law of your fathers . . . . . . Celsus repeats himself about Jesus, saying
> now for the second time that as an offender he was punished by the
> Jews . . . . . . When we had convicted him, condemned him and decided
> that he should be punished . . . .[2]

Independent corroboration of Jewish participation is also provided by the letter of Mara bar Serapion, dated by J. Blinzler [3] in the period around A.D. 73, and furthermore it is entirely proper to ask how Paul could write 1 Thess. 2.15 if Jesus was condemned simply by Roman sentence and execution.[4] The earliness and persistence of this wide-spread tradition of Jewish involvement raises a question-mark over modern development in the opposite direction [5] although it must be stated clearly and categorically that Jewish involvement then can in no sense whatever carry any hint of Jewish guilt at any other time.[6]

As regards the content of b.Sanh. 43a, the most pressing questions concern relationship with the gospels and historicity.[7] Apologetic

---

[1] This matter of Tendenz finds a parallel in the interpretation of Christian sour-ces. It is commonly argued that the Sanhedrin trial narrative was generated by anti-Jewish motives, and that this wish to blame the Jews *increases* from Mark, through Matthew and Luke, to John. But in fact, the development is, on this sequence, from plain Sanhedrin proceedings (Mark and Matthew) to much less plain ones (Luke) and finally to no trial at all in John (at least in ch.18)!

[2] Greek text in P. Koetschau, Die griechischen christlichen Schriftsteller der ersten drei Jahrhunderte, Leipzig 1899, 130ff; English translation by H. Chad-wick, Origen: Contra Celsum, Cambridge 1953, 69,70,73.

[3] Der Prozeß Jesu, 4th ed. Regensburg 1969, 52-56.

[4] J. Blinzler, Zum Prozeß Jesu, Lebendiges Zeugnis 1 (1966), 18.

[5] Blinzler, art.cit. 5.

[6] See later, pp. 263-265.

[7] Reinach, art. 17, impugns the sources because of the unhistorical dating and their late date, and he goes on to make the reconstructed Josephus passage, Ant. 18. 63-64, definitive for the extent of Jewish participation. However, the dating of these traditions three or four centuries after the event runs aground on the fact that b.Sanh. 43a preserves a baraita, and the word 'imprudence' (see footnote 19 above) betrays a modern Tendenz. The evidence of Celsus also damages Reinach's dating.

motives are perhaps not so powerful as is sometimes assumed. It is possible that the unhistorical 40 day appeal by the herald is directed against allegations of haste, so that only accusation and no defence witnesses were heard,[1] but it may simply be aiming to demonstrate how impossible it was to weaken or deny Jesus' offence, and therefore how unavoidable was his condemnation. The timing 'on the eve of Passover'[2] which agrees with Jn 18.28, has been accepted by Blinzler[3] and others as lacking in apologetic Tendenz and therefore as the one historical element; Lindeskog on the other hand is not prepared to allow any historical value.[4] While it is true that apologetic motives are not readily discernible in this time-note, the obstacle in the way of accepting its historicity is the uncertain strength of other evidence favouring an execution on 14 Nisan.[5]

---

[1] The '40 days' reference is so exaggerated that it contradicts the ruling of Sanh. 3.8, 6.1, dating back to R. Simeon b.Gamaliel. The baraita and R. Ulla agree in apologetic method. It is important that the gospels do not accuse the Jewish leaders of infringing their own laws. Rather the reverse: in contrast with the explicit allegation of illegality in the trial of Paul (Acts 23.3), Mk 14.55-59 may impugn the motivation of the court by means of ἐζήτουν, but shows its procedure as strictly honourable by virtue of requiring testimony to agree and rejecting it when it did not (Mk 14.55,56,59). Contra C. Maurer, Das Messiasgeheimnis des Markusevangeliums, NTS 14 (1968), 515-516. Maurer begs the question of whether the laws he mentions were in existence, and he also proposes to work from Mark's own presentation in spite of Mark's failure to explain what the infringements were. This is a critical objection to Maurer's theory since Mark normally explains Palestinian customs if this is necessary, and without such explanation here the Roman readers would scarcely understand his point. As to allegations of illegality in the other gospels, the ψευδομαρτυρία of Mt 26.59 is immediately overshadowed by the slightly contradictiory οὐχ εὗρον, 26.60a, and the careful observance of the two-witnesses rule, 26.60b. Equally, the χρεία μαρτυρῶν, Mk 14.63= Mt 26.65, which the high priest accepts, is matched by the χρεία μαρτυρίας of the Lukan tradition. From the beginning, the Christian traditions clearly believe that an innocent man had been condemned, but this is understood in a kerygmatic rather than simply legal sense (thus the speeches in Acts).

[2] The variant 'on eve of Sabbath' is of course in agreement with all four gospels.

[3] Der Prozeß Jesu, 44,106.

[4] Jesusfrage, 15; similarly, G. Bornkamm, Jesus of Nazareth, London 1960, 28; R. H. Fuller, The New Testament in current Study, London 1963, 40.

[5] It is not possible to appeal to Paul since ἀπαρχή, 1 Cor 15.23, does not allude to any dating of the resurrection on 16 Nisan but, as the context makes clear, belongs to the basic structure of Paul's 'theology of solidarity' (cf. similarly the ἀπαρχή references in Rom 8.23 and 1 Cor 16.15). 1 Cor 5.7, a pre-Pauline formula, is also theological in purpose and does not presuppose a time-scheme. On the contrary, 1 Cor 10.16 indicates that Paul regarded the Lord's Supper as a Passover meal. Johannine data is an equivocal support, since (a) it does not seem possible to eliminate Passover lamb theology from Jn 1.29 and 19.36, and (b) traces of Passover ritual in Jn 6.51c and 13 support Synoptic dating. Cf. J. Jeremias, The Eucharistic Words of Jesus, 3rd ed. London 1966, 107f. The best argument for Johannine dating, apart from b.Sanh. 43a itself, is the balance of astronomical evidence.

Of particular interest is the charge levelled against Jesus, that he practised sorcery and led Israel astray. The allegation of sorcery is attested in authentic Synoptic passages, with the combined testimony of Q (Mt 12.24= Lk 11.15) and Mk 3.22. Thus, whereas there is no evidence in favour of locating this charge in the trial of Jesus, b.Sanh. 43a still reflects an historical tradition, and this element stands as a warning against total dismissal of the content of the Talmudic texts.

Next there is the 'mesith' charge (cf. Dt 13.6-11). Does this have any historical basis? The normal argument is that this must reflect the post-schism situation and be unhistorical. But let us pause. Suppose it were actually true that Jesus was condemned for leading the people astray. A simple and uncritical argument as above would mean that we could not, because of our own presuppositions, ever discover the true ground of Jesus' condemnation. Scholarship would be made the victim of its own methodological vicious circle. For the claim that a statement is born of a certain situation is not an historical judgement, but a statement about the evolution of a tradition *after* historicity has been examined and rejected. Consequently it is necessary to examine the evidence afresh.

Attention has recently been drawn by D. W. Wead to other non-Christian sources which take up the themes of the related passage, Dt 13.1-5.[1] Thus Josephus uses the terms παραδόξων ἔργων ποιητής and διδάσκαλος ἀνθρώπων, and Justin, Dial. 69, contains allusions to Jesus as μάγος and λαοπλάνης. Wead draws a line back from these and b.Sanh. 43a to Jn 19.7, so that the law in question is Dt 13.1-5, and he finds backing in the repeated legal reaction to signs in Jn 5.18 (7.19-24), 7.31f, 10.31-34 and 11.47-53. Within the Jewish proceedings against Jesus, he draws attention to Jn 18.19 and Mk 14.65, the latter being the only Synoptic support.

The πλάνος theme could draw on either Dt 13.1-5 or 13.6-11, and is in fact mentioned in several texts other than those cited, e.g. Mt 27.63f, possibly Lk 23.2,5 (διαστρέφων τὸ ἔθνος ἡμῶν .... διδάσκων), and Jn 7.12,47. However the Synoptic material is not firm and unequivocal, and it is not possible to conclude with Wead until Johannine texts have been subjected to far more critical scrutiny.

(a) Mk 14.65. If the source-critical position proposed in this book is correct, Lk 22.63-65 is a more primitive tradition of the mockery,[2] and there προφήτευσον has a more popular and less technical sense than

---

[1] We have a Law, NovT 11 (1969), 185-189.

[2] See later, pp. 174-183.

allusion to Dt 13 would require. 'Exercise the gift of second sight' is probably an order based on the 'smell and judge' test of messiahship [1] (b.Sanh. 93b), drawn from Is 11.3 by midrashic technique. This test having proved inconclusive, direct interrogation on this theme ensued (Lk 22.66-68).

(b) Mt 27.63f is weak support, though not totally negligible. It belongs with 28.11-15, which contains the doubtless early tradition that the resurrection claim could be dismissed as a hoax since the disciples stole the body, and μέχρι τῆς σήμερον certainly implies circulation over a period. Moreover, if, as is possible, Mt belongs to a pre-schism situation, the πλάνος references cannot be regarded as reflections of the schism.

(c) Lk 23.2,5 is ambiguous and could refer to the charge of political rather than religious subversion. In the former case it would doubtless have been understood by Luke as false, like the accusation of forbidding tribute. Moreover, in view of Luke's keenness on the theme of Jesus' teaching (cf. redactionally 19.47, 20.1, 21.37), and the geographical construction in 23.5, we may have here the hand of the evangelist.

Therefore Synoptic πλάνος references are not strong support, though it is certainly relevant that Jesus' teaching in matters of law and Christology [2] would make a readily understandable background for a Dt 13-formulated charge.

We are left with Johannine data—but this is not automatically to be devalued. In particular, Jn 18.19f merits attention.[3]

There are four features which count in favour of the section Jn 18.19-24: (a) The role attributed to Annas agrees with both the evidence of Acts and the weighty influence he retained by means of family connection even after his own deposition from office. (b) The material is untouched theologically, e.g. there are no Servant-type allusions to silence and a spirited reply is twice given by Jesus. There is also no Christological concentration: indeed comparison with the Pilate hearing, where John has certainly moulded his material, makes this passage seem plain and almost colourless. (c) There is no anti-Jewish Tendenz discernible, such as is often alleged to have influenced John

[1] Cf. J. D. M. Derrett, An Oriental Lawyer looks at the Trial of Jesus and the Doctrine of Redemption, London 1966, 20. Derrett in fact traces this back to Mk 14.65, but reasons of textual criticism deprive Mk of these allusions, and make Lk the text which corresponds most closely. See below. pp. 175f.

[2] See pp. 107ff, 141ff.

[3] Cf. E. Stauffer, Jesus and his Story, London 1960, 100; C. H. Dodd, Historical Tradition in the Fourth Gospel, Cambridge 1963, 95.

powerfully. (d) The slight dislocation caused by editorial activity at 18.13b,14 implies that there is a pre-Johannine tradition here to be redacted.

The specific exchange between Annas and Jesus is of great significance, but is not a piece of Johannine theology.[1] (a) The sense of κόσμος is not that of the typically Johannine created, often hostile, cosmos.[2] As at 7.4,26, which are the only passages parallel to this one, τῷ κόσμῳ is synonymous with (ἐν) παρρησίᾳ.[3] Further, the κόσμος is not in Jn the object of Jesus' teaching.[4] (b) The reference to teaching ἐν συναγωγῇ suggests a constant activity, such as we know from the Synoptics, and as ἐν τῷ ἱερῷ does in Jn (7.14-39, 8.12-20, 10.22-39). But Jn 6.59 is the only Johannine reference to fill it out, and this is hardly enough. (c) The term οἱ Ἰουδαῖοι is used in a simply ethnic sense and not in the normal Johannine sense of the Jerusalem leadership with cosmic overtones. (d) ἐν κρυπτῷ ἐλάλησα οὐδέν again does not fit the Johannine scheme of considerable private teaching.[5]

Jn 18.19f therefore shows clear signs of being pre-Johannine, and what is important about it from a legal angle is the combination of teaching, disciples and secrecy. This conjunction recalls Dt. 13.6-11, and coheres with b.Sanh. 43a. Therefore, while it cannot be affirmed with total confidence that Jesus was condemned on this count, it cannot be reckoned impossible.

The remaining Talmudic Jesus-passages can be dealt with more briefly, and extended comment is not appropriate at this point. An important group are the Ben Stada texts, whose applicability to Jesus has been disputed.[6] The first of these is b.Sanh. 67a (cf. Tos.Sanh. 10.11 and b.Shabb. 104b):

---

[1] Contra W. Bauer, Das Johannesevangelium, Tübingen 1912, 163; R. Bultmann, Das Evangelium nach Johannes, 11th ed. Göttingen 1950, 500; C. K. Barrett, The Gospel according to Saint John, London 1958, 441.

[2] TDNT 3 (1965), 394-395.

[3] It does not, as Bultmann claims, stand for Judaism here.

[4] The normal Johannine view is presented in 14.22, 17.6,

[5] Bultmann, op.cit. 500 traces ἐγὼ παρρησίᾳ λελάληκα τῷ κόσμῳ and καὶ ἐν κρυπτῷ ἐλάλησα οὐδέν to the evangelist redacting his source. He argues that here the thought of 7.4, 10.24 is expressed. But 7.4 concerns miracles, and 10.24 rests on a pre-Johannine tradition (cf. Lk 22.67f). Furthermore, Bultmann argues that the theological bearing is that the authorities have made their decision, and the time for discussion is over: 'Und mit der Antwort, die Jesus v.20f. dem Hohepriester gibt, schneidet er jede weitere Auseinandersetzung mit dem Judentum ab: es bedarf keine Frage, keines Wort mehr!' op.cit. 498. This is scarcely borne out by Jn 18.21: 'Ask them that heard me, what I said to them.'

[6] See pp. 35, 44-47, 61-64.

It has been taught: And for all others for whom the Torah decrees
death, witnesses are not hidden, excepting for this one (a mesith). How
was it done?—A light is lit in an inner chamber, the witnesses are
hidden in an outer one, so that they can see and hear him but he cannot
see them. Then the person he wished to seduce says to him, 'Tell me
privately what you have proposed to me.' And he does so. Then he
remonstrates: 'But how shall we forsake our God in heaven, and serve
idols?' If he retracts, it is well. But if he answers: 'It is our duty and
seemly for us', the witnesses who were listening outside bring him to
the Beth Din, and have him stoned.

And thus they did to Ben Stada in Lydda, and they hung him on the
eve of Passover. Ben Stada was Ben Padira. R. Hisda said: The husband
was Stada, the paramour Pandira. But was not the husband Pappos
b. Judah?—His mother's name was Stada. But his mother was Miriam,
a dresser of women's hair (megaddela neshayia)?—As they say in Pum-
baditha, 'This woman has turned away (satath da) from her husband.'

Very similar to this passage, though with no reference this time to
hanging, is j.Sanh. 7.16 (cf. j.Yeb. 16.6):

'He who entices to idolatry: this means a common man.' Not a sage?
From the time when he entices he is no sage, from the time when he is
enticed he is no sage. How do they deal with him so as to use artifice
against him? They conceal with regard to him two witnesses in an inner
room, and they cause him to sit in an outer room, and a lamp is lit beside
him, so that they can see him and hear his voice. So they dealt with
Ben Sotedah in Lydda; and they concealed two disciples of the sages
with regard to him, and they brought him to the court and stoned him.

To these must be added j.Shabb. 12.4 (cf. Tos.Shabb. 11.15):

He who makes cuts on skin in the likeness of writing is culpable.
R. Eliezer said to them: 'And did not Ben Stada bring sorceries from
Egypt only in this way?' They said to him: 'Because of one fool, are
we to destroy many sensible men?'[1]

The remaining text of importance for our subject is b.Shabb. 116a-
b. Altough this does not mention legal proceedings against Jesus, it is
important for the central quotation which is similar to Mt 5.17:

Imma Shalom, R. Eliezer's wife, was R. Gamaliel's sister. Now a certain
philosopher lived in his vicinity, and he bore a certain reputation that
he did not accept bribes. They wished to expose him, so she brought
him a golden lamp, went before him, and said to him, 'I desire that
a share be given me in my (deceased) father's estate.' 'Divide', ordered

---

[1] Texts in H. L. Strack, Jesus, die Häretiker und die Christen, Leipzig 1910.

he. Said he (R. Gamaliel) to him, 'It is decreed for us, Where there is a son, a daughter does not inherit.' (He replied:) 'Since the day that you were exiled from your land, the law of Moses has been superseded and another book given, wherein it is written, 'A son and a daughter inherit equally.'

The next day, he (R. Gamaliel) brought him a Lybian ass. Said he to them, 'Look at the end of the book, wherein it is written, I came not to destroy the law of Moses, nor to add to the law of Moses, and it is written therein: A daughter does not inherit where there is a son, Said she to him, 'Let your light shine forth like a lamp.' Said R. Gamaliel to him, 'An ass came and knocked the lamp over! '

B. MENDELSSOHN: BEGINNINGS OF THE MODERN PATTERN.

In Moses Mendelssohn [1] the old and the new approaches meet. The old Dt 13 framework is used for the evaluation of Christianity, but the charges drawn from it and reproduced in the Talmud are never applied to Jesus. Firstly, the principle for assessing miracles, expressed there and repeated by Maimonides, is repeatedly adopted by Mendelssohn.[2] Indeed, to the Jewish text is added the Christian one, Mt 24.24, which means not only a rapprochement at this point between Jewish and Christian theology, but also a movement away from the Rabbinic viewpoint on Jesus: he is put firmly on the side of Moses and the law. Indeed, he and Moses can be paired as 'diese beide Gesetzgeber'.[3] Similarly, the formulation used in accusations against miracle workers 'Zauberer und Verführer',[4] recalls b.Sanh. 43a, but Mendelssohn never pronounces such a verdict on Jesus.

Secondly, the relationship between law and assertions of divinity is depicted in terms of the Dt 13 principle. Mendelssohn is prepared to give 'Hochachtung für den moralischen Charakter' of Jesus [5] provided no supra-human claims are attached.[6] This is repeatedly stressed, and

---

[1] All citations from Gesammelte Schriften III, Leipzig 1843. For the debate between Mendelssohn and the Christian writer J. C. Lavater, see G. Lindeskog, Jesusfrage, 34-37; W. Hoch, Das Glaubensgespräch zwischen J. C. Lavater und M. Mendelssohn, Judaica 3 (1947), 44-84,89-122.

[2] Nacherinnerung of 6.4.1770, op.cit. 65f; letter to C. Bonnet 9.2.1770, op.cit. 118f; Betrachtungen über Bonnet's Palingenesie, op.cit. 147.

[3] Letter to Bonnet 9.2.1770, op.cit. 122.

[4] Letter to Bonnet 9.2.1770, op.cit. 119; 'Zauberei' is also the term used for the works of Sabbatai Zevi, Betrachtungen, op.cit. 156.

[5] Letter to Lavater 12.12.1769, op.cit. 42.

[6] Letter to Lavater 15.1.1771, op.cit. 105: 'Hochachtung gegen den Stifter habe ich bezeugt; ja, aber mit der Einschränkung, wenn Jesus von Nazareth nichts mehr als ein tugendhafter Mann hat sein wollen.' Mendelssohn is able to proceed the more safely in this direction because of corresponding tendencies among some Christian theologians of his time.

most emphatically when dealing with the trial of Jesus, where, in a characteristic passage, he declares his willingness 'die Unschuld jenes Religionstifters, so wie die sittliche Güte seines Charakters anerkennen, aber die ausdrückliche Bedingungen dabei voraussetzen: 1) daß er sich nie dem Vater gleich gesetzt, 2) nie für eine Person der Gottheit ausgegeben, 3) daß er sich folglich die Ehre der Anbetung nie angemaßt habe, und daß er 4) die Absicht nicht gehabt, die Religion seiner Väter umzustoßen, so wie er offenbar bei vielen Gelegenheiten das Gegentheil hiervon zu erkennen gegeben zu haben scheint. Diese Bedingungen sind von der äussersten Nothwendigkeit, denn in der That, wenn einige verdächtige Reden und Äußerungen, die das Gegentheil auszusagen scheinen, in dem buchstäblichen Sinne genommen werden müßten, so würde das Urtheil über die moralische Güte seiner Absichten eine ganz andre Wendung nehmen.' [1]

Now this passage is highly significant for Mendelssohn's thought, and also for the spelling out of issues for subsequent writers. (a) Conditions 1 and 2 above reflect Jn 5.18 and 10.30,33 which are thus projected into the debate on the trial, later to be made the cornerstone of Joseph Salvador's theory. (b) Conditions 2-4 express exactly the Dt 13 criteria, so that Mendelssohn in effect sets out the alternatives of the mesith sentence or the view that Jesus said and did nothing to incur condemnation, a scheme which contains in a nutshell the two tendencies, either to maximize Jesus' claims and give substance to the trial,[2] or to minimize Jesus' claims and derogate from the trial. [3] Mendelssohn himself thinks that Jesus did not make extraordinary claims, [4] but this turns out to be heavily qualified because certain sayings rouse uneasy suspicions and would, if interpreted literally, alter the whole case. There is room left for doubt, therefore, and the Maimonides [5] / b.Sanh. 43a pattern cannot be neglected. (c) The way is prepared for a rapprochement between Christianity and Judaism based on

---

[1] Letter to Lavater 15.1.1771, op.cit. 104. Omission of these conditions roused strong indignation and a letter to the Hamburgische Neue Zeitung 19.1.1770—text in M. Kayserling, Moses Mendelssohn: sein Leben und seine Werke, Leipzig 1862, 555f.

[2] Thus Salvador, Saalschütz, J. Cohen and Peynado.

[3] Thus Samuel Hirsch.

[4] Letter to Lavater 9.3.1770, op.cit. 91. Compare here the approach of Troki, who neutralizes Jn 10.30 with Mk 13.32, and Jn 10.33 with Ps 82.6, and any divine claim with the 'son of man' idea: Faith Strengthened, London 1851, 223, 238, 264. See pp. 73-75.

[5] The Code of Maimonides XIV, Yale 1949: 5.xi.4: 'He was instrumental in changing the Torah and causing the world to err and serve another beside God.'

the person [1] and ethic of Jesus. In later writers the mesith element diminishes in direct proportion to the growing stress on the ethic of Jesus. Here in Mendelssohn is the beginning of liberal Judaism's attempt to reclaim Jesus as its own, and here also are the seeds of conflict with the orthodox acceptance of the seduction theme stiffened by fear of apostasy.[2] This fear was scarcely dispelled by the subsequent conversion to Christianity of many of Mendelssohn's descendants. (d) Jesus' attitude to the law is made definitive.[3] Here he was conservative, even with regard to the ceremonial law which Mendelssohn himself discounts, and this, together with the suggestion [4] that Mt 24.24 is more rigorous than Dt 13.2-4, makes Jesus stand well to the right theologically—almost more Mosaic than Moses! (e) The separation between Jesus and later Christianity in the New Testament is foreshadowed in the Christological distinction involved in Mendelssohn's scheme.[5] Nevertheless, Jesus, not Paul, is the founder of Christianity, and Mendelssohn does not himself take the position later to be embraced so enthusiastically by liberal Judaism.

All these five points except the first show how Mendelssohn both turns away from the old Talmudic view of Jesus, and yet treats him in categories dictated by that view. Into the movement away from the Talmud can be inserted his own explicit and distinctive evaluation. Speaking of the responsibility of the Sadducees and Pharisees in Jesus' case, he asks: 'Was weiß ich's, was meine Vorfahren vor 17-1800 Jahren zu Jerusalem für gerechte oder ungerechte Urtheile gefällt haben? ... Wir haben übrigens, unserer Seits, von jener großen Begebenheit keine zuverlässige Nachrichten, keine Aktenstücke, keine Berichte, die wir den Ihrigen entgegensetzen könnten.—Das Toledoth Gischu ist ein Mißgeburt aus den Zeiten der Legenden und ihrer würdig, wird auch von meinen Mitbrüdern dafür erkannt. Im Talmud

---

[1] Note the phrase 'die Religion seiner Väter' which makes Jesus truly a Jew. Cf. later M. Duschak, Die Biblische-Talmudische Glaubenslehre, Wien 1873, 104: 'Jesus held to the unity of God and so gained many adherents among the Jews, and he still does in regard to his humanity.'

[2] See e.g. A. Ginzberg (Ahad Ha-am), Ten Essays on Zionism and Judaism, London 1922.

[3] Letter to the Erbprinz von Braunschweig-Wolfenbüttel, op.cit. 132: 'Der Stifter der christlichen Religion hat niemals mit ausdrücklichen Worten gesagt, daß er das Mosaische Gesetz aufheben und die Juden davon dispensiren wolle.'

[4] op.cit. 121: 'Der Gesetzeber der Juden erkläret sich hierüber mit deutlichen Worten (Deuteron. 13,2.3.4) und Jesus von Nazareth spricht eben so ausdrücklich, vielleicht noch entscheidender von der Unzuverlässigkeit der Wunderwerke.'

[5] Letter to the Erbprinz, op.cit. 129.

finden sich hier und da Spuren von Nachrichten, von denen es aber
sehr zweifelhaft ist, ob sie dieselbe Begebenheit angehen, und die
sicherlich nicht hinreichen, eine Urtheil zu fällen.' [1]

Here again is a passage rich in significance. (a) Only in the context
of the trial are the Rabbinic sources mentioned, and they embody for
him the confrontation of religions. What elsewhere he shuns,[2] here he
introduces. In historical perspective this is not at all surprising, for
charges of guilt and the anti-Talmudic campaign, culminating in Pope
Clement IV's censorship in 1264, together tragically stain the path of
Jewish-Christian relationships. Mendelssohn's dilemma is exposed by
his introduction of, and yet struggle to disentangle himself from, total
Jewish solidarity and confrontation with Christianity. Whereas he
accepts N.T. data on other topics, here he looks for documents 'on
our side'. But the Rabbinic material will not satisfy the need for one
set of documents to set against the other set. Behind this there also lies
the presupposition, later to become almost a cliché in Jewish Prozessforschung, that to a particularly concentrated extent the Passion narratives are infected with a Tendenz which prevents straightforward
acceptance. (b) Doubt is expressed about whether the events are in
fact the same, so that Mendelssohn stands in a line running from the
mediaeval debates [3] to modern debate about the identity of Ben Stada,
Balaam and the pupil of R. Joshua b. Perahjah. (c) In allowing the
possibility of an unjust condemnation, Mendelssohn again diverges
from b.Sanh. 43a, but he modifies this by stating the uncertainty of the
affair, and implying that even modern courts make decisions for which
he would not like to be held responsible.[4]

C. From Jost to Hirsch

The indebtedness to Rabbinic ideas, which appeared in Mendelssohn, reasserts itself in the early 19th century, which is dominated by
Isaac Jost [5] and Joseph Salvador.

Jost, in his earliest work,[6] includes in his description of Jesus nine

---

[1] Letter to Lavater 15.1.1771, op.cit. 103.
[2] Letter to Lavater 12.12.1769, op.cit. 39-49.
[3] e.g. R. Jehiel at the Paris disputation of 1240. See A. Lewin, MGWJ 18 (1869),
193-210. Contrast Maimonides who, living in Islamic territory, does not need to
contest the identification of the person in these passages with Jesus of Nazareth.
[4] Letter to Lavater 15.1.1771, op.cit. 103.
[5] With Jost a new Literaturgattung emerges in which Jesus can be included
within Jewish history: Lindeskog, Jesusfrage, 85.
[6] Geschichte der Israeliten, Berlin 1820. This book gives no explicit citation
of sources.

features which must be attributed to Talmudic influence: (a) The name is spelt Jesu.[1] (b) The idea that Jesus honoured the law, and was even a Rabbi, is set alongside the assertion that he soon taught new ideas about a relationship with God.[2] (c) The idea of novelty is persistently reiterated, e.g. 'das ganze neue Gebäude',[3] 'oft stritt er . . . gegen die herrschenden Lehrsätze, woraus sich seine Gesinnung immer mehr offenbarte',[4] 'seitdem sich Jesus als Stifter eines neuen Bundes zeigte',[5] 'die neue Lehre' contrasted with 'das alte Gesetz'.[6] This picture of deviationist teaching recalls b.Sanh. 107b. (d) Jost defends his inclusion of Jesus in Jewish history [7] on the grounds that his story stands 'mit den Juden im Verhältnisse . . . und Veränderungen im Volke hervorgebracht.' [8] This is certainly a viewpoint adopted from b.Sanh. 43a. (e) A threefold reaction to Jesus' miracles is outlined. Believers regarded them as 'unmittelbare höhere Einflüsse, göttliche Kraft; while the unbiassed 'achteten wenig darauf'. But opponents were more violent: 'Eingebungen des Teufels, Zauberei'.[9] This recalls b.Sanh. 43a as well as Mk 3.22 and Lk 11.15. (f) A development from private to public self-advertisement occured. 'Nun erklärte er sich öffentlich für den Sohn Gottes . . .' [10] Dt 13 also took up the secrecy/openness question. (g) Jost is explicit, as the Rabbinic sources are implicit, that Jesus was not a political offender. He cites Jn 18.36. Even intense cross-examination by the Pharisees (N.B.) could expose no opinion

---

[1] This corresponds to 'yeshu', a hostile truncation of 'yeshua', and may derive from Jewish objections to (a) a parallel with Joshua, or (b) the belief that Jesus was a saviour figure. Parallels for punning or modification of names are Bar Kosiba (b.Sanh. 93b) and perhaps Ben Stada—though in the latter case Babylonian speculation can confirm only the method, and not the accurate interpretation. Cf. A. S. Kamenetzky, Notes sur Jésus dans les sources juives, REJ 59 (1910), 277; J. Z. Lauterbach, Rabbinical Essays, Cincinnati 1951, 481.

[2] op.cit. 296.

[3] op.cit. 296.

[4] op.cit. 296.

[5] op.cit. 297.

[6] op.cit. 298.

[7] This definitely required defence. In a significant comment, all that the orthodox H. H. Graetz said about Jesus in the 1st ed. of his Geschichte der Juden, Leipzig 1856, 260 was: 'Nach Johannes trat Jesus von Nazaret als Messias (Christos) auf und wurde der Stifter des Christenthums, dessen Leben und Wirken aufzuklären, nicht unbedingt die Aufgabe der jüdischen Geschichte ist.' Reluctance to include Jesus remains attested in e.g. M. J. Raphall, Post-Biblical History of the Jews II, London 1856, 373, and D. Cassel, Manual of Jewish History and Literature, London 1883, 73.

[8] op.cit. 296.

[9] op.cit. 296.

[10] op.cit. 297.

dangerous to the State.[1] (h) Jesus attracted many Samaritans.[2] This associates Jesus with schism, as does Galilean and Gentile attachment which is clearly mentioned with negative implications.[3] (i) The gradual emergence of a threat to the foundation principles of Judaism expresses the conflict, and excludes correspondence, between Jesus and Judaism. Thus, for instance, the Pharisees saw in him a threat to the Temple sacrifices, the study of scripture and the divine order. 'Der Jude mußte daher sich noch stärker hinter seine Schranken zurückziehen, als die neue Lehre, früher so ganz der alten Form ähnlich, bald ganz andre, dem Glauben der Juden widersprechende Formen annahm.'[4]

Certain features of this Talmudically-framed picture were swiftly to be rejected. Mt 5.17 and 23.2 emerged in support of a legally acceptable Jesus. Mt 10.5f and 15.24 reversed the relationship with Samaritans and Gentiles. Hostility from Pharisaism was belittled. The political threat overwhelmed Jn 18.36. And for all the influence of passages like b.Sanh. 43a, 107b one striking element stands out: Jost passes over the Sanhedrin trial! 'Jesus of Nazareth practised magic and led the people astray' is there, but no legal proceedings. From the pre-Passion interrogation, the story moves to the Pilate trial.[5] Jost does not draw back from describing Sanhedrin pressure on Pilate, but his reticence about the Sanhedrin trial exposes a natural defensive tendency, like Mendelssohn's. This reticence about the Jewish trial is not, however, worked into a coherent scheme defending the Jews. There is no argument that the Jews had nothing to do with the case, but only the implication that Jesus was indictable because of religious infringements during his career. Whereas Jost held back from interpreting the trial in these Rabbinic categories, the opposite is true of Joseph Salvador, to whom we turn before tracing further developments in the work of Jost.

When Salvador writes: 'Notez de plus que je ne cite que les chroniques d'une des parties de ce grand procès',[6] he, like Mendelssohn, shows his consciousness of the confessional background of each set of sources, although he implicitly sets aside the Jewish documents. Ne-

---

[1] op.cit. 297.
[2] op.cit. 297.
[3] op.cit. 297: 'In Galiläa ward er sehr geehrt, besonders weil ihm Jude und Nicht-Jude gleich willkommen war.'
[4] op.cit. 299.
[5] op.cit. 298.
[6] Histoire des Institutions de Moise II, Paris 1828, 87.

vertheless, like Jost, he takes this semi-conservative attitude to the gospels and injects Talmudic data and assessments, as follows: (a) The Jews were justified in condemning Jesus. This, as noted earlier,[1] is the emphasis in b.Sanh. 43a. (b) Jesus was illegitimate. This is the point of departure for Salvador's discussion of the trial,[2] and means that Jesus is at variance with the law, even though it may not be his fault (that is not the point), from the beginning. The legal bearing of this matter is set out very pointedly.[3] The same view of Jesus' birth occurs in b.Sanh. 67a,[4] and perhaps Yeb. 4.13. It is also part of the stock 19th century apologetic against Divine Sonship,[5] but an allegation which recedes steadily with the emergence of the 'Jewish Jesus' theory. (c) There was a rabbinic/prophetic period. As an interpreter of the law Jesus was listened to gladly, and 'le peuple alors se plaît à leur considérer comme un prophète'. As for the authorities, 'quel que soit leur ressentiment, les chefs se taisent, tant qu'il reste dans le droit'.[6] This pattern strikes two Talmudic chords: b.Sanh. 106a, where Balaam (= Jesus?) is said to have been first a prophet and then a soothsayer, and b.Sanh. 107b, where the disciple only later fell away. (d) 'Jésus, en présentant des idées nouvelles, en donnant de nouvelles formes à des idées déjà répandues, parle de lui-même comme d'un Dieu'.[7] This is very similar to Jost's repeated remarks about newness, 'die neue Lehre',[8] etc., which we traced back to Talmudic influence. Here, this is particularly plain because of the resultant introduction of a new god. It is noticeable that Salvador goes back behind the Troki-type weakening of claims to divinity [9] to the older view that Jesus did make such totally repugnant claims. This shift is the result of approaching Jesus through his trial: necessarily a reason must exist for his condemnation. (e)

---

[1] See above, pp. 4-6.

[2] This is an important indication of a difference in standpoint between Jost and Salvador. For Jost, Jesus' downfall is just one part of his total career. Salvador, on the other hand, is concerned with the trial, and slants the whole of Jesus' career towards it.

[3] op.cit. 81.

[4] Whether or not Ben Stada was originally Jesus is not germane at this point. Salvador does not dispute it.

[5] Cf. J. Salvador, Jésus-Christ et sa Doctrine I, 2nd ed. Paris 1864, 235: 'À Nazareth, Jésus est fait Dieu par la conception de sa mère.'

[6] Histoire II, 82.

[7] op.cit. 82.

[8] This becomes an oft-repeated formulation, cf. J. H. Dessauer, Geschichte der Israeliten, Erlangen 1846, 91, and J. Cohen, Les Juifs Déicides, in La Vérité Israélite 2 (1860), 171. The latter regards Jesus as 'le créateur d'une nouvelle doctrine à la fois politique et réligieuse'.

[9] See pp. 73-75.

Condemnation corresponds to the laws of Lev 24.16, Dt 13 and Dt 18.20.[1] This is most obviously a Talmudic standpoint. But it is also clear that Salvador is compelled to tone down the data he uses for apologetic reasons. In contrast with the procedure of Sanh. 7.10 for dealing with a mesith, he stresses openness and publicity throughout [2] and does not have the very hasty reference to the Beth Din and subsequent execution.[3]

While both Jost and Salvador use Talmudic data, it is striking that their selection within that material does not overlap widely: Jost's list has parallels in only the third and fourth of Salvador's. The subsequent movement in their positions must now be studied.

Jost exhibits a characteristic tendency within Jewish historiography, when facing a Talmudic-type reconstruction of Jesus' career. In his second book, published in 1832,[4] the nine points mentioned above are treated as follows: (a) The name Jesu remains. (b) Jesus was not a danger to Judaism from the beginning. In spite of claims to deity, the clash only came after his death.[5] Here the Hegelian view of history is intruding upon, but not destroying, the scheme already laid down. (c) The oft-repeated mention of 'newness' is dropped.[6] This again stems from the ground-plan in which the schism starts after the crucifixion; as regards Jesus himself, it means that a 'Jesus *is* different' plan is displaced by a 'Jesus *becomes* different' plan. (d) The reason for discussing Jesus is remodelled: 'nur um folgende Grundzüge des eben genannten *sich entwickelnden* Gegensatzes zu liefern, der für die Geschichte der Juden *erst später* von Bedeutung ist.' [7] The centre of gravity shifts,

---

[1] op.cit. 87. That this is part of an influential Jewish scheme is attested by the plan of argument against Christianity in the book of G. B. English (see p. 1, footnote 2). This includes: (a) The two tests of Dt showed Jesus to be a false prophet. (b) The messianic prophecies were not fulfilled. (c) Jesus commanded worship of himself. Of these arguments he writes, op.cit. xii: 'A very considerable number of them were selected from ancient and curious Jewish tracts, translated from Chaldee into Latin.'

[2] op.cit. 85: 'Ce jugement est public; il est connu de tous, de Jésus en particulier.'

[3] Sanh. 7.10 suggests *immediate* reference to the Beth Din, which, in Salvador's reconstruction, does not follow the awful words of Jn 10.30-36. (In later works Salvador places Jn 7.12,43 and 10.20 after the entry to Jerusalem.) Dt 13.8 is often cited in this respect in later discussion, b.Sanh. 29a,33b,43a.

[4] Allgemeine Geschichte des Israelitischen Volkes II, Berlin 1832.

[5] 'Der eigentliche Gegensatz des Christenthumes gegen das Judenthum trat erst dann hervor, als der Stifter desselben seine irdische Laufbahn vollendet hatte.' op.cit. 66.

[6] This, incidentally, confirms its theological significance in the 1820 presentation.

[7] op.cit. 66f. My italics.

therefore, from 'Veränderungen im Volke' caused by Jesus himself, to those of later times. (e) Jost shortens the treatment of miracles. He refers, in words drawn from the 1820 text, to 'mancherlei angestaunte Wunderthaten, die jedoch nicht so tief einwirkten als seine Leben',[1] but the threefold reaction with the climactic reference to 'Zauberei' is dropped. (f) disappears. (g) A Rabbinic viewpoint re-emerges. The Pharisees are said to have opposed Jesus because he criticized the holiness of certain laws, and viewed redemption as a change of heart rather than the establishment of a kingdom.[2] The Sadducees appear alongside the Pharisees as critics during the teaching period.[3] In Jerusalem he often saw his teaching assessed as heresy, though not by any of the famous Pharisaic teachers,[4] and he was also accused of treason. Here then there is a double movement: firstly, bringing in political matters while still allowing religious ones priority, and secondly, discussing debates yet, by stating that the critics were lesser men than the great Pharisaic leaders, avoiding the full confrontation of Judaism and Christianity. In other words, the Rabbinic scheme is being heavily qualified. (h) All reference to Jesus' appeal to Samaritans and Gentiles is omitted. (i) was treated under (b).

A broad trend away from the Talmudic stand is therefore clear. Yet, interestingly, Jost does allow a reference to a Sanhedrin trial this time. 'Ein Synedrium, unter dem römischen Statthalter Pontius Pilatus berufen, fand ihn schuldig. Wider seine Überzeugung ließ Pilatus ihn ans Kreuz nageln, da der gereizte Pöbel darauf drang.'[5] In this matter of initiative, and therefore of responsibility, Jost is sensitive and aims to shield the Jewish leaders;[6] in so doing, he allows a political intrusion to take place, thus conforming to the prevalent trend in Jewish historiography, in which the Rabbinic reconstruction is repeatedly subject to pressure from the political side.

The tendency went even further twenty-five years later.[7] By then the only vestiges of the old pattern to survive were the name Jesu and the treat to Judaism contained in the idea of the new birth.[8] This time,

---

[1] op.cit. 67.
[2] op.cit. 68. Note that the issue was still basically religious.
[3] Here the Geigerian emphasis is foreshadowed, op.cit. 67. See below, pp. 36f.
[4] op.cit. 67.
[5] op.cit. 68.
[6] M. Wiener, Jüdische Religion im Zeitalter der Emanzipation, Berlin 1933, 214, mentions the strong opposition Jost received for ascribing the death of Jesus to the Jews.
[7] Geschichte des Judenthums und seiner Secten, Leipzig 1857.
[8] op.cit. 402.

Mt 5.17 has become the definitive expression of Jesus' attitude to the law, and the political side is dominant. Political considerations arouse the high priest's fear, and the entry to Jerusalem expresses symbolically the purpose of Jesus' activity.

The positive tendency to replace Rabbinic religious ideas with political ones is matched negatively in 1857 by a critical assessment of these sources,[1] in the context of a conservative evaluation of the gospels.[2] In spite of the baraita-type introduction, b.Sanh. 43a is attributed to 3rd-4th century Rabbis, and attention is drawn to its apologetic Tendenz (the 40 days countering illegality) and contradictoriness (i.e. the stoning).[3] Jost notes that Nisan 14 is the date in b.Sanh. 43a and 67a, comments on the chronological error in b.Sanh. 107b, and sees the figure of Pilate behind 'Phinehas the robber' in b.Sanh. 106b. His literary criticism is noteworthy for the following elements: (a) Mendelssohn's choice between the New Testament and Jewish sources reappears, but Jost, instead of being critical of both, accepts the gospels! There is as yet no reference to secular sources; Philippson is the first to make Tacitus, Annals 15.44 the basic source. (b) The criterion for dating the gospels, as well as the harmonizing method, were even then vulnerable to attack from Tübingen.[4] (c) The Tendenz which Jost finds in b.Sanh. 43a also reflects the debate of his own time. Only in 1857 does he mention the illegality question, and he attempts no defence.[5] (d) No doubt exists as to the identity of Balaam, Ben Stada, and the disciple of b.Sanh. 107b.

While Jost, then, moves steadily and firmly away from a fundamentally Talmudic position, Salvador does nothing of the kind. Five elements remain permanently in his composite gospel-Talmudic scheme:

---

[1] op.cit. 403.

[2] op.cit. 403: 'Wir haben keinen Grund, die Treue des Berichtes in Zweifel zu ziehen. Er ist ein zu klares Bild der Zeit, und ist nur durch Missverständniss entstellt und zu ungerechten Urtheilen ausgebeutet worden. Fassen wir die verschiedenen Darstellungen zusammen und sehen, was geschah.' This does not apparently preclude a recognition of the contradictions within the gospels, op.cit. 395.

[3] This stems from filling out the Talmudic passage with N.T. data, so that 'hanging' is interpreted as crucifixion and not as the post-mortem exposure of Sanh.6.4.

[4] D. F. Strauss himself, while using contradictions widely and sceptically, was earlier content with what is 'not historically improbable' in the Passion narratives. This is severely criticized in L. Philippson, Haben wirklich die Juden Jesum gekreuzigt, Berlin 1866, 2nd ed. Leipzig 1901, 27.

[5] op.cit. 406.

(a) Jesus' illegitimacy is maintained.[1] This is the implication of the habitual use of the term 'son of Mary'.[2] It is also quite clear in the discussion about whether the Jewish rumour of illegitimacy or the Christian claim of a virgin birth is prior. Salvador's assumption that the former is earlier shows the influence of dogmatic objections on historical reconstruction, and belongs, theologically as well as historically, to the period before the Jewishness or Pharisaism of Jesus became almost a fixed tenet. It is important, too, that throughout Salvador's works the curtailment of Jesus' civil rights, because of illegitimacy, is reiterated.[3] (b) Attention is focussed on the visit(s) to Egypt, a feature of both b.Sanh. 67a and 107b. Firstly, it is connected with the illegitimacy in that embarrassment was avoided, according to Salvador, by fleeing to Egypt.[4] Secondly, it is connected with influences on Jesus' thought.[5] The presence of this problem in Salvador's mind is telling, and even though he does not insist on a long stay for this influence to gain a firm hold, he does suggest that similar influence was exerted on Jesus by the Essenes.[6] It is not surprising to read in the Passion story of 'le principal dieu de l'Égypte, dont Jésus a recueilli l'héritage et imité en partie la Passion'.[7] Thirdly, the possibility of a second visit to Egypt [8] is canvassed though not finally adopted. But the end-result is still presupposed in the third section. (c) Jesus' teach-

---

[1] Jésus-Christ et sa Doctrine I, Paris 1838, 178: 'Nul rapport de filiation ni de sang n'exista jamais entre Jésus et l'époux légitime de Marie.' The evidence cited is: (a) The 'remarkable' parallel to Mt 13.55 (Mk 6.3), though note that this is not proposed on the basis of a precise evaluation of Synoptic relationships; similarly, op.cit., 2nd ed. Paris 1864-5, 220. (b) The suspicion aroused by the union of an old man and a young woman. (But where is the evidence for Joseph's age?!) (c) The extremely old source, the Protevangelium of James. I(1838), 174-6; I(1864), 218. (d) The testimony of the Tol'doth Yeshu, and the comparability of the Paulina story, adjacent to that of Jesus in Josephus, Ant.18.65-80. 1(1838), 179; II(1865) 230f. (e) The prevalence of rumours as attested in Contra Celsum and the gospel of Nicodemus. (f) The lack of evidence of anything extraordinary in the gospels' presentation of the relationship between Jesus and his mother.

[2] It is also used repeatedly by E. Benamozegh, Jewish and Christian Ethics, San Francisco 1873.

[3] Histoire II, 82; Jésus-Christ I(1838), 172f; I(1864), 218.

[4] I(1838), 186,196; I(1864), 237, 240.

[5] I(1838), 196: 'Mais ce premier voyage fut-il d'assez longue durée pour y chercher les circonstances qui donnèrent l'impulsion à l'esprit et à l'âme du maître nazaréen?' The question is not directly answered, but it is sufficient for it to have been asked.

[6] Compare H.H.Graetz, REJ 20 (1890), 11-15.

[7] II(1865), 5.

[8] This would be instruction in mysteries and magic arts. I(1838), 204-6.

ing. With the judaico-oriental mixtures suggested by Salvador, the mesith picture appears again. Comparison with the later 'Pharisaic Jesus' theory exposes the drift of this mixed Judaism, which was effectively non-Judaism. In spite of statements to the effect that Jesus did not attack Mosaism,[1] and the increasingly familiar battery of texts, Mt 5.17, 10.5f, 15.24 and 23.2f, Salvador still says that Jesus' school aimed to 'dégager de la loi',[2] and that he declared war on the Pharisees from the beginning [3] (even meeting with the disapproval of John the Baptist[4]). 'Mais en aggrandissant, en exagérant même, afin de mieux former le contraste, tous les préceptes moraux de l'ancienne loi, Jésus en changea la direction.' And in the most crucial of all possible changes of direction, Jesus claimed to be God in the oriental manner [5] — which means idolatry. (d) Miracles are seen in the perspective of Dt 13. This is plain from three pieces of evidence. Firstly, the Maimonides-Mendelssohn line on the evidential value of miracles is restated.[6] Secondly, Salvador adds that magic, and especially Egyptian arts, exercised great influence in Jesus' time.[7] Thirdly, and crucially, Salvador notes that Jesus accepted worship at the time of performing these miracles,[8] and the reaction of the Council binds together the whole complex of idolatry, the mesith charge, the law in all its aspects, and finally the trial. (e) The trial of Jesus. Here, as in 1828, the Talmudic citation of Is 43.10 is used to interpret Jn 10.30-36.[9] A second feature is that debates among the people, cited from Jn 7.12,43 and 10.20 as well as Lk 23.5 are located, in spite of Jn, *after* the entry to Jerusalem.[10] Here, the assimilation of Lk 23.5 to the Johannine πλάνος-references is particularly significant. Thirdly, Mt 27.63 is used as ammunition for attacking the resurrection.[11] Fourthly, Johannine chronology is preferred.[12] Fifthly, there is a possible reminiscence of b.Sanh. 43a in the

---

[1] I(1838), 298ff; II(1865), 53.
[2] I(1838), 411.
[3] I(1838), 234.
[4] I(1838), 221.
[5] I(1864), 325.
[6] I(1838), 245.250; I(1864), 403.
[7] I(1864), 396.
[8] Thus the miracles become 'les preuves de la volonté de Jésus à s'approprier la qualité de Dieu, ce qui, à tort ou à raison, passait aux yeux du conseil de Jérusalem et de toute la Judée pour l'acte le plus subversif de la loi réligieuse et nationale'. I(1864), 391.
[9] II(1838), 132; II(1865), 135f, where Dt 13.1-5 is added.
[10] II(1838), 140; II(1865), 147.
[11] II(1838), 197; II(1865), 221.
[12] II(1865), 160.

insistence on the publicity of the arrest warrant.[1] Sixthly, words of
Don Calmet are borrowed to describe the condemnation: 'Les miracles les plus évidents . . . ne peuvent persuader au commun des Juifs la
divinité de Jésus-Christ, et lorsque devant le tribunal du grand Sacrifi-
cateur Jésus avoue qu'il est Dieu, le grand prêtre déchire sa robe comme ayant entendu un blasphème.' [2] Here, only blasphemy is mentioned, and not Dt 13 and 18.20 as in 1828, but this only shows the characteristic tendency to interpret blasphemy in these terms. The argument about miracles shows how Salvador is able to use them with
double force against Jesus. He was doomed on one side because miracles are not proofs, and on the other because, when asked for a miraculous proof, he was unable to supply it.[3] The two approaches cannot
be harmonized.

Before turning from Salvador, some general remarks must be made
about the demonstrable Rabbinic influence upon him. In the narrow
field we see how Lk 23.5, connected already with the mesith theme,
both provides continuity between Jewish and Roman hearings and
allows the intrusion of religious affairs into the latter. [4] Further, there
is no citation of rabbinic sources about Jesus [5] and stress is laid on the
Christian ones. But this calls attention to overlap between the two, an
area of overlap which is important for the historical evaluation of each.
Next, it is particularly in Jn, with support from Lk, that material is
found. Since Salvador regards Jn as the latest of the gospels,[6] this
raises an inconsistency. This inconsistency he ignores, thus proving that
old arguments linger on in spite of newer critical methods. It is specially interesting that he unconsciously uses the correspondences between Lk and Jn, and one recalls the fact that it is in Jn that the closest
parallels with Talmudic views of Jesus are found. More broadly, the
trial is assessed within the confrontation of two religions. For Salvador
this was intensified by his own parentage (his family Jewish but his
mother a Roman Catholic), and also by the contemporary political
situation of the Jews. With this coheres the interpretation of Jesus as a
mesith, and the sense of oneness which leads Salvador to make no
distinction between the Jewish people and their leaders, or between

---

[1] II(1838), 168; II(1865), 193.

[2] II(1865), 197f.

[3] II(1838), 525f.

[4] There are times when Salvador's distinction between 'religious' and 'political'
becomes very thin.

[5] Because of this the appeal to the Tol'doth Yeshu is surprising.

[6] I(1838), 167.

Jesus and his disciples.[1] The law is the unifying concept: there is no need for any section to evade responsibility if the law guided their actions, and Salvador, following the Talmudic passages, finds this the best defence. Consequently there is no need for any distinction between Sadducces and Pharisees, and little even for one between Jews and Romans as far as Jesus' case was concerned.

Jost and Salvador are the outstanding figures in the 1820-1860 period, and before Talmudic data became the subject of an intensified debate through Graetz, Derenbourg and Geiger. Nevertheless there are other scholars, notably Samuel Hirsch and Saalschütz, who show a tendency away from the rabbinic sources and yet remain influenced by them. Such writers as these show how widely different may be the reconstructions within which Talmudic data and presuppositions can be accomodated. Both Hirsch and Saalschütz, like the later Jost, develop the political aspect at the expense of the religious one, and clearly start from a sense of what is common and can bring reconciliation between the two religions,[2] rather than what is in opposition.

When Hirsch claims, immediately after his statement of Jewish-Christian harmony, that the Talmud knows nothing of Christianity, and that the rabbis cited lived in other lands and knew only Persian and Roman heathenism rather than the Christian Weltanschauung, the Jewish sense of unity between Talmudic sources and religious confrontation is again impressively documented. These passages are the first influence on the assessment of Jesus which a Jewish writer has to consider and, if necessary, eliminate. Working from a position diametrically opposite to Salvador's, Hirsch says of the sources: 'Nur in einzelnen, fabelhaften Sagen ist ihnen eine Kunde von einem 'yeshu' geworden, der einst mit Rabbi Jehoschua Sohn des Perachja nach Alexandrien gereist sei und der durch die sehr getadelte Heftigkeit des Rabbi alsdann sich dem Bösen in die Arme geworfen haben soll.' [3] In a footnote he adds that in the Talmud there are some few 'Censurlücken' which people think refer to Christ, and he cites b.Sanh. 107b. But, he adds, 'selbst wenn der Talmud den Stifter des Christenthums hier meint, so ist er doch, wie man sieht, von allen den Gehässigkeiten

---

[1] In Histoire II, 23f, the actions taken against Jesus and the apostles stem from 'les magistrats et la grand majorité du peuple juif'.

[2] Die Religionsphilosophie der Juden, Leipzig 1842, 621: 'Das Judenthum stehet dem Christenthum nicht feindselig gegenüber und hat dieses niemals'—an over-sanguine claim. Compare the title of Saalschütz's earlier book: Zur Versöhnung der Confessionen, Königsberg 1844.

[3] op.cit. 622.

frei, die man ihm anzudichten beliebt'.[1] Now these two citations immediately provoke the following reflections: (a) b.Sanh. 107b is
singled out, though an assimilation of Ben Stada details to it has occurred. Hirsch here follows a trend mentioned earlier, and there are three
possible reasons. Firstly, there is an obvious chronological ground for
disputing the identification with Jesus, which Hirsch indeed proceeds
to do. Secondly, as Hirsch notes, the Rabbi is blamed and Jesus treated
favourably, and so the Jews can regret the exclusion of Jesus. Thirdly,
and very importantly, there is no mention of a trial (and, of course,
b.Sanh. 43a is conspicuously absent). (b) The Talmudic sources are
clearly an embarrassment and have to be played down. Consequently
the old mediaeval non-identification apologetic is used. Hirsch is also
embarrassed by Christian allegations of secret blackening of Jesus and
so declares that the Tol'doth Yeshu is blameworthy and the invention
of a baptized Jew. (c) Hirsch's total approach, which re-Judaizes
Jesus [2] and draws a Hegelian distinction between Jesus and the
Church,[3] necessitates the abandonment of the mesith theme.

In 1865 Hirsch polemized directly against the Rabbinic picture of
Jesus' trial.[4] The two points he isolates are in fact the substance of
'Jesus of Nazareth practised magic and led Israel astray'. Firstly, he
opposes the idea that the Pharisees raised against Jesus an accusation
of healing magically on the Sabbath.[5] Now this must be drawn from
the Talmud because there is no gospel passage which mentions magic
in the context of Sabbath healings. Secondly, Hirsch seeks to demonstrate illegalities in the trial by dismissing the relevance of mesith
legislation (Dt 13.7-12; Tos. Sanh. 10). There is some tension here
with Hirsch's acceptance of the relevance of the Mishnah to the current
legal situation. When Hirsch comes to propose a theory about the
trial he adopts a political scheme, so that he and Jost to this extent
move in parallel.

Joseph Saalschütz, when contrasted with Salvador upon whom he is
dependent, also stands within the process of transition from the religious to the political scheme. The Rabbinic picture remains: (a) Dt

---

[1] op.cit. 622.

[2] The term 'son of God' is rendered inoffensive; Mt 5.17 dispels all newness;
Salvador is criticized for his interpretation of Jesus' preaching of the kingdom.
op.cit. 646-648, 653, 680.

[3] op.cit. 622.

[4] Les Crimitières au point de vue Israélite, Archives Israélites 26 (1865),
383-390.

[5] op.cit. 386, 'magiquement' is italicized by Hirsch.

13.2-4 means that some sign was required of Jesus [1]—a point borrowed from Salvador but scarcely a correct deduction from Dt 13. (b) Jn 11.47-53 also shows an appeal to Dt 13.2-6. (c) Condemnation was based on Dt 13.2-6, i.e. blasphemy and false prophecy are omitted from Salvador's original scheme. Thus Saalschütz manages to combine the Talmudic elements with a political emphasis, as, in the same period, do M. Noah [2] and J. Cohen.[3] Yet Saalschütz's attempt at reconciliation by stressing the Jewishness of Jesus [4] in a theological sense again shows the tension between the needs of contemporary apologetic and the old habits of thought.

To summarize then, the following broad trends characterize the first half of the 19th century. Firstly, the rabbinic sources make Jewish writers feel they have a position already laid down for them. This is often an irksome restriction, but they cannot break away completely until an acceptable alternative is found. This eventually appears in a critically expurgated reproduction of Christian sources— but even then Talmudic features are slow to fade. Secondly, there is a clear preference for not mentioning these texts explicitly. All specific citation is critical: no one both mentions and defends them. Those who use them do not say so. Salvador was particularly noticeable in this respect in that he cited apocryphal gospels, Contra Celsum, and even the Tol'doth Yeshu but never the Talmudic passages. Thirdly, when the passages are cited, there is a slight preference for b.Sanh. 107b, and the possibility of non-identification with Jesus of Nazareth is canvassed though never adopted positively. It is more of an attempt to prevent their being used than a scientific evaluation for its own sake. As a general rule, at least the presuppositions of argument seem to be that Jesus does stand behind Balaam, Ben Stada and the pupil of Rabbi Joshua ben Perahjah. Fourthly, in line with b.Sanh. 43a, there is some intersection of the Talmudic source question and the illegality debate. Lastly, Talmudic influence steadily diminishes, mainly under pressure from the emergent theological Jewishness of Jesus (which tones down dogmatic conflict) and the political elements, with consequent modification or elimination of the Sanhedrin trial. Even 100 years later these two emphases remain definitive.

---

[1] Versöhnung, 40; similarly, Das Mosaische Recht, Berlin 1853, Chap 1, note 16.
[2] Discourse on the Restoration of the Jews, New York 1845, 19-21.
[3] La Verité Israélite 2 (1860), 344.
[4] Versöhnung, 52,57,64.

D. The crisis of the 1860s

In this fresh decade powerful new influences affected the Jewish view of Jesus and his trial. Heinrich Graetz introduced, for the first time explicitly, the full mesith procedure. Joseph Derenbourg denied the identity of Jesus and Ben Stada. Abraham Geiger moved in the opposite direction and attempted to prove the equation, Balaam = Jesus. The last is not so important for the trial of Jesus, and Derenbourg's work achieved greatest permanence, but it was the theory of Graetz which was the most notable landmark in the development of Talmudic influence in the study of the trial of Jesus.

1. *The contribution of Graetz*

A study of the work of Graetz must begin with his adoption of a generally Talmudic pattern. As was true with Jost and Salvador, so with Graetz there are a series of features which are best explained as due to the influence of Talmudic sources:

(a) He calls Christianity 'diese alte Lehre im neuen Gewande, oder richtiger dieses mit fremden Elementen versetzte Essäerthum'.[1] But this has a different bearing for Graetz from that for Jost, Salvador and Dessauer. Firstly, Christianity does remain in some sense 'die alte Lehre'. That means that the deviation from Judaism is modified and lessened as compared with, for instance, Salvador. Secondly, there is a reflection of the Maimonides-Formstecher view of Christianity as the agent of Judaism's world-mission,[2] though it is plain that the clothes worn for this task were not made of Jewish cloth.[3] Thirdly, there is the influence of the Hegelian system which makes what is essentially Jewish the real Jesus. However, Graetz's use of this scheme is not straightforward; if it were, none but Jewish elements would remain attached to Jesus, and the mesith charge would be impossible. Yet Graetz retains both the mesith material and many elements of the 'Jewish Jesus', an inconsistency which is particularly plain in differing

[1] Geschichte der Juden III, 2nd ed. Leipzig 1863, 217.
[2] Maimonides, The Book of Judges, 5.xi.4. It is also adopted by many later scholars, e.g. E. Grünebaum, Die Sittenlehre des Judenthums, Mannheim 1867, 32; E. Benamozegh, Israel et Humanité, Livourne 1885, 5; the manifesto of the 1885 Pittsburgh Conference convened by Kaufmann Kohler (see G. Lindeskog, Jesusfrage, 49); C. H. Levy, Progressive Judaism and Liberal Christianity, New World 8 (1899), 503; S. Dubnow, Weltgeschichte des jüdischen Volkes II, Berlin 1925, 525; J. Klausner, Jesus of Nazareth, E.tr. London 1925, 413; S. E. Rosenberg, Bridge to Brotherhood, New York 1961, 152.
[3] Graetz expresses this view again in Sinai et Golgotha,Paris 1867, 281.

statements about Jesus' attitude to the unity of God.[1] Further, although the quotation above particularly refers to Christianity, Graetz does not simply drive a wedge between this and Jesus, but rather allows some continuity. In all, he attempts to bind together an older and a newer pattern, with resulting acute tension. This tension might possibly be relieved by the idea of two periods within the ministry, one orthodox and the other less so. But apart from remarking that we cannot tell whether the idea of messiahship had been in Jesus' mind before Peter's confession, Graetz does not develop any such scheme.

(b) Jesus was a Galilean. Graetz stresses that Galilee was far from Jerusalem and the temple, and on the wrong side of Samaria—with all that that means! It was much inferior to Judaea in knowledge of the law, and was vulnerable to Syrian superstition. This, sadly, was Jesus' native air and made his teaching inferior to that of Hillel and Shammai.[2]

(c) The miracles made people think of Jesus as an extraordinary being—a man of God 'dessen bloßes Wort magisch wirke' [3] and this accounted for his grip upon them.[4] The mention of magic recalls b.Sanh.43a,67a, and the association of this with the claim that Jesus attached to himself those upon whom he had performed miracles,[5] and in particular exorcisms, is an even clearer sign of a Talmudic orientation. For the only cases in the gospels of Jesus' bringing recipients of miraculous activity into discipleship are Mk 10.52 and par., Lk 5.11 and 8.2. The first of these is not an exorcism and is at the wrong stage of the ministry, so is unlikely to be the case in mind. Similarly Lk 5.11 is not a miracle performed on a person. This leaves only Lk 8.2 or the Talmud as the source of the idea. But this is not a strict alternative because there has frequently been the suspicion that Mary Magdalene

---

[1] Geschichte der Juden, 232: 'An dem bestehenden Judenthum rüttelte Jesus keineswegs, er dachte gar nicht daran, Verbesserer der jüdischen Lehre zu werden, oder überhaupt etwas Neues zu stiften, sondern lediglich die Sünder für die göttliche Lehre, für Gottseligkeit und Lebensheiligkeit zu erziehen und sie für die messianische Zeit würdig zu machen.' Graetz goes on to cite as examples of Jesus' orthodoxy his inoffensiveness to Pharisees, his treatment of law, Sabbath and unity of God, his attitude to the Gentiles and his Passover observance, op.cit. 221, 232f, 239. And yet, op.cit. 232, heterodoxy enters by way of Essenism.

[2] op.cit. 234.

[3] op.cit. 235.

[4] Here is the same ambivalent attitude to miracles as appeared in Salvador. There are circumstances in which, even in a Jewish context, they are impressive. Graetz agrees with Salvador that Jesus could not give the necessary sign of his Messiahship, op.cit. 239.

[5] op.cit. 235.

is alluded to in b.Sanh. 67a. And of course the pattern of the personal attachment of the recipients of miraculous power to a person of doubtful theological bent is exactly what Dt 13 envisages.

(d) An atmosphere of secrecy, cf. Dt 13.6-11, pervades the whole period between the events of Caesarea Philippi and Jerusalem,[1] the period of probable heterodoxy. 'Son of God' was a term used only in the closest circle of the disciples. So the scheme leads naturally to Graetz's view of the arrest and charge.

We can now turn to Graetz's detailed evaluation of Talmudic sources. He begins by assessing favourably the tradition of the hidden witnesses overhearing Jesus' act of enticement.[2] This was an exceptional procedure, and only after Jesus' case did it become part of the mesith legislation. (This is in itself very important: it means that Jesus' trial was itself 'rechtsschöpferisch'.[3]) Graetz then goes on to explain his attitude to the main Talmudic sources. In fact he accepts only b.Sanh. 67a and j.Sanh. 7.16, on the grounds that the Talmud assumes the 'Jesus = Ben Stada' equation, and that mesith trials occured seldom or never during the period of the second temple.[4] All the other sources are, by contrast, criticized. The reference to 40 days in b.Sanh 43a is what makes that passage suspicious, in spite of the fact that Graetz accepts Nisan 14 chronology and goes on to discuss the identity of the disciples mentioned in the latter part of the text. b.Sanh. 107b is even more legendary in suggesting that Jesus went to Egypt in the time of Hyrcanus I (N.B.). The same applies to the bringing of charms from Egypt, b.Shabb. 104b, although 'bemerkenswerth is nur, daß der Talmud wie Matthaeus Jesus in Egypten weilen lassen'.[5] Finally Graetz rejects the Ben Pandera stories stemming from the period of the second revolt and, trenchantly, the Tol'doth Yeshu.[6]

What is noticeable in this analysis is, firstly, that Graetz moves away from giving to b.Sanh. 107b the central position which earlier scholars had done. His criticisms of this text are the usual ones but not all

---

[1] op.cit. 237,239,242.

[2] op.cit. 242: 'Eine jüdische Quelle, die ihrer ganzen Haltung nach alt und glaubwürdig erscheint, setzt die Art ins rechte Licht, wozu dieser Verräter benutzt worden ist.' The procedure is then outlined. The parallel in: Sinai et Golgotha, 338, begins: 'Un document original, dont le caractère et l'authenticité ne peuvent être soupçonnés . . .'

[3] I owe this observation to Dr. E. Bammel.

[4] op.cit. 242: 'Die genannte Mischnah und die Boraita dazu dürften die einzigen authentischen Quellen im Talmud über Jesus sein.'

[5] op.cit. 243.

[6] He describes it as 'ein elendes Machwerk, compilirt aus fragmentarischen Sagen des Talmud über Jesus'.

Talmudic passages are made to stand with this one. Secondly, like Salvador, Graetz feels the attraction of the Egyptian period but does not develop this. Thirdly, he gives no exclusive reasons why Jesus should be Ben Stada. The first of his observations about this complex could no longer stand when the Talmud's assumption was itself criticized as late and unproven, and his second point does not eliminate the possibility of alternative identifications. In addition, the well-known discrepancies, later to become so important, are not tackled.[1] One is left asking why such are important in one passage and not in another, leading to the rejection of one but in no way imperilling the acceptance of the other. Fourthly, Jost's suggestion that the sources belong to the 3rd-4th century is, by implication, resisted. Fifthly, the old confrontation of Talmud and New Testament does appear in the discussion of the betrayal but not as a *general* alternative, and without the overtones of confessional solidarity and opposition.[2] Sixthly, to the very distinctive acceptance of the Sanh. 7.10 procedure for Jesus' delivery to the authorities, Graetz adds that Jesus was stoned. If this is striking, the change in the next edition is equally so, and the two parallel passages merit being set out side by side:

Nach den damals üblichen Strafgesetze solle ein wegen GotteslästerungVerurtheilter zuerst gesteinigt und dann nach dem Verscheiden ans Kreuz genagelt werden. Gewiss ist Jesus auf dieselbe Weise hingerichtet worden, aber dann war er wohl vor der Kreuzigung bereits verschieden. Die christlichen Quellen wollen aber ...[3]	Da Jesus noch vor dem Tode gegeißelt wurde, so folgt daraus, daß Pilatus ihn nach römischen Strafgesetzen behandelt hat; denn nach den judäischen wurde die Geißelstrafe keineswegs einen zum Tode Verurtheilten aufgelegt. Die römischen Büttel (Lictoren) waren es also, die den angeblichen 'König der Judäer' schadenfroh mit Ruthen oder Stricken gegeißelt haben. Diese waren es auch, welche auf Pilatus,

---

[1] He is later forced to tackle them. Cf. Eine Localität Lod bei Jerusalem, MGWJ 27 (1878), 427-432, where he argues not only that there was a suburb of Jerusalem named Lod, but also justifies the Jesus = Ben Stada equation in that (a) b.Shabb. 104b identifies Ben Stada and Ben Pandera, and (b) the hanging on the eve of Passover shows that the case is the same. It is noteworthy that under pressure Graetz is forced to be more positive about b.Shabb. 104b and the Ben Pandera stories.

[2] The Ben Stada eavesdropping technique simply appears as a more convincing explanation of the betrayal than the gospels' version of the identification by Judas of one who had appeared quite publicly as he entered Jerusalem in triumph and taught in the temple, op.cit. 243. This is a little inconsistent as Graetz had earlier dismissed the entry as unhistorical, op.cit. 240.

[3] op.cit. 245.

Befehl ihn ans Kreuz nagelten
und den schimpflichen Tod nach
römischen Gesetzen an ihm anwen-
deten. Denn mit dem Todesspruch
von Seiten des über Leben und Tod
eingesetzten römischen Beamten ge-
hörte der Verurtheilte nicht mehr
seiner Nation an, sondern verfiel der
römischen Staatsgewalt. Nicht das
judäischen Synhedrion, sondern Pla-
tus hat Jesus als Aufwiegler und
Stattsverbrecher hinrichten lassen.
Die christlichen Quellen wollen . . .[1]

Footnote:

Jesus ist demnach als Staatsverbrecher, weil er sich selbst als Messias,
als König der Judäer ausgegeben,
oder dafür gehalten wurde, hinge-
richtet worden. Das Synhedrion hat
lediglich den Prozeß gegen ihn
anhängig gemacht.

The scheme of the 2nd edition is exactly the Mishnaic one, and, in
the history of the discussion, is an extension of the view that the Jews
acted entirely within the framework of their own legislation. It is also
in line with an apologetic tradition running back through Sefer Nizzachon 4.4f.[2] Graetz in fact uses j.Sanh. 7.16 as the textual basis for
'stoning'.[3] But, of course, this whole view stands sharply opposed to
the scheme of argument increasingly adopted by Jewish writers: (a)
Jews accept that Jesus would have been stoned if Pilate had had only to
confirm the sentence, but the gospels' testimony that Jesus was crucified and that Pilate did not merely confirm a sentence previously passed
creates two fixed axioms. Indeed Graetz himself changes 'bestätigte'
to 'verhängte'.[4] The role of Pilate thus becomes more definite and

---

[1] Geschichte der Juden III, 3rd ed. Leipzig 1878, 326. In this 3rd ed. Graetz did
retain the 'eavesdropping by two witnesses' technique.

[2] Text in O. S. Rankin, Jewish Religious Polemic, Edinburgh 1956, 60:
'On the words: 'Of the tree of the knowledge of good and evil'
The Minim base conclusions that lead to evil,
Teaching that all mankind descended to the Underworld,
There to await, until the day of Jesus' death
By stoning and hanging,
His remission of their penalties and curse.'

[3] Sinai et Golgotha, Paris 1867, 344.

[4] 2nd ed. 244; 3rd ed. 325.

more definitive for the course of events. (b) Crucifixion was not a Jewish method of execution. But according to Graetz's 2nd edition the Jews nailed Jesus up—a clear assimilation of New Testament to Talmudic data. (c) The superscription proves that Jesus was condemned for political reasons. This emphasis on 'King of the Jews' begins to make itself felt in Graetz's 3rd edition. (d) The Tendenz of the gospels is all in the direction of blaming the Jews and exonerating the Romans. This point was made before, and accepted by Graetz, but the Tendenz presupposed by the movement from events, as reconstructed in his 2nd edition, to the accounts in the New Testament is not in line at all. And it is also noticeable that Graetz seems to concentrate all his apologetic on the crucifixion, rather than on the death in general terms or on the Sanhedrin trial in particular. It is thus rather muddled to argue: 'Mais s'il résulte de tout qui précède, que Jésus a expiré avant le crucifiement, l'histoire de sa mort, telle que les Évangiles la recontent, est apocryphe. Et cette histoire légendaire, inventée par les ennemis du peuple juif, a été la cause de souffrances innombrables et de supplices de tout genre.' [1]

In the 3rd edition the volte face is complete. In the area of apologetic we can see that Graetz has been able to defend the Jews *for* executing Jesus, and now he is able to defend them because they did *not* execute him! Originally this was achieved by, in effect, blaming Jesus: the latter stands over against the Jews as a law-breaker, exactly as in Salvador. Now, Graetz achieves his purpose by claiming moderation in the Jews' treatment of Jesus, and he uses a stock tripartite pattern: [2] Firstly, the Jews offered him wine to soften the pains; secondly, Romans, not Jews, mocked him and crowned him with thorns; thirdly, with Jesus, the whole nation was scorned, as its messianic hope was mocked. At the same time the centre of gravity is shifted in the direction of the Sanhedrin trial, though involvement is summed up in the phrase 'lediglich anhängig machen'. In Pilate we have a murderer inflicting a barbarous punishment.[3]

---

[1] Sinai et Golgotha, 345. Further ill-assortment is caused by retaining Mt 27.46 even though Jesus was killed before his crucifixion. Thus it is plainly demonstrated that this verse is part of a Jewish dogmatic scheme. Similarly, mention of the superscription placed on the cross by the *Romans* hardly fits.

[2] Salvador, Histoire, 74,89; Philippson, Haben die Juden, 42,61; I. M. Rabbinowicz, Le rôle de Jésus et des apôtres, Bruxelles 1886, 137; M. Joel, Blicke in die Religionsgeschichte zu Anfang des zweiten christlichen Jahrhundert II, Breslau 1883, 71f; M. Fluegel, The Messiah-Ideal, Baltimore 1896, 105; J. Eschelbacher, Die Vorlesungen Harnacks über das Wesen des Christentums, MGWJ 46 (1902), 417; J. Klausner, Jesus of Nazareth, London 1929, 351.

[3] op.cit., 3rd ed., 326, 334.

What explains the change between 1867 and 1878? On the one hand, Graetz's earlier position is so individualistic and against the trend of Jewish research at this point that strong resistance inevitably gathered against it. In particular, Philippson's monograph, published in 1866, attacks at very sensitive places the scheme of Graetz. Objections at the places where the theory is itself inconsistent can be readily understood. On the other hand, it probably produced a difficult situation for an orthodox Jew to heighten Jewish involvement and to open himself to charges of giving opportunity to Christian opposition, when liberal Jews of the standing of Geiger were producing the apologetic of non-involvement. Above all, we see in Graetz the processes whereby, firstly, a stock pattern of apologetic overpowers a distinctive deviation, secondly, the Roman hearing becomes a trial at the expense of the Jewish one, and, thirdly, political affairs squeeze out the religious ones which themselves are heavily dependent on Rabbinic material. In Graetz therefore, we see a miniature of the same process as overtook Jóst, and which steadily alters the orientation of the trial of Jesus in Jewish historiography.

2. The contribution of Derenbourg [1]

Derenbourg's view of the trial must be regarded as to some extent a reaction against the view put forward in Graetz's 2nd edition, but he does not feel the same reserve about the 3rd edition.[2] A critique of Derenbourg can conveniently be grouped into three sections:

(a) General criticism of the sources. 'Nos sources rabbiniques sont presque muettes sur le fondateur du christianisme, et les rares passages qui traitent de Jésus datent d'une époque où l'esprit de parti a dû altérer la tradition.' [3] The word 'nos' should be noted as showing again a confessional solidarity. Further, the general verdict here is not borne out by Derenbourg's actual use of the sources: he is therefore probably repeating a stock formulation.

In detail Derenbourg says: 'L'histoire évangélique se résume pour le Thalmud dans la courte phrase, Jésus fit des prodiges, séduisit et égara les masses.' [4] He, like Graetz, notes that Egypt was the home of miracle technique,[5] and he notes also the gospel record of Jesus' stay

---

[1] Essai sur l'histoire et la géographie de la Palestine, Paris 1867.

[2] He cites it, op.cit. 203.

[3] op.cit. 202.

[4] op.cit. 203.

[5] j.Shabb. 12.4; b.Shabb. 104b; j.Yeb. 15b; b.Sanh. 67b; Josephus, Ant.xx.8.6, B.J. ii.13.5.

in Egypt. He then mentions that it is very doubtful whether the procedure of hiding witnesses was used in Jesus' case.[1] b.Sanh. 43a has only an apologetic purpose, and the Ben Pandera explanations are as odious and ridiculous as those in the Tol'doth Yeshu. In comparison with Graetz, therefore, the same sceptical attitude is adopted towards most of the sources, but b.Sanh. 107b regains prominence at the expense of b.Sanh. 67a.

(b) Jesus' career reconstructed. In spite of his criticisms, Derenbourg's presentation of Jesus' life is almost entirely in line with the Rabbinic scheme. (a) Jesus was in the beginning 'un agadiste' drawing texts from the prophets.[2] Some disapproval was aroused among other teachers because Jesus took away part of their audience, weakened belief in the practise of observances, and used potentially dangerous prophetic texts. But he was not an illiterate, because his teaching can be explained in rabbinic terms, his methods were Pharisaic, and he respected temple and sabbath. All this could well be polemic against the 'Galilean backwardness' theory of Graetz, but its general thrust is more or less as in b.Sanh. 107b: Jesus is rabbinic even though nonconformist. (b) 'Seulement, lorsque plus tard il fit des miracles, que ses discours parurent empreints d'une couleur étrange, et que certaines expressions figurées des anciens voyants reçurent dans sa bouche une application qui heurta et troubla les sévères croyances monothéistes des Juifs, le tribunal lui appliqua la loi de Deutéronome 13.1ff.'[3] In a footnote, Derenbourg adds that it was the term 'Son of God' which moved the judge. We notice firstly that the combination of Dt 13 and 'Son of God' is typical of Talmudic reconstructions.[4] Secondly, why does Derenbourg say 'plus tard'? The gospels have miracles at the beginning, too. Derenbourg is in fact laying down the patterns in which Jesus is at first unexceptionable but later heterodox (b.Sanh. 107b), and in which Jesus' miracles have no significance except when integrated into his condemnation. The objections add up to miracles plus the 'Son of God' claim, i.e. in legal terms, he 'practised magic and

---

[1] He mentions the difficulty of the arrest, op.cit. 469, as does Graetz, but makes the applicability to Jesus of the Sanh. 7.10 procedure dependent on the understanding of Ben Stada as Jesus. This is not strictly necessary as Derenbourg does retain the mesith charge.

[2] op.cit. 202, cf. b.Sanh.107b.

[3] op.cit. 202.

[4] Derenbourg, like Saalschütz, makes Dt 13 stand alone: blasphemy is only mentioned later as an addition when commenting on the stoning prescribed in Lev 24.16 and Sanh. 7.5, op.cit. 203.

led Israel astray'. (c) On the execution, Derenbourg does not shun the suggestion that the Jews would have killed Jesus had the Romans not done so.[1] He thinks the governor decided the mode of execution in capital cases quite arbitrarily, sometimes the Roman form (Jesus), sometimes the Jewish one (Stephen). He mentions the view of j.Sanh. 7.16 that Ben Stada was stoned, but draws back from Graetz's earlier view by insisting that the Jews did not crucify.[2]

(c) Jesus ≠ Ben Stada. Derenbourg's reasoned opposition to the equation has exercised an influence to this day, and within the modern period he stands as the pioneer of this position. He argues firstly from the difference of name, which lacks any rapport with the real name, or reason for replacement (since the Talmud uses Jesus' real name some twenty times). Secondly, j.Sanh. 7.16, the earlier tradition, differs as to place (Lydda), name (Ben Stada), and mode of execution (stoning). Thirdly, the addition 'and they hanged him on the eve of Passover' in b.Sanh. 67a already shows confusion with Jesus, a confusion which later discussion increases. Fourthly, R. Eliezer lived at Lydda and would know what happened around A.D. 100 when Ben Stada was executed.[3]

Derenbourg therefore suggests two originally distinct but analogous traditions:

Jesus	Ben Stada
Son of Mary and Panthera	Son of Sotada and Jehuda ben Pappos
at Jerusalem	at Lydda
for seduction	for seduction

These two traditions were muddled and merged by R. Hisda in 3rd century Babylon, and Jehuda ben Pappos should be read for Pappos ben Judah in b.Sanh. 67a. The former, a contemporary of R. Gamaliel II and R. Joshua, was a pious man[4] but he had a loose wife: here then was the putative father of Ben Stada.

Derenbourg's Jesus-tradition, which he clearly regards as historical, includes illegitimacy as well as seduction, but he draws no attention to it.

---

[1] op.cit. 203.
[2] op.cit. 203.
[3] j.Shabb. 12.4, b.Shabb. 104b.
[4] j.Ber. 2.9, j.B.B. 5.1; Derenbourg, op.cit. 470f.

3. *The contribution of Geiger.*

Abraham Geiger has a double importance for Jewish study of the
trial: firstly he argued for the Jesus = Balaam equation,[1] and secondly
he was the pioneer of the approach based on the legal dominance of the
Sadducees. While the first of these proposals is not directly fruitful in
material for the trial,[2] and the second is not suggested by the Rabbinic
Jesus-passages, yet both features eroded well-entrenched positions
vis-à-vis those passages.

Geiger describes Balaam as 'der Name für den, der Israel zum Ab-
falle verleitet',[3] but does not regard these passages as a source of historical information about Jesus. Rather, this view of Jesus presupposes both Jewish-Christian opposition to Paulinism by applying to him
Balaam categories, and also the historical achievement of Christianity
in disseminating true belief in God. Thus Jesus came to be recognized
by the Jews as doing the work of a prophet among the heathen. This
means that within the Balaam complex there is an attitude both res-
pectful and disapproving—an attitude indeed characteristic of Jewish
scholars of Geiger's time, who are involved in the rescue operation of
reclaiming Jesus from Christianity back into Judaism even though
they are aware that Jesus cannot be totally dissociated from the birth
of the daughter-religion. Geiger plainly finds in the Balaam material
data which can easily be assimilated to both the Formstecher hypothesis and the Hegelian dialectic. Bearing in mind his stress on Jesus the
Pharisee, it is indeed surprising that the theme of leading the people
astray is not entirely relegated to later Christianity. This view of Jesus
as 'ein pharisäischer Jude mit galiläischer Färbung',[4] together with his
preference for political issues in Jesus' downfall, his own reform position, and his dislike of Graetz,[5] all these might be expected to eliminate
the mesith theme altogether. Yet Geiger here stands apart from many
of his followers, and, although reduced, this theme is not obliterated:
Jesus' world view, in which this world was but the forecourt of the

---

[1] Bileam und Jesus, JZWL 6 (1868), 31-37.
[2] The only possible relevance is via (a) the Phinehas = Pilate equation, and (b)
the early death of Jesus, b.Sanh. 106a.
[3] art.cit. 33.
[4] Das Judenthum und seine Geschichte, Breslau 1864, 111. Note again the
attention given to Jesus' Galilean origin and views. It has religious as well as political nuances.
[5] See Die neuesten Forschungen über Judenthum und Christenthum, JZWL 5
(1867), 265.

next, was not Pharisaic; [1] he himself kept the law but allowed his followers to break it,[2] and his Christology was menacing. So Geiger
writes: 'Er griff in die damaligen religiösen Anschauungen ein, erhob
sich zu einer Höhe, die ihm nicht zuerkannt wurde, stellte die Hoffnung
der Zukunft als gegenwärtig und in sich verkörpert dar . . .' [3] And
finally the bearing of all this is exposed: 'So trat die erste Anregung
auf, in welcher zwar nicht eine neue Religion sich zeigt, in welcher
jedoch der Antrieb zu derselben lag.' [4]

Geiger thus holds together in microcosm a mixture of the tendencies—the old and the new, the Talmudic and the political, the mesith
and the Pharisee. Above all, his 'Jesus = Balaam' equation was against
the contemporary tendency in dealing with Talmudic material, but the
divergence must be understood in the light of the much greater pos-
sibilty of rapprochement of contemporary thought with the Balaam
passages than with the other ones. In the long run, however, Derenbourg who stressed the mesith aspect was, ironically, more of a path-
finder by disputing the other equation, 'Jesus = Ben Stada', than
Geiger, who, with undertones only of the mesith theme, yet advocated
the view that Jesus was to be seen behind a Talmudic pseudonym.

Subsequent reaction to this Balaam hypothesis was mixed: criticism from D. Joel, Moriz Friedländer, J. Klausner and M. Goldstein,[5]
and acceptance by M. Hyamson, S. Krauss and A. Danziger.[6] It
exerted no lasting influence on the trial of Jesus in Jewish historiography.

E. From the 1860s to Klausner

In the 1860s the Jewish debate is dominated by Graetz, Derenbourg
and Geiger, all of whom stand out at least partly because of their
treatment of Talmudic schemes, and on the other hand by Ludwig
Philippson, who with Samuel Hirsch heads a formidably long list of

---

[1] Geiger saw in this other-worldly resurrection doctrine of Jesus the kernel of
his heresy.

[2] Sadduzäer und Pharisäer, JZWL 2 (1863), 37.

[3] Das Judenthum und seine Geschichte, Breslau 1864, 115.

[4] Judenthum, 114.

[5] D. Joel, Der Aberglaube und die Stellung des Judenthums zu demselben,
Breslau 1881, 18-20; M. Friedländer, Der AntiChrist, Göttingen 1901, 190;
J. Klausner, Jesus of Nazareth, 32f; M. Goldstein, Jesus in the Jewish Tradition,
New York 1950, 65f.

[6] M. Hyamson, JQR 22 (1931), 211-217; S. Krauss, Jesus of Nazareth in
Jewish Legend, JE 7 (1904), 171; A. Danziger, Jewish Forerunners of Christianity, London 1904, 278.

scholars who move quite decisively away from these sources. In the subsequent period a widely varying permutation of typical elements in Leben-Jesu-Forschung do not, however, obscure certain marked trends closely interconnected with those already observed in the 1770-1870 period.

1. *The influence of Graetz*

Inevitably reaction to so bold a theory as Graetz put forward in his 2nd edition was determinedly hostile,[1] though there were still a number of scholars who persistently followed it in at least some respects. These include A. Weill, M. A. Weill, S. Bäck, A. Franz and J. Jacobs.

Alexandre Weill [2] accepts Graetz's view of the overhearing technique and the stoning, and for the same reasons. The only development of any note is in the direction of more Talmudic influence: b.Sanh. 43a is treated favourably since it is allegedly written in Hebrew of the time of Jesus.[3] Overall, Weill finds no difficulty in speaking of 'les juifs qui l'ont crucifé', and his whole approach is primitive.[4] But he too changes ground in parallel with Graetz, and moves to an interpretation of 'Son of God' based on Dt 14.1, a strictly Jewish theology, and a political fever in Jesus' programme as he stormed the Bastille of political oppression.[5] In the end, Weill ignores the Sanhedrin hearing and stresses Lk 23.2. Here again is the Talmudic scheme yielding to pressure from political factors, as in Graetz but more so.

Neither M. A. Weill [6] nor S. Bäck [7] follow Graetz in the two outstanding features of his version of the Passion, but in other details his influence can be detected. Particularly is this true of Bäck, whose

---

[1] Thus, H. Rodrigues, Le Roi des Juifs, Paris 1870, 243-246; T. Reinach, REJ 35 (1897), 17; S. Bernfeld, Zur ältesten Geschichte des Christentums, JJGL 13 (1910), 89-128, esp.117. At times the critical attitude is so confident that Graetz is mentioned but no effort made to comment, e.g. L.Philippson, op.cit. 33.

[2] Moïse et le Talmud, Paris 1864, 181f.

[3] op.cit. 182-184. This contrasts with b.Sanh. 107b which is said to be written in bad Aramaic and contains the famous anachronism.

[4] Thus in defence of the Jews he argues that if Jesus were God become man in order to be crucified, the Jews were his faithful instruments; but if Jesus were not God they were only guilty of a crime of lèse-humanité. op.cit. 313.

[5] Le faux Jésus-Christ du Père Didon, Paris 1891, 11,24: 'Jésus était un mosaïste pur, prêchant le Jéhovah-Un avec l'égalité et la fraternité pour toutes les nations. Il était contre l'oppression et la tyrannie romaine.'

[6] Le Judaisme ses Dogmes et sa Mission III, Paris 1869, 471-473.

[7] Die Geschichte des jüdischen Volkes, 1st ed. Lissa 1878, 2nd ed. Frankfurt a.M. 1894, 3rd ed. Frankfurt a.M. 1906.

vocabulary even recalls Graetz. For him Jesus was basically orthodox [1] and even where he used the idea of divine Sonship he did not meet opposition, but when it came to be preached openly and when the political temperature rose Jesus' downfall ensued. In Bäck's view the Sanhedrin trial concerned only a political matter, and so the religious mesith aspect is sublimated. In fact the 'Son of God' aspect appears as an intrusion in the scheme of religious orthodoxy/political condemnation in the rest of Bäck's account, and demonstrates the difficulty of disentangling old strands from the newer presentation.

By contrast M. A. Weill takes a step backwards into the mediaeval ideas and debates by connecting the second heterodox stage with the deification of the Messiah.[2] Like Graetz, however, he interprets Jesus' reply to the messianic question before the Sanhedrin as equivocal. For him Jesus' newness was in the interpretation, presumed false of course, of old data rather than theological innovations.

In later times the influence of Graetz is most plainly seen in Jacobs.[3] Yet once more an original Talmudic scheme later has its crucial features withdrawn.[4] In 1895 Jacobs went even further than Graetz in using Talmudic material data, adding also apocryphal gospel material—though he did not cast doubt on the crucifixion. Firstly, he includes the 'mamzer' element, the content of allegations not only in early rumour but also by those who were in the temple [5] (which brings it very close to the passion). Secondly, Jesus is said to have been an haggadist. While not himself a Pharisee, he did the work of one.[6] From an early stage he knew the law outstandingly, but his promise of devotion was not fulfilled, and since he had not learnt from one of the bearers of tradition he was unable to pronounce halakah.[7] At this point in the argument Jacobs inserts b.Shabb. 116a-b, with its saying contrary to the Torah. Thirdly, Jacobs agrees that Jesus did signs but argues

---

[1] 1st ed.135: 'Jesus lebte innerhalb des Judenthums, erklärte die Verbindlichkeit aller Gesetze und Vorschriften desselben und wollte überhaupt nur an das jüdischen Volk als Erlöser geschickt sein . . . . . Und auch als er sich für einen Sohn, für die Inkarnation Gottes ausgab und damit an den Grundfesten des Judenthums rüttelte, einer Gotteslästerung sich schuldig machte, ließ man ihn gewähren, so lange er sich auf den Kreis seiner Jünger beschränkte.'

[2] Le Judaisme, 473. Mk 12.35-37 is the text used.

[3] As Others saw Him: a Retrospect A.D.54, London 1895.

[4] Jesus of Nazareth in History, JE 7 (1904), 160-166.

[5] As Others saw Him, 4,17,154. Graetz did not include this element.

[6] op.cit. 7; JE 7 (1904), 161. At this point Jacobs is out of step with D. Chwolson, who in other places exerts an influence. Jacobs prefers Ebionite to Pharisaic features.

[7] op.cit. 19, 42.

against exorcism and magic.[1] Whereas this would seem to be a rejection of a Talmudic viewpoint, it is plain that the mesith's use of miracles is still near at hand because Jacobs stresses that Jesus used his own name and authority rather than God's.[2] Fourthly, attention is drawn to a later stage of Jesus' ministry (cf. b.Sanh. 107b) when Jesus spoke of himself in a marvellous way, implying that communion with him and with God were identical. He also seemed to identify himself with the great judge, and spoke as if the message were his own rather than using the prophetic introduction, 'Thus saith the Lord'.[3] This combination of legal deviation and the intrusion on the divine is demonstrably the Dt 13 pattern. Fifthly, the interrogation procedure of Sanh. 7.10 is adopted.[4] Sixthly, the trial itself shows a gathering together of themes of blasphemy and leading the people astray: 'Jesus of Nazara, thou art accused before us of blasphemy and leading the people astray'[5] are the words of Caiaphas. According to Jacobs, Jesus replied with the words of Jn 18.20f, which is a most notable positioning and interpretation of those words.

Here then is the old scheme of the Salvador-Graetz period, modified by a highly favourable view of Jesus [6] and a few later advances. For instance, the Sadducees, especially Annas, receive most of the blame (cf. Geiger and Daniel Chwolson [7]), and Nisan 13 is the date of the trial (cf. Chwolson). But whereas the mesith theme differentiates Jacobs from Chwolson in 1895, there is a Chwolson-type change in 1904 to the view that there is little evidence of a messianic claim by Jesus.[8] Further signs of Chwolson's influence are to be seen in the criticism of the Talmud passages as being for the most part as legendary as the apocryphal gospels. Yet this is one more example of conforming to a popular view without conviction, for Jacobs continues to use them.[9]

---

[1] op.cit. 27.

[2] op.cit. 27, 200.

[3] op.cit. 84f, 200.

[4] op.cit. 175: 'Even now as I speak, one of his followers, Judas a man of Kerioth is drawing forth from him his blasphemies before two witnesses, concealed as is the custom.'

[5] op.cit. 179.

[6] op.cit. 199, and the Epilogue.

[7] Das letzte Passamahl Christi und der Tag seines Todes—first published in 1892.

[8] art.cit. 164.

[9] op.cit. 160. The baptism-temptation story in the gospel of the Hebrews is still regarded as 'well authenticated tradition', op.cit. 161,164, though this time he is more slighting about b.Shabb. 116a-b and works from Mt 5.17. For a similar attitude to the gospel of the Hebrews, cf. K. Kohler, The Origins of the Synagogue and the Church, New York 1929, 213.

Again, claims to authority and personal relationship with God are, in the later article, toned down to ordinary personal relationship in the light of Jesus' non-claim to messiahship.[1] Although the fourth gospel is a 'Tendenz-Roman' [2] Jacobs, like many Jewish writers, still finds it very serviceable for the trial.[3] There is a plain synoptic-type arrest and no Sanh. 7.10 procedure, and it must be accidental and only by association of ideas that Sanh. 7.10 is cited as background for the issue of blasphemy, since seduction as such is ignored. Thus Jacobs returns to the conventional Jewish pattern, retaining only the eccentricity of apocryphal gospel material, and toning down the trial to a preliminary priestly hearing, exactly in line with the contemporary Jewish trend once Talmudic reconstructions proved unviable.

Although A. Weill and Jacobs (1895) accept Graetz's first outstanding idea, the witness procedure, no one in this group accepts the second, death by stoning. But we discuss next a parallel movement to this second suggestion.

2. *American development under I. M. Wise*

Wise had read Graetz [4] but it is more accurate to see him as initiating a movement in parallel rather than in direct dependence, for overall the presentations are separate and distinct. Wise is notable for:

(a) Doubt cast on the crucifixion. Whereas Graetz had wrongly interpreted 'hanging' as crucifixion, Wise opposes the two, and from this contrast concludes: 'It is uncertain that the Messiah was crucified at all.' [5] In this he is followed by L. Weiss.[6] The argument of Wise runs as follows. Firstly, crucifixion is three times denied by Peter, Acts 5.30, 10.39, 13.29. Secondly, the tradition is also present in Barnabus and the Basilideans,[7] and reaches the Koran.[8] Thirdly, Rabbinic tradi-

---

[1] op.cit. 163f.

[2] op.cit. 160.

[3] op.cit. 165: 'The author appears to have had access to some trustworthy traditions about the last days.'

[4] Mentioned in The Origin of Christianity, Cincinnati 1868, 228.

[5] Origin, 29; The Martyrdom of Jesus of Nazareth, Cincinnati 1874, 100-107; A Defence of Judaism against Proselytising Christianity, Cincinnati 1889, 92.

[6] Some burning Questions: an exegetical Treatise on Christianising of Judaism, Columbus 1893, 67.

[7] At approximately the same time the same argument was being used by L.Stern, an orthodox Jew, in debate with R. Roberts, a Christadelphian, in Birmingham, October 17-19, 1871. Cf. Was Jesus of Nazareth the Messiah? London 1872, 29. He claims that Simon was crucified in place of Jesus who escaped.

[8] See S. M. Stern, Quotations from the Apocryphal Gospels in Abd al-Jabbar, JTS 18 (1967), 34-57.

tion agrees with Peter in calling Jesus 'the hanged one'. Fourthly, it
was Paul who originated the 'Christ crucified' idea, but then after all
he was not an eyewitness and his testimony is therefore suspect.[1] The
fifth argument is that the whole record is clouded by legal and chronological discrepancies, and the freedom of John to amend the tradition
itself attests widespread uncertainty.[2] Weiss uses the first and last of
these points, and adds the erroneous argument against the gospels
that Roman law did not prescribe crucifixion for thieves, thus misunderstanding the term λῃστής.[3]

Now these claims by Wise stem clearly from an attempt to discredit
the gospels as historical sources,[4] rather than any wholehearted conviction: it is essentially a defensive, debating anti-proselytising technique.[5] This is quite plain from the context [6] and the fact that the
Jews are elsewhere defended on the grounds that not they but the
Romans crucified Jesus.[7] Further, there are inconsistencies of argument which tend to support this suspicion. For instance, the speeches
in Acts are said to be Thucydidean and to reflect non-Petrine Christology [8] and yet Wise uses them as if they were not. Apart from attributing Acts 13.29 to Peter, he conveniently omits Acts 2.23, 36 and 4.10!
Then for polemical purposes Petrine speeches are opposed to Pauline
theology. This is of a piece with his ambivalent attitude to the Pauline
letters, which are treated as primary sources [9] but their evidence rejected. In all, the combination of Hegelian dialectic and Jewish apologetic remains awkward. Lastly, it must be noticed that there are no
specifically legal arguments in favour of hanging as there were in
Graetz. And a quite fundamental difference remains: Wise rejects both
the mesith charge and the Sanhedrin trial.[10]

---

[1] Defence, 69.

[2] Origin, 29.

[3] Weiss, op.cit. 67f.

[4] The approach is diametrically opposite to Salvador's: the time has gone when
the best ad hominem argument works from the professed acceptance of gospel
statements.

[5] This is also true of Weiss. In this respect, and in general argumentation about
the gospels, Weiss follows Troki-type methods. Cf. M. Kulischer, Das Leben Jesu,
Leipzig 1876, 7, who rejects the historicity of Jesus, and plays off the N.T. and the
Talmud against one another in their descriptions of the mode of execution.

[6] Defence, 92. He speaks of the scepticism achieved by N.T. criticism.

[7] Origin, 232; cf. p. 452, where Tacitus, Annals 15.44 is used.

[8] Origin, 85. Acts 5.30 says that the Jews were responsible, but Wise poses
against this the mildness of the authorities, op.cit. 142.

[9] Origin, v.

[10] History of the Hebrews' second Commonwealth, Cincinnati 1880, 267;
Defence, 80.

(b) Treatment of the mesith theme. This also is controlled by pole-mic. Wise claims that Jesus never said he was God or son of God.[1] Dt 13.2-6 merely provides a point against proselytism [2] in the light of the alleged silence of the gospels about it. In the total context of Jewish Prozessforschung this means that the 'leading astray' idea has evolved through the whole spectrum of settings: from the frankly hostile (the Talmud) to the defensive (Salvador, etc.) and on to the dogmatic apologetic (Wise). However close at hand the idea may be in Wise, it is striking that in view of his acceptance of so much Talmudic data, including the Ben Stada tradition, this is the one major element that he cuts out. Once again a clash has taken place between the Rabbinic themes and the Hegelian dialectic.

(c) Centrality of the Rabbinic sources. Ben Stada material and b.Sanh. 107b are primary, certainly apply to Jesus, and are used more extensively by Wise than ever by Graetz. This is partly a reaction to Christian neglect of the Talmud.[3] On the Ben Stada passages, Wise writes: 'If it were not for those rabbinical notices of Jesus, and espec-ially one (j.Shabb. 12.4 and also in Toseptha and B.T.) there would not be any evidence on record that such a person ever lived.' [4] Such heavy reliance on this strand of material is unparalleled. In addition, when discussing j.Shabb. 12.4, he writes: 'R. Eliezer said, Did not Jesus (Ben Stada) bring necromancy from Egypt in this very same manner of writing? . . . Here is an undoubted reference to something like a manuscript of Jesus himself, then well known among the Rabbis.' [5] Wise also has a novel method of waiving objections to b.Sanh. 107b: an 'ignorant transcriber' inserted the words 'ben Perachiah'.[6] He does

---

[1] op.cit. 80.

[2] Defence, 80: 'If Jesus did maintain that he was a god or a person of the trinity, performed those miracles to prove his divinity and exacted of his disciples faith in his own divinity, any criminal court acting under the law of Moses was obliged, the fact being proved, to have him put to death: and yet in the trials preceding the crucifixion, also according to John, no reference to this law is made.' Cf. Weiss, op.cit. 77; P. Goodman, The Synagogue and the Church, London 1908, 263.

[3] Origin, 264.

[4] History, 258. Cf. the use of the Talmud to prove the historicity of Jesus: A. Reichenbach, Die Lehre des Rabbi Jeschua von Nazareth, München 1882, 1; A. L. Sachar, A History of the Jews, New York 1930, 125. Against this, T. Reinach, REJ 35 (1897), 1, and E. G. Hirsch, My Religion, New York 1925, 29.

[5] Origin, 291.

[6] Origin, 291. The Rabbis 'made Jesus a pupil of R. Joshua with whom he went to Egypt and learnt necromancy there.—What that necromancy was, no one can tell in our days: but that Jesus was a pupil of one R. Joshua, and that he went with him to Egypt, that he learnt there much of the Therapeuts . . . cannot well be denied.' In History, 259, he interprets the miracles in terms of 'the arts of Horus

not explain what caused the references to Jannaeus and Simeon ben Shetah, which also determine the dating!

The crucial point about Wise's use of the Rabbinic texts is that he selects only those which say nothing about the trial. The nearest he ever approaches is in the 'hanged one' references. The trial is rejected solely by a critique exposing the contradictoriness and discrepancies he locates in the gospel narratives, and no reason is given for the rejection of other texts like b.Sanh. 43a,67a.

3. *The effect of Derenbourg*

Not all scholars after Derenbourg abandoned the 'Jesus = Ben Stada' equation. Both Jacob Levy [1] and the convert, P. Cassel,[2] maintain it, and its occurrence in R. W. Husband's book,[3] which influenced Jewish scholars so deeply, must also be mentioned. But a trend of acceptances soon gathered strength, first through Grünebaum and then with M. Joel, who thereafter is often bracketed with Derenbourg.

Grünebaum combines a Geigerian reconstruction of Jesus' life with a broadly Philippsonian conclusion.[4] He writes that if Jesus had been tried on religious grounds (which he was not) it would have been as a mesith or a false prophet.[5] This shows not just the retaining force of the Talmudic scheme but also once again that mesith and false prophet are far more natural categories for the Jewish scholar than blasphemy. In assessing the Talmudic sources [6] Grünebaum says that even if Jesus = Ben Stada, which would mean a Jewish condemnation and stoning for Jesus, the gospels and Tacitus, Annals 15.44 are to be preferred to the Talmud. But he then relies on the refutation provided by Derenbourg. It is quite plain from Grünebaum's argument that the Ben Stada trial passages cause particular embarrassment and give powerful impetus to the rejection of all Ben Stada tradition. This was noted above for Wise, and appears similarly in Joel's divergence in detail from Derenbourg, in spite of agreement with him in general.

---

and Serapis in Egypt'. (In Origin, 24, he denied their historicity.) Cf. A. Danziger, Jewish Forerunners to Christianity, London 1904, 77, who thinks there was another Joshua b. Perahjah in Jesus' time, or that the story was not interested in chronology.

[1] Articles in Levy's Wörterbuch I (1876), 236; III (1883), 499; IV (1889), 60.
[2] Apologetische Briefe I: Panthera-Stada-Onokotes, Berlin 1875.
[3] The Prosecution of Jesus, Princeton 1916.
[4] For Philippson's theory, see later, pp. 113f.
[5] Die Sittenlehre des Judenthums, 2nd ed. Straßburg 1878, 273.
[6] op.cit. 296f.

This divergence he himself prefers not to specify,[1] clearly for tactical reasons.

In 1880, Joel's remarks were focussed in two assertions: (a) The chronological discrepancy sabotages b.Sanh. 107b, which in turn renders useless all Jesus-passages.[2] Here is a familiar argument. (b) Jesus affirmed both law and tradition, but the antinomian tendency intruded via Hellenistic Jews. Debates about Trajan's edict about temple-building, which in the eyes of Jewish Christians was bound up with the ceremonial law, brought the schism: hence the disputes with Minim about national regeneration. Such a reconstruction as this removes all monotheistic debate from the schism and, contrary to the evidence, from the Minim passages. This is symptomatic for Joel's avoidance of the mesith factor, and also assumes no debate about messiahship.

Joel's use of b.Sanh. 107b may be contrasted with that of E. Schreiber.[3] The latter also makes this passage central and crucial, and says it proves that Jesus was only a disciple of his master,[4] knowing nothing of Trinity or divine sonship, teaching nothing new, but being finally condemned according to the Philippsonian pattern.[5]

In 1883 Joel dated the Rabbinic references to Jesus in the 2nd century, surprisingly close to Jesus' time. Turning to Ben Stada material, he marshalls all Derenbourg's points [6] and adds only one more. This is that Ben Stada is said to be a fool by Tos.Shabb. 11.6, and foolishness is the reaction of Greeks, not Jews, to Christianity. But it is in the disentangling of the traditions that Joel makes his sharp divergence from Derenbourg: the Ben Stada strand includes the stoning at Lydda for seduction,[7] his character as a fool, the teacher using writings in his skin,[8] and the bringing of magic formulae from Egypt.[9]

---

[1] Blicke II, 58: 'Der kundige Leser erkennt leicht, worin ich in Erklärung der Stellen über Ben Sad'ta von Derenbourg abweiche, in der Hauptsache aber ist seine Bemerkung unanfechtbar.'

[2] Blicke I, II; II, 64: 'Die späteren Talmudisten wissen nichts Genaues über die Vorgänge bei den Anfängen des Christenthums.'

[3] Die Prinzipien des Judenthums, Leipzig 1877.

[4] Schreiber elaborates rabbinic characteristics.

[5] op.cit. 8.

[6] Blicke II, 54-57. In spite of Geiger, the point is repeated that Jesus is always given his real name in the Talmud. Here see the objections of his brother D. Joel to the view of Geiger, Der Aberglaube und die Stellung des Judenthums zu demselben, Breslau 1880, 18-20. Note also that Joel does not mind taking Ben Pandera as Jesus, and that the Bar Kochba/Bar Kosiba case counts against him.

[7] Tos. Sanh. 10.11; j.Sanh. 7.16.

[8] Tos. Shabb. 11.6.

[9] j.Shabb. 12.4; b.Shabb. 104b.

All that remains for the Jesus strand is that he did wonders by magic and had been in Egypt. According to Joel, the words 'they hung him on the eve of Passover' were added after the merging of the two traditions and are themselves drawn from the Christian tradition.[1]

The difference between this reconstruction and Derenbourg's [2] is the more pointed when it is realised that they only agree on the negative aspect, i.e. Jesus ≠ Ben Stada. And the fact that later Jewish writers cite Derenbourg and Joel together means that this is what interests them more than the evolution of the traditions.

Joel's scheme, firstly, shifts the points common to Jesus and Ben Stada right away from the trial, and so avoids not only the mesith theme but all Jewish judicial involvement. This could not be more different from Graetz, for whom the mesith aspect was enough to prove the identity of Jesus and Ben Stada. Secondly, the data contained in the Jesus strand reduces to material which is present in the gospels too, i.e. Joel is attempting to eliminate the independence of the Talmudic witness. His other attempts to deal with the mesith question are: (a) R. Akiba thought Jesus was a mesith and, knowing the synoptic chronology, deduced the exception in the laws for the execution of such an offender at a feast.[3] (b) Hostile remarks about Jesus are the reflection of subsequent events [4] and particularly of the schism. (c) The statement of trial and execution by the Jewish court is a later deduction from Jesus' assumed character as a mesith.[5] (d) In another place Joel argues against the gospel account of the Sanhedrin trial, that it clashes with the mesith account.[6] But Joel is so intent on reaching his conclusion that at times the argumentation shows considerable tension. Thus the issue leading to the schism is described in terms quite different from the normal content of the mesith charge. Again, the fact that R. Akiba regarded Jesus as a mesith in the light of the schism does not take account of R. Akiba's allegedly having lived before the schism,[7] and clashes with the placing of responsibility for

---

[1] Blicke II, 56.

[2] See above, p. 35.

[3] op.cit. 59-63.

[4] Cf. Derenbourg, op.cit. 202. He of course did not include the mesith issue in this category.

[5] Blicke II, 66: 'Natürlich setzt er ... nicht blos eine Verurtheilung, sondern auch eine Vollstreckung durch das jüdische Gericht voraus.'

[6] op.cit. 65.

[7] Joel's treatment of R. Akiba's ruling in Tos. Sanh. 11.7 is criticised, though with not wholly sufficient arguments, by J. Z. Lauterbach, Rabbinic Essays, Cincinnati 1951, 493.

these views of Jesus on the Babylonian Rabbis. Further, point (d) is no argument at all if the mesith trial has already been eliminated.

Joel has not only eliminated the mesith theme but also the 'mamzer' charge. This was the second focal point for Derenbourg who started the separation of the traditions here. The abandonment of both these charges coheres with the twofold reproach from non-Jewish quarters: responsibility for the trial and personal attacks on Jesus. In fact Jesus becomes more and more a true Jew accepted by his fellow-Jews.

In the period following, the work of Derenbourg and Joel conti-nued to be used, e.g. by Kohler,[1] Krauss,[2] and A. Cohen.[3] A new deve-lopment comes with the attempt to identify Ben Stada with the Egyp-tian false prophet of Josephus, Ant.20.167-170, B.J. 2.258 and Acts 21.38. This was suggested, apparently independently, by H. P. Chajes [4] and, hesitantly, by the Unitarian, R. T. Herford,[5] and accepted by B. Z. Bokser,[6] J. Gutmann,[7] K. Kohler [8] (he does so rather ambigu-ously, and adds in Theudas as well) and L. H. Feldman.[9] The identifi-cation of Jesus with Ben Stada was in general terms doubted by S. R. Krauss (though 'The Talmudic account of the manner of executing a person guilty of leading the people astray, Sanh.67a, would be of signal importance if it were certain that it referred to Jesus')[10] and H. Freedman, who returns to Derenbourg's argumentation and rejects the Egyptian prophet theory on the grounds that Pappos b. Judah lived in the century after Jesus.[11] Mantel refers to Derenbourg but does not mention alternative identifications for Ben Stada. [12]

4. The political theory from Philippson onwards

Philippson's political reconstruction is the classic example of its type,[13] and his work can be evaluated from three angles:

---

[1] Christianity in its relation to Judaism, JE 4 (1903), 50.
[2] Jesus of Nazareth in Jewish Legend, JE 7 (1904), 170-173.
[3] Jewish History in the first century, in Judaism and the Beginning of Christia-nity, London 1924, 40.
[4] Unfortunately I have been unable to obtain access to a copy of Chajes' article.
[5] Christianity in Talmud and Midrash, London 1903: 'a hypothesis worth con-sideration'.
[6] Pharisaic Judaism in Transition, New York 1935, 17f.
[7] Ben Satada, EJ 4 (1929), 73.
[8] op.cit. 50.
[9] Josephus: Jewish Antiquities IX, London 1965, 480.
[10] art.cit. 171f.
[11] The Soncino Talmud: Sanhedrin, London 1935, 456f. Freedman differs from Derenbourg in not substituting Judah b. Pappos for Pappos b. Judah.
[12] Studies in the History of the Sanhedrin, Cambridge, Mass. 1961, 309.
[13] Haben wirklich die Juden Jesum gekreuzigt?, Berlin 1866.

(a) His reaction to Graetz. Philippson gives a lengthy survey of previous work (Salvador, Winer, Saalschütz, Strauss, Renan, Graetz and Samuel Hirsch) but apart from the very general comment about Graetz that his chapter on Christianity is 'originell und scharfsinnig und hält dabei die Linie einer gemässigten und besonnenen Kritik ein' he is the only one of the list whose argument receives no scrutiny. Moreover Philippson's startingpoint is accurately stated in his title,[1] which questions almost precisely what Graetz had allowed in his 2nd edition. And the letter which is cited at the beginning of the book, and which provides the starting-point for the whole investigation, implies that there is considerable doubt about crucifixion and the Jews, a doubt which was in no way allayed by Graetz's book.

It would seem therefore that Philippson regarded his theory as a reply in toto to the sort of thing Graetz had written.[2] This reply is founded on the proof that crucifixion was a Roman procedure,[3] and also on the abandonment of the choice between Talmud and N.T. as alternative sources by appealing beyond them both to Tacitus: 'Als historische Thatsache steht also nur fest, was Tacitus Annal.XV,44,4 sagt.'[4]

(b) His conscious attitude to the sources. 'Auch die Jesu betreffenden talmudischen Notizen haben keinen geschichtlichen Werth, weil sie durchaus nicht aus unmittelbaren Überlieferungen, sondern aus späterer Zeit stammen, und sich nur an die christlichen Traditionen anlehnen.'[5] He then points out the divergence in dating, some placing Jesus 100 years earlier, others at the time of the temple's destruction,[6] and he refers to the work of Jost. Here again b.Sanh. 107b. is kept central. And although Philippson cites Jost he differs in claiming dependence on Christian tradition, and in omitting Jost's allegation that the sources have an apologetic intent. If this latter were true, apologetic and a Sanhedrin execution are related in some way, and Philippson apparently is not able to admit that. In line with this he omits b. Sanh. 43a, 67a from the list of sources cited. As to the detailed

---

[1] The emphasis is significant, and slightly different from Klausner's citation, Haben die Juden wirklich Jesum gekreuzigt? (Jesus, 333, 349) or, as in Lindeskog's bibliography, Haben die Juden Jesum wirklich gekreuzigt? (op.cit. 354).

[2] Philippson produces all the objections cited above, pp. 31f, op.cit. 2nd ed. Leipzig 1901, 7, 9, 26, 28, 42, 51, 62.

[3] op.cit. 7-9. For more treatment of Philippson, cf. below, pp. 113f.

[4] op.cit. 41.

[5] op.cit. 23.

[6] b.Sanh. 107b; Midr.Echa.59; j.Ber. 5.1.

consistent working out of his view, Philippson does not explore the
matter. For in fact the view that the Talmud depends on the gospels,
which were themselves written 100 years after the event, can hardly be
maintained in view of the connection of Ben Stada material with
R. Eliezer. Within the gospels Philippson holds a predictably low
opinion of John, but he can still stand as founder member of the large
group of Jewish scholars who make use of John as a crucial witness to
a Roman arrest—this solves the problem which made the Sanh. 7.10
procedure a possibility—and no Sanhedrin trial.[1]

(c) Talmudic influence within his framework. This can be detected
in what he approves in earlier works. Firstly, he accepts that the Jews
would and did act legally as Salvador showed.[2] Unfortunately this is
contradicted by the argument that the time and execution on a feast day
were illegal.[3] So Philippson is caught between two positions: diminish-
ing the illegalities in order to defend the Jews, and heightening them
in order to dismiss the Sanhedrin trial, again in order to defend the
Jews.[4] Secondly, he accepts that 'Son of God' in the Sanhedrin trial
is transcendent in significance, and makes this rather than messiahship
the issue: [5] yet he himself stresses the messianic charge which brought
about Jesus' condemnation by the Romans. For him the Sanhedrin
trial must be presented as purely religious (thus retreating to a pre-
Saalschütz position) and in maximum contrast with Ann. 15.44, i.e.
the purer the religious aspect and the more in line with Dt 13 and
b.Sanh. 43a, 67a, the easier it is to dismiss it.

Philippson thus presents only another variation on the theme of
retreat from a Rabbinic to a political approach. The process is not
complete and the transition involves anomalies. Other scholars follow
him in absorbing the old themes into a political view, e.g. I. M. Rabbinowicz [6] and H. Rodrigues.[7]

In the book of Rabbinowicz, both methodology (general acceptance
of relevant gospel material [8]) and interpretative method involve a

---

[1] op.cit. 55f.   [2] op.cit. 19.   [3] op.cit. 58.
[4] The same combination of Salvadorian arguments and the political theory is
present in Rabbinowicz, Rôle de Jésus, 134.
[5] The sources say that the senate condemned Jesus 'nicht wegen der Behauptung, der Messias zu sein, sondern wegen der zugestandenen dem ganzen jüdischen
Begriffe von der Einheit und Unkörperlichkeit Gottes widersprechenden Lehre
von der Göttlichkeit Jesu'. op.cit. 16.
[6] Le rôle de Jésus et des apôtres, Bruxelles 1866.
[7] Le Roi des Juifs, Paris 1870.
[8] op.cit. 134. He accepts the work of Salvador and has no need to appeal to
Tacitus.

difference from Philippson. Jesus' orthodoxy in religion and his lack
of new doctrines form the starting-point. The theme of newness, earlier so plain an indication of Talmudic influence, is retained but in a
quite different sense: 'Ce qu'il a dit de nouveau, c'est que le Messie
c'était lui' and 'c'est dans l'usurpation de la royauté que consiste la
séduction du peuple'.[1] This means that at Mk 14.61, whereas Philippson
ignored 'Messiah', Rabbinowicz ignores 'Son of God'.

Rodrigues opposes Graetz explicitly,[2] poses a choice between Mt
5.17 and Johannine christology [3] (whereas Graetz had incorporated
both), and lays all the stress on 'King of the Jews'. The mesith theme is
regarded as inconsistent with the continued activity of James the
brother of Jesus in Jerusalem.[4] From the time of Rodrigues onwards it
is in the context of the political reconstruction that repeated dismissal
of all Talmudic sources almost always appears. This holds for M. Güdemann, M. Fluegel (who returns to the old tendency, though with no
new arguments, to prove that the Talmudic passages do not refer to
Jesus), T. Reinach, S. Schindler, J. Bergmann, M. Freimann, Moriz
Friedländer, S. Schechter, H. G. Enelow and S. Bernfeld.[5] The judgement of Enelow is typical: 'Neither his life nor his death is mentioned
in the Talmudic portions of his period. What references there
are in the Talmud to Jesus, originated later on and are in themselves so obscure and doubtful as to be of very little historic value.' [6]

---

[1] op.cit. 139.

[2] Roi des Juifs, 242-246.

[3] Les origines du sermon de la montagne, Paris 1868, 130. He is still able to use
Jn 18.19f against any divine claim, Roi, 42f,146.

[4] Roi, 73. It would, he says, have been impossible to preach 'l'enseignement et
la glorification de celui qui aurait été réellement condamné par un synedrium en
qualité de blasphémateur et de séducteur du peuple'.

[5] M. Güdemann, Das IV (Johannes) Evangelium und der Rabbinismus, MGWJ
37 (1893), 350; M. Fluegel, The Messsiah-Ideal, Baltimore 1896, I,88, II,139-144
(Fluegel gives himself away by using the data of b.Sanh. 43a, op.cit. II, 143, even
though he says it is not about Jesus!); T. Reinach, REJ 35 (1897),1; S. Schindler,
Messianic Expectation and Modern Judaism, Boston 1886, 38; J. Bergmann, Die
Legenden der Juden, Berlin 1919, 122: 'Das erste Merkmal der Legende ist, daß
sie chronologische und historische Tatsachen unbeachtet läßt.' Cf. Jüdische
Apologetik, Berlin 1908, 35-37; M. Freimann, Die Wortführer des Judentums in
den ältesten Kontroversen zw. Juden und Christen, MGWJ 55 (1911), 556;
M. Friedländer, Encore un mot sur Minim, Minout et Guilonim dans le Talmud,
REJ 38 (1899), 197, Der Antichrist, Göttingen 1901, 54-61, Synagoge und Kirche
in ihren Anfängen, Berlin 1908, 141; S. Schechter, Studies in Judaism, 2nd Series,
London 1908, 102; H. G. Enelow, A Jewish View of Jesus (1920), published in
Selected Works III, Kingsport 1935, 484; S. Bernfeld, JJGL 13 (1910), 117.

[6] op.cit. 484.

5. *The position of Jewish converts to Christianity*

The merging of Jewish and Christian viewpoints tends normally to accentuate the stress on specifically Jewish themes. It is symptomatic that Franz Delitzsch, himself strongly influenced by the Jewish approach through Saalschütz, should argue that Jesus was condemned as a mesith,[1] and also that P. Cassel, a Jew, should assume that Ben Stada stands for Jesus, and should set himself to explain the derivation of Stada and Pandera.

Alfred Edersheim shows a similar preoccupation, and with such a polemical attitude to Jews that this phenomenon must be reckoned a likely influence on non-Christian Jewish writers to turn from the mesith idea and towards a negative criticism of the gospels. He begins with b.Sanh. 67a,[2] remarking apropos of Lydda that the tribunal there is declared to have been competent to pass death sentences (the first time a Jewish writer associates b.Sanh. 67a with the question of capital competence [3]), and arguing that Jesus and Mary are introduced with 'studiously and blasphemously altered names'.[4] Although Edersheim regards the Rabbinic sources as, in general, confused, he draws three points of positive value from b.Sanh. 67a: (a) It certainly refers to Jesus and his condemnation 'for supposed blasphemy and seduction of the people', a typically Jewish formulation.[5] (b) It indicates a close connection between Lydda and the founding of Christianity. In an entirely fanciful way, Edersheim locates there the events of Jn 11.47-53 or the negotiations with Judas. (c) The 'eve of Passover' detail confirms the synoptics! [6] The seduction theme is allowed to intrude again when Edersheim alludes to the command in Dt 13.1f, 18.21f to test a prophet by the signs he showed: 'a misapplication of which was made by the Jews in Jn 2.18, 6.30'.[7] (Again Edersheim is careless in his use of sources in that the attitude to signs in Dt 13 is different from that in

---

[1] Untersuchungen über die Entstehung und Anlage des Matthäus-Evangeliums, Leipzig 1853, 109: 'Die Anschauung Jesus als eines Verführers πλάνος Mt 27.64 zeigt, wie man nach jüdischem Gesetze seine Verurtheilung begründet, nämlich aus Deut 13.'
[2] Sketches of Jewish social life in the days of Christ, London 1877, 76.
[3] Cf. P. Winter, On the Trial of Jesus, Berlin 1961, 156.
[4] Sketches, 76.
[5] Sketches, 77.
[6] This is made into a polemical point: 'The Rabbis know nothing of those Jewish scruples and difficulties, by which modern Gentile writers have tried to prove the impossibility of Christ's condemnation on the Paschal night.' op.cit. 77.
[7] op.cit. 101.

Dt 18, and, knowing Saalschütz,[1] Edersheim had additional reason to make this distinction).

The same attraction towards the mesith idea recurs in Edersheim's later works: (a) The exceptional ruling for mesith executions is mentioned as a possibility.[2] (b) The Mk 14.58 saying, a distortion of Jn 2.19, could have been used for a charge of seduction or divine magical pretensions,[3] though technically neither this saying nor the blasphemy made Jesus a mesith (public seducer) or maddiach (private seducer). (c) Edersheim toys with the Sanh. 7 procedure [4] in spite of explicit statements to the contrary [5] and professed agreement with Jost on the lateness of the material. (d) In answer to those who ridicule the mesith/maddiah idea he writes: 'It is indeed true that, viewed as a Jewish charge, it might have been difficult if not impossible to construe a capital crime out of these charges',[6] but the high priest was aiming to formulate a charge which would convince Pilate, and not one defined in terms of Jewish law,[7] so the charge of fanatical seducer would do as well. Thus Edersheim is caught between Roman and Jewish legal contexts and between Jewish and Christian points of view.

Whereas Edersheim is typical of Jewish-Christians who move to a conservative position and high christology, Chwolson is quite the opposite: in him the Jew is always dominant over the Christian. He really knows the Talmudic sources [8] but aims to expunge their influence. He also eliminates any self-conscious claim by Jesus e.g. to be messiah or son of God, and in his 1892 volume is reluctant to give any content at all to the blasphemy.[9] Hence it is not in the least surprising that he says the Pharisees could not possibly have condemned Jesus as a false prophet or seducer.

---

[1] J. L. Saalschütz, Das Mosaische Recht, 2nd ed. Berlin 1853, Kap 1, Note 16.

[2] The Life and Times of Jesus the Messiah, London 1883, 557: 'It might be argued . . . that a process against one who had seduced the people should preferably be carried, and sentence executed, on public Feast Days for the warning of all.' Sanh. 11.4; Tos.Sanh. 11.7.

[3] op.cit. 558.

[4] The Temple: its Ministry and Services, London 1910, 397: 'I agree with Graetz (Geschichte IV, 242 note) that much in Sanh 7 bears, though unexpressed, reference to the proceedings of the Sanhedrin against Christ.'

[5] Life and Times, 559: 'The two stories that witnesses had lain in wait to hear and report the utterances of Christ (Sanh 67a), and that 40 days before his execution heralds had summoned exculpatory evidence in his favour (Sanh 43a) may be dismissed without comment.'

[6] Life and Times, 558.

[7] In any case, Edersheim thinks only of a preliminary hearing.

[8] Über die Frage, ob Jesus gelebt hat, Leipzig 1910, 9, 11.

[9] Das letzte Passamahl Christi, Leipzig 1908, 88.

In Chwolson's scheme there are three points of immediate relevance.
(a) He gives much more precise legal definitions than Edersheim does.
(b) The 'Pharisaic Jesus' theory [1] is the backbone of his view, and he is
almost the classical exponent of its application to the trial of Jesus. He
gives the well-known list of supports for a close relationship between
Jesus and Pharisees: Lk 7.36, 13.31, Acts. 5.34, 15.5, 23.9f and Josephus, Ant. 20.200. (The predominance of Lukan material must be
carefully noted here.) Chwolson also gives an historical basis to the
mesith issue, arguing that the schism only took effect from A.D. 110
onwards: [2] only when Jewish Christians went off into gnostic ideas did
opposition and conflicts arise. This means: only when they left *their
own* true faith (and were no longer true Christians) did division come.
In turn this means: between true Christianity and true Judaism [3] there
is no quarrel. Consequently any mesith accusation against Jesus is unthinkable. (c) The context of controversy between Jews and Christians
is formative for Chwolson. It is possible that his conversion was motivated by a desire to help the Jews.[4] This has led to a toning down of
all issues separating the two religions, something which shows plainly
in his treatment of σὺ εἶπας.[5] The claim to be God and the charge of
leading astray just would not fit. So the Talmudic picture yields this
time to a theological trend and the pressure of the Russian situation. It
is important that Chwolson describes the faith of the Jewish Christians
as Judaism + belief in Jesus 'als Messias oder als Propheten'.[6] This
joining of prophet to Messiah involves a considerable weakening, for
in a prophet there is no offence at all.[7]

In 1901 and 1910 Chwolson stated plainly his view of the Rabbinic
sources: 'Im eigentlichen Talmud finden sich relativ viele Nachrichten
über Christus, diese zerfallen in zwei Klassen, in solche die meist aus

---

[1] Passamahl, 90-92.

[2] op.cit. 102.

[3] A similar distinction within Judaism is that between Pharisees and Sadducees,
which Chwolson presses.

[4] Cf. L. S. Dawidowicz, The Golden Tradition: Jewish Life and Thought in
Eastern Europe, London 1967, 335. Chwolson's christology is certainly not high
enough to supply a cogent reason for conversion, and he was throughout a staunch
defender of the Jews against scandalous persecution.

[5] Cf. D. R. Catchpole, The Answer of Jesus to Caiaphas (Matt. xxvi.64), NTS 17
(1971), 215f.

[6] Passamahl, 108.

[7] Compare Kohler's description of Jesus as the boldest and most unique ethical
teacher, Origins, 218. Also more and more Jewish writers begin at this time to
evaluate Jesus in prophetic categories without thereby relaxing their grasp on
Judaism.

dem 3. oder 4. Jahrh. stammen und absolut keinen historischen Wert
haben und in einige wenige aus dem 1. Jahrh., die historisch sehr
wertvoll sind.' [1] The former are therefore given exactly the evaluation
of Jost and the latter, covering Jewish-Christians, are used to establish
harmony between Pharisees and Christians. From the data contained
in the passages dealing with Jesus, Chwolson accepts only the Nisan
14 chronology, and he opposes specifically the 'quite false' claim that
the execution was at Lydda.

F. The Klausner debate

The book of Klausner[2] marks a turning-point in Jewish evaluation of
Jesus, not because it contained much new material[3] but because it stirred
up and brought to common notice issues which had been debated many
years earlier and whose influence had never been entirely eliminated.

The first striking feature of Klausner's book is that he accepts so
much Talmudic and N.T. material as historical. He summarizes the
reliable Talmudic information as follows: 'There are reliable statements to the effect that his name was Yeshu'a (Yeshu) of Nazareth;
that he "practised sorcery" (i.e. performed miracles as was usual in
those days) and beguiled and led Israel astray; that he mocked at the
words of the wise; that he expounded scripture in the same manner as
the Pharisees; that he had five disciples; that he said he was not come
to take aught away from the law or to add to it; that he was hanged
(crucified) as a false teacher and beguiler on the eve of the Passover
which happened on a Sabbath; and that his disciples healed the sick
in his name.' [4] Now it has been shown that the Talmudic material on
Jesus, while never entirely losing its influence, was nevertheless subjected to intense pressure so that many scholars came to reject it
explicitly and many others simply to ignore it. Of the last group C. G.
Montefiore is the most outstanding example, and at no point is the
contrast between him and Klausner greater than here. But this contrast has to be seen within the context of the attack levelled against
Montefiore by A. Ginzberg [5] under whose influence Klausner wrote.

---

[1] Über die Frage, 11; cf. Die Blutanklage und sonstige mittelalterliche Beschuldigungen der Juden, Frankfurt.a.M. 1901, 60f.

[2] Jesus of Nazareth, London 1925.

[3] Klausner's opponents were emphatic that he had said nothing new. S. Zeitlin,
Studies in the Beginning of Christianity, JQR 14 (1923), 132; M. Guttmann,
MGWJ 75 (1931), 250-257.

[4] op.cit. 46.

[5] Ten Essays on Zionism and Judaism, London 1922.

The relevant essay by Ginzberg shows how a debate *within* Judaism disturbs the evaluation of issues outside Judaism. Montefiore is here accused of estrangement from the essential nature of Judaism [1] and of having led English Reform Judaism along a path of error which minimizes the difference between Christianity and Judaism. The Christian message, Ginzberg argues, is essentially a deviation, and intrinsically tends to idolatry: 'If the heathen of the old story, who wished to learn the whole Torah standing on one leg, had come to me, I should have told him: 'Thou shalt not make to thyself any graven image or any likeness—that is the whole Torah, and the rest is commentary' . . . It matters not whether he (Jesus) be called Son of God, Messiah or Prophet: Israel cannot accept with religious enthusiasm, as the Word of God, the utterance of a man who speaks in his own name—not "thus saith the Lord" but "I say unto you". This "I" is in itself sufficient to drive Judaism away from the Gospels for ever.' [2] Ginzberg then goes on to cite Mk 10.2-12 as indicative of an un-Jewish view of the law. Here then we see, firstly, an approach more rigid than that of Mendelssohn who accepted Jesus' legal teaching, provided no unorthodox Christology was added. Ginzberg sees *within* that legal teaching the mesith deviation. Secondly, this is an interpretation of the early development of the Christian church quite opposite to that of Chwolson. The period of overlap with Judaism is not so significant as the final rupture which was emphatically a necessary rupture and exposed the true and original character of Christianity.[3] Thirdly, the rapprochement, constructed by means of the Golden Rule, is devastated. Even the positive form is said to be essentially different from Hillel's negative form and contrary to the moral basis of Judaism.[4]

Now Klausner cites Montefiore only once [5] and alludes to the article

---

[1] op.cit. 228: 'The general atmosphere of the book (of C. G. Montefiore) is so utterly alien from the essential character of Judaism as to make one fact clear beyond a shadow of doubt to any Jew in whom Judaism is still alive—that the Gospels can be received only into a Judaism which has lost its own true spirit and remains a mere corpse.'

[2] op.cit. 229, 232. Cf. T. Weiss-Rosmarin, Judaism and Christianity, New York 1943, 130, 147; P. E. Lapide, The last three Popes and the Jews, London 1967, 19. We may compare here the opposition of Paul Winter to the authenticity of this I-saying, again opposing even the prophetic status of the true Jesus and making him only a Jewish rabbi. Μονογενὴς παρὰ πατρός, ZRGG 5 (1953), 2-23, esp. 12.

[3] There is a striking coincidence between these views and the position of E. Stauffer.

[4] op.cit. 235. This position is also adopted by R. Learsi, Israel: a History of the Jewish People, Cleveland 1949, 159.

[5] Jesus, 114. See S. Sandmel, We Jews and Jesus, London 1965, 93.

by Ginzberg. Clearly he accepts that Montefiore's exposition of the gospels for Jews and his evident sympathy with Jesus had gone too far. He himself criticizes the attempt to show parallels for gospel material in Talmudic literature and the whole intention of showing that 'the gospels are generally superior to the Talmud and are Hebrew works which should be acceptable to Jews',[1] as well as comparing Montefiore with H. G. Enelow whose book is labelled 'virtually Unitarianism'. It is therefore natural for Klausner to give attention to the distinction between Jesus and Jews, and to Judaism's verdict on him. Thus the seeds of apostasy, which are almost imputed to Montefiore, are detected in Jesus by means of a revival of the orthodox Talmudic position. In Ginzberg is revealed the source of the reaction to which Klausner subscribes. Moreover Klausner, like Ginzberg, was a Zionist [2]—again a contrast with the positive liberalism of Montefiore. The national assessment of Jesus, in line with this, plays a part, and with this also coheres a return to the Talmudic sources. Different aspects of nationalism explain how Klausner is able to see both Jesus 'the nationalist' and Jesus the one who had something out of which arose non-Judaism.[3]

A storm was raised not only by Klausner's use of Talmudic sources but also by his conservative 'in dubio pro traditione' attitude to the gospels. Within the general charge of bypassing the tools of Leben-Jesu-Forschung,[4] he was particularly accused of over-conservative methods in treating the Passion events.[5] Thus these last events become the nub of the debate.

Attitudes to the New Testament and to the Talmud do not for Klausner belong to two separate categories; rather he sees a connection between the two.[6] Here again he was severely criticized, and his position deserves to be outlined. He recognized that in part both N.T. and Rabbinic passages are unhistorical, and yet respect for both leads to difficulty about critera. On the one side Klausner gives the Hebrew

---

[1] op.cit. 114.

[2] Criticized as such by M. Dienemann, Zur Leben-Jesu-Forschung, Der Morgen 6 (1930), 376.

[3] Jesus, 413.

[4] Dienemann, art.cit. 375: 'Das Charakteristische und Neue an Klausner innerhalb der kritischen wissenschaftlichen Forschung ist nur, daß er die Glaubwürdigkeit der Evangelien als Niederschlag einer gegründeten Überlieferung bejaht.' Cf. M. Guttmann, MGWJ 75 (1931), 250, and repeated criticism of Klausner by Sandmel.

[5] Dienemann, art.cit. 378-380; S. Zeitlin, JQR 14 (1923), 136-138.

[6] M. Guttmann, art.cit. 250-257.

sources priority because they spring from Jesus' own environment [1] whereas the gospels are said to be biassed and not objective. Yet the Talmud too has inherent defects, through polemical intention and consequent unhistoricity: [2] the passages often late, depend on popular versions and are not a true recollection. Nevertheless Klausner thinks the earliest of them are earlier than the latest of the gospels. [3] Talmud and N.T., therefore, stand in certain respects on opposite sides of the divide, and Guttmann rightly remarks that Klausner attempts to build a bridge between them. [4] The relationship he claims exists between Talmudic assertions and N.T. material at its oral stage. The former are replies to the latter. Hence the gospel material is earlier in date than its literary form, so 'the accounts in the first three Gospels are fairly early', and Jesus' existence and general character as described there can be accepted—'this is the single historical value which we can attribute to the early Talmudical accounts of Jesus'. [5] Two examples of the way in which Talmudic statements reply to N. T. ones are provided by Klausner: firstly, Jesus is said to have been illegitimate, not born of the Holy Spirit, and, secondly, he is said to have done wonders through magic. These two examples, however, show the tension in Klausner's position, for three reasons. (a) The illegitimacy taunt is earlier than the virgin birth claim, as Mk 6.3 shows. Klausner's argument moves from the earliness of one claim he does not accept as historical to the historicity of other claims which he declares by this argumentation to be early. (b) The magician accusation is also reflected in the gospels, as Klausner does recognize, and this time he does accept it as historical. [6] (c) Both Jewish comments occur in the gospels (Mk 3.22, 6.3) and in neither case as the answer to a Christian claim.

Whereas other scholars had used the Talmud to support the existence of Jesus, Klausner's attempt to use it to vindicate the gospels was new and plainly in contradiction to the older pattern, which saw them as in certain senses in opposition. Once the Talmud has been used to vindicate the N. T., the latter then becomes the criterion for assessing the Talmud. There is therefore a two-way relationship. The most

---

[1] Jesus, 17.
[2] op.cit. 18f.
[3] op.cit. 19.
[4] art.cit. 252.
[5] op.cit. 20.
[6] It is noticeable that Klausner dilutes the sorcery charge, op. cit. 46, rendering it harmless, i.e. 'he performed miracles, as was usual in those days', while including it among the reliable Talmudic insights.

trenchant criticism of this came along two different lines: (a) Zeitlin proposed that the Talmudic passages are all later than, and dependent on, the gospels.[1] He writes, polemizing against Klausner: 'All passages which, according to Herford and Klausner, prove that the early Tannaim not only knew about Jesus but also knew that he was executed in Lydda on the eve of Passover as a deceiver . . . . are of late period and were brought into the Tannaitic literature under the influence of the gospels.'[2] This is, however, not a just criticism because Klausner opposes the Ben Stada equation which is necessary for Zeitlin's statement to be true, and he never says that the Tannaim knew Jesus was executed at Lydda—in fact he opposes the view that they even *thought* so. (b) The force of Guttmann's criticism is that the Talmudic passages must be considered first in toto and not piecemeal *before* comparison with the gospels. This excludes a policy of accepting some parts and rejecting others. This total picture, he feels, is wholly other than the N.T. Jesus,[3] and so the way is prepared for a wholesale rejection. In fact Guttmann is producing in a slightly different form the argument that all the sources are to be dismissed because of an objection to b.Sanh. 107b.

Two examples of Klausner's method must now be cited. The first concerns b.Sanh. 43a.[4] Klausner argues in the following manner: (a) The Talmud does not deny Jesus' miracles but interprets them as sorcery. The source is found in the gospels: Mk 3.22, Mt 9.34, 12.24. Here then agreement with the gospels is the authenticating factor. (b) In the statement that Jesus was executed as seducer and beguiler the Tannaim were in fact projecting back the schismatic situation of their own day. At this point Klausner is in a position of tension between the normal view, which is what he here states, and his elsewhere expressed view which sees the schism as deriving from Jesus. This latter is something which he stresses, e.g. in criticism of Geiger.[5] (Klausner rejects the tendency to stress the evolution/continuity argument on the Jewish side through and in Judaeo-Christianity, but instead transfers it to the Christian side, thus preventing a wholly

---

[1] Studies, 132.

[2] Jesus in the early Tannaitic Literature, Abhandlungen zur Erinnerung an H. P. Chajes, Wien 1933, 295.

[3] op.cit. 252f.

[4] Four of the eight propositions accepted by Klausner from the Talmud are drawn from b.Sanh. 43a. See above, p. 54.

[5] op.cit. 115. This is also not a totally fair criticism of Geiger, who had allowed some interference by Jesus with the basic faith of Judaism.

orthodox Jesus. Earlier scholars had made a break and discontinuity within Christianity, often with Paul. Klausner also has a development from Paul [1] but in his theory Paul is not the founder of Christianity). In fact, Klausner's rule that Tannaitic statements may be historical provided there is no controversy with Christian opinions or the gospel accounts, should really disallow this dismissal of the seducer issue. Of N.T. πλάνος references, Klausner ignores Jn 7.12,47, and Mt 27.62-66, although cited,[2] receives no comment. However retention of the πλάνος idea elsewhere is in line with Klausner's account in which Jesus himself sows the seeds of apostasy. (c) The herald's 40-day appeal is dismissed because it contradicts the gospels' record of haste and is tendentious. Here the above rule is applied consistently. (d) Chronology, agreeing with Jn 19.14, is accepted. But this is not easily harmonized with his earlier statement about the relative order of the Talmudic sources and Jn. In so far as the Talmud establishes the gospels, it is the synoptic gospels alone. (e) The five disciples. Here again Klausner departs from his own rule and prefers this to the figure of twelve, which reflects the parallelism with Israel.[3] From this detailed survey of how Klausner treats one important source it can be seen that his practice is far from consistent.[4]

The same emerges from Yeb. 4.13:

> R. Simeon b. Azzai said: I found a family register in Jerusalem, and in it was written, 'Such-a-one is a bastard through (a transgression of the law of) thy neighbour's wife.'

Klausner readily admits that this text refers to Jesus,[5] and explains the omission of his name by the fact that disciples were healing in that name. He dates it at the time of Celsus, and concludes: 'That there is

---

[1] op.cit. 392.

[2] op.cit. 357.

[3] He allows that some of the names are inaccurate but makes the following equations: Mattai = Matthew, Naqai = Luke, Netzer = Andrew (or Nozrim), Buni = John, Todah = Thaddaeus, op.cit. 30. Elsewhere he accepts 12 tentatively when describing the commissioning of the disciples, op.cit. 283.

[4] On the other hand Zeitlin's reply to Klausner on this passage is no more convincing. He admits that the first part is a baraita, but draws no conclusion from this. Instead, he introduces against the whole an argument applying only to the second half. He concludes: 'This story has no historical bearing on the execution of Jesus. It is quite evident from the story itself that it belonged to a later period when the Jews obtained their knowledge from the Gospel narratives.' Jesus in the Tannaitic literature, 302f.

[5] op.cit. 35. Against this Zeitlin, art.cit. 300; M. Goldstein, Jesus in the Jewish Tradition, New York 1950, 68.

no historical foundation for the tradition of Jesus' illegitimate birth, and that the tradition arises from opposition to the view that Jesus was born without a natural father—all this we have repeatedly seen.' [1] Yet this tradition would appear to satisfy Klausner's usual criteria: firstly, it is early [2] (because of the date of Ben Azzai, A.D.90-130) and, secondly, although it contradicts the virgin birth, it agrees with Mk 6.3. [3] In view of this, specific reasons must be sought for Klausner's avoidance of the old Jewish viewpoint: firstly, he is anxious to avoid any attack on Jesus, and secondly, the illegitimacy / Aryan descent theory [4] leads to a defensive acceptance of normal birth.

We can now turn to issues converging specifically on the trial. (a) Jesus and the law. The summary of reliable Talmudic data does not give an unequivocal account of Jesus' attitude to the law. On b.Shabb. 116a-b Klausner writes that the same ambivalent attitude is imputed to Jesus and to Christians; [5] and in spite of claims to the contrary, Jesus did actually set aside ceremonial laws. [6] Although Klausner cites all the usual pro-Pharisaic verses [7] like Mk 12.28-34, he retains some mixedness in Jesus, and the beginnings of the subsequent rupture. Like Ginzberg he brings Jesus' attitude to the law closely in line with the confession of monotheism, [8] so that the πλάνος theme is not discarded. Jesus, he says, gave excessive emphasis to the Fatherhood idea, [9] and *arising from this* was his insistence on 'But I say unto you' rather than 'them of old time', i.e. the law of Moses, the prophets and the Pharisees. Similarly, Jesus' setting of miracles on a level with teaching was non-Pharisaic. [10] Klausner does however modify the unsoundness [11] of Jesus with three

---

[1] op.cit. 36, 252.

[2] Klausner himself allows that it is the earliest statement in Hebrew literature dealing with Jesus, op.cit. 35.

[3] Klausner cites Mk 6.3, op.cit. 282, but the scandal is passed over quickly, and amplification drawn from Mt 13.54, Lk 4.22.

[4] Cited, op.cit. 233.

[5] op.cit. 45.

[6] op.cit. 255. Jesus taught little beside the oral law—a point separating him from the Pharisees. Yet, op.cit. 275: 'Jesus remained steadfast to the old Torah: till his dying day he continued to observe the ceremonial laws like a true Pharisaic Jew.' Cf. Zeitlin's criticism, Studies, 132, that Klausner recites contradictory opinions without deciding between them.

[7] op.cit. 319.

[8] op.cit. 378f.

[9] Similarly combining these themes, S. Dubnow, A short History of the Jewish People, London 1936, 117.

[10] op.cit. 255,266.

[11] J. Jocz, The Jewish People and Jesus Christ, London 1949, 29-31, criticizes Klausner at this point for indecisiveness.

qualifications. First, it was in the development that trouble came. Second, in Jesus it was unintentional.[1] Third, it came from over-emphasis. This means not that Jesus said wrong things, but that he said right things in misleading proportions. Klausner thus tries to hold together Jesus the Jew and Jesus who 'led Israel astray'. (b) Jesus' trial. Here the points outlined above converge. Speaking of Jesus' insistence on Divine Fatherhood, Klausner writes: 'It was precisely this excessive emphasis which made Kaiaphas the High Priest rend his clothes.'[2] This is said in spite of his having removed 'Son of the Blessed' from what the high priest said, and is drawn from Jesus' non-rejection of the coming messiah role and heavenly session. Again therefore the Talmudic perspective is controlling gospel interpretation.

In all this b.Sanh. 43a is the primary passage, but some discussion of b.Sanh. 107b and the Ben Stada complex is prefixed.

Klausner applies to b.Sanh. 107b the technique which had previously been used on Ben Stada material, i.e. two traditions have been conflated, and in this case j.Hag. 2.2 preserves the earlier form. This was taken up by H. Stourdzé,[3] who suggests that R. Ulla first applied the tradition to Jesus, and also by J. Z. Lauterbach and M. Goldstein.[4] Surprisingly, Zeitlin at this point represents an earlier view, arguing from the chronology: 'From this story we can only see how meager and vague was the knowledge of the Tannaim about Jesus.'[5] Once again Zeitlin evades the force of a baraita by translating the final sentence as 'And a teacher Yeshu (of N.) ...' instead of 'And a teacher said ...'—an unvarnished avoidance of the 'amar' which Zeitlin has in his Hebrew text.

On Ben Stada, Klausner follows the Chajes-Herford equation of Ben Stada and the Egyptian false prophet.[6] There are three external reasons: (a) No proof exists that the Tannaim thought he was Jesus. This is similar to the old point about two different names, though Klausner could not argue in that way since he regards Ben Pandera as

---

[1] op.cit. 391: 'the breach which all unintentionally Jesus would have made in the defences of Judaism'. Similarly, S. Rosenblatt, The Crucifixion of Jesus from the Standpoint of Pharisaic Law, JBL 75 (1956), 315-321.

[2] op.cit. 378.

[3] La fuite en Égypte de Jesué b. Perahya et l'incident avec son prétendu disciple Jésus, REJ 82 (1926), 133-156, esp.149f.

[4] J. Z. Lauterbach, Rabbinic Essays, Cincinnati 1951, 486-488; M. Goldstein, Jesus in the Jewish Tradition, New York 1950, 75f.

[5] Jesus in the Tannaitic Literature, 303f.

[6] G. Lindeskog, Jesusfrage, 11, also accepts Klausner's argument for the non-identity of Jesus and Ben Stada.

a mockery of υἱὸς τοῦ παρθένου.[1] (b) The Tol'doth Yeshu never calls
Jesus Ben Stada. This, says Klausner, means that even at that late
stage Ben Stada was not regarded as 'a habitual synonym for Jesus'.
But he then destroys this point by admitting that the Tol'doth attributes to Jesus the introduction of spells from Egypt in a cut in his flesh.
This could only be drawn from the Ben Stada material. Further, it
is inconsistent to reject the opinion of R. Hisda in favour of a mediaeval source. (c) Rabbenu Tam (b.Shabb. 104b) declared: 'This was not
Jesus of Nazareth.' But his view, from the 12th century, constitutes no
evidence whatever. There follow three Joel-type internal arguments:
(a) Lydda clashes with Jesus' execution at Jerusalem. (b) The Talmud
authorities regarded Jesus as a dangerous beguiler, not a 'shoteh'
(madman). But this attempted distinction between Jesus and Ben
Stada is only one between two Ben Stada passages since Ben Stada is
regarded as a beguiler in Tos. Sanh. 10.11, j.Sanh. 7.16, and Klausner
himself [2] argues that the Egyptian prophet was a beguiler. (c) They
could not say Jesus was stoned by the Jewish Beth Din when in reality
the Romans crucified him.[3] Here the insertion by Klausner of 'Jewish'
and 'Roman' is significant, reflecting the stock argument that crucifixion was a Roman punishment. Further, b.Sanh. 43a also has stoning
but Klausner does not dispute the reference to Jesus there.

If the negative side of Klausner's argument is inadequate, his alternative identification has still to be examined. Firstly, it is necessary to
set this in the context of the reasons put forward by Herford [4]: (a)
'This man is called a sorcerer; at least he promised that the walls of
Jerusalem should fall at his approach. Ben Stada, by comparison,
brought magic from Egypt.' (b) The description 'fool' applies better to
him than to Jesus—the converse of Joel's point.[5] (c) R. Eliezer does
not say that Ben Stada was put to death at Lud; and Josephus says he
escaped.[6] This last is the most noteworthy point, because it means
that b.Shabb. 104b alone is taken as definitive for Ben Stada. This
means that Klausner in his external reasons (a) and (c) weakens Herford's very straightforward position by allowing more Ben Stada

---

[1] op.cit. 23f.
[2] op.cit. 22.
[3] Similarly, S. Zeitlin, Jesus in the early Tannaitic Literature, 300f, though
without the identification with the Egyptian prophet.
[4] Christianity in Talmud. 345.
[5] See above p. 45.
[6] 'The execution of Ben Stada at Lud is the result of identifying Ben Stada with
Jeshu Ha-Notzri.' This is an extraordinary argument.

material as primary even though he draws two more contrasts.

Klausner's positive arguments on the Egyptian false prophet are the following: (a) He was a beguiler and led the people into the wilderness. In connection with this he remarks that the Tosephta lacks the argument, 'How can we leave our God who is in heaven and worship idols?' which appears in the Babylonian Talmud but 'is not possible in the case of the Egyptian false prophet'.[1] (b) He performed acts of foolishness and madness in promising that the walls of Jerusalem would fall. (c) 'It is possible' that after his escape he was found at Lud and far from Jerusalem, and stoned by the Beth Din after the use of the concealment procedure.

These arguments can only stand if the meaning of 'mesith' is devalued. Thus (a) the Tosephta statement, regarded by Klausner as inapplicable, is consistent both with the passage as it stands and with the legal background in Dt 13. If this element of mesith terminology does not apply, neither does the mesith context of Tos.Sanh. 10.11 and j.Sanh. 7.16. (b) Leading into the wilderness is no content for the legal definition of beguiler, for although the wilderness has messianic/political associations,[2] the religious position of those who went there was one of fanatical loyalty to, and certainly not apostasy from, Yahweh. Further, the foolish acts of b.Shabb. 104b hardly correspond to the promise that the walls of Jerusalem would fall. Nor do the magical acts attributed to Ben Stada find any parallel in the deeds of the Egyptian. Finally, as regards his (supposed) recapture, unsubstantiated conjectures are no substitute for evidence.

With Klausner at this point stand J. Z. Lauterbach, J. Jocz and M. Goldstein.[3] Goldstein adds speculatively a new comment, allowing for an impact by Jewish tradition on Christianity here, rather than, as is more usual, the reverse. 'Is it possible that passages of the Gospel account of Jesus attribute to him some of the trials and tribulations of Ben Stada, the disappointing saviour of the middle of the 1st century?' Now Goldstein sees in both Jesus and Ben Stada 'a disappointing Saviour',[4] but is at pains to stress differences and consequent non-

---

[1] op.cit. 22. Contrast here J. Z. Lauterbach, Essays, 520, who follows Klausner in arguing for 'Ben Stada = the Egyptian prophet', but allows the former to be a mesith.

[2] Acts 21.38 mentions that those influenced by this prophet were sicarii, who, if zealots, were devotees of the sole lordship of God.

[3] J. Z. Lauterbach, Rabbinic Essays, 520-525; J. Jocz, The Jewish People and Jesus Christ, London 1949, 59; M. Goldstein, Jesus in the Jewish Tradition, New York 1950, 26-28.

[4] op.cit. 28.

identity; moreover, the details of the religious trial in the gospels are understood to diverge not only from the true course of events (Roman trial and execution [1]) but also from the b.Sanh. 43a details.[2] It would therefore be interesting to know what *gospel* details are drawn from the Ben Stada ones. That Goldstein should so end his treatment of Ben Stada testifies to the intuitive link between the two in spite of contrary argument.

The points of similarity between Jesus and Ben Stada persist in spite of the arguments of Klausner, Lauterbach, Zeitlin and Goldstein. (a) Both are connected with Egypt: Mt 2.13-19 (the gospel known to Jews), b.Sanh. 107b, b.Shabb. 104b. (b) Both are regarded as magicians (whereas the prophet was not): Mk 3.22, Mt 12.24, b.Sanh. 43a, Tos. Shabb. 11.15, b.Shabb. 104b. (c) Both are regarded as mesiths: Mt 27.64, b.Sanh. 43a, Tos.Sanh. 10.11, j.Sanh. 7.16. The prophet was not. (d) Both are wrongly alleged to have been stoned: b.Sanh. 43a, Tos.Sanh. 10.11. The prophet's fate is unknown. In view of all this overlap it is difficult to believe that Ben Stada does not stand for Jesus.

G. From Klausner to the present day

During this period of 40 years the cycle of Talmudic reconstructions and rejections repeats itself. Jewish approaches can be analysed as follows:

1. *Later Klausnerian/Talmudic schemes*

Klausner is cited, and his general approach accepted often,[3] in spite of the heavy criticism directed at him.[4] It is partially under the influence of Klausner that Dubnow [5] put forward a reconstruction heavily biassed towards the Talmud, and at times reminiscent even of Graetz. Dubnow is severely critical of theories which had in fact minimized Talmudic influence, e.g. the attempts to make Jesus either an orthodox (Chwolson) or a Galilean (Geiger) Pharisee.[6] In the process of resur-

---

[1] op.cit. 26.

[2] op.cit. 26f. These details are themselves 'an unhistoric tradition', op.cit. 96.

[3] e.g. S. Cohon, The Place of Jesus in the Religious Life of his Day, JBL 48 (1929), 82; E. R. Trattner, As a Jew sees Jesus, London 1931, 3, 173; A. L. Sachar, A History of the Jews, New York 1930; J. Schechter, Soncino Talmud: Tractate Sanhedrin, London 1935, on b.Sanh. 43a.

[4] M. Dienemann, M. Guttmann, S. Zeitlin, cited above.

[5] Weltgeschichte des jüdischen Volkes II, Berlin 1925.

[6] op.cit. 581. He is particularly scornful of Chwolson: 'In dem Bestreben, seine ehemaligen Glaubensgenossen von der Schuld des Gottes-mordes reinzuwaschen, versucht der apostatische Apologet Daniel Chwolson ...' Similar words are voiced by S. Zeitlin, JQR 14 (1923), 136.

recting the pre-Geigerian assessment, Dubnow interjects the following features which were seen earlier to be Talmud-inspired: (a) The
rumour of illegitimacy.[1] (b) Jesus' home was in Galilee, not Jerusalem,[2]
and therefore in a hotbed of mystical religion and politics (cf. Jost and
Graetz). (c) The description 'the new teacher' reappears in the context
of the conflict with Sadducees and Pharisees. The suggestion of deviation from official normative religion is confirmed, pace Mk 12.28-34,
by the statement of a fundamental cleavage between Jesus and the
Pharisees [3]—this causes Mt 5.17 to be adjusted by Mt 5.20! [4] All this
coheres with Dubnow's view of history. Of the suggested three phases in
Christianity, corresponding to John the Baptist, Jesus and Paul, the
second is the phase of revelation and of inner break with national
Judaism. Thus the Hegelian dialectic is cracked and the principle of
continuity applied to the differences from Judaism. There is nothing of
Chwolson's attempt to apply it to the similarities. All of this recalls
Klausner's criticisms of Geiger [5] as well as the former's revival, under
Ginzberg's influence, of the nonconforming element in Jesus, all
coupled with a sympathetic use of Talmudic passages. (d) Jesus'
conciousness as 'jener Übermensch, der Gesandte Gottes, der die Herr-
schaft Gottes auf Erden zu begründen berufen sei'.[6] A prophet and
wonderworker in Galilee, Jesus struck the capital like lightning with
his claim to be messiah, Son of God or king of the Jews.[7] Here is the
old pattern of offensive Christology, dominated by the Sonship idea.[8]
(e) The view of some associates of Jesus (the story mentions Judas)
who were willing to denounce him and point out that by his *speeches*
and *wonders*, the *new prophet* had caused *unrest among the people*. Not only
do the italicized words add up to the Dt 13 pattern, but the preference for plural betrayers, instead of the single individual Judas, who
tell about the content of Jesus' activity rather than his geographical
whereabouts and identity—all this is very close to Sanh. 7.10. (f) The
Sanhedrin's condemnation of Jesus 'als einen sich "Messias" und

---

[1] op.cit. 531.

[2] op.cit. 532-534.

[3] op.cit. 538.

[4] op.cit. 582. Mt 23.2, the verse usually associated with Mt 5.17, is not covered,
and is free to be used by I. Elbogen in criticism, cf. Zu S. Dubnows Geschichts-
werke, MGWJ 70 (1926), 153.

[5] Jesus of Nazareth, 115.

[6] op.cit. 534.

[7] op.cit. 534.

[8] Dubnow agrees with Klausner about Jesus' over-emphasis on the Fatherhood
of God.

"Gottessohn" nennenden falschen Propheten und Gotteslästerer'.[1]
The bearing of this is made clear by Dubnow's shorter work,[2] where
the sentence parallel to the above citation omits to mention messiah
and blasphemy. Clearly false prophecy is primary.[3]

The Klausnerian picture of inherent deviation from Judaism, alongside the Mt 5.17, 23.2 scheme, is frequently repeated during this period
e.g. by A. L. Sachar, L. I. Edgar, T. Weiss-Rosmarin, R. Learsi, S.
Rosenblatt, J. Jocz and P. E. Lapide.[4] There is agreement here that
Jesus cannot be integrated into the Judaism of his own time, but disagreement exists as to whether this prevents his reception into present-
day Judaism (the presupposition of which had so exasperated Ginzberg). Thus Edgar retains Jesus as a prophet [5] faithful to Judaism's
basic principles (Mk 12.28-34) but critical within the legal sphere (Mk
1.22, 3.6, 7.1-19, Mt 5.21-48).[6] His message was 'one which made
some Jews unbounded in their devotion to the prophet Jesus, and
which made others hate Jesus as a heretic and regard his teaching as
subversive of Judaism'. But, concludes Edgar, liberal Judaism takes
the same line and can sympathize with Jesus.[7] This type of presentation
is markedly divergent from that which rejects any kernel of opposition
to the law in Jesus, whether on historical grounds (the later faithfulness of James) by Hugo Mantel [8] or on form-critical grounds by Paul
Winter.[9]

Of those who espouse Talmudic themes during this period, there
are three of very great interest: T. Weiss-Rosmarin, H. E. Goldin and
P. E. Lapide.

---

[1] op.cit 535.

[2] A Short History of the Jewish People, London 1936, 117: 'He was accused of
considering himself the 'Son of God' (because he frequently used the expression
'My father in heaven'), 'the king of the Jews' and 'the Messiah' and he was committed for trial by the Sanhedrin. The court condemned him as a false prophet and
handed him over to the Roman procurator ...'

[3] Similarly already, M. L. Margolis—A. Marx, A History of the Jewish People,
Philadelphia 1927, 183.

[4] A. L. Sachar, A History of the Jews, New York 1930, 129f; L. I. Edgar, A
Jewish View of Jesus, London 1940, 9-13; T. Weiss-Rosmarin, Judaism and
Christianity, New York 1943, 126-134; R. Learsi, Israel: a History of the Jewish
People, Cleveland, Ohio 1949, 159; S. Rosenblatt, art.cit. 315; J. Jocz, The Jewish
People, 27; P. E. Lapide, The last three Popes and the Jews, London 1967, 18f.

[5] op.cit. 9.

[6] Although dismissing a Sanhedrin trial, Edgar is prepared to allow that the
Pharisees were not sorry about Jesus' death because of his attitude to the law.

[7] op.cit. 9-12.

[8] Studies in the History of the Sanhedrin, Cambridge, Mass.1961, 281.

[9] ZRGG 5 (1953), 12; On the Trial of Jesus, Berlin 1961, 135.

The book of Weiss-Rosmarin makes specially interesting reading in the light of the diametrically opposite convictions of Ginzberg and Edgar. He feels obliged to point out that Judaism and Christianity are not the same, and to refute any attempt to reclaim Jesus as a faithful son of the Jewish people and their religion.[1] Even the most liberal Christian, he argues, will not allow that Jesus is only a teacher, prophet or rabbi. And he himself would go further: not only did Jesus fail to live up to the standards of Hebrew prophecy [2] but it is damagingly inaccurate to apply even the the title of rabbi to him. 'Jesus, in fact, was opposed to, and attacked all and everything the Rabbis of his time stood for . . . In all respects Jesus placed himself in opposition to the faith into which he was born.' [3]

The detailed argumentation within this framework is sometimes familiar and always arresting. (a) Weiss-Rosmarin is singularly unimpressed by Mt 5.17-19 and the deduction Jewish scholars have made from it, i.e. that Jesus believed in the eternal validity of the Torah and observed all its minutiae.[4] This simply collapses under the weight of counter-examples seen in Jesus' practice: Mt 12.1-8 is a healing in no way demanded by an emergency (such as the Talmud provided for); [5] Jesus prohibited divorce, except on grounds of adultery, on his own authority; [6] he viewed negatively the dietary laws, and he did not wash hands as required.[7] Particularly offensive in this context was the 'I' which preceded teaching with no authority but his own, and implied that he was acting as if he were God. Indeed he even went so far as to claim to forgive sins. All of this is typically old-fashioned, not only in terms of gospel-criticism (predominace of Matthaean references is to be noted) but also in terms of pattern. This is sealed by the ultimate appeal to Maimonides, who declared that a prophet must not add to or subtract from the Torah. (b) Miracles are also offensive. These were done without reference to God and were intended to make people believe in himself.[8] But, according to Jewish conviction, miracles prove nothing—as Maimonides and Mendelssohn said! [9]

---

[1] Judaism and Christianity, 126.
[2] op.cit. 130.
[3] op.cit. 150.
[4] op.cit. 82,148.
[5] op.cit. 82,146.
[6] op.cit. 147.
[7] op.cit. 147f.
[8] op.cit. 136.
[9] op.cit. 36,137.

(c) Teaching and acts both led to a subversion of monotheism. Mt 11.27-30 contradicts the Jewish democratic conviction that all men are equal and none exclusively singled out as divine sons.[1] Jesus also omitted the first four commandments, Mk 10.17-19, in a most dangerous manner.[2] Furthermore, Messiahship was a crux. Jesus cannot have been Messiah because he did not fulfil the prophecies (mediaeval argument![3]), and his additional claim to be Son of God (especially Mk 14.61-64) 'placed him in eternal opposition to Judaism'.[4]

Weiss-Rosmarin here draws attention to material which is of great moment, as the new quest for the historical Jesus has made clear. What is of special interest within our present context is the revival of extremely ancient material in opposition to Jesus. The derivation stretches back, as we have repeatedly seen, through Ginzberg, Mendelssohn, mediaeval and Maimonidean apologetic to the Talmudic characterisation of Jesus as a mesith. And it is important to see how, for Weiss-Rosmarin, Mk 14.61-64 crystallizes the whole problem.

Perhaps the most fervent of all espousals of Talmudic themes during this period comes from H. E. Goldin.[5] This is the more remarkable in that his total rejection of the Sanhedrin trial makes it quite unnecessary for him to list the offences with which Jesus might have been charged. Goldin also argues contrary to the main trend in Jewish historiography, in that he refuses the theory of Sadducean involvement to the exclusion of the Pharisees. Basically, his is an old-fashioned Troki-type approach,[6] devoting considerable space to proving Jesus' falsity, and treating the evangelists as separate persons capable of legal cross-questioning rather than as writers of documents requiring literary and theological evaluation. He argues that possible charges against Jesus were seduction, false prophecy and Sabbath profanation, and particular attention is devoted to Jesus' irregular treatment of the law. (a) Seduction (Dt 13.7-12). Some tension is apparent here, for Goldin argues in one place[7] that 'Jesus did not introduce a new Testament to replace the law of Moses' since this would infringe Dt 13.1 and contradict

---

[1] op.cit. 131,144.
[2] op.cit. 83.
[3] op.cit. 129f.
[4] op.cit. 130.
[5] The Case of the Nazarene Reopened, New York 1948.
[6] Thus, see the texts being used to exploit Jesus' subordination to the Father, his praying, and his weakness in Gethsemane, op.cit. 32, 666, 687, 740.
[7] op.cit. 356f.

Mt 5.17f. But in detail the mesith charge would have fitted since Jesus set himself up as a god (Mt 4.3, Jn 10.36), assumed divine prerogatives [1] (Jn 5.17, Mk 2.5-7), enticed people to believe in and pray to him (Mt 11.28-30, Jn 8.12) and was indeed worshipped (Mt 14.33, 15.25, 17.14).[2] (b) False prophecy (Dt 13.2-6, 18.20-22).[3] Here again Jesus incited people to idolatry, claimed to be a prophet (Jn 7.28f, 8.42), though his prophecies did not come true (Mt 24.34, 26.64, Mk 9.1) and he three times abrogated Mosaic laws (Mk 2.23-28, 7.14-19, 10.2-12).[4] (c) Sabbath profanation (Jn 9.1-6,14).[5]

Goldin's work is significant, not only because he ignores the development of Jewish Jesus-Forschung at crucial points, but for several other reasons too: Firstly, his title expresses the growing pressure among Jews for a re-trial.[6] Secondly, he adopts the old apologetic method of using subordinationist sayings and the denial of any claim by Jesus, and yet attempts to add the transcendent claims required to support the mesith charge. Thirdly, he is typical of a tendency among Jewish scholars, and lawyers whether Jewish or otherwise, to be out of date in gospel criticism.[7] For Goldin, contradiction and discrepancy are the main target.

The last person in this section who deserves to be mentioned is Pinchas Lapide. He thinks of two eras in the career of Jesus, a Torah-centric one earlier and a deviationist one later. The deviation is crystallized in three pieces of evidence: (a) The formula 'But I say unto you . . . ', which is an unprophetic equation of God's message with the messenger; (b) Jn 14.6, which no Jewish God-fearer could possibly utter, and (c) Jesus' failure to pray for divine intervention in raising Jairus' daughter.[8]

2. *Total dismissal of the Talmudic sources*

This is carried out with varying degrees of firmness by M. Joseph, E. Jacob, S. Ben-Chorin, Jules Isaac, A. I. Polack, S. Sandmel, H.

---

[1] Contrast op.cit. 666: 'Jesus never claimed to be divine.'
[2] Cf. b.Sanh. 90a.
[3] op.cit. 424-433.
[4] op.cit. 436-440.
[5] op.cit. 441.
[6] Cf. S. Ben-Chorin, Die Christus-Frage an die Juden, Jerusalem 1941, 23.
[7] This applies even to R. W. Husband, certainly to J. C. McRuer, The Trial of Jesus, London 1963, and also at times to A. N. Sherwin White, Roman Society and Roman Law in the New Testament, Oxford 1963.
[8] The last three Popes and the Jews, London 1967, 18f.

Mantel and H. J. Schoeps.[1] This is usually, but not always, in the context of a heavy stress on a political downfall and no Sanhedrin trial.

3. *The political reinterpretation of the sources*

According to this attempt, the sources are themselves made to yield political data. It must therefore be differentiated formally from the tendency to make a political reconstruction exclude the Talmudic sources althogether. As an approach it was present already in the work of Rabbinowicz, but now it reappears in various forms. One representative of this approach is Robert Eisler, who is both original and unique in treating the name Ben Pandera in this way. He cites the fantastic parallel of Panderos in the Iliad, a person who broke an armistice. 'Ben Pandera was then a not unfitting designation of the man, who by his triumphal entrance into Jerusalem had broken the truce existing between Romans and Jews since 4 B.C.' [2] This vagary is rejected by Goldstein,[3] who nevertheless himself succumbs to a parallel tendency in the interpretation of πλάνος. He interprets b.Sanh. 43a in terms of Mt 24.11,24, Josephus, B. J. 2.258-260 and Ant.20.167-170, and also the disappointment of Jewish political hopes by Jesus (Mt 27.63). This is taken to reflect the historical condemnation of Jesus as a rebel, as well as tradition from the time when religious conflict had retrojected the Christian view of Jesus as divine.[4]

Somewhat related is Winter's understanding of the mesith charge in b.Sanh. 43a as 'leading Israel to revolt—possibly stemming from Lk 23.2'.[5] Clearly this is not what b.Sanh.43a means, but viewed against

---

[1] M. Joseph, Jesus von Nazareth genannt Christus, JL 3 (1929), 240: 'Die Erzählungen über das Leben Jesu, die sich zerstreut im Talmud, und zusammenhängend im "Toledot Jeshu" finden, haben, wie die aus heidnischen und christlich-ketzerischen Kreisen, keine historische, sondern nur polemische Bedeutung.' E. Jacob, Christentum, EJ 5 (1930), 526; S. Ben-Chorin, Christus-Frage, 23; J. Isaac, Jésus et Israel, Paris 1948, 428; A. I. Polack—W.W. Simpson, Jesus in the Background of History, London 1957, 65; S. Sandmel, A Jewish Understanding of the New Testament, Cincinnati 1957, 194: 'Jesus is mentioned in the Rabbinic literature but the passages are rather late retorts to post-N.T. Christian claims. They are of no value for the history of Jesus.' Similarly, We Jews and Jesus, London 1965, 28; H. Mantel, Studies. 280; H. J. Schoeps, Paul, London 1961, 165f; The Jewish-Christian Argument, London 1963, 19, 24f.

[2] The Messiah Jesus and John the Baptist, London 1931, 407f.

[3] Jesus in the Jewish Tradition, 36.

[4] op.cit. 28f. This is in spite of criticisms by Goldstein, op.cit. 12, 109, of Herford's view (resting on a mistranslation) that the Pharisees regarded Jesus as a revolutionary.

[5] On the Trial, 144, (remarkable in so far as Winter evaluates negatively the Talmudic sources in general). Compare the view of S. Zeitlin, that in the Bar

the background of Jewish historiography it does suggest a possible reason for the characteristic preference for Lk 23.2, as against Mk 15.2, for the definition of the charge in the Roman court. Perhaps subconsciously, the mesith approach to Jesus may dictate the choice. Be that as it may, the whole approach of this group of writers is a more refined method of establishing a political as against the Talmudic scheme as normally understood, only this time the sources are not replaced but reinterpreted.

Kochba period the Jews were compelled to fight even fellow Jews when they opposed the idea of a Jewish state, and they called those who broke down the unity of the Jewish nation, beguilers or blasphemers. Jesus in the early Tannaitic Literature, 300-308. This interpretation confuses the unity of the nation with the unity of God.

CHAPTER TWO

THE QUESTION OF THE CHARGE AGAINST JESUS IN THE SANHEDRIN

Although all four gospels agree that Jesus died as a messianic claimant, at least in Roman eyes[1], they are by no means so clear as to the ground of his condemnation by the Sanhedrin. As it stands, the Markan tradition is ambiguous and does not specify whether the offence lay in Messiah-Son of God or in the ἐγώ εἰμι or in the Son of man logion. Matthew, while depending on Mk and in no way clarifying this issue within Mt 26.57-66, nevertheless by redaction draws attention to Messiahship in 26.68 and to divine Sonship in 27.40-43.[2] The independent Lukan tradition, Lk 22.70, and the Johannine implication, Jn 19.7, agree in making a claim to be Son of God the cause of Jesus' downfall. The situation which presents itself to Jewish as well as to Christian scholars is therefore enigmatic, and the more so in that the least clear texts, Mk-Mt, have been accepted as the point of departure. Our survey in this chapter is consequently bound to take into account reactions to the Christological cluster which we have in this tradition, and particularly the relationship between Messiah and Son of God which Mark, though not Luke, presents. Historically, however, it was the 'Son of God' issue which was initially dominant, and it is with this, and the dialectic within it between Jewish and non-Jewish backgrounds and interpretations, that this study must begin.

A. THE SON OF GOD QUESTION

The preceding chapter made clear that Jewish evaluation of the Sanhedrin trial showed a tendency towards polarization in dealing with the Son of God question. Whether or not Jesus made such a claim, and if he did, whether or not he understood the term in its Jewish sense, continually moulds the debate. This is because Jews in our period are the heirs to a double tradition. On the one hand the Talmudic approach normally maximizes the theological sense of divine Sonship, and on the other hand the Emancipation attitude, represented

---

[1] Mk 15.26; Mt 27.37; Lk 23.38; Jn 19.19.

[2] Cf. D. R. Catchpole, The Answer of Jesus to Caiaphas (Matt. xxvi. 64), NTS 17 (1971), 226.

long before by Isaac of Troki [1] minimizes it. These two attitudes focus on Jn 10.33 and Dt 14.1 respectively. Since the former has already been discussed at length, the latter must receive attention here.

Troki uses both O.T. and N.T. in order to refute Christianity [2] and aims to prove that Jesus neither claimed to be God nor is represented by the N.T. as such. (a) The first thesis is argued on the basis of Jesus' calling himself Son of man,[3] his loyalty to the monotheistic principle,[4] various subordinationist sayings [5] and in particular Mk 13.32, the parallelism between his relationship and that of the apostles to the Father,[6] his alleged equivocation in Jn 10.33-36 [7] and his equality with his brothers. Thus on Jn 20.17 Troki writes: 'It cannot be asserted on the authority of this passage that Jesus meant anything more by styling himself the Son of God than the Holy Scriptures indicate in such passages as Dt 14.1.' This means, of course, that Jesus never ventured outside the confines of Judaism. But what is specially notable in view of Troki's methodology, and of the perennial reappearance of these arguments, is his treatment of verses which jeopardize his whole structure. Examples of such are Jn 10.30, 13.3 (cf. 16.15) and Mt 28.18—all of which are dismissed [8] by reference to Mk 13.32. But this is only done at the cost of abandoning his declared claim that the

---

[1] His work is available in Faith Strengthened, London 1815. Lindeskog rightly depicts Troki as 'ein Emanzipationsphänomenon vor der eigentlichen Emanzipation', op.cit. 19.

[2] For a survey of the work of Troki in its historical setting, see G. Lindeskog, op.cit. 19-22 and E. L. Dietrich, Das jüdische-christliche Religionsgespräch am Ausgang des 16. Jahrhunderts nach dem Handbuch des R. Isaak Troki, Judaica 14 (1958), 1-39. Of particular interest is the fact that Troki was indebted for much of his material to Christian anti-Trinitarian sects.

[3] op.cit. 237, using Mt 8.19f; Lk 9.57; op.cit. 262 using Jn 8.40: 'In every part of the New Testament where Jesus speaks of himself he represents himself as the Son of Man, and not as God.' Cf. earlier use of the term Son of man in this way in Sefer Nizzachon 5.12f:

> He who has been hanged and buried
> And his form altered by death,
> Can he save anything at all
> Who was not delivered in the day of his own death?
> When he cried out, 'Why hast thou forsaken me?'
> Who also declared, 'Am not I a son of man
> And have nowhere to lay my head?'

Text in O. S. Rankin, Jewish Religious Polemic, Edinburgh 1956, 63.

[4] op.cit. 243, on Mt 19.16f.

[5] op.cit. 244, on Mt 20.23; op.cit. 268 on Jn 17.3.

[6] op.cit. 266.

[7] op.cit. 265.

[8] op.cit. 266.

N.T. never deifies Jesus.[1] The same tension is apparent in the treatment of Jn 6.38: here Troki argues that if Jesus only meant the descent of the soul from heaven to inhabit a body, he was uttering a mere commonplace, but if he meant descent in the flesh he was contradicting the fact of birth by a woman in Bethlehem—but in any case, Troki argues, divinity cannot be intended since Jesus regarded himself as the agent of him who sent him.[2] Troki's uneasiness is apparent. (b) The second thesis is based on the fact of temptation,[3] the Lukan genealogy,[4] Jesus' disappointment with the fruitless fig-tree [5] and above all the cry of dereliction. The last-mentioned reveals a difference of design from the Father, and Jesus' need to invoke God in the time of trouble. Not only is this use of the N.T. evidence against Jesus also documented in Islamic writings,[6] possibly in dependence on Jewish apologetic, but Mk 15.34 becomes the climax of the standard Jewish account of Jesus.[7]

Here then is the other half of the Jewish background which exerts an influence on the Son of God question.[8] The attempt to devalue balances the primary confessional instinct to maximize in line with the Talmudic viewpoint. But it is transparently clear in the development of the discussion that the Achilles heel of Troki's view is the backbone of the theory of such as Salvador. In spite of Mk 13.32, Troki cannot within his framework deny that Jesus said Jn 10.30, and in spite of his proposed interpretation of Jn 10.33-36 he has to take liberties with the

---

[1] In a similar way Salvador starts with the declared intention of arguing from the gospels as they stand, but has quietly to abandon it when he reaches the mockery, Histoire II, 81,88.

[2] op.cit. 261.

[3] op.cit. 234, arguing from Mt 4.1-11.

[4] op.cit. 254.

[5] op.cit. 250.

[6] See S. M. Stern, Quotations from Apocrypal Gospels in 'Abd al-Jabbar, JTS 18 (1967), 34-57, esp.36.

[7] J. Cohen, La Vérité Israélite 3 (1861), 30; H. H. Graetz, Geschichte, 2nd ed. 245; Rabbinowicz, Rôle, 114; M. Schlesinger, The historical Jesus of Nazareth, New York 1876, 86; L. Weiss, Some burning Questions, Columbus 1893; J. Krauskopf, A Rabbi's Impressions of the Oberammergau Passion Play, Philadelphia 1901, 128; E. G. Hirsch, My Religion, 44; E. Jacob, Christentum, 528; Klausner, Jesus, 377.

[8] Troki-type argumentation often reasserts itself. See e.g., P. Goodman, Synagogue, 264; L. Weiss, op.cit. 75f; S. Pick, Judentum und Christentum, Frankfurt a.M. 1913, 6-8; M. Brod, Heidentum Christentum Judentum II, München 1922, 215; L.I. Edgar, op.cit. 5; H. E. Goldin, The Case of the Nazarene reopened, 687-740.

context. He takes Elohim in Ps 82.1 as angels [1] rather than the divine Being, but argues that Jesus has forgotten here that the alleged sons of God betray by their nature that they delude themselves and others.[2] When Salvador, on the other hand, uses this passage he is not concerned about the exegesis of Ps 82 nor with the relevance or otherwise of Mk 13.32, but with the theological conclusion and the Jewish interpretation, as in Jn 10.33,39. There is also a circumstantial matter which deflects Salvador from Troki. The latter's system could give the Jews no defence against the charge of unlawfully condemning Jesus. Indeed, if he made no claim, how could he reasonably be convicted? Hence there emerges a totally different scheme, different because it starts with the trial rather than, as Troki did, ignoring it. For Troki the Passion is only of interest in so far as Gethsemane or the final cry expose the ordinariness of Jesus, or the prayer, 'Father, forgive them . . . ' condemns anti-Semitism. So this general structure cannot be serviceable for Jewish apologetic as long as a trial is assumed to have taken place. Yet, *once destroy this assumption*, as modern Judaism has generally done, and Troki-type arguments come flooding back.[3] The only intermediate position is that of Rabbinowicz [4] who borrows much of Troki's material but locates the uniqueness of Jesus in his messianic claim. Yet while subsequent Jewish writers are virtually unanimous that Jesus claimed messiahship, this is neutralized by their agreement that this constituted no legal offence.

The difference between Troki and the Talmudic assessments can be seen in broadest terms as based respectively on a totally O.T. as against a non-O.T. interpretation of 'Son of God'. The debate, especially in the 19th century, has to be seen as a dialectic between these two interpretations, between the Jewish or even prophetic Jesus and the teacher whose self-consciousness or legal heterodoxy produced a

---

[1] Thus far this interpretation would seem to be correct, cf. J. A. Emerton, The Interpretation of Psalm lxxxii in John X, JTS 11 (1960), 329-332, and Melchizedek and the Gods, JTS 17 (1966), 399-401. The alternative proposed by A. T. Hanson, who sees behind Elohim the recipients of the Divine Word, is weakened by the fact that Jesus is speaking of his own divinity rather than that of the recipients of what he says. John's Citation of Ps lxxxii, NTS 11 (1965), 158-162 and John's Citation of Ps lxxxii reconsidered, NTS 13 (1967), 363-367.

[2] op.cit. 265.

[3] The contemporary tendency towards Troki at a popular level became clear to me when visiting a private Jewish bookseller in Golders Green in December 1965. He had an impossibly long list of orders for Faith Strengthened.

[4] Rôle, 35,43, etc.

collision with Dt 13.[1] It is now necessary to investigate the two corresponding evaluations of 'Son of God'.

1. *The background of the term*

(a) A non-Jewish background. The two outstanding exponents of
this are Salvador and Graetz. The former persistently sees a mixture
of Jewish and Greek ideas in Jesus' teaching and locates Jesus' theological error in the severance of Hebrew ideas from their native roots.
Thus: 'Jésus, en présentant des idées nouvelles, en donnant de nouvelles formes à des idées déjà répandues, parle de lui-même comme
d'un Dieu'.[2] Now firstly, this analysis was only possible, at least in
the form in which it was proposed by Salvador, in the pre-Hegelian
period or before Wellhausen's famous dictum distinguishing the
Christian and the Jew in Jesus. Later any tinge of Hellenism is a
straightforward guarantee of unauthenticity.[3] Secondly, it could only
be defended before the abandonment of the fourth gospel as the
product of late theological reflection. Lastly, it required a situation
before books dwelling on the parallelism between the teachings of Jesus
and his contemporaries or predecessors had made their full impact.

For Graetz the foreign background makes itself felt via the Essenes
who belong to the Alexandrian-Judaean complex. Throughout Graetz's
work on Christianity this is assumed, but the full rationalization
is expounded only at a late stage,[4] which in itself suggests that the
Talmudic scheme is more primary. The basis, when it was detailed,
included (a) the Essene veneration for Moses, almost on a level with
God (B.J.2.145),[5] (b) the expectation of a messianic Moses-figure ac-

---

[1] Hence Jews remain alert against the suspicion of lapsing into neo-Christianity:
thus the David Friedländer incident (Lindeskog, op.cit. 38), the inter-war controversies (Lindeskog, op.cit. 53), the indistinguishability of the views of the
convert Daniel Chwolson from many assessments of Jesus by reform Jews, and
the bitter denunciations of A. Ginzberg, op.cit. 227.

[2] Histoire II,82; cf. Jesus-Christ I(1838), 235: 'La spécialité de cette pensée est
le dernier terme du mariage qui s'était opéré depuis plusieurs siècles entre les
croyances importées de la Babylonie et de la Perse, et les textes sacrés des Juifs.'
I(1864),213: 'Il y a une grande différence entre cette manière tout hébraïque d'entendre les expressions, homme de Dieu, fils de Dieu, image et ressemblance de
Dieu, et celle qui a prévalu en la personne et sous le nom de Jésus-Christ.'

[3] Cf. Gerald Friedländer, Hellenism and Christianity, London 1912, 48; S.
Sandmel, A Jewish Understanding of the New Testament, Cincinnati 1956, 129.

[4] Un mot sur la dogmatique du christianisme primitif, REJ 20 (1890), 11-15.

[5] op.cit. 12: 'Le législateur Moise, l'organe de la Révélation, méritait la plus
grande vénération après la Divinité, puisqu'il était d'une nature semblable à celle
de la Divinité ou des anges.'

cepted by primitive Christianity (Dt 18.18, Jn 1.46, Acts 3.22, 7.37), (c) misguided excesses of exegesis which predicated divine Sonship of the messiah (b.Sukk. 52a, Midr.Pss.2) or applied Is 53 to him, with the dangerous exaltation idea leading to ὁμοουσία![1]

(b) The Jewish background. Salvador's interim definition of 'Son of God' in the Jewish sense was 'l'homme d'une haute sagesse, d'une haute piété',[2] but he later explained more fully. Son of God and messiah both belong to the principle of divine election, the creation of man (and the nation) to be 'une image et ressemblance de Dieu'. However, the gap between 'l'état réel' and 'l'état idéal et divin' of Israel led to the prophetic vision of uniting the two in an Israel truly messiah and Son of God. Thus an element of process is introduced into the term.

Various aspects of this understanding reappear in later writers. The creation theme is adopted by Samuel Hirsch, I. M. Wise and D. Philippson.[3] Cohen applies the term to 'l'homme d'une intelligence qui semble inspirée par Dieu lui-même'.[4] Others stress the quality of righteousness (Soloweyczyk [5]) or the relationship of love (Rabbino-wicz,[6] drawing on Troki's interpretations of Johannine material). But the constant and uniform trend throughout is to apply the term to Israel, a process which exegetically is entirely justified [7] but which also historically adopts the primitive method of applying to Israel all that Christians apply to Jesus. So Saalschütz for instance mentions not only the relationship of love, bordering on the idea of God's image in man, but stresses the moral content implied when related to Israel.[8] And D. Chwolson, most strikingly, writes even from within the Christian confession: 'Dass Christus Gott "seinen Vater" nannte, konnte doch

---

[1] op.cit. 13f.

[2] Histoire II, 82.

[3] S. Hirsch, Religionsphilosophie, 648; I. M. Wise, Origin, 176, and Martyr-dom, Preface: 'the world's people are all God's children.' D. Philippson, letter cited in G. Croly, Tarry thou till I come, New York 1899, 566: 'Judaism holds that every man is the son of God. Jesus was a Jew of the Jews.'

[4] art.cit. 318, cf. M. Noah, Discourse, 20.

[5] Kol Kore, Paris 187ᐱ, 180f, using both O.T. (Dt 14.1, Lev 25.42) and N.T. (Lk 6.35; Jn 1.12; 10.34; Acts 17.29; Rom 8.14). Cf. his evaluation of Peter's confession: 'Par tes rares vertus, tu es véritablement Maschiach, l'Élu du Seigneur, et tu mériterais d'être appelé non pas fils de l'homme, mais fils de Dieu.' Even on Mk 14.61 he writes of Son of God 'en tant que juste; car tous les justes et les hommes d'élite . . . . partagent cette glorieuse qualification'.

[6] Rôle, 35.

[7] Ex 4.22, Dt 1.31, 8.5, 14.1, 32.6, Jer 31.9,20, Ps 2.7,12 are repeatedly cited.

[8] Versöhnung, 24.

sicher den Juden nicht auffallen'.[1] Although he makes use of the
normal battery of proof-texts to show the usage for Israel and for
individuals, his preference for the Fatherhood end of the relationship
shows him fighting to exclude the less easily avoided element of uniqueness in the Sonship sayings.

Samuel Hirsch is the most distinctive in his incorporation of process
into the concept of sonship.[2] Israel, he writes, consists of God's sons
by redemption as well as creation.[3] He cites Ex 4.22, Dt 14.1 to show
that Israel as son was reared by God,[4] and also applies 2 Sam 7.14
to Solomon. Sonship therefore describes Israel as the people to be
brought up by God, the first-born Son through whom ofter sons are
to be brought up. Ultimately, therefore, it means the true Israelite.
Hence Hirsch's repeated reference to 'der erzogene Sohn Gottes' [5] and
the absolutizing of the term's moral content.

2. Jesus and divine Sonship

There are three basic groups into which Jewish writers form themselves when discussing Jesus' use of the idea of Sonship.

(a) The view that Jesus used the term in a non-Jewish sense. According to early writers Jesus and his disciples attached to the title Son of
God 'une idée très-réelle d'origine et d'essence divines'.[6] In view of
this the Jewish sense of divine Sonship cannot contain Jesus' meaning
and so Salvador, for instance, opposes such an understanding, adding
in support other arguments: (a) It would not have produced such a
sensation if Jesus had only used the term in its normal way. (b) An ad
hominem argument: If Christians say 'Jésus ne se proclamait pas dieu
d'une manière expresse . . . pourquoi donc le croyez-vous?' The first
of these arguments is noteworthy in that it clashes with the later position of Salvador and other Jewish writers who claim, in connection
with a denial of the Talmudic sources or the silence of contemporary
historians, that Jesus made little impact.[7] Apologetic, a feature common to both these arguments, produces a tension. The second reason

---

[1] Passamahl, 88.

[2] Les Crimitières au point de vue Israélite, Archives Israélites 26 (1865),
383-390, esp. 385.

[3] On the theological background of this motif within Judaism, cf. Lindeskog,
Jesusfrage, 81-83.

[4] Dt 14.1 is also cited in connection with Jesus' trial. This is undoubtedly the
key verse for him, as for Troki. Cf. art.cit. 388: 'Tout homme pieux pouvait
prétendre à cette disposition.'

[5] Religionsphilosophie, 648, 669, 678, 713.

[6] Cohen, art.cit. 318; cf. later, Learsi, op.cit. 160f.

[7] Salvador, I(1838), 156f; Cohen, art.cit. 244.

also shows the impact of current controversy and presupposes a slight
movement in Christian apologetic too. This is part and parcel of a
recurrent phenomenon: Jews are both pressed and, later, helped by
Christian claims.

In the early part of our period, Jews associate the term Son of God
with Jesus' birth. Sonship is taken to mean literal descent and therefore to arouse a clash with 'Son of David' or 'Son of Joseph'. Thus
Salvador speaks of Jesus' claims: 'Jésus en effet ayant dit un jour "Je
suis descendu du ciel pour faire toutes ces choses" ', received the
reply, 'N'est-ce point Jésus fils du charpentier Joseph et de Marie?
Nous connaissons son père, sa mère et ses frères, pourquoi donc dit-il
qu'il est descendu des cieux?' [1] So the clash with human parentage is
clearly felt. But, more important is Salvador's assimilation of Jn 6.42
to Mt 13.55 by the specific mention of Mary by name and the reference
to his brothers. This latter passage, behind which lies Mk 6.3 with its
insinuation of illegitimacy, is never far away in Jewish writings about
Jesus during these years.

In both 1828 [2] and 1838 [3] Salvador moved immediately from the
exchange recorded in Jn 6.42 to Jn 10.33. In 1865, the prehistory of
Jn 10.33 [4] has been widened [5] to include the claim to be the absolute
master of the sabbath (Jn 5.16-18),[6] the claim to forgive sins [7] and
finally the debate about David's Lord, which was intended to establish
the theological and absolute identity of the Messiah, Jesus and the
God of the Bible.[8] But that the virgin birth is still the real issue is plain
from two considerations: (a) In Salvador's first work the discussion
of the trial was prefaced by an allusion to Jesus' unfortunate birth.[9]
(b) In his last work he writes : 'Il y a une chaîne non interrompue d'un

---

[1] Histoire II, 83; cf. Jésus-Christ II(1838), 130: 'Ils lui reprochaient de soutenir
que Dieu était son père naturel, immédiat, de faire égal à Dieu, de se prétendre
descendu positivement du haut du ciel, tandis que chacun pouvait connaître son
père, sa mère, ses frères.'

[2] op.cit. 83.

[3] II(1838), 130f.

[4] The crucial significance of Jn 10.33 is underlined by its solitary selection in
Salvador's other treatment of this theme, Histoire de la Domination Romaine,
Paris 1847, 470. This pattern is adopted by Derenbourg, Essai, 202f.

[5] Cf. I(1864), 393, where evidence is adduced from all four gospels and mention
made of Jesus' tendency to allow people to worship him at the time of miracles,
Mt 14.33—a case where Matthaean priority is necessary—Mt 15.25, Mk 5.6, Jn
9.35-38.

[6] I(1864), 80.

[7] I(1864), 89.

[8] I(1864), 89.

[9] Histoire II, 81. See above, p. 17.

bout des Évangiles à l'autre, et les témoignages que je viens de repro-
duire lient parfaitement la conception miraculeuse ou Nazareth,
l'adoration des Mages ou Béthléem, avec l'aspect tout opposé que la
Judée attachait à la même histoire, c'est-à-dire avec la cause pour
laquelle, selon l'usage antique et officiel de ce pays, le grand sacrifica-
teur Caïphe fut conduit à déchirer ses vêtements.' [1] So only two foci in
the career of Jesus are necessary, the birth and the trial. The same
scheme is adopted by Saalschütz, Stern and Wise,[2] to mention but
three examples, and of course it also has a long history behind it.[3]

Details which should be noted here are the following: (a) It is only
later that Salvador gives synoptic backing to Johannine citations. The
latter provide the basis for Jesus' trial, even though Salvador regards
Jn as 'le réprentant de la troisième et dernière phase' of Christianity.
This necessarily leads to a weakening as other scholars increasingly discarded Jn,[4] and also as there was a diminution of the solely defensive or
polemical considerations which led Salvador to cite the N.T. uncritically and at random simply because he was trying to convince Christians. (b) There is a development beyond Salvador, particularly in
Cohen who uses the former's key texts [5] but without the judaico-
oriental backing for Jesus. What was to Salvador a three-stage
development in Christianity is for Cohen a three stage scheme in
the life of Jesus corresponding to the gospels Mt-Mk: Lk: Jn.[6] Jn,
therefore, describing the last phase of the ministry of Jesus, can be
used for issues culminating in the trial, and it is here that the full
impact of Jn 5.15, 19, 21, 6.40, 51, 10.30-32, 36 can be felt.[7] Cohen
stands within the era when Jesus' Jewishness is emerging, and by

---

[1] I(1864), 393.

[2] Saalschütz, Versöhnung, 24: 'Nur jener dogmatische Begriff, in welchem
Gottes Sohn von Christus, als einem in nicht gewöhnlich menschlicher, sondern
wunderbarer Weise Erzeugten und nur menschlich Geborenen verstanden wird,
wobei man sich auf die Verkündigung dieses Wunders bei Jes 7,14 beruft—dieser
Begriff des Wortes ist ein neu hinzugekommener, den das Judenthum nicht aner-
kennt.' L. Stern, Was Jesus of Nazareth the Messiah?, London 1872, 30: 'this
beautiful Son of God and Mary, this man without a father'. This indicates the
filtering through to the popular level of this kind of attack. I. M. Wise, History,
258: 'The biographers of Jesus . . . . in their anxiety to make him also a Son of
God . . . . branded him as a bastard.'

[3] Cf. Nachmanides in the Barcelona debate: text in O. S. Rankin, op.cit. 202.

[4] Graetz at this point stands in an intermediate position. The extreme but logical
conclusion is evidenced throughout the writings of I. M. Wise.

[5] art.cit. 293.

[6] Les Déicides, Paris 1864, xxv,409.

[7] op.cit. 415-417.

means of his inconsistent scheme is able to smooth out another inconsistency in Salvador, and so to accept both the Jewishess of Jesus and Salvador's trial theory.

Thus the way is paved for presenting divine Sonship as the crux of Jesus' trial, a trial which in the view of Salvador, Saalschütz, Derenbourg, Cohen and Bäck, did take place. There is another group of scholars, e.g. S. Hirsch, L. Philippson and K. Kohler, who think that the Sanhedrin trial did not take place but who still regard the Son of God claim as the issue in the synoptic records, often combining this with an obliteration of the messiahship issue. Philippson in particular is insistent about this, urging strenuously that, according to the records, Jesus was only condemned 'wegen der zugestandenen, dem ganzen jüdischen Begriffe von der Einheit und Unkörperlichkeit Gottes widersprechenden Lehre von der Göttlichkeit Jesu'.[1] This represents a step back from Saalschütz,[2] whom he otherwise commends for stressing the political side more than Salvador did. The reason for this recessive step in the opposite direction to what he in fact approves is that his argument depends on establishing a complete discontinuity between the Jewish and Roman hearings. It must be noted that this belongs to the period before Jn 18.31 is questioned, and therefore the difference in subject matter, rather than legal awkwardness, is most important. The highly religious content of the claim in the Sanhedrin must be maintained in order to exacerbate the contrast with the reason for the mockery and the superscription.[3] It is for the same reason that he corrects what is in fact his own misunderstanding of Samuel Hirsch.[4] At the same time the continuing influence of Salvador is seen in Philippson's acceptance of the latter's arguments on the illegality question. Philippson, in essence, adopts the Salvador position on the Sanhedrin trial in order to detach the whole event from the political proceedings.

Samuel Hirsch and Kaufmann Kohler basically rule out the Sanhedrin trial because of the illegalities, but only the former uses the theological content of Jesus' claim as an argument against it. Kohler is not

[1] Haben die Juden, 16.

[2] For an outline of the views of Saalschütz, cf. pp. 25ff, 87.

[3] op.cit. 42. Mt 27.17-37, Mk 15.16-20, 26, Lk 23.38, Jn 19.2, 19 are used in standard Jewish arguments.

[4] Philippson, op.cit. 33. Hirsch in fact says, 'toujours l'aveu que Jésus se regardait comme fils de Dieu, amène sur-le-champ sa condamnation', and goes on to explain that it is a Christian μονογενής-type conception, Archives Israélites 26 (1865), 388.

entirely clear. But the significant point is that Philippson on the one hand, and Hirsch and Kohler on the other, reach the same end by completely opposite paths in so far as arguments from the account of the Sanhedrin trial are concerned. Philippson takes the theological count and excludes the legal one which Hirsch and Kohler underline.

(b) The view that Jesus used the term in a totally Jewish sense, but did not claim it for himself. This is Samuel Hirsch's mediating position.[1] According to him, Jesus' hopes were expressed thus: He aimed from the time of his baptism to bring in the kingdom of God.[2] To this end he aimed to be the Son of God and the suffering Servant. He did not claim to be the Son of God 'denn nur wer bis in seine Todesstunde treu blieb, war der vollkommene Sohn Gottes'.[3] Jesus not only kept this aim before himself but aimed to inspire others towards it.[4] So when more and more people aimed to realize the Son of God / suffering Servant ideal, the messianic time, already imminent (Mt 10.23),[5] would come. It was because this messianic time had not yet come [6] that Jesus did not claim to be the messiah. But, equally, he could not say that he was not messiah, since messiah could not be more than he himself was, 'der erzogene Sohn Gottes'.[7]

There are several reasons why this view is important. Firstly, it carries through thoroughly the Jewish idea of Son of God, even to the extent of incorporating process and development in the interests of the distiction between what is and what should be. Lindeskog rightly remarks: 'Sein Sohn-Gottes-Begriff ist jüdisch, nicht christlich, wie seine ganze Darstellung judäozentrisch ist.' [8] Secondly, it carries through in Jesus' career the pattern of Jewish eschatology, e.g. the view expressed in b.Sanh. 97b: 'If Israel repent they will be redeemed'.[9]

---

[1] Cf. Lindeskog, op.cit. 257f.

[2] Religionsphilosophie, 647.

[3] op.cit. 648. The danger of falling away precludes such a claim; hence also Jesus' reply to the rich young ruler, op.cit. 676.

[4] op.cit. 678.

[5] op.cit. 666.

[6] op.cit. 669. Here Hirsch touches on a very typical and very ancient Jewish objection to Jesus' messiahship.

[7] But see Hirsch's treatment of the confession at Caesarea Philippi, op.cit. 673. Peter's reply surprised and delighted Jesus, and he saw himself within reach of his ultimate purpose. Even though a claim to be Son of God was not strictly possible Jesus allowed it so that after his death people would recognize that he had been the embodiment of righteous Israel.

[8] Jesusfrage, 258.

[9] Compare also his emphatic assertion against Salvador that Jesus' expectation of the kingdom of God was wholly Pharisaic, op.cit. 681; Archives Israélites 26 (1865), 385-387.

Thirdly, it carries through a rejection of Jn.[1] Emphatically and repeatedly this is made clear, and hence a break with the Salvador technique carried out. 'Jesus trat . . . nach Johannes, überall nicht als die bloße Idee Jisraels, als der erzogene Sohn Gottes, sondern als der Eingeborene (μονογενής) Sohn Gottes auf. Jesus tritt nicht als der werdende und sich entwickelnde Messias auf, sondern als der Fertige, Gewordene, vollkommen Gerüstete.'[2] The authenticity of such sayings as Jn 5.17f is therefore rejected.[3]

The view of Samuel Hirsch is maintained by his son E. G. Hirsch,[4] although the idea of process is minimized with the result that it can be emphatically claimed that Jesus said he was *a* son of God.[5] On the other hand, process does figure in the view of Soloweyczyk, though with less subtlety. He mentions that Solomon's enjoyment of the title depended on obedience, and his N.T. citations are intended to prove that the title was allowed to a man who triumphed over his passions.[6] Mt 16.16f is understood as follows: 'Telle était sa vertu et sa piété, qu'il eût mérité d'être le Messie ou l'Élu de Dieu, si d'autres considérations (indiquées par le Talmud) n'eussent pas prévalu à l'encontre.'[7]

The application of this view to the trial leads in two directions. Hirsch makes it one reason for unhistoricity;[8] Soloweyczyk looks elsewhere for the content of the blasphemy. The former stresses in this context that every Jew has the right to call himself son of God,[9] but to a later Christian 'der den Ausdruck "Sohn des lebendigen Gottes" in seinem Sinn nahm, konnte allerdings nichts plausibler sein, als Jesus dieses Ausdrucks wegen verurtheilen zu lassen'.[10] This position raises the following criticisms: (a) Philippson takes up Hirsch's point about the Dt 14.1 sense of Son of God and disputes its applicability here because of the addition of the Son of man saying: this, he argues,

---

[1] op.cit. 720: 'Beim Matthäus stehen wir auf dem historischen Boden des Judenthums; bei Johannes fehlt dieses Moment.' He is more sceptical about Mt in 1865, art.cit. 384.

[2] op.cit. 708.

[3] op.cit. 720.

[4] My Religion, New York 1925, 51.

[5] Mk 14.61, with its definite article and the parallelism with messiah is not an embarrassment, since Hirsch only accepts the historicity of the Roman trial, art. Crucifixion, JE 4 (1903), 373f.

[6] Kol Kore (Vox Clamantis): the Bible, the Talmud and the New Testament, London 1868, 180.

[7] op.cit. 1870, 294.

[8] Cf. M. Joel, Blicke II, 64-66.

[9] Religionsphilosophie, 685, and art.cit. 388.

[10] op.cit. 685; similarly S. Bernfeld, JJGL 13 (1910), 116.

shows that Jesus is not using the expression in its ordinary sense alone.[1] This criticism is partly valid in that, except for Mk 15.39, the synoptic usage includes the definite article, but it is not totally so because Hirsch does not dispute the Christian sense of Mt 26.63. Both Philippson and Hirsch agree actually in taking Son of God and none other as the decisive climax of the Sanhedrin trial, thereby showing their conformity to the older pattern which is held almost unanimously by Jewish scholars in the 1828-1868 period. (b) Hirsch says 'Sohn des lebendigen Gottes', thereby, perhaps accidentally, citing the Petrine confession, not the statement in the Sanhedrin. This draws attention to an inconsistency, for he allows the historicity of the former but not that of the latter. This is because he retreats from his view of 'der erzogene Sohn Gottes' when commenting on Mt 26.63. Here there is no longer any idea of progress or of absolute moral categories. It is a more developed meaning than his normal one and represents a retreat to the old pattern of Troki.[2] The only difference between Jesus' acceptance of Peter's confession (according to Mt) and of the high priest's suggestion is the following saying about the Son of man. This, which could have proved Hirsch's point, is instead used by Philippson against him. (c) Son of God is rejected, not on legal grounds (Sanh. 7.5) but for theological reasons. (d) Whereas in other places Hirsch does consider the relationship of messiah and Son of God, he does not do so here. Such an omission, necessary for the sake of maintaining discontinuity between the Jewish and Roman hearings, combines with the evidence above to show a difference in critical method when treating the trial. (e) Hirsch, as noted in chapter I, shows himself to be fighting the mesith charge, for it is in this context that he argues that 'Jésus n'a jamais proclamé un autre Dieu que celui des pères'.

(c) The view that Jesus understood and claimed for himself the title Son of God in its Jewish sense. The effect of this view on the trial is to open up three possibilities: either to argue against the whole idea of a trial,[3] or to locate the blasphemy elsewhere,[4] or to allege an illegality.[5]

[1] Haben die Juden, 39.
[2] This pattern evinces itself elsewhere in Hirsch's elimination of claims to deity, and his stress on Mt 19.17. This last verse (though better in the Markan and Lukan parallels) could be regarded as providing a N.T. starting-point for Hirsch's conception of absoluteness and of progress in connection with Jesus' intentions.
[3] Wise, M. Joel, M. Fluegel (with variation), and A. Weill (finally, in Le faux Jésus-Christ, 11).
[4] Rabbinowicz, Chwolson (later).
[5] Chwolson (earlier).

The position of Wise at this point is most typical. Having explained the Jewish background of the term, he attributes any other meaning to Paul.[1] Any pre-Pauline passages in the gospels or Acts are interpolations if the non-Jewish sense is intended, for neither Jesus nor his Jewish followers could have entertained a conception so foreign and repugnant to the Jewish mind.[2] Here again is the intensely Jewish Jesus, and a thorough application of the Hegelian dialectic—indeed, much more thorough than in Graetz who, while adopting that framework, is still ideologically in transit towards it from the older position by having Jesus himself drawing the term from an unorthodox environment.

Whereas the normal protagonist of this position rejected Jn outright, Rabbinowicz is an exception. He absorbs the Johannine view into the Jewish one, retains the Jewishness of Jesus, and lays stress on Jesus' messianic consciousness. 'Jésus lui-même, né juif, a voulu rester juif . . . Ce qu'il a dit de nouveau, c'est que le Messie c'était lui.' [3] The term Son of God he assimilates to Son of man, so that Jesus' answer to the high priest is interpreted as implying that he is at the same time Son of God and Son of man, 'le fils de Joseph et le protégé de Dieu'.[4]

M. Joel, writing in 1883, is beyond the stage when Son of God is the only possible candidate for the blasphemy. He considers as well the claims to be messiah and Son of man coming with the clouds, and adds: 'Selbst unter der Annahme, die nicht leicht ein Kritiker macht, daß Jesus sich vor dem Synedrium bereits in höherer als menschlicher Würde (Gottessohn) bekannt habe, ist eine Anklage auf "Gidduf" nicht verständlich.' [5] Son of God clearly implies something superhuman, and the use of Dan 3.25 in this connection suggests Talmudic influence through j.Shabb. 8, but this time the argument is less theological than legal. Blasphemy must be 'die direkte Schmähung des Gottesnamens',[6] yet the theological aspect is not absent in that blasphemy is dismissed as conflicting with the reason given in the Jewish sources and reflecting the schism between Judaism and Christianity.

---

[1] Origin of Christianity, 333; similarly, M. Brod, op.cit. 208-215; M. Guttmann Das Judentum und seine Umwelt, Berlin 1927, 256, 354; for criticism of this role attributed to Paul, cf. Jocz, Jewish People, 5.

[2] op.cit. 177; Defence, 80: 'The Messiah of the Synoptics never said he was a, God or a Son of God.' Cf B. Felsenthal, Concerning Jesus, surnamed the Christ, repr. in: Bernard Felsenthal: Teacher in Israel, New York 1924, 190.

[3] Rôle, 31.

[4] Contrast the argument of Philippson, who took the conjunction of Son of God and Son of man in exactly the opposite sense.

[5] op.cit. 65.

[6] op.cit. 65.

It is noticeable that several scholars who give Son of God a devalued sense outmanoeuvre themselves by making σὺ εἶπας evasive.[1] This suggests that, subconsciously at least, the old Johannine sense remains.

To draw together the evidence so far, there is by no means a uniform picture presented by Jewish evaluation of the Son of God question. Nevertheless it is clear that the interpretation of almost every writer so far considered stems from an attempt to place Jesus' usage somewhere with reference to a totally Jewish structure or one which has become quite separated from the limits of Judaism. A transcendent Son of God conception flourishes in close association with Talmudic influence. But both the Dt 14.1 and Jn 10.33 interpretations often involve taking liberties with the precise parallelism of the Mk 14.61 formulation σὺ εἶ ὁ χριστὸς ὁ υἱὸς τοῦ εὐλογητοῦ;. This would not be so important if the Lukan version were taken as primary, but while the dependence on the Mk-Mt strand persists this parallelism must be taken seriously and imprecision of whatever type carefully examined. This is the starting-point of our next section.

B. Messiah and Son of God

In treating these two titles, several permutations of view appear among Jewish scholars. Some make the two titles express two separate charges; others absorb messiahship into the transcendence presumed to be inherent in Son of God, so that messiahship itself becomes superhuman in character; a third group, more loyal to the Mk 14.61 formulation, understand Son of God as only a title of the entirely human messiah. The final position of this third group is also reached if the words Son of God are thought to reflect an anachronistic parallelism, and so are deleted.

1. *Two different charges: Messiah and Son of God*

This scheme is most clearly proposed by Saalschütz, who, as Philippson correctly noticed,[2] stresses the political aspect more than his

---

[1] e.g. Soloweyczyk, Kol Kore (1875), 357; Chwolson, Passamahl, 88; N. S. Joseph, Why I am not a Christian, London 1907, 5; A. Danziger, Jewish Forerunners of Christianity, London 1905, 279; M. Fluegel, Messiah Ideal, 103, says the high priest could not have been serious in asking his question, and Jesus could have replied like every other Israelite, 'Yes, for we are all sons of God.' Nevertheless Jesus did not decidedly affirm. (Note the passing over of messiahship.) Rabbinowicz, Rôle, 38, allows a definite claim to be messiah, but by means of the σὺ εἶπας suggests that Jesus preferred not to use the term Son of God. Again the relation of σὺ εἶπας to Messiah as well as to Son of God is completely obscured, this time because of the concentration on the political side.

[2] Haben die Juden, 17.

predecessor Salvador had done. We shall show later that while Salvador laid all the stress on Son of God, his account nevertheless contained the seeds of the political development. Saalschütz however says that Jesus' condemnation followed his claim to be messiah and Son of God—a formulation markedly different from that of Mt and Mk. He adds: 'Die Hauptanklage für die Juden lag in dem zweiten, der Einführung einer neuen Gottheit.' [1] He then briefly gives the prehistory of each count, dwelling especially on messiahship. The fact that neither messiah nor Son of God is simply dropped is important,[2] but the lack of relationship between them is due to the fact that they confront one another as Jewish and Christian concepts respectively. In his earlier work Saalschütz had argued that Christians accepted the Davidic messianic expectation but had super-humanized it. The Jewish idea 'abstrahirt ganz von der Idee des Gottessohnes' and presupposes a real descent from David.[3] Saalschütz and his contemporaries seem to think that Son of God can be taken in its ordinary Israelite sense, or in a Trinitarian sense, but never in the intermediate messianic sense. This may be because of centuries of debate in which the Jewish side had argued that messiah was not divine.

From this position of Saalschütz we have to look back to Salvador and forward to later proponents of this theory. Salvador divided the high priest's question, but less carefully: 'Est-il vrai que tu sois Christ, que tu sois fils de Dieu?' [4] The insertion of the second 'que tu sois' subtly makes Son of God the climax, so that he avoids discussion of messiahship and goes on to urge that 'l'expression fils de Dieu entraînait ici l'idée de Dieu-même'.[5] Later however, Salvador does touch on the messiah/king of Israel theme. He cites Mt 27.42, though he does not draw out any connection between the two names—and indeed Matthew's redaction does make Son of God the climax here.[6] Only in one other place, but that a significant one, is 'le roi des juifs' mentioned. This is where Salvador comments on the Herodians: 'Ce sont eux qui insistent sur ce que Jésus se prétendait roi des juifs: mais ce chef d'accusation ne fut compté pour rien devant le sénat, et n'était

---

[1] Das Mosaische Recht, 625. He like Salvador, appeals to Jn 10.33.

[2] This doubling of charges contrasts with Samuel Hirsch and Philippson, whose arguments depend on there being only one charge in the N.T. accounts.

[3] Versöhnung, 38f.

[4] Histoire II, 87.

[5] op.cit. 87.

[6] Salvador accepts Matthaean priority, of course, but the point could still have been made.

pas de nature à entraîner seul la peine capitale.'¹ That means that in spite of its inadequacy messiahship was mentioned in the Sanhedrin. And there is clearly no connection with Son of God. Consequently, Saalschütz's development beyond Salvador consists in making messiahship a separate charge, though not the main one, and giving it a prehistory in Jesus' ministry—something which Salvador only gave to the Son of God idea.²

Fundamentally, Salvador's inability to consider any relationship between these two titles is due to his view that Jesus severed ideas from their Jewish roots. Only as long as the background is Jewish can some common conceptual background be considered possible. Yet there is a relatedness in some places in Salvador's work which throws into relief the places where the assumption is made that there is none. (a) The two terms are said to relate to different aspects of the principle of election.³ (b) Both together are suitable to be applied to the purified and ideal Israel, i.e. Israel realizing her destiny.⁴ (c) Most strikingly, both are connected with Jesus at his baptism: 'L'objet de Jean est de constater dans le fils de Marie l'existence de l'élection divine . . .; son objet est . . . de le lancer dans la carrière comme le fils bien-aimé de Dieu, c'est-à-dire comme l'homme supérieur et libérateur, le roi de justice, de magnificence et de paix, que le pays appelait de toute son âme.'⁵ This is of great moment because, firstly, Son of God is here a predicate of the messiah, and secondly, the baptism of Jesus is regarded as an anointing, which is by no means necessary.⁶ Yet it must be remembered that this description is, because of John the Baptist, still within the circle of Jewish ideas.⁷ On the other hand, because presumably Caiaphas stands equally within that circle, it is the more arresting that the equivalence of terms cannot be allowed in the question he poses to Jesus. Such is the influence of the old heritage of Son of God and Dt 13 ideas affecting the trial.

In both Salvador and Saalschütz there are therefore two charges mentioned though with differing weight attached to each, and only

---

¹ Histoire II, 89.
² Salvador, op.cit. 82-85; Saalschütz, Mosaische Recht, 625.
³ I(1838), 224.   ⁴ I(1838), 224.   ⁵ I(1838), 230.
⁶ What action of *John* can strictly be regarded as an anointing? There is nothing corresponding to e.g. 1 Sam 16; cf. Justin, Dial. 49, where Trypho acknowledges that Elijah is expected to come and anoint the messiah, but denies that Elijah has in fact come or that his spirit was in John.
⁷ Cf. II(1865), 274, where John is said to have dissented from the views of Jesus, and certainly to have repudiated the equation of himself with Elijah.

one of them is carried through to a condemnation. The same applies to Peynado and Cohen among those who are also to be considered in this section, but not to Franz who has, by implication, condemnation on both counts.

Peynado, arguing in a dogmatic rather than historical context,[1] says that 'Jesus was brought before (the high priest) on the charge of having asserted that he was the Messiah and the Son of God'. The latter was judged to be blasphemous. The formulation is identical to Saalschütz's though the law invoked is different. All connection between messiah and Son of God is severed not only by the legal separation as charges and the fact that Son of God is the content of the blasphemy while messiah is not, but also by the context, in which Peynado is opposing a dogma, i.e. the view that the Jews expected the messiah to be the Son of God.[2]

Cohen, writing under the strong influence of Salvador, ends up with a position close to Saalschütz. Like Peynado he argues that the Jews thought of the messiah as only a man.[3] This again suggests that any equivalence is excluded almost from the beginning on dogmatic grounds within the religious confrontation. Even though Cohen allows that David is often called Son of God in the Psalms and even, with an exaggerated metaphor, told, 'This day have I begotten thee', he yet stresses that David is never called God by himself (sic) or by others. This is the nearest Cohen gets to a relationship when discussing the background. Nevertheless his account of the trial is distinctive. Again two charges are considered, one religious and the other political. 'On accusait Jésus d'avoir violé la loi d'Israël en se déclarant fils de Dieu; on l'accusait aussi de vouloir renverser les pouvoirs établis et usurper, à leur place, l'autorité souveraine.'[4] Clearly, no connection is suggested here, and the same applies to the structure of the proceedings:

> Question of the high priest: Is it true that you are the Christ?
> Reply: If I tell you, you will not believe + Son of man saying.
> Question by the judges: Are you then the Son of God?
> Reply: You say so, I am. (Vous le dites, je le suis.)
> Verdict of blasphemy.

Although Cohen does not here draw out any connection, he hints at one in a later work [5] when he says that if Jesus' messiahship, disengaged from the divinity question, had alone been in question, consider-

---

[1] An Examination of Bishop Pearson's Exposition of the Apostles' Creed, Occident 5 (1847), 548f.   [2] op.cit. 548.   [3] art.cit.(1860), 220.
[4] art.cit. (1861), 10f.   [5] Les Pharisiens II, Paris 1877, 34.

ably less opposition would probably have been aroused. This leads to
some incoherence, however, because any connection at all clashes
with his original scheme. However, Cohen's version of the trial stands
out because it is fundamentally the Lukan account with a slight interpretative alteration of ὑμεῖς λέγετε ὅτι ἐγώ εἰμι, together with two
adaptations drawn from Mk: First, the high priest asks the first question, and, second, the sentence is for blasphemy. This is the first time
the Lukan account had been preferred (Cohen does not appear to be
aware of this), though clearly it would be serviceable to Jews of this
era because of the separation of messiah and Son of God, with the
latter in a climactic position. In Cohen, however, the existence of the
pair of charges causes complication because it is not clear why messiahship was mentioned at all if the religious matter was the concern of
the Sanhedrin, and the political charge was for Herod or Pilate.[1]

Two accusations are adopted by Franz [2] but this time Jesus is convicted on both counts. This treatment is interesting because (a) he
speaks of 'ein Sohn Gottes', yet this is sufficient for conviction. Hence
Franz is situated at the confluence of two streams, the different Jewish
views of Son of God. (b) He writes: 'Als Jesus hier erklärte, er sei ein
Sohn Gottes und König der Juden, kamen Kaipha und seine Genossen
überein, ihn bei dem Römischen Gericht dem Landpfleger, wegen
Volksaufwieglung und Hochverrat anzuklagen.' [3] This order, with
Son of God first, reveals the old pattern where this is dominant. (c) He
reverts to the mesith theme, corresponding to this Son of God charge.
Like Saalschütz he does not mention blasphemy in the actual context
of the trial, even though earlier he had connected blasphemy with
divine Sonship. Once again it seems that 'mesith' includes blasphemy
and is more natural to the Jewish assessment of Jesus.

2. *Messiah transcendent with variations on the Son of God theme*

As mentioned above,[4] the argument of Graetz depends on a close
association of messiah and Son of God, and his absorption of messiahship into transcendent Sonship marks the break with the older apologetic stress on the complete humanity of the Jewish messiah. He also
virtually ignores the O.T. sonship references, citing only Ex. 4.22 and
that just once,[5] and never giving it interpretative weight. Son of God

---

[1] art.cit. (1861), 11.
[2] Das Buch der Religionen, Stuttgart 1889, 109.
[3] op.cit. 109.
[4] pp. 76f.
[5] Sinai et Golgotha, Paris 1867, 61.

is always messianic or more. Yet there are cracks in the structure
which interrelates messiah and Son of God: (a) Although Son of God
was a current Jewish messianic title,[1] the possibility is allowed that it
was separated from messiah in the usage of Jesus. This is in fact a
Salvadorian pattern, placing Son of God in the foreground though
introducing it this time by way of messianic ideas.[2] (b) Graetz draws
back into the Markan version of the Petrine confession,[3] although he
had no secure source-critical warrant for doing so. (c) Jesus is said
never to have clarified whether by Son of God he meant simply messiah.[4] Not even at his trial, when he was condemned on the Son of
God charge, did he reveal his meaning. Uncertainty was the order of
the day: 'Der Schein war gegen ihn.' [5] But it was divine Sonship that
was the issue [6] even though the connection with messiah was and is
doubtful. This doubt stems theologically from the variety of messianic
conceptions at the time: it could be the Essene type [7] or it could be
messiah ben David.

The uneasy tension in Graetz is caused by his attempt to bring too
many strands together, particularly by means of Essenism. He is essentially trying to amalgamate the Jewish Jesus and the Talmudic mesith.[8]
Within a Hegelian framework, which Graetz himself implicitly acknowledges,[9] this is strictly not possible. Johannine references should
go,[10] yet Graetz gives no synoptic support for the divine Son of God

[1] Geschichte III, 2nd ed. 238.

[2] e.g. b.Sukk. 52a.

[3] Geschichte III, 2nd ed. 237: 'Im Markus-Evangelium 8.27-30 ist die Nach-
richt viel ursprünglicher gehalten.' Normally Graetz prefers to use Mt.

[4] Geschichte III, 2nd ed. 238: 'Hat Jesus diesen Ausdruck blos bildlich für
Messias oder im eigentlichen Wortsinn genommen wissen wollen? Er hat, so viel
wir wissen, sich nie darüber erklärt.'

[5] op.cit. 244. Although the Son of man logion is said, in the 2nd ed., to have
provided confirmation, its authenticity is doubted in the 3rd. ed. 325.

[6] Un mot. 11: 'Là était véritablement le point sensible de la situation . . . La
qualité de fils de Dieu était . . . . en opposition avec la conception de Dieu d'après
le judaïsme.'

[7] Un mot, 11-15.

[8] Thus for instance, although Jesus affirmed the unity of God, 'eben an diesem
Punkte bot Jesus dem Angriff eine schwache Seite dar'. Geschichte III, 2nd ed.
232, 241.

[9] Op.cit. 2nd ed. 225: 'Im Allgemeinen läßt sich festhalten, daß diejenigen
Äusserungen Jesu, welche einen gesetzesfeindlichen Charakter haben oder dem
Christenthum eine universelle Bedeutung auch für die Heiden beilegen, durchaus
unecht sind.'

[10] It is necessary for him to appeal to Jn 19.7, op.cit. 2nd ed. 244. Less significant
are his references to Bread of heaven, alleged, without evidence, to be an Essene
messianic title, op.cit. 238, and Jn 12.6, with reference to the Essene community
of goods, op.cit. 227.

theory. So again it is clear that Graetz is primarily coloured by Talmudic interpretations, and yet feels the effect of current Christian and philosophical trends which lead elsewhere. He is tossed by the waves of transition from one approach to another, but the consistent underlying influence is the older one. The Essene hypothesis [1] cannot quite, even with Rabbinic support, bind the theory into a unity. He moves too quickly from Essene to Rabbinic or Christian ideas for clarity as to the precise significance of a given term in the mind of a given speaker at a given moment. So, although messiahship can be transcendent, we are left in doubt as to what Caiaphas meant in framing his question.

The next scholar to use the idea of a transcendent messiah is Edersheim,[2] but again the argument has damaging inconsistencies for which an explanation must be found. In fact, in this case they stem from the tension between the Jew and the Christian in Edersheim, and the influence of Christian arguments in the Jewish-Christian dialogue and mission to which Edersheim, in his conversion, is the heir. Consequently apologetic and historical faithfulness coexist with some difficulty, particularly in the link he tries to prove between messiah and Son of God, and in the application of this to the trial. 'The high priest adjured the True One by the living God, whose Son he was, to say it, whether he were the Messiah and Divine—the two being joined together, not in Jewish belief but to express the claims of Jesus.'[3] This sentence is sufficient to show that he takes the parallelism seriously, and yet divides the two. His remark that Jewish belief did not join them is an admission of the normal Jewish claim which he had earlier attempted to demolish.[4] Formerly, he argued for the divinity of the Messiah on four grounds: (a) The names of the messiah. From Is 9.6 LXX μεγάλης βουλῆς ἄγγελος he deduces a person of greater dignity than the angels or men, and appeals to the Targum in support of premundane existence, eternal continuance and superhuman dignity. The weakness of this argument is apparent not only in the use of ἄγγελος which itself excludes any idea of superiority to the angels, as well as the fact that eternal rule by no means implies divinity, but also because Edersheim's citation of the Targum is onesided and omits such aspects as the messiah's study of Torah and the possibility of a messianic

---

[1] Acid criticism of this was meted out by F. Delitzsch, Jesus und Hillel, 2nd ed. Erlangen 1867, 25, who claimed that nothing was actually known about Essene messianism.

[2] The Life and Times of Jesus the Messiah, London 1883.

[3] op.cit. II, 559f.

[4] op.cit. I, 171-179.

dynasty rather than the eternal rule of one messiah.[1] Edersheim goes on to cite Ps.Sol. 17.36 χριστὸς κύριος which he claims is identical with Lam 4.20 LXX. But this belongs to a pre-critical period in the treatment of the Psalms of Solomon; against this is Rahlfs' view that in Lam 4.20 the reading should be κυρίου, since κυ was written for both nominative and genitive. Moreover, the normal O.T. usage is 'the Lord's anointed', and since χριστὸς κύριος in Ps.Sol. 17.36 is to be taken as a mistranslation of the construct 'anointed of the Lord',[2] Edersheim's argument collapses. His next example, b.Sanh. 38b, 'the very curious concessions in a controversy with a Christian' is also disabled by its late date [3] (R. Idith belongs to the 3rd-4th century) and the fact that Metatron rather than messiah is the subject. The last case is Lam R.I.16(51),[4] but the parallel b.B.B. 75b overturns this suggestion by applying the name of God not only to the messiah (Jer 23.6) but also to the righteous (Is 43.7) and Jerusalem (Ezk 48.35). (b) The origin of the messiah. The sending of the messiah from heaven (Sib. Or.III.285f) or from the sun (Sib.Or.III.652) are here emphasized. But again, the sun probably stands for the east,[5] the heavenly sending refers to authorization with heaven a periphrasis for God, and the messianic reference is in any case neither undisputed nor supported by the general interest in God's activity throughout sections 625-807. (c) The pre-existence of the messiah is proposed in an essential sense on the basis of Ps 72.5, 110.3 and Targ.Mic 5.2. That Edersheim's conclusion is unjustified is sufficiently demonstrated by the extensive list of other pre-existent entities [6] in Midr. Prov 8.9, b.Pes. 54a etc., the view of Billerbeck [7] that the old Synagogue knew nothing of messianic pre-existence except among those who from 250 B.C. onwards believed in the pre-existence of all souls, and finally Edersheim's failure to distinguish the fixing of messiah's name from the ontological

---

[1] Billerbeck II, 332.

[2] This then agrees with Ps.Sol. 18.8.

[3] See the strictures of S. Schechter, Studies in Judaism: Third Series, Philadelphia 1924, 168, who criticizes Edersheim for inattention to the dating of Rabbinic texts.

[4] Soncino Midrash Lamentations, 135: 'What is the name of the King Messiah? R. Abba b. Kahana (A.D. 310) said: His name is 'the Lord' as stated in Jer 23.6.' Cf. Midr. Pss.21.2.

[5] Cf. R. H. Charles, Apocrypha and Pseudepigrapha, ad.loc: 'from the sunrise', Is 41.25.

[6] The list includes besides the messiah, the Torah, repentance, the garden of Eden, Gehinnom, the Throne of Glory and the Holy Place.

[7] Handkommentar II, 333.

existence of his person. (d) The supernatural kingdom of the messiah.[1]
The sources cited are Gen 49.10 LXX, Ps 72.5-7 LXX, Syb. Or.
III.625-807, Enoch (in spite of nervousness about dating), Ps. Sol. 17,
18—'this is not an earthly kingdom nor yet an earthly king' [2]—4 Esdras
and Ap. Baruch. He does occasionally distinguish between 'essential
sonship' and 'infinite superiority over all other servants of God',[3] and
he also admits that Divine personality is an idea foreign to Jewish
messianology in the first century,[4] but the vague use of terms like
'superhuman', 'superior dignity', 'not earthly', 'elevated above the
ordinary conditions of humanity' gives ample scope for argument,
imprecision and no clear indication of where the frontier between
'greater than human' and the 'divine' is crossed.

The trend towards the idea of a supernatural messiah gathers momentum in the works of some outstanding Jewish scholars of the 20th
century, e.g. J. H. Greenstone, C. G. Montefiore, S. Zeitlin, S. Dubnow, M. L. Margolis and A. Marx, I. Mattuck, J. B. Agus, Jules Isaac,
A. I. Polack and, with modification, J. Klausner. I Enoch, presumed
to be pre-Christian, is the main source,[5] though S.Zeitlin appeals

---

[1] 'That a supernatural kingdom of eternal duration . . . . should have a superhuman king seems almost a necessary corollary.' Edersheim's view at this point is
adopted by J. H. Greenstone, The Messiah Idea in Jewish History, Philadelphia
1906, 70-72.

[2] Life and Times. I, 174.

[3] 1 Enoch 105.2, where messiah is called Son of God, is explained by reference
to 90.28.

[4] op.cit.I, 171.

[5] J. H. Greenstone, op.cit. 72: 'almost a supernatural being'. He does not say
how this affects the trial. C. G. Montefiore, The Synoptic Gospels I, London 1909,
94,99: 'a supernatural being pre-existent in heaven before his appearance on earth,
and different from the old purely human monarch of Is xi'. Similarly op.cit. 351:
'In the age of Jesus the purely human character of the Messiah was not insisted
on . . . . as it was . . . . after the development of Christianity.' S. Zeitlin, Studies in
the Beginnings of Christianity, JQR 14 (1923), 111-139, esp. 127; The Crucifixion
of Jesus re-examined, JQR 31 (1941), 327-369, esp.333; The Origin of the Idea
of the Messiah, in the A. H. Silver Festschrift, New York 1963, 456; Moriz
Friedländer, Die religiösen Bewegungen innerhalb des Judentums im Zeitalter
Jesu, Berlin 1905, 323; M. L. Margolis—A. Marx, A History of the Jewish People,
Philadelphia 1927,180; I. Mattuck, The Trial of Jesus, London 1929, 6; J. B. Agus,
The Evolution of Jewish Thought, London 1959, 107: 'a heavenly being . . . .
the son of man of Daniel or Enoch'; S. Dubnow, Weltgeschichte II, 534; J. Isaac,
Jésus et Israel, Paris 1948, 239, speaks of the Danielic Son of man as 'un être
céleste'; A. I. Polack, Jesus in the Background of History, London 1957, 77-79.
J. Klausner's position is in opposition to the view of a supernatural messiah
within Judaism, but he sees a link between Jesus and the Essenes in a mystical
concept of messiahship, and he thinks that at the time of his trial Jesus was convinced of 'his Messiahship in a supernatural sense'. Jesus of Nazareth, 256, 411 and

(erroneously) to Test.Reuben 8.6, Ps.Sol.17.6,23,36, 18.8 as well.[1] This approach marks a reversal of two traditional Jewish tendencies: (a) It marks a further disintegration of Judaism's united front. No longer are the Sadducees and Pharisees alone contrasted, but now a division even within Pharisaism is postulated by the theory of many of these writers that the apocalyptic Pharisees formed a distinct group.[2] (b) Centuries-old Jewish stress on the humanity of the messiah is abandoned.

As would be expected, the balance of the two terms Son of man and Son of God is adjusted. No longer does the straight contrast survive in the form in which Troki proposed it. A greater unity is seen between the messianic question (Mk 14.61f) and the Son of man saying, so that the latter becomes a messianic affirmation along the lines of I Enoch.[3] Indeed the outstanding significance of this saying is such that Klausner can even incorporate it into a summary of the Roman proceedings.[4] It is true that Zeitlin disputes this interpretation of Mk 14.62, stressing exclusively the political aspect of messiahship,[5] but this is untypical of

The Messianic Idea in Israel, London 1956, 277. He takes 1 Enoch as an Essene book, Jesus, 209, and like Dubnow (op.cit. 534) stresses the dreamy mystical side of Jesus' character. Jesus, 253,342.

[1] Who crucified Jesus? 4th ed. New York 1964, 99; Origin of the Idea of the Messiah, 450-452. Zeitlin is not only wrong in his reconstruction of the historical development of the idea, taking too little account of the O.T. (cf. F. Hahn, Christologische Hoheitstitel, Göttingen 1963, 133-140) but also misunderstands the texts. For instance, it remains true that the messiah in the Psalms of Solomon is no more than a man, as shown already by H. E. Ryle—M. R. James, The Psalms of Solomon, Cambridge 1891, lv and J. Viteau, Les Psaumes de Salomon, Paris 1911, 71. Zeitlin's 'concretizing of the apocalyptic tendency into a group' is criticized in a review by S. Sandmel, JBL 87 (1968), 98; cf. W. D. Davies, Apocalyptic and Pharisaism, in Christian Origins and Judaism, London 1962, 19-30.

[2] Margolis-Marx, History, 180; Dubnow, Weltgeschichte, 532; Montefiore, Gospels I(1909), 51-53; Agus, Evolution, 114; Polack, Jesus, 50.

[3] Margolis-Marx, op.cit. 180; J. Klausner, From Jesus to Paul, London 1944, 258.

[4] op.cit. 258: 'Jesus was crucified by the Romans because he persisted in the belief that he was Messiah and would appear as Messiah "at the right hand of power".' Cf. Jules Isaac, whose approach is basically Klausnerian, and who wrote in 1948 that the theory of a pre-Christian messiah—Son of man equation is overbold; yet in 1959 he thought it possible within a limited circle, cf. Jésus et Israel, 2nd ed. Paris 1959, 590. But even in his 1st ed. he wrote: 'Face au Sanhédrin, Jésus n'aurait donc prononcé qu'une affirmation explicite et souveraine, l'affirmation que les textes éclatants du psaume de David et de la vision daniélique étaient désormais réalisés, et, sans le dire explicitement, qu'ils l'étaient en sa personne. La revendication de cette messianité transcendante, suprahumaine, étroitement associée à Dieu peut-être—peut-être—est-ce là le blasphème . . . .?', op.cit. 442.

[5] Who crucified Jesus?, 4th ed. 153; The Ecumenical Council Vatican II and the Jews, JQR 56 (1963), 93-111, esp. 95f. He argues from Ps 110.1 (surprisingly!) that many pious Jews looked forward to sitting in God's company in the future world.

this group of scholars. A further point of importance is that there is a diminution of the importance of Son of God, so that it is either unauthentic [1] or simply messianic. Here Mattuck is the exception, when he explains that to the Jews messiah meant 'at the same time an earthly king and a superhuman being: Son of God if you will'.[2] Usually these two strands of messianic expectation are separated, at least for purposes of analysis.

If this transcendent pattern of messiahship had a Jewish background, even if in nonconformist circles, there is still the problem of why it should in Jesus' case constitute a crime.[3] This is solved either by emphasizing the political side (so that there is either no Jewish hearing, or only one before a political Sanhedrin [4]) or by underlining the monstrous presumption and falsity of the claim when made by Jesus on behalf of himself. In the latter case appeal is made either to a background of conflict [5] or to the circumstantial evidence against Jesus.[6] But it is interesting that the definition of the offence varies, and even here the old religious objections to Jesus reappear. Thus Margolis-Marx [7] and Dubnow [8] speak of false prophecy,[9] and Klausner toys

---

[1] e.g. Klausner, Jesus, 342 and art. Jesus von Nazareth, EJ (1932), 66; J. Isaac, Jesus, 1st ed. 235f, 440f.

[2] op.cit 6.

[3] Claims to messiahship are normally regarded as non-criminal: I. Mattuck, The Trial of Jesus, London 1929, 6; Edgar, op.cit. 7; S. Zeitlin, JQR 31 (1941), 362. Montefiore however saw a messianic claim as a bone of contention with all groups, since Sadducees feared the political menace and Pharisees took note of the implied criticism of the law, cf. Gospels I(1909), lxxxix, 102, 204; I(1927), 83.

[4] Zeitlin, Who crucified Jesus? 163-165, followed by Polack, op.cit. 62f; E. L. Ehrlich, A concise History of Israel, London 1962, 136.

[5] e.g. Margolis-Marx, op.cit. 183: 'The assumption of power beside the Deity by one who had made light of the things hallowed by religious sentiment was blasphemous in the eyes of the court.' This presupposes, of course, a loose definition of blasphemy.

[6] Klausner, Jesus, 343: 'To the High Priest the answer was sheer blasphemy—a Galilean carpenter styling himself "Son of man" in the sense of the Book of Daniel and saying that he should sit on the right hand of God and come "with the clouds of heaven".' Similarly, Agus, op.cit. 117; Polack, Jesus, 102; C. G. Montefiore, Gospels II(1909), 350; I(1927), 357: 'The claim to be Messiah without any of the ordinary qualifications of the Messiah—a claim admitted by a solitary prisoner in the full power of his enemies—must have seemed a presumptuous insolence.' Cf. I(1909), 351: 'If it was blasphemy for the real Messiah to be spoken of, and to speak of himself, as the Son of God in the Jewish and contemporary sense, it might conceivably be regarded as blasphemy for a man to claim to be that Son when he was not.'

[7] op.cit. 182f.

[8] Weltgeschichte, 535; A Short History of the Jewish People, London 1936, 117.

[9] For details, see above, pp. 54-61.

with the mesith possibility.[1] It is noticeable that scholars in this group are not so devoted to the theory of Jesus' orthodoxy in practice, however much they use the Mt 5.17 proof-text.[2]

Finally, some supplementary attention to the theories of Montefiore[3] and Klausner is appropriate. Montefiore's scheme is as follows: (a) The two strands of messianic expectation correspond respectively to Is 11 and 1 Enoch.[4] (b) A reminiscence of Samuel Hirsch is provided by the assertion that 'the consciousness of Messiahship never meant anything else than a consciousness of something he would become'.[5] (c) Son of God meant no more than messiah to Jesus.[6] Indeed both Son of God and Son of man were 'but synonyms of Messiah'; [7] yet with tantalizing ambiguity, Montefiore also remarks that Son of God may *not* have been a current messianic term.[8] It is significant here, firstly, that he is able to accept the Mk 14.61 parallelism 'because the later metaphysical and more developed conception of the term Son of God had not yet arisen'.[9] Secondly, when Montefiore does allow for messianic Sonship, this is but an intensification of a 'spiritual sense' appropriate to all Israelites or even to all men.[10] But on other occasions he is in some difficulty over which of messiah and Son of God is the basic concept. Against Harnack on Mt 11.27 he urges that Jesus was only Son of God because messiah,[11] but elsewhere he regards Jesus' messiahship as the consequence of intensified filial consciousness.

Klausner proposes a different evaluation of the messiah-Son of God

---

[1] See pp. 54 ff.

[2] See e.g. Montefiore, I(1909), lxxxix; I(1927), 370f; Polack, op.cit. 98; Klausner, From Jesus to Paul, 3-5—the profession of agreement with the Wellhausenian dictum that Jesus was not a Christian but was a Jew, is scarcely borne out by the contents of his book on Jesus.

[3] Cf. Lindeskog, Jesusfrage, 164, 254-256.

[4] I(1909), lxxxix,xcviii,51-53, 99; II(1909), 1046.

[5] I(1909), 105.

[6] In 1927 he suggested that the term was probably not used by Jesus anyway—but not so strongly in I(1909), 277.

[7] I(1909), 111, 351.

[8] I(1909), 111.

[9] I(1909), 351.

[10] I(1909), xcix,105; II(1909), 606; cf. on Lk 3.38, II(1909), 869.

[11] He regards Mt 11.27 as a gospel exaggeration with metaphysical implications, I(1909), xciii,105; II(1909), 605; I(1927), cxxviii. See also J. Eschelbacher, Das Judentum und das Wesen des Christentums, Berlin 1905, 15. On the other hand, Mt 11.27 is accepted as genuine and certainly repugnant by I. Elbogen, Die Religionsanschauungen der Pharisäer, Berlin 1904, 63; S. Pick, Judentum und Christentum, Frankfurt a.M. 1913, 8. H. G. Enelow, Jewish View, 428 regards it as both genuine and acceptable.

question. He is adamant that the parallelism in Mk 14.61 is inconceivable [1] because, firstly, 'Son of the Blessed' is not a Hebrew expression [2] and is not an abbreviation of 'the Holy One, blessed be He', and, secondly, a Jewish high priest, and he a Sadducee, could not possibly have said these words.[3] Now we note that Klausner does not have the same objections to Mt 16.16. There he regards the phrase 'the living God' as entirely Hebrew, and traces the addition of Sonship to the title 'messiah' back to Ps 2.7; indeed he says the reference of this text to the messiah was never doubted in Jesus' time.[4] Hence it is the formulation and the person involved, rather than divine Sonship as such, which constitute the objection. However, τοῦ εὐλογητοῦ can hardly be anything other than Jewish, and an argument about the parallelism would be stronger since this is only attested in marginal Judaism,[5] and in Klausner's time was not known to be attested at all. In the Markan formulation ὁ υἱὸς τοῦ εὐλογητοῦ could easily be redactional, as in Mt 16.16, but any attempt to eliminate it from the exchange between Jesus and the Sanhedrin is jeopardized by its independent attestation in Lk 22.70 (cf. Jn 19.7).[6]

Like Montefiore and Dubnow, Klausner still sees the seeds of Jesus' apostasy in the title Son of God [7] and consequently does not interpret the parallelism strictly.[8] All the commonplace texts, Ex 4.22, Dt 14.1, Ps 82.6, are mentioned, but there remains in the words of Jesus an emphasis and a claim to literal nearness to God, and in this consists the offensiveness of Jesus.[9]

3. *Son of God a title of the normal messiah*

The assertion of this parallelism gains momentum[10] in time with

---

[1] He notes en passant the differentation in Lk 22.67-70 but makes nothing of it. Jesus, 342.

[2] So already, H. P. Chajes, Markus-Studien, Berlin 1899, 77; Abrahams, Studies, 212; A. Marmorstein, The old Rabbinic Doctrine of God, London 1927, 87.

[3] Cf. Grünebaum, Sittenlehre, 159.

[4] op.cit. 299,378.

[5] F. Hahn, Christologische Hoheitstitel, Göttingen 1963, 281-287; E. Lohse, art. υἱός TWNT 8 (1967), 361; O. Michel—O. Betz, Von Gott gezeugt, in: Judentum Urchristentum Kirche, Festschrift J. Jeremias, Berlin 1960, 3-23.

[6] See chapter III.

[7] See above, pp. 60f.

[8] Jesus, 378.

[9] op.cit. 378,392. Similarly, Polack, op.cit. 110-114.

[10] Apart from those scholars mentioned in the text, the following propose this link: Rodrigues, Roi, 38, 230; Rabbi Jeshua, London 1881, 140; M. Joseph, Jesus, JL 3 (1929), 237-243; E. Jacob, EJ 5 (1930), 528; E. R. Trattner, As a Jew sees

political emphases, but in view of historical legacies in debate [1] is put forward with some raggedness about the edges.

Jost is a good example, and an important one, since it is with him that detailed and consecutive treatment of the life of Jesus begins among modern Jews. In 1820 he made no definition of the relationship between messiah and Son of God, but since he ignored the Sanhedrin trial there was no pressing need to do so. Some connection between the two is, however, occasionally implied. Firstly, Jesus is said to have called himself the Son of God, the promised messiah, the redeemer from sin.[2] Secondly, we note the statement: 'Seitdem sich Jesu als Stifter eines neuen Bundes zeigte, ward er Christos (der Gesalbte) genannt, und seine Anhänger sahen in ihm eine in menschlicher Hülle erschiene Gottheit.'[3] Jost, however, regards Son of God as implying divinity, in that Jesus' teaching assumed forms different from Judaism: and the Jews must oppose bodily ideas, the divinity of Jesus, his sending and redemption.[4] Yet clearly there is the suggestion of a messiah/Son of God relationship at the pre-Christian stage.

In his first book, Jost explained Jesus' downfall in political terms, and he did so again in 1832,[5] though this time he spoke of a Sanhedrin called by Pilate. In 1857 the Sanhedrin trial is more precisely described, and the high priest's question 'Are you the messiah, the Son of the blessed?' reported though not explained.[6] Yet in the context Jesus causes a political upheaval which comes to a head in the entry to Jerusalem and the messianic claim. To this Jost adds an older idea by commenting on the condemnation, that Jesus' words should have been scrutinized before he was sentenced for blasphemy and leading the people astray.[7] Only loyalty to the older lines of defence prevents

---

Jesus, London 1931, 75-78; and with qualifications, H. J. Schonfield, The Passover Plot, London 1965, 41.

[1] The old approach is typified by M. A. Weill, Le Judaïsme ses dogmes et sa mission III, Paris 1869, 471, claiming that deification of the messiah is the essential difference between Jewish and Christian views.

[2] Geschichte der Israeliten I, Berlin 1820, 297; similarly in Allgemeine Geschichte II, Berlin 1832, 67. J. H. Dessauer, Geschichte der Israeliten, Erlangen 1846, 90, has a comparable though undeveloped formulation: 'Er nannte sich den Sohn Gottes, den verheissenen Messias (Christos) und den König des göttlichen Reiches.' His outline is heavily influenced by Jost (1820) and he also omits to mention the Sanhedrin trial.

[3] op.cit. 297.

[4] op.cit. 299.

[5] op.cit. 68.

[6] op.cit. 404.

[7] op.cit. 408.

Jost from fully identifying messiah and Son of God in line with his heightened political emphasis.

The necessary step forward is evidenced actually within the development of Grünebaum's thought. He writes of the messianic issue: 'Das war der Gegenstand der Anklage und der Grund seiner Verurtheilung.'[1] In line with this he originally expunged 'Son of God' from Mk 14.61 because, firstly, messiah was only called the root from Jesse and not Son of God, and secondly, the expression 'the blessed' is not Jewish and 'the blessed God' was not a current term. Grünebaum is at least taking seriously Mark's parallelism. In his next edition, however, he makes a notable step forward.[2] While dealing with the Sanhedrin hearing [3] he argues: (a) Jesus never called himself Son of God in the Pauline sense but only in the messianic sense. Taken in the Pauline sense, the high priest's question is meaningless. He could have said, Are you a mesith? or, Are you a blasphemer? but never, Are you the Son of God? (b) The high priest would understand Son of God only in the sense of messiah, as indeed the preceding reference shows. The expression was already used of the messiah, he says, in Ps 2.7, Wisd 2.16,18, Mt 16.16. (c) The messianic claim was not a blasphemy (cf. Bar Kochba).

This notable advance is made possible by not taking 'blasphemy' as the fixed point of reference, and by respecting the order of the narrative. He does not deny that the high priest rent his clothes and accused Jesus of blasphemy, but 'allein offenbar war es weder ihm, noch den Besitzern Ernst mit dieser Anklage'.[4] If they had been serious, proceedings before the Great Sanhedrin would have been instituted.

The same ambivalence between messianic and transcendent Sonship, which we see in Jost, appears also in Kohler, though he conforms to a growing Jewish tendency to exclude a Sanhedrin trial[5] and to confine involvement to the arrest and the handing over of Jesus to Pilate. Sonship in Mt 11.27 is interpreted as mediation between God and

---

[1] Die Sittenlehre des Judenthums, Mannheim 1867, 158.
[2] op.cit. 2nd ed. Straßburg 1878, 274.
[3] He thinks it was a priestly court and not the Great Sanhedrin.
[4] op.cit. 2nd ed. 273.
[5] The Origins of the Synagogue and the Church, New York 1929, 227: 'The statements that the high priests found him guilty for having claimed to be the Son of God, or that the Pharisees accused him of violation of the Sabbath or of having spoken against the Temple, must be dismissed as spurious.' Similarly, Grundriss einer systematischen Theologie des Judentums auf geschichtlicher Grundlage, Leipzig 1910, 319.

men, and yet, because of its O.T. application to Israelite kings
and to the messiah (Ps 2, where it only implied 'a distinction from
others, an aloofness above the rest of men'), Jesus 'appears to have
regarded it as inseparable from Messiahship, yet only in a spiritual sense'.[1] Both these suggestions are somehow welded into the
earlier view that Jesus claimed to be no more than a prophet.[2] The
historical reconstruction is similar to Samuel Hirsch's treatment of the
trial: Son of God is the central claim, but the whole episode is a fiction.

C. THE MESSIANIC CONDEMNATION

This section may appropriately be begun with the agreed conclusion
of a Christian and a Jewish scholar. Lindeskog has rightly remarked:
'Die Eigenart der jüdischen Forschung zeigt sich nun auch darin, daß
sie fast ohne Ausnahme in Jesus den Messiasprätendenten sieht.'[3]
Similarly Jacob Jocz has declared that 'it reveals a good sense of real-
ism on the part of Jewish scholars that they invariably admit the
Messianic consciousness of Jesus'.[4] It is therefore the influence of
Christian scholarship which moves such as Joel Carmichael and Paul
Winter to the opposite view,[5] a view already resisted explicitly by
C. G. Montefiore.[6] Yet if, as the normal view asserts, Jesus claimed
and was executed for claiming messiahship, there is still some variation
in the reconstruction of the preceding events, and in the opinion about
whether or not the Sanhedrin participated. This section must therefore
deal with the two political trends: that which allows a Jewish hearing,
and that which does not.

1. *A Jewish condemnation for a messianic claim*

The attractiveness of this position to Jewish scholars is quite clear.
It avoids a dogmatic clash, and it is an intermediate position between
the old stand, according to which there were theological differences
between Jesus and his contemporaries, and the new stand, according
to which Jesus and his contemporaries agreed in matters of religion
and only clashed in the political sphere. It can therefore stand as a

---

[1] Origins, 230.

[2] Art. Christianity in its relation to Judaism, JE 4 (1903), 49-59.

[3] Jesusfrage, 251.

[4] Jewish People, 147.

[5] J. Carmichael, The Death of Jesus, London 1963, 193; P. Winter, On the
Trial of Jesus, Berlin 1961, 148.

[6] Gospels I(1909), xcv-xcvii.

halfway position between a full-blown Sanhedrin trial and no Sanhedrin hearing at all.

Features of this view are the following: first of all, a movement towards Jesus' religious orthodoxy. The issue is put at its sharpest by Rodrigues. Between the saying of Jesus that he will not change the law at all, and the statement of John that Jesus declared himself equal with God 'il faut absolument choisir'.[1] He also writes of Jesus' agreement with Hillel as a 'concordance qui détruit absolument l'allégation d'une condamnation purement religieuse de Jésus par le synédrium'.[2] It is clear, then, that Mt 5.17 epitomizes the 'orthodox Jesus' theory, and that this is the the the starting-point [3] for the political condemnation view, whether Jewish involvement alongside the Romans is allowed [4] or not.[5] The list of those who follow this path is extremely long.[6]

[1] Les origines du sermon de la montagne, Paris 1868, 130.

[2] Le Roi des Juifs, Paris 1870, 59.

[3] From Geiger onwards, the insistence on understanding Jesus through a true assessment of his environment makes itself felt at this point. Cf. Lindeskog, op.cit. 102f.

[4] Rodrigues, Roi, 56; Grünebaum, Sittenlehre, 1st ed.150; K. Magnus, About the Jews, London 1881, 68 (cf. Outlines of Jewish History, London 1892, 51: 'Jesus himself probably never denounced Pharisees or Judaism.' The controversies are said to be those of a later time; in the revised ed. London 1958, 30, controversies are however accepted.). L. Weiss, Burning Questions, 17; Ackermann, op.cit. 11; I. Ziegler, Der Kampf zwischen Judentum und Christentum in den ersten drei christlichen Jahrhunderten, Berlin 1907, 10; M. Hyamson, JQR 11(1920), 91f; J. Z. Lauterbach, The Pharisees and their Teachings, HUCA 6 (1929), 69-134, esp. 71-74; S. Zeitlin, Who crucified Jesus?, 114-143. Cf. A. Finkel, The Pharisees and the Teacher of Nazareth, Leiden 1964, 130-139, who thinks that Jesus took a Pharisaic position, and disagreed only with the Shammaite school. He does not apply this in any way to the trial. R. Leszynsky, Die Sadduzäer, Berlin 1912, 284 thinks that Mt 5.17 is evidence of a Sadducean approach.

[5] Those rejecting a Sanhedrin hearing and insisting on Jesus' orthodoxy in terms of Pharisaism or Mt 5.17: Wise, Martyrdom, 76: 'Jesus the Pharisean Jew'; Schreiber, Prinzipien, 108; Krauskopf, Impressions, 72; Enelow, Jewish View, 432, who takes πληρῶσαι as 'to grasp the full content and aim of the law' and makes Jesus closest to, though not united with, Pharisaism; A. Cohen, Jewish History in the first Century, London 1924, 42; M. Hunterberg, The crucified Jew, New York 1927, 17-32; M. Joseph, JL 3 (1929), 237f; E. Jacob, EJ 5 (1930), 526; M. Guttmann, MGWJ 77 (1933), 24; S. Ben Chorin, Christus-Frage, 9,30; S. W. Baron, A Social and Religious History of the Jews, 2nd ed. New York 1952, 67f; B. J. Bamberger, The Story of Judaism, New York 1957, 98; E.L.Ehrlich, A concise History of Israel, London 1962, 136; S. Umen, Pharisaism and Jesus, New York 1963, 119-126; J. Isaac, Revue Historique 85 (1961), 126; P. E. Lapide, The last three Popes and the Jews, London 1967, 17-21,28, dismisses the Sanhedrin trial and insists on Jesus' Pharisaic upbringing—but in between has a deviation by Jesus from the sound basic principles of Judaism.

[6] An exception to the 'Pharisaic Jesus' view is the suggestion of S. S. Cohon, The Place of Jesus in the religious life of his Day, JBL 48 (1929), 82-108, that Jesus was an Am-haarez hasid.

In the case of Rodrigues it is clear that the dichotomy between law and Christology is in fact the old one discussed by Moses Mendelssohn a hundred years before.[1] Lindeskog's perceptive words are here worth remembering: 'Das Religionsgespräch zwischen dem Judentum und dem Christentum hat uns gelehrt, wo—wenigstens nach jüdischer Auffassung—die Grenze zwischen den beiden Religionen geht. Die Grenze ist die Christologie, die nach jüdischer Überzeugung keineswegs mit der Lehre Jesu identisch oder aus ihr herzuleiten ist.'[2] Everything stems from or turns on the teachings of Jesus and his christological claims, and the suggested balance between the two.

Two other factors about Rodrigues are important at this juncture. It might appear that he is pressing a dichotomy between Jn and the synoptic gospels, but this is only partly true. Even where Jn is explicitly dismissed Rodrigues, like many Jewish scholars after him, still uses the fourth gospel when convenient.[3] Then a further point is the governing influence that the pre-history has on the evaluation of the trial. The balance of this argument is in striking divergence from the modern approach of, for instance, Samuel Sandmel or Paul Winter. The former thinks that the whole attempt to discover the historical Jesus is an effort 'to put a somewhat uncertain figure into an uncertain background'.[4] And while Winter's book states boldly that Jesus was a Pharisee, it also regards the pre-history of the trial as practically unknowable and in any case not very germane to the trial itself.[5]

Not all Jewish scholars found the simple choice posed by Rodrigues to be acceptable, although it is certainly true that in varying degrees there is a movement towards it. Thus Geiger already, the pioneer of the 'Pharisaic Jesus' theory, who does not mention Son of God in connection with Jesus (for μονογενής is a later development), and who makes the Sanhedrin hearing hinge on messiahship, — even Geiger

---

[1] Gesammelte Schriften III, 91: 'Jesus ein Jude? Ja, wenn er, wie ich glaube, das Judenthum nicht hat aufheben wollen.'

[2] Jesusfrage, 91.

[3] Rodrigues dates Jn at A.D. 170, Roi, 143; but Jn 18.19f is used in support of Jesus' orthodoxy, Jn 10.35f for the devaluation of the term Son of God, op.cit. 214, Jn 6.15, 11.47-50,19.12 for the political evidence, op.cit. 122, 141, Jn 18.3,12 for a Roman arrest, op.cit. 223.

[4] A Jewish Understanding of the New Testament, Cincinnati 1957, 20f. Sandmel's agnosticism in this matter is part of his view that Jews tend to accept the authenticity of gospel material more than Christians do. Cf. The Jewish Scholar and early Christianity, JQR 75 (1967), 472-481.

[5] On the Trial, 135: 'The grounds for his arrest had nothing to do with personal or religious differences between Jesus and any other Jews. Rather than the content of his teaching, it was the effect . . . .'

still says that Jesus intruded in religious matters in a damaging way
and lifted himself up in an unacceptable manner.[1] Schlesinger too,
following Geiger, argues that the messianic claim was blasphemy.[2]
Such a suggestion, which is against the stream of Jewish insistence
that there is no offence in claiming to be messiah, is revived later by
K. Magnus, M. Freimann, H. J. Schonfield and, with modifications,
S. Grayzel.[3]

Further evidence of the difficulty that the political theory had in
shaking off the religious interpretation is provided by Rabbinowicz.
He too stresses the political data and yet (a) cites Jn 5.18 as evidence
of the real Pharisaic complaint against Jesus [4] leading to the allegation
of seduction, Jn 8.57-59, 10.25-33, and (b) cites Lk 22.70f on the
Sanhedrin trial itself,[5] thus omitting in toto the messianic interrogation. To this extent a Salvadorian view is retained,[6] but according to
Rabbinowicz's real view the Sanhedrin trial was concerned with 'une
grave accusation de révolte contre l'autorité établie et surtout contre
le gouvernement romain'.[7] One could easily dismiss Rabbinowicz as
muddled, but the fact that he preserves two such ill-fitting and, in
themselves, significant pictures makes him important in the development of Jewish historiography.

A final point about Rodrigues' dichotomy: it rests on the classic interpretation of Mt 5.17 as expressing a fully conservative position.[8] This
is indeed the normal view adopted by most Jewish writers, though not

---

[1] Judentum, 115.

[2] The historical Jesus of Nazareth, New York 1876, 77f.

[3] K. Magnus, About the Jews, London 1881, 76; M. Freimann, MGWJ 55
(1911), 166; H. J. Schonfield, The Passover Plot, London 1965, 148; S. Grayzel,
A History of the Jews, Philadelphia 1966, 134f: he argues that an informal Sadducean hearing turned on the messianic claim which was interpreted as implying an
intention to start a revolt against Rome. However, some of the crowd, seeing
Jesus on the way to excution 'may have heard that this poor Galilean Jew had
claimed to be the Messiah, and so they justified his fate as befitting a blasphemer'.

[4] Rôle, 132.

[5] op.cit. 139.

[6] This debt to Salvador is acknowledged, op.cit. 134. Another parallel with
Salvador is the argument that Jesus gave no clear proofs that he was the messiah.
Cf. J. Isaac, Jésus, 134f.

[7] op.cit. 135. Similarly in S. Bäck, Die Geschichte des jüdischen Volkes, Lissa
1878, 135, where the Sanhedrin trial centres on 'sein Vergehen gegen den römischen Kaiser', though Jesus had previously called himself Son of God, a blasphemy
tolerated only as long as it was kept private.

[8] Cf. D. Daube, who thinks that Mt 5.17 is to be interpreted on the basis of
πληρῶσαι = qiyyem, and consequently as upholding the law. The New Testament
and Rabbinic Judaism, London 1956, 60.

by all. There are two complicating and weakening factors: (a) the other possible interpretations of πληρῶσαι, and (b) Jesus' method of treating specific laws. On (a) we have at one extreme the view of Joseph Hamburger[1] who takes πληρῶσαι as 'to fulfil in the sense of destroy'. This shows the effect of centuries-old debate, since the contrast of πληρῶσαι and καταλῦσαι in Mt 5.17 is ignored. On the other hand Schoeps interprets 'fulfilment' as the exposure of the true will of God, i.e. Jesus goes back behind the letter to the real essence of divine requirement.[2] On (b) several scholars do see the seeds of disruption in Jesus' assertion of personal authority over the law.[3] Yet a few examples show how reluctantly this is pushed through. Klausner, for instance, attempts to have it both ways, asserting [4] and yet qualifying [5] the traditional Mt 5.17 approach. A. H. Silver argues [6] that Mt 19.9 reflects the true attitude of Jesus (i.e. Mt 5.17) better than Mk 10.2-12. Jesus, he says, did not even oppose tradition, but only inconsistency of life (Mt 23.2f), and as for Mk 7.19, this gloss depends on Pauline influence and is not in keeping with Jesus' positive attitude. More surprisingly, Sandmel in spite of critical apparatus still asks whether Jesus' attitude is shown by Mk 10 or Mt 19.[7] On the other hand there do exist writers who emphasize the qualification to Mt 5.17 provided by specific cases of legal activity on Jesus' part.[8]

The strongest assertions of the Pharisaism of Jesus have come from Paul Winter. Winter's view was already made plain in 1953 when he wrote: 'The famous formula by which the Jesus of Redactor Matthaei's creation introduces his discourses, "It was said to them of old time . . . but I say unto you", has no place in the life of Jesus of Nazareth.'[9] This was underlined in 1961: Jesus' teaching 'in its general tenor

---

[1] Jesus von Nazareth, Real-Encyclopädie des Judentums, Abt.III, Supplement IV, Leipzig 1897, 43,47.

[2] Aus frühchristlicher Zeit, Tübingen 1950, 212-220. Cf. also S. Umen, Pharisaism and Jesus, New York 1963, 109f. Schoeps's view is set out at length in: Jésus et la loi Juive, RHPR 33 (1953), 1-20. He regards Mt 5.17 as traceable back, via Matthaean mistranslation, to the form of the legal saying in b.Shabb. 116b, where the terminology of Dt 4.2, 12.32, is adopted.

[3] E. Benamozegh, Jewish and Christian Ethics, San Francisco 1873, 4,12,87; Dienemann, op.cit. 382; Sachar, op.cit. 130.

[4] Jesus, 366-368.

[5] op.cit. 409, cf. the influence of Ginzberg upon him.

[6] Where Judaism differed, Philadelphia 1956, 90-96.

[7] We Jews and Jesus, 25.

[8] S. Rosenblatt, The Crucifixion from the Standpoint of Pharisaic Law, JBL 75 (1956), 315-321; Edgar, op.cit. 9-12.

[9] Μονογενὴς παρὰ πατρός, ZRGG 5 (1953), 12.

corresponds with the Pharisaic pattern: on the ethical side quite obviously, and on the eschatological conceivably . . . . . In historical reality Jesus was a Pharisee. His teaching was Pharisaic teaching. In the whole of the New Testament we are unable to find a single historically reliable instance of religious differences between Jesus and members of the Pharisaic guild, let alone mortal conflict.' [1]

This point more than any other was criticized in reviews of Winter's book,[2] and in particular a critical review by E. Stauffer aroused a heated debate.[3] This, together with Winter's claim about the Pharisaism of Jesus, must be examined in detail.

Stauffer argued that Jesus preached emancipation from the law with his 'Amen, I say to you', and he pressed this principle in action in the discussion of food-laws (Mk 7.15), and divorce (Mk 10.9), as well as in his treatment of the adulteress, Jn 8.11. This confrontation between Jesus and the law has been the object of an attempt by Matthew to tone it down, but even he cannot allow that Jesus was a Pharisee, Mt 5.20, 15.1ff, 23.4ff. Mk also contains at least one controversy story which is not a retrojection of later Christian practice, i.e. Mk 2.18f (contrast Acts 21.20, Josephus, Ant. 20.200 and Mt 4.2, 6.16-19). Lk 18.9ff adds its testimony to the evidence that Jesus was critical of the Pharisees.[4]

---

[1] On the Trial, 133. Similarly, H. Mantel, Studies, 280f: 'The Gospel stories of Jesus' defiance of Pharisaic law are not historical but evangelical.' Mantel opposes Klausner's suggestion of unorthodoxy in Jesus by alluding to James the Just. Against this, it must be proved that James reproduced Jesus' position. With Winter and Mantel stand Y. Baer, Some Aspects of Judaism as presented in the Synoptic Gospels, Zion 31 (1966), I-III and F. E. Meyer, Einige Bemerkungen zur Bedeutung des Terminus 'Synhedrion' in den Schriften des Neuen Testaments, NTS 14 (1968), 548.

[2] P. Benoit, RB 68 (1961), 598; O. Betz, JR 44 (1964), 181f; G. Lindeskog, in: Abraham unser Vater, Leiden 1963, 327,334; E. Lohse, Gnomon 33 (1961), 626; P. Mikat, BZ 6 (1962), 304f; E. Schweizer, EvTh 21 (1961), 239; J. B. Soucek, CommViat 6 (1963), 201; H. van Oyen, Christlich-jüdisches Forum 26 (1961), 3.

[3] Heimholung Jesu in das jüdische Volk, ThLZ 88 (1963), 97-102. The difference between Stauffer and Winter, which led to the subsequent debate, is already evident in Winter's review of Stauffer's book, Jerusalem und Rom, in NovT 2 (1958), 318f. There Stauffer's claim that Jesus was, in relation to Judaism, 'ein Ketzer' was criticized and opposed with the counter-claim: 'Einzig und allein vom Standpunkt des Christentums aus gesehen, ist Jesus ein Ketzer, da die von ihm gepredigte Lehre im Gegensatz zu den der Kirche offenbarten Glaubenswahrheiten steht.' Here is the old Hegelian reconstruction of Christian origins. The same interest leads Winter to insist that 'heresy' is not a Jewish concept, On the Trial, 130.

[4] Stauffer's view is repeated in Jesus und seine Bibel, in: Abraham unser Vater, Festschrift O. Michel, Leiden 1963, 440-449.

Winter's cause was subsequently championed by H.-W. Bartsch in an article whose tone and whose accusations that a straight line leads inevitably and directly from the view that a religious trial of Jesus occurred to the pogroms are less valuable than the taking up of detailed points of evidence and argumentation.[1] Bartsch criticizes Stauffer's thesis at four points. Firstly, he takes up Stauffer's own view that Jesus did not claim to be the messiah, and asks what then, if a religious trial took place, can have been the blasphemy.[2] This is scarcely a compelling approach since (a) the history of research is itself sufficient to show there are a number of other candidates for the content of the blasphemy; (b) messiahship is in any case a fairly unlikely candidate for it; [3] (c) the assumption that βλασφημία in Mk 14.64 is used in a technical legal sense rather than in a looser and more general sense as in Mk 2.7, must be recognized as an assumption. Secondly, Bartsch takes exception to Stauffer's claim that the trial was from a legal point of view 'in Ordnung'. Bartsch does not give a full examination of this issue, and it will be argued later that Stauffer's view is not so unrealistic, though perhaps for different reasons.[4] Thirdly, Bartsch charges Stauffer with inattention to literary-critical questions. At this point Bartsch certainly goes too far, much as when he links Lietzmann and Blinzler as defenders of the Sanhedrin hearing. Finally, Bartsch argues that Winter's view of Mk 2.18 is preferable since it is based on the work of Bultmann and since Acts 21.20 is less primitive.[5] This must be dealt with in the wider context of criticism of the view that Jesus was a Pharisee.

It is frequently urged that the Jerusalem church provides crucial evidence of the stance that Jesus must have taken. However, the appeal to subsequent Christian viewpoints must not concentrate on James and the Jerusalem church to such an extent that the positions of Paul and also of the Stephen group are neglected. Arguments for continuity must take into account the circumstantial pressures and theological climate. Whereas the position of James coincides with tendencies in Judaism, that of Stephen and Paul does not, and some starting-point for the divergence from Torah-centricity in e.g. Acts 6.13 and Rom 14.14 must be found.[6] Such can only be convincingly

---

[1] Wer verurteilte Jesus zum Tode? NovT 7 (1964), 210-216.

[2] art.cit. 211.

[3] See later, p. 132.

[4] See later, pp. 258-260.

[5] art.cit. 213.

[6] C. K. Barrett rightly points out the agreement between Paul's attitude and Mk 7.14-23, and its disagreement with orthodox Judaism: A Commentary on

located in the teaching of Jesus, and together with the fact of Paul's earlier implacable opposition as a Pharisee[1] to Christianity, must indicate that Jesus was not a Pharisee. But in this case, the divergence of the Jerusalem church from Jesus is in no way a problem: the Acts-Galatians problem shows the circumstantial pressure to which that church was subjected,[2] while Matthaean redaction of Mk is an altogether sufficient parallel for the re-Judaizing tendency.

The attitude to Torah expressed in Mk 7.15, is very clearly crucial for the evaluation of Jesus. Here the work of Merkel has demonstrated conclusively that we have here a saying of the historical Jesus and more than that, 'ein torakritisches Kampfwort'.[3] Käsemann was entirely right in his interpretation of this devastating saying: 'The man who denies that impurity from external sources can penetrate into man's essential being is striking at the presuppositions and the plain verbal sense of the Torah and at the authority of Moses himself.'[4]

A similar deviation unpalatable to Pharisaism is preserved in Mk 2.19a, almost certainly a saying of Jesus, and a saying which coincides with the attitude of neither Jewish Christianity nor Judaism [5] but which corresponds with well-authenticated features of Jesus, Mt 11.18f = Lk 7.33f.[6]

Mk 10.2-9 is particularly important as a controversy story which calls in question the assertion of P. Winter [7] and F. E. Meyer [8] that this whole genus as represented in Mk is unauthentic. For Winter, 'all the Marcan controversy stories without exception reflect disputes between the Apostolic Church and its social environment and are devoid of roots in the circumstances of the life of Jesus'. The most

---

the Epistle to the Romans, London 1957, 263. W. D. Davies, Paul and Rabbinic Judaism, London 1958, 138, regards the agreement as stemming from dependence by Paul upon Mk 7.15.

[1] H. Merkel, Jesus und die Pharisäer, NTS 14 (1968), 194-208, esp.196.

[2] B. Reicke, Der geschichtliche Hintergrund des Apostelkonzils und der Antiochia-Episode, Gal 2.11-14, in Studia Paulina (Festschrift J. de Zwaan), Haarlem 1953, 172-187.

[3] Markus 7,15—das Jesuswort über die innere Verunreinigung, ZRGG 20 (1968), 340-363, esp.351f; cf. earlier, W. D. Davies, Christian Origins and Judaism, London 1962, 41.

[4] Essays on New Testament Themes, London 1964, 39; cf. J. Schmid, The Gospel according to Mark, Cork 1968, 138.

[5] E. Haenchen, Der Weg Jesu, Berlin 1966, 117.

[6] J. Jeremias, The Parables of Jesus, London 1963, 160-162.

[7] On the Trial, 125.

[8] Einige Bemerkungen zur Bedeutung des Terminus 'Synhedrion' in den Schriften des Neuen Testaments, NTS 14 (1968), 548.

that he will allow is that Mk 10.6-9 contains traditional material (a view also expressed by Bultmann [1] and Haenchen[2]) but that Mark has himself constructed out of this material a conflict between Jesus and the Pharisees. However, a clash between Jesus and Pharisaism does not vanish with the declaration that the setting is secondary. The legal decision involved certainly stems from Jesus [3] for it lacks parallels within Judaism and contains no christological assertion. Since the addition of vv. 10-12 shows itself to be indeed an addition, both because of its difference in content from vv. 2-9 and because of the completeness of the latter in terms of form, the material to which it is added cannot be a Markan construction. Further, the argument from creation presupposes that the principles governing the Urzeit can now be re-applied. Therefore the Endzeit must be present, a conclusion well-attested in genuine sayings of Jesus.[4] At this point, of course, the assertion that Jesus' eschatology was Pharisaic [5] is as firmly refuted as the parallel evaluation of his ethics. For Jesus' ruling on divorce is a ruling against Moses [6] and therefore against Pharisaism. In the light of this, objections to the setting become less convincing, for the asking of the question about the allowability of divorce as such, rather than about detailed grounds for divorce, does not express Mark's view (in the light of the Roman adaptation in vv.10-12) nor would it stem from strict Jewish Christians who would also revere Dt 24.1f. But whatever the truth about the setting, the ruling itself is utterly non-Pharisaic.

Thus far the material demonstrating the divergence of Jesus from Pharisaism in legal matters has been drawn from Mk, though each instance is demonstrably pre-Markan. Rom 14.14 shows the pre-Markan existence of the cleanness saying; the possibly secondary Mk 2.19b-20 with its difference from 2.19a shows the earlier existence of the latter; the divorce ruling is found also in Q, Mt5.31f = Lk 16.18, once the παρεκτὸς λόγου πορνείας is removed as Matthaean redaction. This pre-Markan character is itself important evidence against the reconstructions of Winter and Brandon, both of whom make Mk occupy a hinge position (though it must be noticed that in neither of

[1] Synoptic Tradition, 49.
[2] Der Weg Jesu, 338.
[3] Cf. H. Merkel, Jesus und die Pharisäer, 206f.
[4] W. G. Kümmel, Promise and Fulfilment, London 1959, 105-109; E. Käsemann, Essays, 41-43.
[5] Winter, On the Trial, 132f.
[6] Bultmann, Synoptic Tradition, 27.

his volumes[1] does Brandon refer at all to Mk 7.15 or 10.2-9). But more can be said. Other strands of gospel material provide emphatic evidence for a clash between Jesus and Pharisaism, especially in matters of law. This extends even beyond the general controversy between the two to which the parables testify.[2]

Mt 23.16-19,23-26 contains anti-Pharisaic material, strongly supporting Mk 7.15, and originating not simply in pre-Matthaean stock[3] but indeed with the historical Jesus.[4] The same conclusion must be drawn in respect of the antitheses of the Sermon on the Mount. E. Käsemann in his essay[5] works simply from the antitheses concerning murder, adultery and swearing, and correctly draws attention to the unprophetic and unrabbinic ἐγὼ δὲ λέγω [6]—a claim shattering the framework of Jewish piety.[7] This is so in spite of the fact that in the first and second antitheses Jesus' position does not clash with, but rather strenghens almost intolerably, the Decalogue. In the third and fifth antitheses (drawn probably from Q) an attitude sharply critical of the Torah can be found. παρεκτὸς λόγου πορνείας must be removed from Mt 5.32 as Matthaean redaction,[8] and in consequence a tradition emerges which coheres precisely with Mk 10.2-9. Similarly in Mt 5.38-42, there would appear to be a ruling highly critical of the lex talionis.

Such a conclusion has been vigorously opposed by David Daube.[9]

---

[1] Jesus and the Zealots, Manchester 1967; The Trial of Jesus of Nazareth, London 1968. In the former volume, p.268, Brandon allows for Pauline influence in Mk 7.6f. It is certainly correct that the Is 29.13 quotation comes from liberal/Hellenistic Judaism (cf. E. Schweizer, Das Evangelium nach Markus, Göttingen 1967, 81) yet Mk 7.15 belongs to a different layer of the tradition within Mk 7.1-23.

[2] J. Jeremias, The Parables of Jesus, London 1963, passim. Jeremias's treatment of Lk 18.9-14a, op.cit. 139-144, entirely justifies Stauffer's reference to it. Similarly, Merkel, Jesus und die Pharisäer, 207; E. Lohse, Jesu Worte über den Sabbat, in Judentum, Urchristentum, Kirche, Festschrift J. Jeremias, Berlin, 1960, 79-89.

[3] G. Strecker, Der Weg der Gerechtigkeit, 2nd ed. Göttingen 1966, 133.

[4] R. Bultmann, Ist die Apokalyptik die Mutter der christlichen Theologie? in Apophoreta (Festschrift E. Haenchen), Berlin 1964, 66.

[5] Essays, 37.

[6] Cf. J. Jeremias, Characteristics of the ipsissima vox Jesu, in The Prayers of Jesus, London 1967, 114f; E. Stauffer, Jesus und seine Bibel, op.cit. 442f; E. Haenchen, Weg. 86f.

[7] Similarly, J. Jeremias, The Sermon on the Mount, London 1961, 10: 'Jesus even goes so far as to set his teaching over against that of the Torah.'

[8] Cf. μὴ ἐπὶ πορνείᾳ, Mt 19.9; G. Barth, in Tradition and Interpretation in Matthew, 94.

[9] The New Testament and Rabbinic Judaism, 254-265.

The formulations of the contrasts in Mt 5.21-48 he finds to be between 'the 'hearing', the 'literal understanding' of a rule, and what we must 'say' it actually signifies'.[1] In the words 'and (only) he who shall kill shall be in danger of the judgement' and 'thou shalt hate thine enemy' there is embodied the interpretation which Jesus rejects.[2] Matthew therefore, illustrating Jesus' position as upholder of the law, uses legal material having a two-fold form: a first part containing a scriptural rule narrowly interpreted, and a second part containing a wider demand made by Jesus. This is in line with the summary generalization in Mt 5.17, of which all the cases in 5.21-48 are examples.[3] Daube rightly points to the great distinguishing first person 'I say', and the lack of reasoning by Jesus, both of which show him as the supreme authority.[4] This is certainly crucial and should lead to Käsemann's conclusion. But on other points one must raise doubts. For instance, the fourth antithesis concerning swearing does not proceed from the same contrast as Daube finds in the first. Rather does a Pentateuchal regulation suffer by being made redundant. Again, Mt 5.31f, while assuredly being a softening of an earlier form, and having also been made antithetical by Matthew, plainly deviates from Dt 24.1f.[5] Finally, one must distinguish between the Matthaean structure (dominated as it is by Mt 5.17) and the forms safely traceable to Jesus. Daube has clearly established that the statement of a principle, followed by a number of illustrative cases, is Rabbinic,[6] but this cannot securely take us behind Mt unless it can be demonstrated that Mt 5.17 is Dominical in its present form, and that πληρῶσαι does render 'qiyyem' and have the sense of 'uphold'.

Stylistic traits characteristic of Mt are plainly present, and these include the verb πληρῶσαι. The parallel form, Mt 10.34 = Lk 12.51 is sufficient to show that this does not mean that the whole saying is a Matthaean creation. But the editorial activity which includes 'the law and the prophets' and 'to fulfil' clearly coheres with the remodelling carried out by Matthew on Mt 5.18, and more widely in 7.12, 22.40 and the fulfilment-formulae of 1.22, 21.4 and 26.56. E. Schweizer and G. Barth must therefore be right to interpret this in terms of a fulfil-

---

[1] op.cit. 57.

[2] op.cit. 56.

[3] op.cit. 60.

[4] op.cit. 58.

[5] Cf. W. D. Davies, Christian Origins and Judaism, London 1962, 39; Jeremias, Sermon, 39.

[6] op.cit. 63-66.

ment through Jesus' bringing the love commandment into distinctive legal prominence.[1] That this agrees with pre-Matthaean and Dominical teaching in e.g. Mk 12.28-34 still does not permit Mt 5.17, in whatever form it may originally have existed, to be used as evidence of a straightforwardly conservative attitude of Jesus to the law. And the whole complex of material within which Jesus' attitude to and treatment of the law is unfolded, makes it transparently plain that Jesus was no Pharisee.[2]

This discussion of the alleged Pharisaism of Jesus arose within the context of the first feature of the view that Jesus was involved in a messianic condemnation, namely the movement towards the religious orthodoxy of Jesus. There are two more elements of this theory which are important. One is that scholars in this group are emphatic that Son of God is not a possible charge. In this again, those who reject any Sanhedrin hearing[3] are at one with those who envisage a political investigation by the Jewish authorities. Among the latter group, some simply ignore the question,[4] while others explicitly deny the possibility.[5] Finally, the Lukan account, paradoxically, receives more notice from this group of scholars. It is a paradox because, according to Lk, Jesus refused to be drawn on the messianic topic and the hearing came to a climax with the Son of God confession. Lk therefore supports a political interpretation rather less than Mk does. But the appeal of the Lukan version is found in its timing in the morning as well as the lack of an explicit sentence, and since it can be interpreted as less than a trial it fits the preference of scholars in this group for a preliminary hearing.[6] The distinctive features of Lk, however, are not treated

---

[1] E. Schweizer, Matth.5.17-20—Anmerkungen zum Gesetzesverständnis des Matthäus, ThLZ 77(1952), 479-484; G. Barth, op.cit. 64-73.

[2] E. Lohse, Die Frage nach dem historischen Jesus, ThLZ 87 (1962), 196f, agrees that Jesus was no Pharisee, and rightly points out that his teaching and his death must be seen as congruent to one another.

[3] Schreiber, Prinzipien, 80; Eschelbacher, Vorlesungen, 417; E. G. Hirsch, My Religion, 50f; Goodman, Synagogue, 208-211; Bernfeld, art.cit. 116; G. Friedländer, Hellenism, 48f; M. Joseph, JL 3 (1929), 240; Rosenblatt, art.cit. 319; Sandmel, Jewish Understanding, 129; Goldstein, Jesus, 26 (though he appeals to Zeitlin, Who crucified Jesus?, 168, where however the only evidence cited is 1 Enoch 105.2). Krauskopf, Weinstock and Kroner ignore the matter.

[4] Sachar, History, 132; Ziegler, op.cit. 35; Freimann, op.cit. 166.

[5] Rodrigues, Roi, 59; Fluegel, Messiah-Ideal I, 90,97; Hamburger, Jesus, 50; M. Radin, The Trial of Jesus of Nazareth, Chicago 1931, 46; H. Zucker, Studien zur jüdischen Selbstverwaltung im Altertum, Berlin 1936, 86; Mantel, Studies, 275.

[6] M. Schlesinger, Historical Jesus, 77; J. Hamburger, Jesus, 49,52; J. Lehmann,

uniformly. Thus Radin argues from them to the superiority of Mk,[1] and C. H. Levy dismisses all versions: 'Since the statements of Mt and Mk conflict with Jn's and Lk's, and both the Roman and the Jewish law are opposed to any such trial, I believe that Jesus was tried by the Romans.'[2]

2. *The full political reconstruction*

Scholars discussed in the preceding section are often involved in what is essentially a movement away from one position, rather than a positive assertion and proof of the validity of another one.[3] The stress frequently lies on what cannot be true in a theory more developed than their own. This means that there is only a difference in degree between them and the group which deny a Sanhedrin hearing altogether. Although Saalschütz prepared the ground, and Samuel Hirsch made a great deal of progress in this direction, credit for the classical form of political reconstruction certainly belongs to Ludwig Philippson,[4] and his argument will now be outlined. It hinges on the following affirmations:

(a) Crucifixion was not a Jewish method of execution.[5]

Quelques Dates importantes de la Chronologie du 2[e] Temple, REJ 37 (1898), 1-44, esp.16; M. Hyamson, JQR 11 (1920), 90; Sachar, op.cit. 132; H. Zucker, Studien der jüdischen Selbstverwaltung im Altertum, Berlin 1936, 87.

[1] The Trial of Jesus of Nazareth, Chicago 1931, 161-166.

[2] Progressive Judaism and liberal Christianity, New World 8 (1899), 497-506, esp. 504.

[3] There are outstanding exceptions, e.g. Zeitlin and Winter.

[4] Haben wirklich die Juden Jesum gekreuzigt?, Berlin 1866. Citations from the identical 2nd ed. Leipzig 1901. On Philippson, cf. Lindeskog, Jesusfrage, 280.

[5] op.cit. 7-9. Followed by E. Grünebaum, 2nd ed. 296; M. Joel, Blicke II, 67f; T. Reinach, art cit.17: 'Du caractère de la peine on peut déduire avec sûreté le motif de la condamnation et la nature du tribunal qui la prononça.' Philippson's pattern of argument is also taken up by Schindler, Messianic Expectations, 47; Krauskopf, Impressions, 91; Eschelbacher, Judentum, 43; E. G. Hirsch, Crucifixion, 373; H. M. Cohn, Sein Blut komme über uns, JJGL 6 (1903), 85; J. L. Levy, Addresses: Series 14, Pittsburgh 1914, 23; H. G. Enelow, Jewish View, 490; E. Jacob, art.cit. 528; M. Hyamson, JQR 22 (1931), 215; C. Roth, A short History of the Jewish People, London 1936, 141; Rosenblatt, Crucifixion, 318; M. Dimont, Jews God and History, London 1964, 142; Winter, On the Trial, 62-66.

Further appeal is often made to the superscription: Philippson, op.cit. 42; Eschelbacher, Vorlesungen, 417; E. G. Hirsch, Crucifixion, 374; Magnus, Outlines, 52; Goodman, History, 37; J. L. Levy, op.cit. 23: 'Are not these words the defence of the Jews against the charge which has age after age been brought against them?' Sandmel, Jewish Understanding, 130; Goldstein, Jesus, 26; Zucker, op.cit. 87; Winter, op.cit. 107-110; Mantel, Studies, 288; Learsi, Israel, 161.

(b) The gospels are unreliable and contradictory, and Tacitus, Annals 15.44 alone is a trustworthy historical source.[1]

(c) The execution implies that Pilate sentenced Jesus as a political rebel against the Roman authority.[2] This is supported, so runs the argument, by the fact that Jesus provoked no religious opposition but only roused political danger by his messianic entry,[3] and also by the fact that Pilate's character was entirely different from what the gospels claim,[4] and finally by the fact that Roman procurators put down all other known messianic movements with uncompromising ferocity.[5]

(d) The Jews neither persecuted nor tried Jesus, nor did they cry for his death.[6] They may have warned Pilate, but that is all. Jesus was arrested by the Romans, Jn 18.3,12,[7] and executed by them. Hence: 'Allein ein wirklicher Prozeß vor dem Synedrium wie die tumultuarische Forderung der Hinrichtung Jesu seitens des jüdischen Volkes haben nicht stattgefunden.'[8]

It can readily be seen that Philippson lays down here a pattern which becomes standard for the concentratedly Roman reconstruction. His arguments and affirmations have suvived almost without opposition, except for the reliance on Tacitus to the total exclusion of other sources, the matter of religious opposition and the question of the trial itself. Yet even here it has been shown already how powerful is the trend towards agreement on the religious assessment of Jesus. The only other point which has divided scholars who reject a Sanhedrin hearing is the extent of Jewish involvement: some think the Jews handed Jesus over to Pilate [9] while others claim no Jewish contribu-

---

[1] op.cit. 41.

[2] op.cit. 42.

[3] op.cit. 43f.

[4] op.cit. 45-51.

[5] op.cit. 47f.

[6] op.cit. 60.

[7] Similarly Rodrigues, Roi, 221; Krauskopf, Impressions, 84; Enelow, Jewish View, 488; M. Hunterberg, The crucified Jew, New York 1927, 40; S. Landman-B. Efron, Story without End, New York 1949, 97; Dimont, op.cit. 141, is an exception in thinking that the Jews arrested Jesus as a protective measure but were forced to hand him over. Lindeskog, Jesusfrage, 293, is incorrect in claiming Jewish unanimity for the view that the high priest and his party arrested Jesus.

[8] op.cit. 61.

[9] Rodrigues, Origines, 135; Rabbinowicz, Rôle, 145; T. Reinach, art.cit. 16; Eschelbacher, Judentum, 418; Enelow, Jewish View, 482; Franz, op.cit. 109; E. Jacob, Christentum, 528; S. W. Baron, A social and religious History of the Jews, New York 1937, 70; Rosenblatt, art.cit. 319 (perhaps some Pharisaic quislings); B. J. Bamberger, The Story of Judaism, New York 1957, 95; P. Winter,

tion at all.[1] These two positions correspond respectively to the reconstructed Josephus and Tacitus patterns.

Although this reconstruction of Jesus' end became so standard, the pre-history of that end has been the subject of a wide variety of interpretations. Broadly, four theories have been proposed.

(a) The 'misunderstanding' theory. This is primarily based on Mk 12.17 and Jn 18.37. Jesus, a mystic dreamer,[2] claimed messiahship and preached the kingdom of God in a spiritual, non-political sense.[3] The masses however were disappointed with this sophisticated hope, and their political longings were frustrated,[4] or on the other hand they did not understand at all.[5] In either case the Romans were quite clear that Jesus was a menace, and took action accordingly.[6]

(b) The 'messianic claim' theory. Most Jewish authors, as has already been noted, believe that Jesus claimed messiahship [7] and did so particularly at the entry to Jerusalem. In varying degrees this is coupled with the view that Jesus aimed to restore national independence, an aim largely erased by the gospels.

On the Trial, 137f: 'after being conducted to a local administrative authority'; Edgar, A Jewish View, 15.

[1] C. H. Levy, art.cit. 503f; H. Weinstock, Jesus the Jew, New York 1902, 34; T. Kroner, Geschichte der Juden, Frankfurt a.M. 1906,28; Goodman, Synagogue, 229; S. Bernfeld, art. cit. 90f; J. L. Levy, Addresses, 20; A. Cohen, The Parting of the Ways, London 1954, 45; M. Joseph, JL 3 (1929), 240; C. Raddock, Portrait of a People, New York 1965, 173; S. Sandmel, Jewish Understanding, 205, thinks the circumstances beyond recovery.

[2] Magnus, About the Jews, 74; J. Hamburger, Jesus, 42; Trattner, As a Jew sees Jesus, 64.

[3] Hamburger, art.cit. 42-46; S. W. Baron, History, 69; V. G. Simkhovitch, Towards the Understanding of Jesus, New York 1921, 41; Magnus, About the Jews, 73-75; Learsi, Israel, 158f. This idea (basically a Christian one) has repeatedly been opposed by Jews, for it is part of the 'fulfilment of prophecy' debate that Christians claimed a spiritual fulfilment and Jews a straight non-fulfilment.

[4] Enelow, op.cit. 480; Trattner, op.cit. 127.

[5] Hyamson, JQR 11 (1920), 93.

[6] Hyamson, art.cit. 93; Enelow, op.cit. 480; S. W. Baron, History, 70.

[7] Philippson, Haben die Juden, 43,61; Ziegler, Kampf, 33f; Freimann, MGWJ 55 (1911), 312; Schreiber, Prinzipien, 131; Krauskopf, Impressions, 54f; Weinstock, Jesus, 34; Kroner, Geschichte, 28; Goodman, Synagogue, 229; J. L. Levy, Addresses, 22; A. Cohen, op.cit. 42; Hunterberg, op.cit. 20,78; M. Joseph, Jesus, 237-239 (he thinks, however, that the entry is legendary); E. Jacob, art.cit. 526; Roth, History, 98; Landman-Efron, Story without End, 95; Bamberger, Story of Judaism, 95; Dimont, Jews, God and History, 139; Magnus, op.cit.77; Schechter, Studies III, 38; Edgar, Jewish View, 7; Learsi, Israel, 160; Grayzel, History, 134. Exceptions are Goldin, Case of the Nazarene, 724; S. Reinach, A short History of Christianity, London 1922, 12; P. Winter, On the Trial, 148.

(c) The 'popular unrest' theory. This is proposed by Paul Winter. He tones down the political aspects of Jesus' career and argues that it was his effect upon people rather than any deliberate claims which provoked police action.[1] Political aspirations were present,[2] but there was no messianic claim, not unequivocally even before Pilate.[3] 'That he was executed as a rebel together with others who were executed on the same charge by no means proves that he did work for the overthrow of the existing political system.'[4] Winter treats what were apparently the three crucial events in the gospels as follows: Mk 8.27-30 tells us only the views of Jesus' followers and not his own;[5] the entry to Jerusalem marks an event undiscoverable to us now;[6] the temple cleansing was merely 'a disturbance of the peace'.[7]

This theory of Winter means that even the comparison with Theudas, which had proved useful to some earlier scholars, no longer applies. He does not even use the verses scattered through the gospels which would possibly support a political motif, and there is a wide gap between what he says and the theory that Jesus was either a Zealot or sympathetic to Zealotism. But what is at once the most characteristic and the most vulnerable feature of this scheme is the divorcing of Jesus' earlier activity from his trial, and this was several times treated critically in reviews.[8]

(d) The 'Zealot' theory. This is the very extreme version of (b). In its classic form it was championed by Eisler,[9] though it had been suggested tentatively before.[10] Occasionally also the interpretation of Mk 12.13-17 as an avoidance of Zealotism had been questioned.[11] In

---

[1] On the Trial, 135: 'Rather than the content of his teaching it was the effect which his teaching had on certain sections of the populace that induced the authorities to take action against him.'

[2] On the Trial, 138f: Jesus was a nationalist and had politically-inclined friends.

[3] op.cit. 148f.

[4] op.cit. 148.

[5] op.cit. 140.

[6] op.cit. 142f. Goldin, op.cit. 459, also thinks this event a fiction.

[7] op.cit. 143f.

[8] Betz, JR 44 (1964), 182; W. D. Davies, Commentary 33 (1962), 541; Lohse, Gnomon 33 (1961), 626; Soucek, CommViat 6 (1963), 201f; van Oyen, Christlich-jüdisches Forum 26 (1961), 2f.

[9] The Messiah Jesus and John the Baptist, London 1931.

[10] Cf. Rodrigues, Roi, 104-113; Fluegel, op.cit. 84,98. On Rodrigues, see Lindeskog, Jesusfrage, 263.

[11] Rabbinowicz, Rôle, 91; A. Weill, Le faux Jésus-Christ, 21. Rodrigues, Roi, 125, thought that Mk 12.13-17 was an evasion whereas Mt 17.24-27 showed the truth, i.e. a grudging attitude. Similarly, Grünebaum, 164.

addition, it is relevant to mention that Lk 23.2 is continually cited by
Jews of all schools of thought for the indictment before Pilate, rather
than Mk 15.2. This would suggest some attraction towards the different interpretation of Jesus' attitude to the payment of tribute, though
it is admittedly more likely to be towards the perversion theme,
whether interpreted politically or theologically.

Eisler's theory has recently been republished by Joel Carmichael,
with only three changes of any significance: (a) For Carmichael, Jesus
did not make a messianic claim, and was only a herald of the Kingdom.[1] (b) The Jews did have capital competence.[2] (c) There was no
Sanhedrin meeting. Eisler thought there was, though not the improbable trial of the gospels.

Depending heavily on the reconstructed original of the Slavonic
Josephus, the original version of which he dated at A.D.72, Eisler's
theory ran as follows: John the Baptist was a Zealot leader,[3] praised by
Jesus as such at Mt 11.12. His baptism initiated a political association
aiming to purify from the cardinal sin of serving the Romans. Jesus
originally took a more pacifist line and preached 'the higher righteousness',[4] but, stirred by his fervent eschatology[5] (here Eisler draws
heavily on A. Schweitzer), oppressed by his failure in Galilee,[6] and
challenged by the incident of the standards (which is, incidentally,
reflected in Mk 13.14-17 [7]), he set out to seek a verdict in Jerusalem.[8]
Won over by the persuasion of his friends he led an armed insurrection,[9] interpreted theologically as a second Exodus. To cries
of 'Free now' (Hosanna) [10] he entered the city and occupied the
temple by armed force,[11] while supporters seized the tower of Siloam[12]
(reflected in Lk 13.1-4). The rebellion was however put down by the

---

[1] The Death of Jesus, London 1966,51,63,148,152; cf. Eisler, op.cit. 371.

[2] op.cit. 36; cf. Eisler, op.cit. 500.

[3] Eisler, op.cit. 264; cf. Carmichael, op.cit. 139.

[4] Eisler, op.cit. 356, 362-369; cf. Carmichael, op.cit. 146-148.

[5] Eisler, op.cit. 350; cf. Carmichael, op.cit. 75.

[6] Eisler, op.cit. 370; cf. Carmichael, op.cit. 110. Note that here Caesarea
Philippi is not, as for most Jews, the turning-point in Jesus' career.

[7] Eisler, op.cit. 325-327; cf. Carmichael, op.cit. 157.

[8] Eisler, op.cit. 370; cf. Carmichael, op.cit. 110.

[9] Reflected in Mk 15.7. Eisler, op.cit. 10,472; cf. Carmichael, op.cit. 121. The
formulation of Brandon is slightly weaker (Jesus and the Zealots, 339: 'Jesus'
action in the Temple coincided with an insurrection in the city') but the general
drift is the same.

[10] Eisler, op.cit. 480; cf. Carmichael, op.cit. 149-152.

[11] Eisler, op.cit. 482f; cf. Carmichael, op.cit. 111,114,119,131.

[12] Eisler, op.cit. 502; cf. Carmichael, op.cit. 120.

Romans who arrested Jesus [1] and had him executed as a rebel.[2]

This theory has been revived at many points by S. G. F. Brandon.[3] It is sufficiently important to merit full summary in order that its distinctive features and argumentation may be exposed.

While maintaining that Jesus himself was not a Zealot,[4] Brandon claims that his movement was closely parallel to and at times overlapped with Zealot aims and principles. This view is based on the following arguments: (i) Zealotism was firmly religious and theological in complexion, and closely associated with Pharisaism.[5] (ii) Mk occupies a pivotal position in the development of the Christian tradition. It emerged as an apologia out of the events of A.D. 71, intent on minimizing the political danger inherent in Jesus' movement.[6] This tendency was followed by the other evangelists who developed the picture of the 'pacific Christ'.[7] Brandon outlines this theory with special reference to Mt, calling attention in particular to Mt 26.52-54, the Beatitudes Mt 5.3,5,7,9, and Mt 5.41,43.[8] (iii) The Baptist movement was 'an apocalyptic movement which the Jewish ruler of Galilee regarded as politically dangerous'.[9] With such was Jesus connected. (iv) The theme of eschatological imminence, expressed in such sayings as Mk 1.15, 13.29f, was common to both Jewish Christianity before A.D.70 and Jesus himself.[10] This implied 'the overthrow of the existing political and social order'.[11] Lk 24.27 and Ac 1.6 confirm that Jesus awakened in his disciples the conviction that he was the Messiah who would restore the kingdom to Israel. After his death the Jerusalem Christians venerated him as a martyr for that cause but, more than that, were convinced of his ultimate return to effect this task and establish this ideal.[12] (v) Of extreme importance for Brandon's theory is the fact that

---

[1] Eisler, op.cit. 512; cf. Carmichael, op.cit. 24.

[2] Eisler, op.cit. 335,358; cf. Carmichael, op.cit. 213.

[3] Jesus and the Zealots, Manchester 1967; The Trial of Jesus of Nazareth, London 1968; similarly, The Trial of Jesus, in: History Today 16(1966), 251-259; Pontius Pilate in History and Legend, in: History Today 18(1968), 523-530; Jesus and the Zealots, Studia Evangelica 4(1968), 8-20.

[4] Zealots, 355.

[5] Zealots, 38.

[6] Zealots, 21f,247,322. Cf. earlier, The Date of the Markan Gospel, NTS 7(1961), 126-141.

[7] Zealots, 149,221,280; Trial, 64,107.

[8] Zealots, 306-309; Trial, 77,109.

[9] Trial, 143.

[10] Zealots, 50.

[11] Trial, 143; cf. treatment of Mk 8.34, Zealots, 344.

[12] Zealots, 18,167,177,182,324; Trial, 21.

one of Jesus' disciples was a Zealot.[1] (vi) Alongside sayings of the
'turning the other cheek' variety can be set another more violent series
including Mt 10.34 and Acts 5.9.[2] (vii) Jn 6.15 indicates that Jesus
aroused strong popular enthusiasm which took a political form.[3]
Moreover, the authorities clearly inferred as much, in view of Jn 11.47f,
18.19f,33-39. In the first case their view was that 'the precarious
balance of Jewish relations with the Roman occupying power was
imperilled by Jesus'.[4] Brandon goes on to argue that Jn 18.19f
indicates an attempt by the high priest to discover 'the exact nature
of his aims and the identity of his main supporters'.[5] In the case of
Jn 6.15, it is conceded that Jesus resisted the popular pressure, but
the argument maintains that such resistance could not be, and indeed
was not, carried through permanently.[6] (viii) In Mk 12.13-17 is
recorded a saying of Jesus which has been given a new setting in
line with Mark's apologetic. This saying was originally 'a definitive
condemnation of the giving of the resources of the Holy Land in
tribute to the heathen Emperor of Rome'.[7] As such it was a saying of
which any Zealot would have approved.[8] (ix) The Cleansing of the
Temple: 'This beyond doubt was one of the most crucial actions
of Jesus; but unfortunately its true significance has been obscured
in the Gospel records.'[9] Properly interpreted, it amounted to 'a
dynamic political action of a revolutionary kind'.[10] (x) In Gethsemane
Jesus had checked that his disciples were armed—like the sicarii.[11]
When the time came, resistance was offered. (xi) Evidence of a
political disturbance at this time is provided by Mk 15.7 (ἡ στάσις)
and 15.27 (the two λῃσταί crucified with him).[12] It is significant that
Jesus was crucified, rightly or wrongly, as King of the Jews.[13]
(xii) Confirmation is provided by subsequent events. The adoption
of a Zealot oracle (Mk 13.14-20) attests a notable agreement between

[1] Zealots, 10,16,43,78f,200,205,243-245,264,324,355; Trial, 40,65,144.
[2] Zealots, 202f.
[3] Zealots, 16f.
[4] Trial, 127f.
[5] Zealots, 336.
[6] Zealots, 18,353.
[7] Trial, 146,cf. 66-68.
[8] Zealots, 347.
[9] Trial, 83f.
[10] Trial, 147; cf. Zealots, 324-339.
[11] Zealots, 10,16,203,306,324,340-342; Trial, 148.
[12] Zealots, 78,257; Trial, 40,94-103.
[13] Zealots, 328; Trial, 141.

Jewish Christians and Zealots. So also does the execution of James the son of Zebedee with the sword, and the elimination of James the brother of Jesus.[1]

This theory is persuasively and plausibly argued, but it fails to carry conviction on a number of counts.

Firstly, Brandon has certainly been successful in establishing the theological basis of Zealotism. But the association of this movement with zeal for the law or Pharisaism is fatal for a parallel association of Jesus with it. The views which divided Jesus from Pharisaism and from unconditional acceptance of the Torah, divide him equally from the Zealots.[2]

Secondly, Brandon proposes a neat linear pattern of tradition-history, beginning at Mk and proceeding on the basis of Mk through Mt and Lk to Jn. But closer examination shows that this straight line is an illusion. On the one hand, several passages incorporated by Brandon into Mt, often stem from Q and therefore from a primary, not a secondary, source. It is true that Mt 5.4 has no precise literary parallel in Lk 6, but it is paralleled in content at Lk 6.21 and therefore, stemming from an earlier tradition, cannot be the product of the Alexandrian refugees, bereft of home and families.[3] Mt 5.3, dealing with the πτωχοί, also stems from Q. Mt 5.39-41 is drawn from a pre-Matthaean tradition, and demonstrates that the witness of Q makes Jesus a pacifist opposed to any resort to violence.[4] Again it is a tour de force to regard Mt 5.43 as a change from the Levitical injunction to hate foreigners, a change arising apparently in the Alexandrian situation. As has often been pointed out, not least by Jewish scholars, the Levitical regulations do not contain the whole citation in Mt 5.43, and it is to be interpreted against the background of Qumran.[5] And once again, although the precise legal formulation is due to Matthew, the tradition of the 'loving enemies' saying is already in Q (Lk 6.27-35). Equally clear is the origin in Q of Mt 23.37-39,[6] and the consequent impossibi-

---

[1] Zealots, 115-125.

[2] See above, pp. 107-112. Cf. M. Hengel, die Zeloten, Leiden 1961, 385.

[3] Zealots, 309. I leave aside at this point the Alexandrian theory as a whole, which has been dealt with elsewhere.

[4] Cf. D. R. A. Hare, The Theme of Jewish Persecutions of Christians in the Gospel according to St. Matthew, Cambridge 1967, 90.

[5] K. Stendahl, The School of St. Matthew, 2nd ed. Lund 1969, 137; W. D. Davies, The Setting of the Sermon on the Mount, 245-248.

[6] Brandon is compelled to admit that this saying is well-established in the Jewish-Christian tradition, Zealots, 315.

lity of regarding it as an explanation ex eventu of the significance of the destruction of Jerusalem or its Temple.[1]

While the above evidence requires us to modify the pivotal role of Mark in the apologetic [2] and remoulding of Jesus' career in general, there must be added to it a parallel correction in the analysis of the accounts of the Sanhedrin hearing. Brandon argues that Mk 14.55-64 has as its base the Jerusalem church's version, which aimed to refute the suggestion that Jesus criticized the Temple and to assert that he would after all return as messiah.[3] Mark's account here also is pivotal; although Brandon acknowledges that Luke may have had supplementary information about the Passion, this is relegated as a minor and insignificant possibility. Lk 22.66-71 is regarded as 'curiously indeterminate'.[4] In particular, Lk's dependence on Mk is shown by the unsupported pronoun in the account of the mockery.[5] In all, it is a 'careless inconclusive summary of a Sanhedrin investigation held in the morning', [6] and the original Jerusalem apologia is prior in every way. To this one may reply that while it is certainly true that parts at least of Mk 14.55-64 stem from a Semitic environment, so too does Lk 22.66-71 if my later source-analysis is correct.[7] And if so, we have two very different versions which are not dependent on one another, and it is extremely probable that in tradition-history it is the Markan version which is the later of the two.

We therefore have 'pacific Christ' passages well before Mk, and not stemming from the apologetic purpose Brandon claims. We also have a separate Passion narrative largely independent of Mk which must be given very great consideration in any historical reconstruction.

---

[1] Rightly, G. Strecker, Der Weg der Gerechtigkeit, 2nd ed. Göttingen 1966, 113-115. It is a remarkably weak argument against these verses that they clash with the lack of indication in the gospels that Jesus frequently proclaimed his message in Jerusalem (Brandon, Zealots, 315). For the pilgrimage custom makes it overwhelmingly probably that Jesus had visited and worked there before. The single visit is only a Markan device for concentrating on the Passion.

[2] Also worthy of note is the point made against Brandon by M. Brockett with reference to the anti-Jewish and pro-Roman Tendenz of the Pilate narrative: Since Pilate was eventually exiled for maladministration, it would scarcely aid the Roman Christians to know that such a man recognized Jesus' innocence. Cf. History Today 16 (1966), 475.

[3] Zealots, 251; Trial, 22f.

[4] Trial, 118.

[5] On this, see p. 174.

[6] Trial, 119.

[7] See pp. 183-203.

A third criticism of Brandon's theory concerns his treatment of 'imminent eschatology'. Not only is there no support for the suggestion that the overthrow of the political order was in mind,[1] but also Jesus' insistence on the present process of the kingdom's realization makes necessary a drastic correction to Brandon's theory. Sayings such as Mt 11.12, 12.28, Lk 17.20 are impossible to merge with Zealot attitudes while the Romans controlled the land, and indeed the stress on present realization marks Jesus out from all contemporaries in a way which could not fail to be offensive.[2] At this point it must also be noted that the allegedly hostile attitude to Gentiles which Brandon attributes to the Jewish Christians (and by implication therefore to Jesus) would fit an anti-Roman attitude, but is in fact flatly negated by Jesus' treatment of the Gentile theme [3] and the inroads which he was prepared to make into Israelite privilege at the same time (e.g. Mt 8.11f).[4] Hahn has firmly demonstrated that Jesus' attitude to the Gentiles was positive and primarily conditioned by the eschatological event beginning to be realized.[5]

Fourthly, a Zealot's membership of the band of disciples must be seen in the context of Jesus' appeal to all strata of society and in particular to those repugnant to both Pharisees and Zealots, namely the prostitutes and tax-collectors.[6] This appeal to the outcasts is not only particularly firmly embedded in the gospel tradition,[7] but also, by bringing against Jesus an accusation framed in the language of Dt 21.20, could not fail to carry with it Zealot opposition.[8] The attach-

---

[1] Bornkamm, Jesus, 66, rightly remarks that the expectation voiced in Lk 24.27 and Ac 1.6 was disappointed by Jesus. Cf. P. Winter, The Trial of Jesus as a Rebel against Rome, JQ 16 (1968), 37: We can say without hesitation that Jesus's followers cherished aspirations of Jewish national independence. We cannot say whether they were encouraged to such aspirations by Jesus himself.'

[2] E. Linnemann, Parables of Jesus, London 1966, 38-41.

[3] J. Jeremias, Jesus' Promise to the Nations, London 1958, 40-54.

[4] Bornkamm, Jesus, 78; F. Hahn, Mission in the New Testament, London 1965, 34-36.

[5] Mission, 29-41.

[6] Already John the Baptist had accepted tax-collectors for baptism and allowed them to go on collecting taxes, (Lk 3.12f)! Cf. W. Foerster, Palestinian Judaism in New Testament Times, London 1964, 110.

[7] Jeremias, Parables, 124-127,139-144; E. Schweizer, Lordship and Discipleship, London 1960, 13; Bornkamm, Jesus, 78-81; Hengel, Zeloten, 385; Hahn, Mission, 30.

[8] On the authenticity of Mt 11^{19} = Lk 7^{34}, C. Colpe, art. ὁ υἱὸς τοῦ ἀνθρώπου, TWNT 8 (1967), 434.

ment of Simon to Jesus' person therefore in no way implies the attachment of Jesus to Simon's politics.

Fifthly, Mt 10.34 (a later version of Lk 12.51) must be interpreted in the light of the division among men recognized by Jesus as the necessary corollary of his message. Men are divided from men in accordance with their response or otherwise to the preaching of imminent catastrophe, the demand for repentance and the call to discipleship.[1] Division in fact means opposition (Mt 11.12), an opposition of which Jesus shows awareness in his treatment of the cosmic struggle.[2] Yet he makes clear that the struggle is not political.

Sixthly, the 'revolt in the desert'. Jn 6.15 already depends on pre-Johannine tradition and agrees with the indications provided by Mk 6.30-44. What is particularly important, as H. Montefiore has stressed,[3] is that Jesus and the crowds parted company over his resolute refusal to yield to the political pressure. Brandon attempts to qualify this by alluding to later incidents indicating that this position could not be sustained, and also to later Johannine material. But the matter is not so straightforward. Brandon's reconstruction has *already* put Jesus close to the Zealots (cf. John the Baptist, Simon the Zealot, and the political aspirations abroad in Galilee) and therefore Jn 6.15 represents something of an interruption. Again, the Johannine passages cannot without more ado be cited as historical evidence. Jn 11.47-53 and 18.33-37 are shot through with Johannine theology, and whereas Jn 18.19f may depend on better historical material [4] it probably refers to theological [5] rather than political interrogation.

Seventhly, Mk 12.17 cannot bear the weight Brandon places on it. Bultmann already showed that the form of the pericope is a unity and that the saying is bound up with it and did not circulate independently.[6] Certainly Mark is not responsible for the setting,[7] and the first part of the saying itself, following the discussion about the ownership of the coin (Mk 12.16), clearly affirms the duty of paying tribute,[8] while

---

[1] Cf. G. Bornkamm, Jesus, 82-84; W. Michaelis, art. μάχαιρα, TDNT 4 (1967), 526.

[2] O. Betz, Jesu heiliger Krieg, NovT 2(1958), 125-132.

[3] Revolt in the Desert?, NTS 8(1962), 135-141.

[4] For the opposite view, E. Lohse, Die Geschichte des Leidens und Sterbens Jesu Christi, Gütersloh 1964, 75.

[5] Cf. E. Stauffer, Jesus and his Story, London 1960, 100,171; C. H. Dodd, Historical Tradition in the Fourth Gospel, Cambridge 1963, 95.

[6] Synoptic Tradition, 26.

[7] Daube, New Testament and Rabbinic Judaism, 158-169.

[8] E. Stauffer, Christ and the Ceasars, London 1955, 130-134.

the second part refuses to set this duty outside the scope of God's dominion.[1]

Eighthly, the Temple Cleansing is notoriously difficult to interpret [2] but the political interpretation proposed by Brandon is altogether lacking in textual support.

Ninthly, the data connected by Brandon [3] with Jesus' arrest must be examined. For the interpretation of Lk 22.35-38 the source-critical work of Heinz Schürmann is fundamental.[4] Schürmann has argued that these verses show signs of having been drawn from a pre-Lukan source but have been subsequently redacted by Luke.

The difficulty for interpretation lies in the fact that it is virtually impossible to get behind the Lukan viewpoint even if a Vorlage exists here. One finds this, for instance, in v.38 where the present form of Jesus' reply is probably Lukan. Now ἱκανόν ἐστιν probably means 'sufficient' in line with the quantitative tendency in Luke's use of the word, as well as the example in Ac 20.11.[5] If this means that Jesus declares two swords to be enough, then it certainly does not envisage realistic preparation for an uprising led by twelve men.[6] Consequently a Zealot-type interpretation must be discounted, with which coheres Jesus' rejection of forceful intervention at 22.51 (which is also pre-Lukan).[7] If on the other hand, ἱκανόν ἐστιν indicates a cutting off of the conversation,[8] there remains an implied rebuke to the disciples. So the net result of either of these two interpretations is that Jesus is aiming to distract the disciples from the use of force.[9]

In connection with v.36, Schürmann suggests that πωλησάτω τὸ

---

[1] O. Cullmann, The State in the New Testament, London 1957, 18f; Bornkamm, Jesus, 121-124; J. Schmid, Mk, 221; L. Goppelt, The Freedom to pay the Imperial Tax, Studia Evangelica 2(1964), 183-194.

[2] For various attempts, cf. O. Betz, Jesu heiliger Krieg, 134; Hahn, Mission, 36-38.

[3] It is not certain that 22.35-38 originally belonged here. H. Schürmann, Jesu Abschiedsrede, Münster 1957, 134ff.

[4] op.cit. 116-142.

[5] op.cit. 132.

[6] Brandon here has to retreat into the claim that 'it is scarcely likely that it was only two'. Zealots, 341.

[7] F. Rehkopf, Die lukanische Sonderquelle, Tübingen 1959, 56-65.

[8] Cf. Dt 3.26; Hahn, Hoheitstitel, 168; Schmid, Lk, 335.

[9] K. Rengstorf, art. ἱκανός, TNDT 3(1965), 296. This means that Betz, Jesu heiliger Krieg, 136, cannot be followed in interpreting vv.36,38 along with Mk 15.34, as signs that God would intervene at the highpoint of the Holy War to save Jesus. Cf. the eschatological interpretation of C. K. Barrett, Jesus and the Gospel Tradition, London 1967, 47f.

ἱμάτιον αὐτοῦ καί could be Lukan redaction.[1] But the linguistic
arguments fall short of proof and clearly the sentence is deficient
without this phrase. Hahn is probably right that, because of the basic
indispensability of the cloak, this saying foresees the coming of a time
of severe privation and opposition which will overturn even the most
fundamental criteria of life.[2] Consequently the μάχαιρα reference is
metaphorical [3] as in Mt 10.34, and it has only become associated with
the literal reference in v.38 by means of the catchword μάχαιρα.[4]

The lack of support within the Gethsemane complex for Brandon's
theory is reinforced by the fact that none but Jesus was arrested.[5]
Indeed this has been noticed by Betz[6] as a fact distinguishing Jesus'
end from that of all known messianic claimants. The ineptitude and
incompetence of the arrest party, if it is true that 'they succeeded in
seizing Jesus, but in the darkness and confused fighting they failed to
arrest the disciples who made good their escape' [7] defies all credibility.
Such a suggestion is further damaged by the unhindered presence of
Peter in the neighbourhood of the high priest's house, as witnessed by
Mk 14.53/Lk 22.55, a happening whose historicity is hardly in doubt.

Tenthly, the occurrence of an uprising at approximxately the same
time (the exact time-scheme is not stated in Mk 15.7) by no means
proves a link between it and Jesus. The historicity of the Barabbas
incident is in itself so doubtful [8] that no firm conclusions can be drawn
from material connected with it.

Finally, criticisms have already been urged against Brandon's often-
repeated argument from subsequent history. The case of James the
Just will be dealt with later.[9] Here it is sufficient to remark that the case
was probably religious rather than political. The execution of James
the son of Zebedee by the sword has been convincingly shown by
Blinzler [10] not to be political either: it was the charge of leading the

---

[1] op.cit. 123.
[2] Hoheitstitel, 170.
[3] Similarly, Rengstorf, Lk, 249; Schmid, Lk, 334. Otherwise, O. Cullmann,
The State in the New Testament, London 1957, 32 who takes the references as
literal and having in mind a defensive necessity.
[4] On the compositeness of the block vv.35-38, see also Rengstorf, Lk, 248,
Schmid, Lk, 333.
[5] Blinzler, Prozeß, 180.
[6] Jesu heiliger Krieg, 135.
[7] Trial, 149.
[8] Winter, On the Trial, 91-99.
[9] See pp. 241-244.
[10] Rechtsgeschichtliches zur Hinrichtung des Zebedaïden Jakobus (Apg xii.2),
NovT 5 (1962), 191-206.

people astray ('maddiah') which prompted the Sanhedrin, with the final confirmation of Herod, to have him executed.

In conclusion then, the reconstruction of Brandon must be rejected. Jesus was no Zealot, nor was he close to the Zealots. It is altogether in excess of the evidence to regard his movement and Zealotism as parallel or in sympathy with one another.

D. Evaluation of the Charge

Within the accounts of the Sanhedrin hearing, only once is the definition of the crime stated: βλασφημία (Mk 14.64 = Mt 26.65). It has already been indicated that this term may not be intended in a technical and legal sense, but rather along the lines of Mk 2.7: that is, a general offensive encroachment on the prerogatives of God. Mention was also made of what is at least a possibility, that the 'mesith' charge should be given more attention than has often been the case.[1] However, with these provisos in mind, it is still necessary to work, at least tentatively with the concept of blasphemy and to analyse again what might be its content. There are five possibilities in all.

1. *Speaking against the Temple*

Only very rarely since Salvador, who laid stress on the claim to deity implicit in the rebuilding,[2] has Mk 14.58 played any part in Jewish study of the trial. Apart from the pressure of political considerations upon it, it has either been set in the pre-history (cf. Mk 13.2) of the passion,[3] or regarded as nullified by the breakdown of witnesses,[4] or attributed under Lietzmann's influence to the theology of Stephen.[5] Exceptions are Hyamson, who makes it the turning-point in a priestly hearing (yet even he has to scale it down by arguing that this saying was an attack on the priests and would not have counted as blasphemy before the Sanhedrin),[6] and G. Solomon, who equated Jesus ben Ananios (Josephus B.J. 6.300-309) and Jesus of Nazareth who was killed for predicting the temple's destruction.[7]

---

[1] See pp. 7-9.
[2] Histoire II, 87.
[3] Dubnow, Weltgeschichte, 535; Polack, Jesus, 97.
[4] E. Jacob, art.cit. 528; Lehmann, Quelques Dates, 15; Edersheim, Life and Times, 558.
[5] Freimann, MGWJ 55 (1911), 166; Zucker, Studien, 86.
[6] JQR 11 (1920), 92.
[7] G. Solomon, The Jesus of History, London 1880, 119, and The Heresies of the Church, London 1896, 191. Similarly apparently M. J. Bin-Gorion, cited by

More generally, the treatment of this saying by Jewish scholars accords with the political movement. For this reason it is either dismissed as unauthentic,[1] or taken as a threat of political upheaval.[2] The two most interesting cases of this are Zeitlin and Mantel. Firstly, Zeitlin seems deliberately to ignore this theme in the trials of both Jesus and Stephen. He lists and criticizes the possible blasphemies in Jesus' trial but omits this one,[3] and in his interpretation of the religious Sanhedrin's dealings with Stephen, he again ignores it and regards Stephen as having been condemned as a beguiler and deceiver for his attitude to God and to Moses.[4] The significance of this emerges when Zeitlin interprets the charge against Paul that he defiled the temple, as political![5] Secondly, Mantel argues that plotting against the temple was a crime unknown to Judaism, because (a) the idea of a replacement messianic heavenly temple is pre-Christian, and (b) Jeremiah and Ezekiel had predicted the first temple's doom, and R. Johanan b. Zakkai, R. Zadok and others had foreseen the destruction of the second. Concerning Jesus ben Ananios, B.J. 6.300-309, Mantel argues that he committed a political offence 'for who else but the Romans could destroy Jerusalem?'[6] So again political pressure deprives the temple threat of any significant role. The weakness of these arguments, which leave open the door to the opposite interpretation, is that Jeremiah at least suffered for his predictions,[7] that Jesus ben Ananios' predictions would scarcely appear a political crime to the Roman authorities, and that Jesus' statement, at least in its Mk 14.58 form, is extended beyond mere foresight to the personal involvement of Jesus himself.

Two questions remain to be asked: Firstly, does the textual evidence suggest that Jesus' trial turned on the issue of his speaking against the

---

S. Ben-Chorin in: Das Jesus-Bild im modernen Judentum: Eckert-Ehrlich, Judenhass, 144.

[1] Krauskopf, Impressions, 72; Kohler, Origins, 277. Graetz, Geschichte, 2nd ed. 243, explicitly questions the authenticity of this saying with no political overtones, but this is unusual.

[2] Mattuck, Trial, 6; M. Brod, Heidentum Christentum Judentum, München 1921-22, 227.

[3] Who crucified Jesus?, 104.

[4] op.cit. 189.

[5] op.cit. 201,203. This throws doubt both on Zeitlin's distinction between religious and political, and also on his two Sanhedrins theory.

[6] Studies, 273; cf. p.297, on Paul.

[7] Cf. G. D. Kilpatrick, The Trial of Jesus, London 1953, 11; J. Wellhausen, Das Evangelium Marci, Berlin 1903, 106.

temple, and secondly, does evidence unconnected with the trial of Jesus imply that speaking against the temple would be considered a blasphemy or some other legally definable offence?

Examination of the first of these questions involves discussing a number of subsidiary questions about the evolution of the traditions. We begin with Mk.

E. Schweizer has argued that there are two layers of tradition within Mk 14.55-64, and that certain features are later or Markan. This applies to vv. 57b,59 which simply repeat v. 56 and do so in almost identical language: [1] hence Mark is responsible for the claim that the testimony was false. It also applies to vv.60f which present a parallel with 15.4f and very improbably equate 'Messiah' and 'Son of God'. Schweizer argues that Messianic claims were also not offensive, and that the Son of man saying does not belong to the earliest traditions: it is 'das Endprodukt einer langen Beschäftigung mit der Bibel'.[2] Consequently the most primitive layer consisted of the temple saying, the sentence of death and the delivery to Pilate. Messiahship was indeed implicit in the idea of rebuilding a new temple, and therefore some link exists between the decisive issues in the proceedings before the Sanhedrin [3] and before Pilate.

Schweizer's theory in fact revives certain elements of Bultmann's analysis according to which vv.57-59 particularize and rather feebly repeat v.56; [4] but v.58 is now retained since it is claimed quite rightly that this must be at least based on a genuine saying of Jesus.[5] There are also certain similarities to Wellhausen's view which associated the temple saying and the blasphemy, though the latter grounded the association between the two on the omission of both by Luke! [6] The separation of the narrative into strata is certainly preferable to the argument of G. D. Kilpatrick that the temple saying was the crux for

---

[1] Das Evangelium nach Markus, Göttingen 1967, 188.

[2] op.cit. 189.

[3] 'Zwar mußten für die Pharisäer die Worte Jesu gegen die Gesetzesgerechtigkeit weit schwerer wiegen als eines gegen den Tempel; doch konnten sich in dieser Anklage sämtliche Mitglieder des Gerichtes finden, da der Tempelkult für die Sadduzäer zentral, für die Pharisäer wenigstens ein Punkt innerhalb des Gesetzesgehorsams war.' op.cit. 189.

[4] Synoptic Tradition, 120; cf. M. Dibelius, From Tradition to Gospel, London 1934, 182 and recently F. Hahn, Christologische Hoheitstitel, Göttingen 1966, 177.

[5] Schweizer, Markus, 187; similarly E. Lohse, art. συνέδριον TWNT 7(1964), 867. On the evolution of the saying R. A. Hoffmann, Das Wort Jesu von der Zerstörung und dem Wiederaufbau des Tempels, in Neutestamentliche Studien für G. Heinrici, Leipzig 1914, 130-139.

[6] Das Evangelium Marci, Berlin 1903, 133.

the Jewish court and that the subsequent interrogation about Messiahship aimed simply at formulating a charge which would convince
Pilate.[1] It is also preferable to Wellhausen's critique, in that the omission of two elements does not establish a legal connection between
them, and the theory that Luke redacts Mk at this point is very questionable. But there are still difficulties in the way of accepting it.
Certainly Mk 14.62 may not belong to the oldest layer of the report [2]
(though reasons will be adduced in favour of the saying's authenticity). But the discussion about messiahship and Divine Sonship is not
eliminated by the doubtful parallelism of the two in Mk 14.61 and the
similarity of Mk 15.4f. Schweizer himself allows that Luke may preserve independent and valuable traditions,[3] and this is indeed the case
as will be argued later in detail in respect of the messianic and Divine
Sonship issues. These therefore cannot be eliminated from the trial,
and the Temple saying can only play a definitive or crucial role if in its
original form and context it was included in the trial [4] and associated
with one of these two.[5] But then we shall soon indicate reasons for
doubting that a messianic claim could bring about condemnation.[6]

The original form of the saying did not contain χειροποίητος and
ἀχειροποίητος[7], since these are absent from Mk 15.29 and the Johannine tradition (Jn 2.19). Whereas ἀχειροποίητος may indicate God
over against man rather than 'inner' over against 'outer'[8] and so cohere
with Jub 1.17,27f, yet the awkward combination of God and Jesus
as subjects of the action reinforces the secondary character of these
words. That the original form exceeded the Mk 13.2 parallel by making
Jesus the subject [9] is suggested by the fact that embarrassment was
caused to the early Christians at precisely this point (cf. the meaningless [10] λύσατε, Jn 2.19), and also by the awkwardness of a general inex-

---

[1] The Trial of Jesus, London 1953, 13-16.
[2] See pp. 157-159.
[3] op.cit. 187.
[4] This is doubted by E. Lohse, Die Geschichte des Leidens und Sterbens
Jesu Christi, Gütersloh 1964, 84.
[5] This position is urged on the basis of the use of 2 Sam 7 in 4QFlor, by O.
Betz, Die Frage nach dem messianischen Bewusstsein Jesu, NovT 6(1963):
20-49; also, What do we know about Jesus? London 1968, 87-92; R. J. McElvey,
The New Temple. London 1969, 67.
[6] See below, p. 132.
[7] E. Lohmeyer, Mk, 326; R. A. Hoffmann, art.cit. 133.
[8] Contra Schweizer, Markus, 187.
[9] Otherwise, O. Michel, art. ναός, TDNT 4(1967), 883 and O. Betz, What
do we know about Jesus?, 91.
[10] It is unlikely that McElvey, op.cit. 71, is right in regarding Jn 2.19 as closest

plicit subject for the destruction part but clear statement of Jesus as
the subject for the rebuilding part.[1] Further, there is no need to see in
ἐν τρισὶν ἡμέραις (Mk 15.29; Jn 2.19)/ διὰ τριῶν ἡμερῶν (Mk 14.58)
a Christian vaticinium ex eventu, since the form contrasts with Mark's
μετά in Passion predictions (8.31; 9.31; 10.34) and in itself means
quite ordinarily 'a short time'.[2] Consequently Mk 15.29 probably indicates both the most primitive form of this saying and its association
with the trial.

Consideration of the role of the Temple saying must now turn to
Luke. In particular it must be asked whether Luke may have omitted a
report of this saying from his Sonderquelle, perhaps from a position
between 22.66 and 22.67. Samuel Sandmel, working from the same
literary standpoint as Wellhausen, has indeed suggested that Luke
omits anything which might imply disloyalty on Jesus' part towards
any Jewish institution, and he compares Luke's glossing over the
Temple cleansing and his omission of reference to the priestly hostility
which followed.[3]

Sandmel is in fact correct in proposing a very positive Lukan
evaluation of Jesus' attitude to the Temple. Redaction of the Temple
Cleansing incident yields the following evidence. Whereas Mark en-
closed the Cleansing within the Cursing of the Figtree, thus making
the Temple the object of a hostile attitude of judgement,[4] Luke has
omitted the surrounding material (Mk 11.12-14,20-23). He has also
softened πεποιήκατε (Mk 11.17) to ἐποιήσατε (Lk 19.46) and therefore removed the suggestion of a permanent state of apostasy. The
positive corollary, that the Temple is the place of prayer for the Jewish
people (thus πᾶσιν τοῖς ἔθνεσιν Mk 11.17 omitted) and Christians, is
borne out by Lk 24.46, Acts 3.1 and 22.17. To prayer by both we must
add teaching in an evangelistic sense (20.1): thus the redactional λαός [5]
of 19.48, who alone, by virtue of the transposition of the διδάσκειν

to Jesus' original wording, the interpretation being that the Jews would destroy
the Temple by turning from Jesus to policies which led to war with Rome,
which would in turn lead to the Temple's destruction. The connection with
A.D. 70 is altogether too subtle. Mt 26.61 δύναμαι καταλῦσαι shows how embarrassing concepts can be modified and at the same time made to serve positive
theological ends, cf. D. R. Catchpole, The Answer of Jesus to Caiaphas (Matt.
xxvi.64), NTS 17(1971), 223f.

[1] For a different view, see R. A. Hoffmann, art.cit. 133f.
[2] Kümmel, Promise, 67.
[3] Jewish Understanding, 186.
[4] McElvey, op.cit. 65.
[5] Cf. Lk 20.1,9,45; Acts 5.20.

reference from Mk 11.17 to Lk 19.47, hear. Hence according to Luke Jesus acts as βασιλεύς to take over the Temple for his own purposes [1] because the kingly Entry has as its immediate goal the Temple.[2] The destiny of the Temple contrasts sharply with that of the City.[3] Jesus weeps over the latter (19.41) and deplores its ignorance and failure to partake of the messianic peace (19.42). The καὶ σύ (19.42) is both a reproach and an emphatic contrast with the disciples who do know and who alone (contrast Mk 11.8f) have sung praise.[4] Whereas Luke certainly takes over the λίθος ἐπὶ λίθῳ prediction of damage to the Temple in Lk 21.6 (Mk 13.2) the important distinction emerges that the city's doom is pre-eschatological (as are all the events of Lk 21.12-24) while the Temple is only harmed at the End in the strictest sense. In history the City has rejected Jesus (19.39-44), therefore in history the City will be punished (21.20-24; 23.27-31, especially v.28).[5] But not so the Temple, which can in this context be separated from the City.

These passages preserve the personal Lukan view-point on Jesus' evaluation of the Temple. In line with its role in Lk 1-2,24 and Acts 1-5, this is very positive. Does this mean that Luke may, consistently with this view, have omitted material similar to Mk 14.58 from Lk 22.66-71? Almost certainly not, because there are several instances of his retaining material on the Temple even though that material diverges from his own attitude. This applies to Lk 13.35, 23.45, Acts 6.13 and 7.48. In conclusion, therefore, we cannot find within or behind the Markan or the Lukan traditions evidence which suggests that the trial of Jesus hinged on his alleged claim to destroy the Temple.

As to whether such a claim would have been regarded as blasphe-

---

[1] Lk 19.38, cf. Mk 11.9. Thus far rightly Hans Conzelmann, Luke, 77f.

[2] W. Grundmann, Luke, 370; H. Flender, op.cit. 86f.

[3] The two are not to be separated in the manner proposed by Conzelmann who claims, op.cit. 75, that Luke does not connect the Entry with the City at all, and that Jesus does not enter Jerusalem before the last supper. The plain statement of Mk 11.11 (which Luke had before him), the obvious data of the O.T., the inclusion of 19.39-44 at this place, the connection of 24.52 'they returned to Jerusalem' with 24.53 '. . . and were continually in the temple', the similar association in Ac 22.17f, the parallelism of 'in the Temple teaching', Ac 5.25 with 'you have filled Jerusalem with your teaching', Ac 5.28—all these demonstrably refute the suggestion that Luke had an inaccurate idea of the relative positions of the temple and the city.

[4] The Pharisees and the ὄχλος belong together in opposition. A similar contrast with disciples is apparent within Lk 9.18-50.

[5] Cf. G. Braumann, Die lukanische Interpretation der Zerstörung Jerusalems, NovT 6(1963), 120-127.

mous, Kilpatrick [1] and Blinzler [2] are probably correct that it would. But this becomes less important for our purpose here in view of our conclusion that such a charge does not seem to have been the direct reason for Jesus' condemnation.

2. *The claim to be Messiah*

Here it must be agreed that Jewish scholars are correct in declaring that a messianic claim is not blasphemous even if the term βλασφημία is given a looser definition than that in Sanh. 7.5. For against the view of Blinzler that this was the offence it must be noted that a messianic claim is no insult to God in the same way as the N.T. examples often cited are (Mk 2.7, Jn 10.33-36, Acts 6.11); [3] that in view of b.Sanh. 38b it cannot be affirmed certainly that the tighter definition of blasphemy was formulated before the time of Bar Kochba, thus freeing him of the offence;[4] that emphasis on the failure of Jesus to conform to or vindicate the popular messianic pattern,[5] in contrast with Bar Kochba, neither proves that blasphemy was the crime nor takes account of the subsequent disillusionment with Bar Kochba; and that the purely human character of the messiah makes this charge unlikely. Moreover, a correlation between messiahship and blasphemy only applies to the condemnation of Jesus if it can be established that this claim was actually made and that it was the climax of the trial. Mk 14.61-63 states the first, though the second is only a possible and not a necessary inference. But the independent Lk 22.66-71, which certainly appears more primitive in dealing with the messianic question, suggests neither.

3. *The assumption of the Divine Name*

Jewish scholars have, with very few exceptions, ignored the possibility that ἐγώ εἰμι = Ani Hu, and that Jesus, by thus pronouncing the Divine Name, may have committed the crime of Sanh. 7.5. In the modern period it has been proposed in the anonymous book entitled

---

[1] The Trial of Jesus, 11-13.

[2] Prozeß,147f. For the contrary view, see D. R. A. Hare, The Theme of Jewish Persecution of Christians in the Gospel according to St. Matthew, Cambridge 1967, 26f.

[3] Re Mk 2.7, the reaction of the hearers is sufficient to throw doubt on Mantel's claim, Studies,269, that Jesus was merely echoing an Essene-type idea that sufferings wash away men's sins (b.Ber. 5a).

[4] J. Blinzler, Prozeß, 154f.

[5] Blinzler, op.cit. 154.

Rabbi Jeshua,[1] though there it is interpreted as a malicious miscon-
struction put by the high priest on a straightforward answer to the
preceding question. There is here, as later in Kohler, some influence of
the Toledoth Yeshu, in that he mentions a later claim that Jesus had
penetrated the Holy of Holies and read there the Sacred Name.[2]

It was the Swedish Rabbi G. Klein [3] who most notably laid down
the foundations for the Ani Hu theory of E. Stauffer, by understanding
ἐγώ εἰμι as the Divine Name. He stressed the background in Is 52.6 [4]
and the central role of the Divine Name in Jesus' preaching, Jn 10.30,
17.6f,26, associated in particular with the feast of Tabernacles.[5] The
theory of T. W. Manson [6] was here anticipated by setting the entry to
Jerusalem and the cleansing of the temple at Tabernacles, though
Klein relied on Johannine data.[7] Indeed, in the form presented by
Klein it is as a whole a theory based on Jn. The fourth gospel also
plays a dominant role for H. J. Schoeps, who accepts the work of
Stauffer and is the latest Jewish adherent of this theory. Schoeps however assimilates the Divine Name and other possible contents of the
blasphemy by arguing that the Ani Hu claim was an assertion of Divine Sonship, to which was added the suggestion that Jesus would come
and sit at the right hand of power,[8] i.e. a literal interpretation of Ps
110.1.

The following comments must be made on the developed form of
this theory as proposed by E. Stauffer. Firstly, even this theory does
not satisfy precisely the Sanh. 7.5 ruling, for Ani Hu in Sukk. 4.5 is
itself a periphrasis for the full Divine Name,[9] and its public pronuncia-
tion, regarded from the angle of explicit wording, is in that place

---

[1] London 1881, 140.

[2] Kohler, Synagogue, 158: 'And who can tell whether at that moment, so
full of awe, he may not, while referring to that ancient prophecy of the nozrim
in Jeremiah (Jer 31.6) have spelled forth the holy name of Jehovah, combining it
with his own name, Joshua of Nazareth, so as to fill the very air about him with
sights and visions of the Son of man in the clouds, and at the same time shocked
and alarmed the bystanders with the blasphemous word or act of a 'seducer',
'corrupter', 'blasphemer' and 'magican'.' The Mk 14.62 scheme is very obvious.

[3] Der älteste christliche Katechismus und die jüdische Propagandaliteratur,
Berlin 1909.

[4] op.cit. 44.

[5] op.cit. 51f,55,58.

[6] BJRL 33 (1951), 271-282.

[7] Katechismus,51f; Ist Jesus ein historische Persönlichkeit? Tübingen 1910,
41-43.

[8] Paul, London 1961, 161f. He compares Jn 5.18, 10.33 and Acts 7.45-60: a
confession of 'faith in a heavenly Son of God'.

[9] H. Danby, The Mishnah, Oxford 1933, 178.

unexceptionable. Secondly, not all texts cited by Stauffer in support may be retained. Thus in his view Jn 4.26 is to be regarded as a theophanic formula rather than a messianic affirmation.[1] But against the argument that there is no other messianic affirmation in Jn stands not only Jn 18.37 but also the analogous fact that there is but one Son of man self-affirmation (Jn 9.35-37 ὁ λαλῶν μετὰ σοῦ ἐκεῖνός ἐστιν), and the similarity of the formulation of these two replies suggests that one, like the other, affirms the previously mentioned title; although Jn 4.25 uses the verb ἀναγγέλλω which appears in Deutero-Isaiah as a theophany word, yet the other Johannine uses do not wholly support this sense (Jn 5.15), and the woman only uses εἶπεν subsequently (Jn 4.29,40), her question in Jn 4.29 showing plainly that messiahship alone is involved; the parallel of the Qumran text of Is 52.6 is inadequate to interpret Jn 4.26; patristic variants at Is 52.6 are probably christologically formed and can in no way be regarded as an independent tradition, confirming a given exegesis of Jn 4.26; although Jesus starts with current titles and goes beyond them sometimes, he does not always do so, e.g. Jn 10.24-36; and finally, Jn 4.26 is presupposed in the suggestion that Jesus is messiah, Jn 4.29, for the revealing of secrets is evidence only of a prophet, 4.19, and more than this is needed to identify Jesus with the messiah. Thirdly, although j.Taan. 65b is to be taken, on grounds of schematic order, as an interpretation of Mk 14.62 rather than Jn 8.28,[2] yet it is not thereby proved to be a correct interpretation, and is certainly not understood in this way by Matthew (σὺ εἶπας, 26.64), who elsewhere is not opposed to the theophanic sense of εγὼ εἶμι[3] or to the assimilation of the divine presence to Jesus.[4] Fourthly, ἐγὼ εἰμι is several times used in acceptance of a previously mentioned role,[5] and this is the best sense for Mk 14.62 (cf. Lk 22.70). Fifthly, there is not a secure enough base in the general teaching of Jesus for this to be a likely feature in the trial. Sixthly, Lam.R. 1.16, cited by P. Borgen as an example of the use of 'I am' as 'a midrashic formula for identifying Old Testament words with a person in the

---

[1] Jesus and his Story, London 1960, 152.

[2] Contra W. G. Kümmel, Promise and Fulfilment, London 1961, 51.

[3] Mt 14.27,33.

[4] W. D. Davies, The Setting of the Sermon on the Mount, Cambridge 1964, 224f.

[5] Mt 26.22,25 (cf. Lk 1.18f), Acts 10.21, 13.25, 26.29. Stauffer himself allows this at Jn 18.5-8, op.cit.191, though this is surprising and unnecessary since this must be a case of Johannine double entendre, in view of the reaction of the hearers.

first person singular',[1] shows that even Ani Hu does not always carry overtones of the Divine Name. The text refers to the arrival of Trajan to slaughter the Jews, and reads:

> On his arrival he found the Jews occupied with this verse: 'The Lord will bring a nation against thee from far, from the end of the earth, as the vulture swoopeth down' (Dt 28.49). He said to them: 'I am (Ani Hu) the vulture who planned to come in ten days, but the wind brought me in five.'

This must be the sense behind Mk 14.62: an identification of Jesus with the messiah of the Old Testament. Schematic considerations of the Markan gospel would support this: an identification of Jesus as messiah and Son of God appears at the crucial points of the beginning, 1.1,11, and the middle, 8.29, 9.7, and the end, 14.61f, leading to 15.26,39. Seventhly, if the Lukan version is more primitive and employs a semitic idiom, as will later be argued, any idea of the involvement of the Divine Name must be shelved.

4. *The self-exaltation as the enthroned Son of man*

The Son of man saying, Mk 14.62, does not play a large part in Jewish treatment of the trial, though at one time or another almost the whole spectrum of Christian Son of man research is covered. Thus we find the following views:

(a) Repeatedly it is stressed that this is not blasphemy.[2] Here there can still be observed the influence of the old Troki-type opposition of Son of man to Son of God,[3] and also the traditional counterthrust to Christian claims by applying to all Israelites what Christians apply to Jesus. Thus Zeitlin argues that many Israelites looked forward to the future world when they would sit in God's company.[4] But here again there is a tension with his analysis of the trial of Stephen. Firstly, he allows, in spite of reiterated insistence on the letter of Sanh. 7.5, that 'these words would still be in the category of blasphemy'.[5] Secondly, there is a difference alleged between the words of Jesus and of Stephen: 'Jesus made a prediction while Stephen made a statement that he saw

---

[1] Bread from Heaven, Leiden 1965, 73.

[2] Joel, Blicke II, 65; Bamberger, Story of Judaism, 50; Kohler, Christianity, 51; Danziger, Jewish Forerunners, 48; Lauterbach, Pharisees, 74; Klein, Katechismus, 59; Goldstein, Jesus, 25; Hamburger, Jesus, 51, argues from Akiba's application of it to the messiah, without taking account of R. Jose's protest.

[3] Rabbinowicz, Rôle, 38; Schreiber, Prinzipien, 80; N. S. Joseph, Why I am not a Christian, London 1907, 4; Goldstein, Jesus, 26, turns the use of Ps 110.1 so that this, reflecting David's allusion to himself, is innocuous.

[4] Who crucified Jesus? 153; though Zeitlin considers, op.cit. 191, that this is what Mt and Mk regard as blasphemy.

[5] op.cit. 191.

the Son of man standing on the right hand of God; that is, he considered Jesus the founder of a new religion'.[1] Not only is it hard to accept
such a distinction, but it is the more surprising in that from a theological angle Jesus' statement involving καθήμενον as against ἑστῶτα,
Acts 7.55, is the more christologically intense of the two.

Not far from this group of scholars is Daniel Chwolson. Only in
Beiträge (1910) did he give any indication of what it was that the high
priest considered blasphemous. The superimposition of a Jewish background on his Christian confession had made him devalue Son of God
and dismiss the messianic question. Even then his theory that the
heavenly session idea is blasphemous is qualified by Sadducean
injustice: it was not really a blasphemy and was wrongly made so by
Caiaphas.[2]

(b) Another group of scholars take the Son of man saying as a
confirmation either of messiahship [3] or divine Sonship.[4]

(c) M. de Jonge [5] argues that the *coming* Son of man is someone
other than Jesus. Like Chwolson, de Jonge was a convert,[6] and also
denied both messianic consciousness and any sonship other than that
on the Dt 14.1 pattern for Jesus.[7]

(d) Occasionally authenticity is denied.[8] This is done emphatically
by Winter [9] who argues, firstly, that the combination of the Son of man
text (Dan 7.13) and the messiah text (Ps 110.1) betrays a conflation of
theological viewpoints, hammered out in debate between two factions
possibly within Mark's community, and secondly, that the impossible
combination of 'sitting' and 'coming' demonstrates that an unnatural
merger has occured.[10] It may be remarked immediately that the first

---

[1] op.cit. 191.

[2] op.cit. 47.

[3] Grünebaum, Sittenlehre, 159; Fluegel, Messiah-Ideal I, 277; Klausner,
Jesus, 343; Trattner, op.cit. 132; Polack, Jesus, 102; Margolis-Marx, History,
183; Isaac, Jésus, 238 (basically because he finds here a point at which he feels
all the synoptics agree).

[4] Graetz, Geschichte, 2nd ed.244; H. J. Schoeps, Paul, 162.

[5] Messias der kommende jüdische Mann, Berlin 1904, 88.

[6] Cf. A. Schweitzer, The Quest of the Historical Jesus, London 1911, 321f.

[7] op.cit. 13,68,70,82: σὺ εἶπας is interpreted as 'Du sagst Du', i.e. a denial.
De Jonge argued that messiah would come early in the 20th century.

[8] Rodrigues, Roi, 230f; Wise, Martyrdom, 76; S. Sandmel, Son of Man, in:
In Time of Harvest, A. H. Silver Festschrift, New York 1963, 335-367; Goldin,
Case of the Nazarene, 370; L. Baeck, Judaism and Christianity, Philadelphia
1958, 29f, who thinks that the term Son of man was only applied to Jesus at the
end of the 1st or the beginning of the 2nd century.

[9] On the Trial, 148.

[10] JTS 14 (1963),100. M. Buber, Two Types of Faith, London 1951, 108, also

argument is weakened by the complete absence of evidence for the existence of a group or community which took Jesus only as the Son of man,[1] and that the second argument is over-literal and does not consider the alternatives, namely that each is an expression of the Son of man's vindication[2] or that two consecutive insights are intended.

Before a decision on the theological and legal bearing of Mk 14.62 can be reached, the problem of its authenticity must be further examined. Objections to this move along well-known lines. Firstly, there are doubts stemming from the setting of this saying in a passage unsupported by eyewitness reports, secondarily inserted within the report of Peter's denial, and weakened legally by the problem of Jewish capital powers.[3] The questions of setting in the Markan narrative, witnesses of the event, and the legal problems are dealt with elsewhere in this book, but the fact is that these are simply irrelevant to the matter of Mk 14.62. For form-critical criteria themselves allow a saying to be genuine without regard to its setting. By the same token Mk 14.58 might be regarded as suspect, but its genuineness is widely accepted. So this kind of argument must be firmly rejected. Secondly, Tödt has argued that a scriptural formulation like Mk 14.62 is not attested in the authentic Son of man sayings, Lk 12.8f, Mt 24.27,37,39, nor in other evidence of Jesus' use of the Old Testament: hence it is not here to be attributed to Jesus.[4] But against this, C.F.D. Moule has raised important criticisms of Tödt's attempt to discount the overwhelmingly probable background in Dan 7.13,[5] and in that case citation of the associated passage is entirely natural. Jesus can scarcely be proved not to have quoted scripture verbatim, cf.Lk 4.18f (a passage not produ-

---

notes this awkwardness and takes out the 'sitting' clause. He accepts the rest as genuine in spite of agreeing with Lietzmann's dismissal of the surrounding pericope.

[1] Certainly no appeal may here be made to the Q community which clearly regarded Jesus not only as Son of man but also as ὁ ἐρχόμενος (Mt ‖11.3 = Lk 7.19), a figure who is clearly not the Son of man (cf. citations of Is 29.18f, 35.5f, 61.1), and also regarded Jesus as the Son (Mt 3.17 = Lk 3.22, Mt 4.1-11 = Lk 4.1-13, Mt 11.25-27 = Lk 10.21f). Nor may appeal be made via the Hegesippus tradition to the Jerusalem church, for messiahship is almost certainly traceable there by means of 1 Cor 15.3-7 and maybe Rom 1.3f. There are certainly no grounds for postulating such an apocalyptic group in the Roman community.

[2] Cf. M. D. Hooker, The Son of Man in Mark, London 1967, 167-171.

[3] P. Vielhauer, Gottesreich und Menschensohn in der Verkündigung Jesu, reprinted in Aufsätze zum Neuen Testament, München 1965, 72; H. E. Tödt, The Son of Man in the synoptic Tradition, London 1965, 36f; E. Schweizer, Der Menschensohn, ZNW 50 (1959), 189.

[4] op.cit. 36.

[5] Theology 69 (1966), 172-176.

ced by redaction of Mk 6.1-6), 7.22. As in the first objection, a question of criteria is involved,[1] and in particular, the over-speedy division of Son of man sayings into groups, followed by the abandonment of all but one of the groups. An analysis of the sayings one by one would not only be better procedurally, but would also give sound reasons for doubting the theory that Jesus in some sayings spoke of the Son of man as someone other than himself. It would also face more squarely the fact that some sayings do combine elements from more than one of the three classical subdivisions, e.g. Lk 9.58 combines suffering and earthly activity, Lk 11.30 combines present activity and the eschatological bearing, Lk 7.34 combines opposition (and therefore the beginning of suffering) and present activity. As regards Tödt's basic grouping, according to which the supreme criterion is agreement with the 'Jesus ≠ the Son of man' scheme, several points can be made: (a) If Lk 12.8 was in Q in its present form, it clearly was not there interpreted as distinguishing Jesus and the Son of man, and moreover Luke clearly did not take it this way; this throws doubt on any suggestion that it was ever taken as implying a distinction. (b) Jeremias has rightly pointed out that in the development of the tradition, there is not one single case of the title being dropped but a substantial number of examples of its being added.[2] In the light of this, Mt 10.32 must be regarded as the earlier form, and Lk 12.8 the form produced by Lukan redaction. (c) In treating Mk 8.38, Lohse has rightly asked how there is room in the eschatological preaching of Jesus for a coming Son of man different from Jesus, when he certainly saw in the appearance of John the Baptist the breaking in of the dividing line between the ages.[3] (d) There are a number of sayings which not only imply that Jesus is the Son of man, but which also have every claim to authenticity. Among these is Lk 7.34, with its origin in Q its setting of the Baptist and Jesus side by side,[4] its reproach against Jesus in terms of Dt 21.20

---

[1] Cf. the further evidence of inconsistency in the use of strict form-critical procedure on the Son of man problem, discussed by Hooker, op.cit. 4-7.

[2] Die älteste Schicht der Menschensohn-logien, ZNW 58 (1967), 159-172. In view of this careful documentation it is scarcely permissible for A. J. B. Higgins to avoid this argument and simply comment that 'the suggestion that the Son of man is not an original element in the saying is a hypothesis which cannot be proved, and need not be pressed'. Is the Son of Man Problem insoluble? in Neotestamentica et Semitica: Festschrift M. Black, Edinburgh 1969, 85.

[3] Die Frage nach dem historischen Jesus, ThLZ 87 (1962), 169f.

[4] Cf. C. Colpe, ὁ υἱὸς τοῦ ἀνθρώπου TWNT 8 (1967) 434; I. H. Marshall, The Synoptic Son of man Sayings in recent Discussion, NTS 12 (1966), 327-351, esp. 339f.

which no Christian community is likely to have fashioned and which coheres with a completely secure feature of the ministry of the historical
Jesus (i.e. the mission among tax-collectors and sinners). Again, Lk 9.58
is not a general proverb, pace Bultmann,[1] because it is not true of man in
general that he has nowhere to lay his head and moreover this is a
saying which lacks all theological embroidery. Finally for the present,
Lk 11.30 which there is no reason to divide from its setting: the theme
of Jesus as an eschatological preacher of repentance is accepted as
authentic; the comparison with Jonah appears nowhere else in the
Christian tradition apart from this Q instance (and Mt 12.40 shows a
quite different train of thought being extracted from it); and that Jesus
is here the Son of man follows from the parallel with Jonah, who
operates on the earthly level (if a comparison is to be drawn with
Lk 12.8, it should be with verse 8a and not verse 8b), and also from
the associated statement in Lk 11.32: ἰδοὺ πλεῖον ᾿Ιωνᾶ ὧδε.[2] From the
preceding argumentation it follows that the construction of blocks of
tradition out of some Son of man sayings, with the result that others
are automatically excluded, is questionable. It may be added here that
Mk 14.62 is well in line, not only with Dan 7.13, but also with the
absorption of kingship ideology into the Son of man concept in pre-
Christian times.[3] (Ps 80.17, which very probably refers to the king, may
well be a conceptual predecessor of Mk 14.62 by combining the ideas
of Son of man and enthronement at the right hand.[4]) At this point it is
appropriate to remark that it is extremely difficult to accept that an
Old Testament term *cannot* have been used by Jesus in terms of its
Old Testament content and context.[5]

The third reason for doubting the authenticity of Mk 14.62 is the
christological concentration at Mk 14.61f, which includes the unattested attribution of the term Son of God to the messiah, regarded as
un-Jewish and unattested in Q and the earliest stratum of gospel tradition. The linking of messiah and Son of man is also thought to be

---

[1] Synoptic Tradition, 28.
[2] It is doubtful whether Jeremias is right, art.cit.160, to regard Lk 11.29-32
as a secondary development from Mk 8.11f.
[3] Cf. Hooker, op.cit. 17-32.
[4] F. H. Borsch, The Son of Man in Myth and History, London 1967, 116f.
[5] Although there are sayings attributed to Jesus which belong rather to the
earlier or contemporary thought of Judaism, neither probability nor proof can
be attached to the criterion for genuineness that a saying must not be paralleled
in Jewish tradition. So correctly, W. D. Davies, Setting, 381; H. M. Teeple,
The Origin of the Son of Man Christology, JBL 84 (1965), 217.

suspect.[1] But against this there is firstly the unmistakably Jewish over-tone in τοῦ εὐλογητοῦ and τῆς δυνάμεως, and secondly, that the chris-tological union between Son of man and the other concepts is not achieved by a merging of them as ideas but by application of them to Jesus, i.e. a personal rather than a conceptual unity. In fact, the kingly theme is one common factor joining messiah and Son of man but, more importantly, there is the probability that the original form, of Lk 22.67-71 did not contain the Son of man saying,[2] and therefore, as the tradition has developed from its Lukan stage to its Markan form this saying has been added. Hence once again, it must not be prejudi-ced by its setting. The fourth and final objection is the psychological difficulty which is felt in the claim of a normal man to be the Son of man.[3] Here it is sufficient to refer to Hooker's criticism of this argu-ment.[4]

Since then objections to the authenticity of Mk 14.62 fall consider-ably short of proof, and if the Markan implication that this saying played a part in the trial is right, the further question remains: could it have been regarded as blasphemous? Several scholars affirm this,[5] and there are a number of passages in Jewish literature which support it. The main text is b.Sanh. 38b in which R. Akiba and R. Jose discuss the text Dan 7.9, included already in a list of passages taken, because of reference to plurality, by the Minim as grounds for their heresy. The crucial section of the text runs:

> How explain: 'till thrones were placed'?—One throne was for himself (the Ancient of Days) and one for David. Even as it has been taught: One was for himself and one for David: this is R. Akiba's view. R. Jose protested to him: Akiba, how long will you profane the Shechinah? Rather, one throne for justice and the other for mercy.

---

[1] Vielhauer, op.cit. 72; Tödt, op.cit. 37; similarly, Teeple, art. cit.219f, whose argument from the incompatibility of the pre-existent Son of man with the human earthly messiah is questionable, since in Dan 7 there is no apparent heavenliness (the 'clouds of heaven' should not be confused) or pre-existence but rather, by virtue of the regal embodiment of the people of the saints, a thorough humanity, cf. Ps 8, where the identical kingly features appear.

[2] See pp. 157-159.

[3] Teeple, art.cit. 221. Winter's assertion in this context that Jesus was 'the norm of normality' seems to reflect implicitly this objection, On the Trial, 148.

[4] op.cit. 183-187; cf. I. H. Marshall, Synoptic Son of man Sayings, 328f.

[5] R. A. Hoffmann, Das Wort Jesu von der Zerstörung und dem Wiederaufbau des Tempels, in G. Heinrici Festgabe, Leipzig 1914, 136-139; Strack-Billerbeck I, 1017; O. Linton, The Trial of Jesus and the Interpretation of Psalm CX, NTS 7 (1961), 258-262; P. Lamarche, Le Blasphème de Jésus devant le Sanhédrin, RSR 50 (1962), 74-85; cf. W. Foerster, κύριος, TDNT 3, 1089: 'the very fact of sitting in God's presence implies divine dignity'.

What is significant is the strenuous resistance put up against the idea of a man's sitting in heaven, and the terminology of the reproach, 'profanation of the Shechinah'. The allegation by R. Jose that such a suggestion is blasphemous must be contrasted with the lack of objection to the idea of sitting in God's presence in the view of R. Levi (a 3rd generation Amora of Tiberius, c. A.D.300) in Midr.Pss 18.29, and in the same text, the view of R. Hama (of Sepphoris, c. A.D. 260) according to which David's session at God's right hand in line with Ps 110.1 is unexceptionable. On the other hand R. Jose's opinion is also supported by a 3rd-century tradition that 'there is no sitting in heaven', attributed to R. Samuel (who died A.D.254), as well as the anonymous traditions in Ex.R. 15.26 and Midr.Pss. 108.1. R. Jose may therefore be echoing a viewpoint which later faded, according to which the session of a man in heaven is sacrilegious. R. Akiba, on the other hand, was a fiery opponent of Christian theology, and the voicing by him of a view usable on the Christian side is puzzling. It may be an older exegetical tradition attached to Dan 7.9, which fell into disrepute under pressure from the Minim and other sectarians. The case of Elisha b. Abujah (b.Hag. 14b-15a, 3 Enoch 16.2-4) is here relevant, in that he is alleged to have fallen into apostasy after a vision of the sitting Metatron in heaven, from which he deduced the existence of two deities. Unfortunately the age of this tradition is sufficiently insecure to prevent firm conclusions. All that can be said is that there is the possibility that a claim such as that in Mk 14.62 might have been regarded as blasphemous.

5. *The claim to be Son of God*

It would, of course, be impossible for Jesus to have been condemned on this count if the title Son of God originated in connection with the parousia in Palestinian Christianity.[1] Ferdinand Hahn has urged this on the basis of three texts: Lk 1.32f, Mk 14.61f and I Thess 1.9f. However, Lk 1.32f, although certainly rightly regarded by Hahn as a classic Jewish formulation, does not indicate the point in time when inauguration to this messianic office would occur.[2] Mk 14.61f makes only a very loose connection between parousia and divine

---

[1] F. Hahn, Christologische Hoheitstitel, 3rd ed. Göttingen 1966, 288-292; with modifications, R. H. Fuller, The Foundations of New Testament Christology, London 1965, 164-167.

[2] On the Jewish interpretation of the Davidic king, cf. E. Lohse, Der König aus Davids Geschlecht, in Abraham unser Vater, Festschrift O. Michel, Leiden 1963, 337-345.

Sonship, but in any case must be dismissed as evidence since a comparison of Lk 22.67-71 and Mk 14.61f indicates that the Son of man logion was originally unconnected with the material to which it is now joined in Mk.[1] Hahn is however right when he remarks that the formulation 'Son of the blessed' goes back to old Palestinian tradition.[2] But this, together with the Lukan evidence, which also reflects a Semitic milieu,[3] means that variation in the use of Son of God is present already at the Palestinian stage. Such variety is further supported by the probability that Rom 1.3f also stems from a Semitic background;[4] for although T.Levi 18.11 proves that the term πνεῦμα ἁγιωσύνης could survive in a Hellenistic milieu,[5] yet this neither proves a Hellenistic origin for the formula in Rom 1.4 nor demolishes the improbability that a Semitism should be incorporated into a Hellenistic credal statement.[6] If then the σάρξ/πνεῦμα antithesis was present in the non-Hellenistic background of this formula, even more fluidity in the use of Son of God must be allowed in Palestinian christology.[7]

Hahn's argument on 1 Th 1.9f depends essentially on this block of material being a pre-Pauline formula. This has also been proposed recently by Kramer [8] on the basis of two observations: Firstly, εἴδωλα here corresponds to the Jewish polemical position, as in Is 44.9-20, and not to the Pauline view of the powers, whose existence is not disputed but whose ultimate influence is regarded as vanishing in subjection to God. Secondly, Jesus' function as redeemer is understood purely eschatologically as the rescuing of the believer from before the judgement.[9] This also is said to be out of keeping with the general trend of Pauline theology. Now it must be noticed that even if

---

[1] Hahn, op.cit. 289, stresses that the evidence of Mt and Lk should under no circumstances be used to reconstruct the trial. This is true for Mt, but becomes the more unsatisfactory for Lk as evidence accumulates in favour of Lukan independence: see chapter III.

[2] op.cit. 289.

[3] See p. 200.

[4] Cf. W. Kramer, Christ Lord Son of God, London 1966, 108-111.

[5] Hahn, op.cit. 255; Fuller, Foundations, 180.

[6] It is also necessary to stress that the non-Pauline σάρξ/πνεῦμα antithesis is not Hellenistic, contra Fuller, Foundations, 180. Cf. E. Schweizer, Lordship and Discipleship, London 1960, 59.

[7] Similarly Paul can use such an adoptionist formula and superimpose pre-existence (E. Schweizer, The Concept of the Davidic Son of God in Acts and its O.T. Background, in Studies in Luke-Acts, Festschrift P. Schubert, London 1968, 186) without seeing the two perspectives as divergent.

[8] Christ Lord Son of God, 123-125.

[9] op.cit. 124.

these suggestions were sufficient to establish 1 Th 1.9f as a pre-Pauline formula, Hahn's suggested Palestinian origin is impossible since ἐπεστρέψατε πρὸς τὸν θεὸν ἀπο τῶν εἰδώλων is meaningless in such a setting,[1] and belongs to the environment of the Gentile mission.[2] But in any case, against Kramer's view there are objections which must be raised: (a) The nature of the εἴδωλα in 1 Th 1.9f is not defined, and there is nothing to mark off this passage from 1 Cor 8.4,7, 10.19 (cf. Rom 2.22, 2 Cor 6.16), and the sense is particularly close to 1 Cor 12.2. (b) The eschatological function of redeemer is paralleled in Rom 5.9f (cf. with God as subject, 2 Cor 1.10), which is not a credal passage.[3] Consequently, 1 Th 1.9f should be regarded as only a Pauline statement with no pre-history, and this text, together with the other two, does not suggest an original emergence of the term Son of God in connection with parousia ideas in a Palestinian setting.

It has been necessary at several stages in the argument to assume the results of the following chapter, which seeks to prove the independence of the Lukan narrative. In that essentially non-Markan source, it must be noted that the separation of messiah and Son of God fits precisely the distinction between these titles in contemporary Judaism. This is a factor to add to those mentioned above which bring the Sonship concept back into a Palestinian setting. And according to the Lukan and Johannine traditions the claim to be the Son of God was the crucial issue (Lk 22.70/Jn 19.7). But does such a tradition cohere with the sayings of Jesus in the earlier stage of his career?

Once again attention must focus on the three famous synoptic sayings: Mk 12.6, 13.32 and Mt 11.27.

Mk 12.6. It is certainly apparent that critical surgery [4] has to be performed on the parable of the wicked husbandmen, but when this has taken place the kernel which remains still contains the reference to the Son.[5] W. G. Kümmel has urged that this is not traceable to Jesus [6] for

---

[1] Thus far, rightly P. Vielhauer, Ein Weg zur neutestamentlichen Christologie? EvTh 25 (1965), 65.

[2] R. Bultmann, Theology of the New Testament I, London 1965, 74,80f, notes the parallelism of 1 Th 1.9f and Ac 17.31.

[3] C. K. Barrett, The Epistle to the Romans, London 1962, 107: 'final deliverance at the last judgement'. Both R. Bultmann, Theology I, 288 and P. Althaus, Der Brief an die Römer, Göttingen 1959, 45, pair 1 Th 1.10 and Rom 5.9.

[4] Jeremias, Parables, 70-77.

[5] Similarly B. M. F. van Iersel, 'Der Sohn' in den synoptischen Jesusworten, Leiden 1961, 124-145.

[6] Promise, 83.

two reasons: firstly, Jesus could not be referring to himself by introducing the 'only' Son into the parable since Judaism did not known the messianic name 'Son of God', and secondly, the transference of the promise from the Jews to the new people of God is normally made by Jesus to hinge on rejection of him in general terms without specifically concentrating on his death. But against this, there is nothing messianic in the sonship of Mk 12.6, and it is altogether too forced to divide rejection of Jesus in general from rejection by his death, particularly in view of Mt 23.37-39 for which Kümmel convincingly argues as an independent saying of Jesus from the oldest tradition.[1] It is therefore at least probable that Mk 12.6 is a saying of Jesus.[2]

Mk 13.32. The objections to this saying are well-known. Firstly it is argued that since the context is apocalyptic the underlying idea is probably 'Son of man' corresponding to the 'angelic Trinity' in Mk 8.38.[3] Secondly, Jeremias [4] has argued that the absolute ὁ υἱός is a Christological title which established itself rather late (1 Cor 15.28 is the first example) and in a Hellenistic [5] context, in view of the Palestinian non-use of the term as a designation for the messiah. He thinks the more primitive form is in Ac 1.7 where the words οὐδὲ ὁ υἱός are lacking. But once again it is necessary to urge that nothing in this saying recalls the messiah. And one cannot appeal to the Lukan writings because Luke in fact recoils from the ignorance of the Son and omits Mk 13.32 in toto. Moreover, it is not credible that οὐδὲ ὁ υἱός would be inserted into an original form which lacked it.[6] Nor are 'angelic Trinity' parallels in themselves sufficient to prove that this was the original form here. Mk 13.32 would therefore seem to be most probably an authentic saying.[7]

---

[1] Promise, 81.

[2] It is difficult to follow R. H. Fuller, The Foundations of New Testament Christology, London 1965, 114, when he argues that even if the parable is authentic, 'sonship' must not be taken as direct self-designation but 'simply stands for God's final eschatological mission. A similar position is reached by C. K. Barrett, Jesus and the Gospel Tradition, London 1967, 27, when he suggests an original simpler form emphasising God's present decisive claim on his people and the judgement of Israel. In spite of the signs of compilation to which he alludes in treating 12.9-12 and the position, answering the question of 11.28 and leading to the pronouncement of 12.17, all of which suggests Mark's editorial hand, there is no intrinsic reason for excluding the sonship reference.

[3] Fuller, Foundations,114; E. Schweizer, art. υἱός TWNT 8(1967), 373.

[4] Prayers, 36f.

[5] Otherwise, Schweizer art.cit. 374.

[6] Cf. I. H. Marshall, The Divine Sonship of Jesus, Interpretation 21 (1967), 94.

[7] Similarly, van Iersel, 'Der Sohn', 117-123.

Mt 11.27 = Lk 10.22. This saying is far more crucial than the two dealt with above. With one degree of certainty or another it has been regarded widely as unauthentic and Hellenistic,[1] partly because of the idea of 'mutual recognition . . . quite foreign to Judaism'.[2] In addition, Barrett has argued that although the idea of nothing in the appearance of Jesus to demonstrate his authority has strong claim to historical trustworthiness, yet the wording is probably secondary because of its unlikely setting. Consequently 'the neat Father-Son formulation cannot be confidently traced back to Jesus'.[3] From a different angle van Iersel [4] has recognized the importance of finding a setting and has suggested, not wholly convincingly, a link with the Nazareth rejection (Mk 6.1-6 and par.).

Jeremias has demonstrated convincingly that structure, language and style place this saying in a Semitic setting.[5] Moreover, the mutual knowledge is itself expressed in a Semitic form[6] and several scholars have rightly pointed to a background in the Semitic 'yadha'.[7] All of this is sufficient to remove both the suspicion of a Hellenistic background and uncertainty as to which of Mt 11.27 and Lk 10.22 is the original version.[8] Luke's γινώσκει τίς ἐστιν reflects a Hellenistic adaptation in line with his redaction of Mk 4.11 (Lk 8.10).[9] To these considerations must be added the repeated use of terms connected with Rabbinic legal instruction both in this saying and in Mt 11.25f. Thus παρεδόθη is certainly to be understood in connection with the transmission of Rabbinic material,[10] and its interpretation is not to be deflected by the partial parallel

---

[1] Bultmann, Synoptic Tradition, 160; Bornkamm, Jesus, 227; H. Conzelmann, An Outline of the Theology of the New Testament, London 1969, 103.

[2] Kümmel, Promise, 41.

[3] Jesus and the Gospel Tradition, 26f.

[4] op.cit. 151-157.

[5] Prayers, 46.

[6] Jeremias, Prayers, 47. This in itself makes it difficult to follow J.C.O'Neill's view that 'no one knows the Son save the Father' is a gloss. The Charge of Blasphemy at Jesus' Trial before the Sanhedrin. The Trial of Jesus, Festschrift C. F. D. Moule, London 1970, 72-77, esp. 76f.

[7] van Iersel, op.cit. 159; Hahn, Hoheitstitel, 325; Schweizer, art.cit. 374; see in particular W. D. Davies, 'Knowledge' in the Dead Sea Scrolls and Matthew 11.25-30, in Christian Origins and Judaism, London 1962, 119-144.

[8] van Iersel, op.cit. 159.

[9] Conzelmann, Luke, 103. W. Grundmann, Luke, 218, is therefore not correct in suggesting no difference in meaning between ἐπιγινώσκειν in Mt and γινώσκειν in Lk.

[10] van Iersel, op.cit. 158; W. Grundmann, Luke, 217; A. M. Hunter, Crux Criticorum—Matt.xi.25-30—a Re-appraisal, NTS 8(1962), 243; Jeremias, Prayers, 49. Otherwise, Hahn op.cit. 323.

ἐδόθη πᾶσα ἐξουσία, Mt 28.18, which is certainly not as old as Mt 11.27. Similarly, even the fatherhood/sonship metaphor is attested in Rabbinic contexts (Mt 12.27, Ac 23.6).[1] It would appear therefore that Jesus is here taking up a current metaphor and deepening it in the light of unique filial consciousness.[2]

Although the unity of 11.25-26 with 11.27 is disputed,[3] it is nevertheless notable that the overlap between the two is not confined to the possible catchword ἀποκαλύπτειν. For in vv.25f we have further legal language, especially in the contrast of σοφοί καὶ συνετοι with νήπιοι. The σοφοί are clearly the Pharisaic teachers,[4] and the νήπιοι are those who stand in need of legal instruction.[5] Here then Jesus, praying out of well-authenticated filial consciousness, gives thanks for the Father's design of teaching and bringing certain selected persons into a personal relationship. Thus in both vv.25f and v.27 we have material bound together by legal language, the idea of ἀποκαλύπτειν, and the concept of sonship. This latter is expressed explicitly by πάτερ/ὁ πατήρ = Abba in vv.25f, and even among those who dispute, as well as among those who accept,[6] the authenticity of the logion v.27 there has been a tendency to regard it as a formulation generated by the Abba consciousness.[7]

In spite of the intrinsic connexion of v.27 with a strongly based element of Jesus' own language, there still remain doubts as to its authenticity. Firstly, does not the affirmation of authority expressis verbis contrast with Jesus' own practice of simply assuming it?[8] Here it must be urged that the statement of authority in Mt 28.18, introduced by ἐδόθη, is to be distinguished from 11.27. The latter does not expressly mention ἐξουσία, though it certainly would provide a rationale for the authoritative Ἀμήν and ἐγώ. This rationale, it must be stress-

---

[1] E. Schweizer, art.cit. 366; also Mt 23.9, S.Dt.6.7. Cf. W. Grundmann, Die νήπιοι in der urchristlichen Paränese, NTS 5 (1959), 197.

[2] Jeremias, Prayers, 47f, argues that the definite articles are to be understood in a generic sense, so that v. 27b-d was originally a statement of general experience adopted by Jesus. This is not convincing in that the truth of such a general statement is doubtful! Moreover, v. 27a points the statement Christologically.

[3] Against it, Bultmann, Synoptic Tradition, 159; Kümmel, Promise, 41; Jeremias, Prayers, 48f. On the other hand, A. M. Hunter, art.cit. 244: 'The connexion with the preceding verses seems logical and natural.'

[4] Grundmann, art. cit. 202.

[5] Cf. Rom 2.20 διδάσκαλος νηπίων applied to the law-teaching Jew; Gal 4.3, where the νήπιοι are those under the law. Similarly, Hunter, art.cit. 243.

[6] Jeremias, Prayers, 48.

[7] So Hahn, Hoheitstitel, 329; Fuller, Beginnings, 115.

[8] Hahn, op.cit. 324.

ed, is must be located somewhere because the consequences stemming from it, involving a divergence from orthodoxy within Judaism,[1] cannot have been entertained without some justification in Jesus' mind. It is here that the question of setting becomes important. 11.25f is a prayer and private—and if v.27 belongs to a similar setting, which is probable, this difference of setting may explain differences in procedure. Jesus is explicit in secret, though implicit in public. With this coheres the fundamental restriction of Abba to Jesus and, only in derivation from him, to disciples,[2] as well as material such as Mk 4.11f and 11.28-33. In sum, παρεδόθη provides a link with the public and authoritative teaching of Jesus and explains the origin of his distinctive message, whether viewed in terms of authority or of content. Here Jesus gives the private explanation. Hence v.27 is earthed even more firmly in the historical practice of Jesus. Secondly, is Barrett correct to argue that the historically suspicious setting suggests secondary wording?[3] This is extremely doubtful. By virtue of content, vv.25f clearly belong to a situation where Jesus reflects on the rejection of his teaching by the Pharisees, and v.27 deals with what led in practice to such rejection. Therefore a setting for 11.25-27 emerges to neutralize this objection, and on the other hand, if v.27 does not belong with vv.25f, then objections in terms of its present position cannot be sustained.

In conclusion, Mt 11.27 is to be taken as a genuine saying of Jesus, coherent with the Abba complex and providing private explanation of what went unexplained in public. Here Jesus deals with legal and didactic matters, in which we have already seen a clash between him and the Pharisees,[4] and a rationale of his abnormal procedure is disclosed. From here a line leads naturally and directly to Lk 22.70/Jn 19.7 [5] and the final public declaration which secured his downfall.

---

[1] See above, pp. 110-112.

[2] Jeremias, Prayers, 53. That Jesus' Abba-consciousness was exceptional has recently been questioned by Hans Conzelmann, Outline, 103. Reliance on the fact that Jesus did not restrict to himself this form of address to God does not, however, meet the point that the use of it by others was derivative from Jesus and therefore in a special relationship to him. Moreover, the distinction between Jesus and disciples, implicit in the lack of 'our Father' references associating him with them, together with the nature of the Lord's Prayer as a distinguishing feature of Jesus and his circle (Jeremias, Prayers, 77; Marshall, 89-90; this is implied even by Rom 8.15, Gal 4.6) combine to show the distinctiveness of this usage in respect of Jesus.

[3] Jesus, 26f.

[4] See above, pp. 107-112.

[5] J. C. O'Neill, Charge of Blasphemy, 72-77, has argued that the formula-

At this point we have to set over against one another the varying
traditions, represented basically by Mark and Luke. It is the question
of literary relationship between these two sources which is of major
importance in determining whether Jesus was condemned on this
count. If Lk is totally dependent on Mk, it is possible but no more.
But if Lk is independent of Mk and provides a version not only stemming from a Semitic milieu but also earlier than Mk's version, which
itself also stems from a Semitic milieu, then, all other things being
equal, the case for condemnation on this count is extremely strong.
The next chapter will attempt to present the evidence.

APPENDIX: JEWS AND ROMANS IN THE ARREST OF JESUS

The arrest of Jesus plays a significant role in solving the problems
of the trial of Jesus, and in particular the balancing of religious and
political issues. It is important to know who did arrest him. From
Salvador to Winter it has been taken for granted by most Jewish scholars that the Romans arrested Jesus, Jn 18.3,12, though not all have
completely discounted Jewish participation. Christian scholars have
also frequently assumed without question that Jn intends to describe
Roman personnel by the terms σπεῖρα and χιλίαρχος [1] though such a
view was questioned by R. W. Husband and now again recently by
Josef Blinzler.[2]

---

tion of Jn 19.7, together with Mt 11.2-6, Mk 10.40, Ps. Sol. 17.22 and the saying
in Mt 11.27 = Lk 10.22 (when relieved of 'No one knows the Son save the
Father'), is to be understood in terms of God's exclusive right to reveal the identity of the messiah, and the consequent presumption and blasphemy of any man's
anticipating the divine decision and claiming this dignity for himself in advance.
But against this, (a) Jn 19.7 does not indicate that messianic ideas are connected
with this reference to Sonship; (b) if I understand the argument correctly, it is
precisely in the clause of Mt 11.27 which O'Neill regards as a gloss that the idea
of God's revealing the identity of the messiah would ex hypothesei be found,
but it would not be in the statement once this part were removed; (c) the statement in Ps. Sol. 17.22 that God knows the time when his messiah will be
raised up is not quite the same as the view that a man must wait for God before
claiming to be messiah; (d) σὺ λέγεις in Mk 15.2 would have to be interpreted
as evasive, which is not easy, cf. D. R. Catchpole, The Answer of Jesus, NTS
17, (1971), 213-226.
[1] e.g. W. Bauer, Das Johannes-evangelium. 2nd ed. Tübingen 1925, 203-205;
A. H. McNeile, The Gospel according to St. Matthew London 1915, 393; J. Wellhausen, Das Evangelium Johannes, Berlin 1908, 80; R. H. Lightfoot, St. John's
Gospel, Oxford 1956, 322; O. Cullmann, The State in the New Testament,
London 1957,45; C. H. Dodd, Historical Tradition in the Fourth Gospel, Cambridge 1963, 74; J. Schmid, Das Evangelium nach Markus, Regensburg 1963,
278; S. G. F. Brandon, Jesus and the Zealots, 329; J. Jeremias, Jerusalem in the
Time of Jesus, London 1969, 210.   [2] Prozeß, 4th ed. 90-95.

If σπεῖρα and χιλίαρχος do describe Roman persons, then Winter is almost certainly right that this rests on historial tradition [1] rather than a theological intention of showing Jesus' supremacy over the cosmic forces ranged against him,[2] or his relationship to the Roman state.[3] But against the immediate conclusion that Jn records a Roman or partly Roman arrest, it must be noticed that σπεῖρα describes a Jewish band in Jdth 14.11, 2 Macc 8.23, 12.20,22 (commanded by one of the Maccabees), and Josephus, Ant.17.215 where the σπεῖρα is commanded by a χιλίαρχος and sent by Archelaus. This last example is specially important as rebutting any attempt to argue from the cumulative force of the combination of σπεῖρα and χιλίαρχος in Jn 18 that these must be Roman in their implication. To these references must be added those where χιλίαρχος is certainly a Jewish officer, 1 Macc 3.55, Josephus B.J. 2.578 and Mk 6.21, and the texts where no national identity is implied, Rev 6.15, 19.18. These examples, balancing those where the words certainly indicate Roman persons,[4] are sufficient to neutralize the terms as terms. Even when B.J.2.224 and 5.244 speak of ἡ Ῥωμαικὴ σπεῖρα watching from the temple roof at Passover time, the specific limitation Ῥωμαική is required. And that these terms in Jn 18.3,12 are not intended to indicate a Roman party at all is suggested by the following considerations: (a) πρὸς ὑμᾶς ἐν τῷ ἱερῷ fits if Jesus is addressing Jews in general, or the temple police in particular,[5] but not if the main participants are Romans. Bultmann's suggestion that Mk 14.48f sounds like church apologetic and dogmatics [6] is not sufficient to dismiss a saying whose liability to misunderstanding about the political role of Jesus is sufficient authentication. (b) It is unlikely that Judas, particularly if Iscariot stems from the sicarius idea,[7] would have betrayed Jesus to the Romans and actively cooperated with them. Winter argues that λαβών, Jn 18.3, puts Judas in charge of the cohort and introduces a discrepancy between this verse and Jn 18.12, and further that because Judas plays practically no part in the pericope the mention of his name is secondary within the literary structure of the passage, the result of an

---

[1] On the Trial, 45f.

[2] So C.K.Barrett, John, 431-433, who regards Roman involvement as improbable since Jesus would then have been taken to Pilate immediately.

[3] So R. Bultmann, Jn, 493. (It is hard to see how Jn 18.1-12 does show anything of this relationship.) Similarly, H. W. Bartsch, NovT 7 (1964), 215.

[4] Acts 10.1, 21.31,33, Mk 15.16, Josephus, B. J. 2.205,318 etc.

[5] Contra the objection of J. Schmid, Mk, 279, that the saying does not fit its context.

[6] Synoptic Tradition, 269,282.

[7] Cullmann, State, 15; though against this, Hengel, Die Zeloten, 49.

attempt to harmonize the Johannine and synoptic accounts.[1] But against this Barrett's comment is correct, that λαβών probably indicates only the role of guide and instigator,[2] and the mention of Judas in 18.5 is theologically deliberate,[3] aiming to include him among those who bow at the divine Name spoken by Jesus. (c) That a Roman arrest party should have conveyed Jesus to Annas [4] is inherently unlikely, especially in view of Annas' deposition by the Romans, and it cannot claim support from Lysias' action in Acts 22.30 for the latter envisages a meeting of the Sanhedrin, the legally recognized authority, which Annas could not claim to be.[5] (d) The failure to arrest Peter, particularly after his provocative action—attested in both the Mk and Lk-Jn traditions [6]—is incomprehensible if Romans were acting against a supposed Zealot threat,[7] but reasonable if Jesus alone were the target for Jewish objection. (e) The passage Jn 18.4-11 may supply clues to the evangelist's interpretation of the event, and the retreat before the divine Name, although theological in conception rather than historical, suggests that the evangelist interpreted his material in the sense of a Jewish audience. The strong probability that the arrest party was Jewish is in no way weakened by Jn 18.12 where σπεῖρα and χιλίαρχος are distinguished from οἱ ὑπηρέται τῶν Ἰουδαίων, for οἱ Ἰουδαῖοι is not so much an ethnic term in much of Jn as a description of the Jeru-

---

[1] On the Trial, 44f. Winter stands apart from the conjecture of Loisy, The Origins of the New Testament, London 1950, 100, that Judas is an imaginative invention produced for the elaboration of the drama.

[2] John, 433.

[3] He already stands on the side of the Satanic opposition, Jn 13.2, which is being judged, Jn 12.31.

[4] Note that Annas is mentioned within the same sentence as that which includes the σπεῖρα and χιλίαρχος at 18.12. Winter does not discount the report that Jesus was detained in the high priest's house, op.cit. 47.

[5] Winter seems to be aware of this difficulty, op.cit.29: 'There is nothing incredible in the account of Jn 18.12,13,28a, which states that a Roman military commander, having arrested Jesus, conducted him to a local Jewish official with the order to prepare the judicial proceedings for the Procurator's court.' But any local Jewish official would hardly do, and only a legally recognized body would be allowed this function by the Romans. Winter's suggestion that both Annas and the χιλίαρχος are exaggeratedly high officials is unconvincing, raises more problems than it solves, and neglects the evidence from Acts of the prominent participation of Annas in anti-Christian proceedings.

[6] For a suggestion as to the intention of this action, cf. D. Daube, Three notes having to do with Johanan ben Zakkai, JTS 11 (1960), 61f. If Mark, for instance, were as politically sensitive as is often suggested (cf. Brandon, Trial, passim), he would hardly have invented this. Moreover, it serves no purpose within the church, either liturgical, kerygmatic, didactic or ethical.

[7] Winter, op.cit. 49f.

salem authorities, particularly when they range themselves against Jesus. With this correlates the proof by Blinzler [1] that ὑπηρέται represents legal officers attached specifically to the Sanhedrin. Nor does the possession of weapons constitute an objection (Edersheim)[2] or an illegality (Chwolson,[3] and recently Stauffer [4]) on the basis of Shabb. 6.4, supported by 1 Macc 2.34ff, 2 Macc 15.1ff, Josephus Contra Apionem 1.22, Ant. 14.63, B.J. 1.146 and Dio.Cass. 27.16. For Barrett [5] rightly draws attention to R. Eliezer's permission for carrying weapons, also cited in Shabb. 6.4; and the Maccabean examples agree with Josephus, but against Shabb 6.4, in prohibiting fighting unless in necessary self-defence. An arrest force could hardly go unarmed, and possession of weapons could be justified there too as a precaution in case self-defence was necessary, though not for active aggression. Against the view of Edersheim [6] that the temple guard were merely unarmed and untrained police stands Josephus, B.J. 4.293 τοὺς πλείονας ὄντας ἀνόπλους and Midd. 1.2.

The second focal point of the arrest narrative, Mk 14.48b,49, is used by Winter in the attempt to find 'trustworthy indications of the grounds for the arrest'.[7] He tries to prove that the 'crucial words' καθ' ἡμέραν should be translated 'in the hours of daylight', 'in the course of the day', 'by day', 'die' or 'tagsüber', rather than the more usual renderings 'day by day', 'quotidie' or 'täglich'.[8] Three reasons are

---

[1] op.cit. 126-128, as earlier Husband, op.cit.83f, Strack-Billerbeck, I, 290, against Winter's understanding of the ὑπηρέται as the temple guard, On the Trial, 45-48. In one point only does Blinzler's argument need modification: he restricts the temple police to the temple site and relates the normal activities of the ὑπηρέται to affairs outside. But this causes difficulties in Jn 7.32,45ff where, contra Blinzler's argument from silence, it does appear that the ὑπηρέται came to arrest Jesus actually inside the temple (cf. Acts 5.24-27). And Lk 22.52 must be placed against the use of the Acts 4.1 involvement of the στρατηγός τοῦ ἱεροῦ as evidence of the participation of the temple guard within the temple alone. It is very likely (especially in view of the relatedness of the Passion traditions in Lk and Jn, which Winter himself admits, op.cit.48), that the χιλίαρχος of Jn 18.12 and the στρατηγός of Lk 22.52 are identical. This would mean that the arrest party consisted of the Sanhedrin's officers and the temple guard under the leadership of the 'segan'.

[2] The attempt of Winter to find traces in the synoptics of Roman participation by way of the references to swords miscarries on the possession of swords by the disciples. Cf. Blinzler, op.cit. 92.

[3] Passamahl, 6.

[4] Jesus and his Story, 99.

[5] John, 39,42.

[6] Life and Times, 541.

[7] On the Trial, 49.

[8] When reviewing Winter's book, E. Schweizer criticized this theory in general

adduced for this: (a) In the Markan context Jesus had only been in the temple twice. (b) Jn 18.20 is a parallel saying using παῤῥησία, and καθ᾽ ἡμέραν should be understood as similarly stressing the public and open character of Jesus' activity. (c) In the context Jesus reproaches those who have come upon him by night as upon a guerilla fighter, and sets his role as διδάσκαλος over against the λῃστής question; to this corresponds the καθ᾽ ἡμέραν/κατὰ νύκτα contrast.

This view cannot be maintained. For the Markan scheme which shows signs of a theological structure [1] cannot be used to interpret a saying which Winter himself rightly regards as non-theological. Furthermore, Lk 19.47, 21.37, which Winter adduces in support,[2] say something quite opposite. Lk 21.37 reads ἦν δὲ τὰς ἡμέρας ἐν τῷ ἱερῷ διδάσκων, τὰς δὲ νύκτας ἐξερχόμενος ηὐλίζετο, and the plural and accusative (=extent of time) [3] prove that the sense is distributive.[4] The phrase τὸ καθ᾽ ἡμέραν in Lk 19.47, which is Lukan redaction, is proved by the parallel instances of the 'meaningless article',[5] Lk 11.3, Acts 17.11, 28(D), 19.9(D), not to have the meaning Winter wishes to draw from Mk 14.49. Similarly, Lk 9.23, redacting Mk 8.34, clearly uses καθ᾽ ἡμέραν as part of the Lukan adaptation to a long period of time, and therefore again the phrase is distributive. As regards the argument from Jn 18.20, Winter is correct that παῤῥησία deals with the charge of clandestine teaching,[6] but in Mk 14.49 the issue is not whether the teaching was secret or not, but that obvious opportunities to arrest the teacher had been neglected. The third point does not add any material evidence but does draw attention to the emphasis placed by Winter on λῃστής. Here he finds a trace of an early tradition that represented the arrest as a precaution against possible insurrectionist activities,[7] but this rests on two questionable assumptions: firstly, that the statement in Mk 14.48b is indicative (as in Luther's version) and not interrogative (as in Nestle-Kilpatrick, Nestle-Aland, R.V., R.S.V., and N.E.B.); secondly, that these defensive words of Jesus also express the legal ground of indictment. It follows that at this point, as well as where he argues for Roman involvement in the arrest party, Winter's interpretation of the arrest is open to question.

---

terms, EvTh 21 (1961), 238-240; but cf. Mk, 183: 'statt täglich ließe sich vielleicht tagsüber übersetzen; doch ändert sich damit sachlich kaum etwas'.

[1] D. Daube, The New Testament and Rabbinic Judaism, London 1956, 158-169.
[2] On the Trial, 173.   [3] C. F. D. Moule, Idiom Book, 34.
[4] Winter's interpretation would require a genitive singular.
[5] Blass-Debrunner, 88.
[6] On the Trial, 49; cf. above, p. 9.   [7] On the Trial, 50.

CHAPTER THREE

THE PROBLEM OF THE SANHEDRIN HEARING IN LUKE

A. INTRODUCTION

It is quite clear that the strongest objections raised against a Sanhedrin trial apply to the Markan account. Not only did Hans Lietzmann try to show that this was the only primary source [1] and that the Sanhedrin trial stood or fell with it, but more recently Eduard Lohse has adopted the same pattern of argument: firstly, to show the dependence of Lk 22.54-71 on Mk, and secondly, to explain Mk 14.55-64 as the result of Christian reflection.[2] The first of these has also frequently been adopted by defenders of the historicity of the trial.[3]

Very few of the difficulties in Mk apply, however, to Lk 22.54-71.[4] This can be seen at seven points: (a) Lohse argues that the temple saying Mk 14.58 is a floating logion which originally belonged elsewhere (perhaps in the cleansing of the temple),[5] and Lietzmann also thought it had been displaced, this time from its original setting in the Stephen material.[6] But wherever it came from, it is not in Lk 22.66-71. (b) Lietzmann and Lohse agree that the question: 'Are you the messiah, the Son of the Blessed?' is unthinkable in the mouth of a Jewish high priest [7] and stems from the later debate between Judaism and Christianity. But Lk has two separate questions and does not assimi-

---

[1] Der Prozeß Jesu, in Kleine Schriften II: Studien zum Neuen Testament, Berlin 1958, 251-263. Similarly, Lietzmann's pupil, J. Finegan, Die Überlieferung der Leidens- und Auferstehungs-Geschichte Jesu, Gießen 1934,35; 'Mt und Lc haben keine historische Quelle für die Leidensgeschichte ausserhalb Mc.' T. A. Burkill, The Competence of the Sanhedrin, VC 10 (1956), 80: 'Mark's gospel, where the Passion narrative is evidently presented in its earliest extant form.'

[2] Der Prozeß Jesu Christi, in Ecclesia und Res publica, Festschrift K. D. Schmidt, Göttingen 1962, 24-39; also in Die Geschichte des Leidens und Sterbens Jesu Christi, Gütersloh 1964, 84-86, and συνέδριον, TWNT 7 (1964), 868.

[3] e.g. J. Blinzler, Der Prozeß Jesu, 4th ed. Regensburg 1969, 170-173.

[4] H. Danby already posed the question in terms of the contrast of Mk and Lk in The Bearing of the Rabbinical Criminal Code on the Jewish Trial Narratives in the Gospels, JTS 21 (1920), 51-76, esp.60-64. See also W. E. Bundy, Jesus and the first three Gospels, Cambridge, Mass. 1955, 515-517.

[5] Prozeß, 35; Geschichte, 84.

[6] op.cit. 255.

[7] Lietzmann, op.cit. 255; Lohse, Geschichte, 85.

late the two concepts. (c) Following H. E. Tödt, Lohse regards Mk
14.62 as unauthentic.[1] It is however likely that Lk 22.69 is dependent
on Mk 14.62 and that its present position is secondary; [2] hence, objections to Lk 22.69 would not apply to Luke's original account if this is
independent and the saying itself an interpolation. (d) Lietzmann
stressed Mk's imprecision as to the content of the blasphemy, Mk
14.64.[3] Lohse also raises this objection: [4] the temple saying is not, pace
Kilpatrick,[5] the blasphemy, and nor is the messianic claim. Here it is
sufficient to note that Lk does not mention the term βλασφημία. (e)
Five legal infringements are, according to Lohse, presupposed by Mk
14.55-64.[6] These are: a session at night, a trial on a feast day, the omission of the statutory second session, the discrepancy between the
blasphemy and Sanh. 7.5, and finally the setting in the high priest's
house.[7] But the first, fourth and fifth vanish if we consider Lk,[8] and
the second and third could apply only if this is the record of a formal
trial and if the laws in question existed.[9] (f) Lohse says that the
conclusion is unavoidable 'daß die Perikope Mk 14.55-64 nicht als
historischer Bericht gewertet werden darf, sondern eine Bildung der
christlichen Gemeinde ist'.[10] He cites the O.T. passages which have
given rise to the material: Mk 14.62 is derived from Dan 7.13 and Ps
110.1, the false witnesses from Ps 27.12, the silence of Jesus from Is
53.7, and the mockery from Is 50.6. But, provided Lk 22.69 is discounted, none of the first three appear in Lk, and whereas Mk 14.65 is influenced from a literary point of view by the Servant motif, Lk 22.63-65

---

[1] Prozeß, 37.
[2] See below, pp. 157-159.
[3] op. cit. 255f.
[4] Geschichte, 80.
[5] The Trial of Jesus, London 1953, 11f.
[6] art. συνέδριον, 866. The same scheme is adopted by G. Haufe, Der Prozeß
Jesu im Lichte der gegenwärtigen Forschung, Die Zeichen der Zeit 22 (1968), 95.
[7] Lohse, Geschichte, 80, mentions that the 'Quaderhalle' was unavailable at
night because the Temple gates were shut. But Josephus, Ant. 18.29 mentions
that on Passover night, the gates were opened at midnight—and the Lukan
narrative certainly agrees with Nisan 15 chronology. Cf. Blinzler, op.cit.
168. Although b.A.Z. 8b mentions the movement of the Sanhedrin forty years
before the temple destruction, and is supported by Acts 22.30-23.10, there is no
proof that this move had already taken place at the time of Jesus. If it had, a
session elsewhere cannot be regarded as an irregularity in any Passion narrative.
Contra P. Winter, The Marcan Account of Jesus' Trial by the Sanhedrin, JTS
14 (1963), 99.
[8] συνέδριον 22.66, is almost certainly to be taken as a place. See pp. 191f.
[9] See pp. 258f.
[10] Prozeß, 37; Geschichte, 85-87; art. συνέδριον. 867.

is not. (g) Both Lietzmann and Lohse regard the lack of a known eye-witness source for the trial as a serious handicap.[1] This does apply equally to Mk and Lk, though Kümmel has questioned its seriousness.[2]

A very similar pattern of argument emerges therefore in the work of Lietzmann and Lohse, but it is a pattern almost totally integrated with the Markan material. Whereas the comparative insignificance of the objections to the Lukan narrative is sufficient to draw attention to its distinctiveness,[3] the arguments put forward by Lietzmann and Lohse are insufficient to demonstrate its dependence on Mk.[4] These, together with critique, are as follows:

(a) The transpositions of the Denial and Mockery reflect Luke's own judgement, as do similar changes in connection with the mockery in Mk 15.16-20 and the eschatological saying Mk 14.25/Lk 22.15-18. Such transpositions are not discordant with Lk's usual method[5] as shown, for instance, in his secondary ordering of the temptations, Lk 4.5-12, and the descriptions of the illness of the Gadarene demoniac, Lk 8.29 = Mk 5.4f. This view of Luke's method is also adopted by Blinzler, who writes of 'die schriftstellerische Technik des Evangelisten' and Luke's attempt to give the story 'den Charakter eines fortlaufenden Berichtes'.[6] But against these arguments several points must be made. Firstly, the original order of the temptations is scarcely demonstrable, but the likelihood is that Luke preserves and Matthew changes the original order of Q.[7] Secondly, Lk 8.29 = Mk 5.4f is a small change

---

[1] Lietzmann, op.cit. 254; Lohse, Geschichte, 83; similarly, G. Bornkamm, Jesus, 163; P. Winter, On the Trial, 6.

[2] Promise and Fulfilment, London 1961, 50.

[3] So even Lohse, Prozeß, 38; 'Der lukanische Bericht kommt dem tatsächlichen Verlauf der Vorgängs näher als die Berichte bei Markus und Matthäus.' This statement crystallizes the marked divergence between Lietzmann and Lohse in historical reconstruction.

[4] Lietzmann, 251: 'Lukas verfährt aber mit größerer Freiheit als Matthäus bei seiner Benutzung, und zeigt ein bemerkenswertes Geschick in der Gestaltung der Erzählung.'

[5] Lietzmann, op.cit. 252; cf. H. F. D. Sparks, St. Luke's Transpositions, NTS 3 (1957), 220.

[6] Prozeß, 171.

[7] It is scarcely convincing when E. E. Ellis, The Gospel of Luke, London 1966, 93, argues that Luke wishes to construct a climax at the temple: against this, K. H. Rengstorf already, Das Evangelium nach Lukas. 11th ed. Göttingen 1966, 63. The argument of E. Haenchen that Luke wishes to bring Jesus down after a spell 'in die Höhe . . . in die Luft' (Der Weg Jesu, 72), is no stronger, since the same rationalizing would apply after a period on a pinnacle of the temple. It is more likely that the Matthaean order is secondary, and stems from this evangelist's keen interest in mountains as places of Jesus' authority, cf. 5.1, 28.18-20.

within one incident, rather than a change in the relative order of two separate incidents. Thirdly, Lk 22.15-18 has been shown by Heinz Schürmann [1] to be independent of Mk 14.25, therefore the question of transposition does not arise. Fourthly, Jeremias has argued convincingly that Luke is the enemy of transpositions,[2] and to the evidence cited by Jeremias can be added reasons for believing that on the two occasions when Luke does transpose Markan incidents he is forcibly constrained to do so, and would have given what he would regard as a seriously distorting impression had he not done so.[3] Fifthly, when dealing with transpositions Blinzler refers favourably to the suggestion of Conzelmann [4] that the change in relative order of Petrine denial and Sanhedrin hearing is intended to contrast Confessor and Denier. But such a contrast could hardly be sharper than in Mk 14.53-72, as Paul Winter has correctly seen.[5] In fact the connection and

---

[1] Der Paschamahlbericht, Münster 1953, 1-74; similarly, Jeremias, Eucharistic Words, 160-164.

[2] Perikopen-Umstellungen bei Lukas?, NTS 4 (1958), 115-119; similarly, A. M. Perry, The Sources of Luke's Passion Narrative, Chicago 1920, 25; F. Rehkopf, Die lukanische Sonderquelle, Tübingen 1959, 1-5.

[3] 1. Lk 6.17-19. This occurred before Lk 6.12-16 in the Markan source, and without the transposition the Q-L material in the Sermon on the Plain would have followed the call of the twelve apostles. The contents of the sermon prohibited this, since some of it, e.g. 6.24-26,46, is demonstrably inappropriate. Hence the audience had to be broadened to others beside disciples, cf.7.1. At the same time, Luke is concerned to extend the circle of disciples who hear. Hence, whereas Mk 3.8 had a movement towards Jesus on the part of those who *had* heard, i.e. in general terms about Jesus' miracle-working activity, Lk 6.17 has them coming to Jesus *in order to* hear. And the personnel involved are not merely 'disciples', Mk 3.7, but 'a great multitude of disciples'.

2. Lk 8.19-21. This occurred before Lk 8.4-18 in the Markan source. Had Luke not transposed, he would have moved out of L material Lk 8.1-3, 'The ministering women', straight into the 'Christ's real brethren' incident. The juxtaposition of the two would suggest not merely that family ties were less valuable than those of discipleship, but also, by the contrast with distinct persons, imply the total rejection of Mary and the brothers. Such a view is certainly not Luke's (pace Conzelmann, Theology, 48). Lk reflects the situation in which Jesus' family do belong to the church, cf. Acts 1.14; ref. J. M. Creed, The Gospel according to St. Luke. London 1942, 118. Luke's internal redaction of Mk 3.31-35 carefully avoids any contrary suggestion. The question τίς ἐστιν ἡ μήτηρ μου καὶ οἱ ἀδελφοί Mk 3.33, is expunged, and so is the expansive gesture towards οἱ περὶ αὐτὸν κύκλῳ καθημένοι which gives an explicit personal contrast, disciples v. family. In Lk, the higher family relationship can and does include earthly family whereas in Mk there is no indication that it does. (The alleged parallel between ἰδεῖν Lk 8.20 and σημεῖον ἰδεῖν 23.8 is fanciful: contra Conzelmann op.cit. 48.)

[4] The Theology of Saint Luke, London 1960, 84.

[5] On the Trial, 23-25.

contrast are actualy weakened in Lk by the intervening mockery, 22.63-65.

(b) Dependence on Mk is shown, according to Lohse, by the repetition of the Son of man saying. Luke retains the Dan 7.13 + Ps 110.1 connection but characteristically omits the reference to the Parousia. Hence his version is shown to be less old than that of Mk.

A different approach to Lk 22.69 has been opened up by E. Bammel,[1] and also subsequently by C. Colpe.[2] Bammel argues that Lk 22.69 is an independent tradition, since: 1. This form contains the minimal statement.[3] 2. A Lukan Tendenz is not perceptible. 3. The text-form is pre-Lukan, modified only by the redundant θεοῦ.[4] 4. The work of Rehkopf,[5] demonstrating that Luke has used old material for the Passion narrative, gives to the Lukan text the status of an independent source. And Lk 22.69 is closer to the form of Acts 7.56 which is probably the best tradition of Jesus' wording.

I would venture, if I may, to disagree with these arguments. Certainly Lk 22.69 says less than Mk 14.62, but there are analogous examples of redactional compression,[6] e.g. Lk 9.27 = Mk 9.1. The absence of καὶ ἐρχόμενον μετὰ τῶν νεφελῶν τοῦ οὐρανοῦ in fact coheres with the wording ἔσται as against ὄψεσθε. And it is precisely in the ἔσται that Luke avoids the unfulfilled prediction of the Sanhedrin's vision of the Son of man, and also reveals his Tendenz. This Tendenz consists in the correction of the Son of man's present humiliation and suffering by the immediate exaltation—two features bound together in time by the Passion itself, and eternally by the divine δεῖ.[7] Further on

---

[1] Erwägungen zur Eschatologie Jesu, TU 88 (1964), 3-32.

[2] art. ὁ υἱὸς τοῦ ἀνθρώπου TWNT 8 (1967), 438.

[3] Colpe has a different view from Bammel of the original sense of the term Son of man, but in dealing with Lk 22.69 the argumentation is fairly parallel: 'Die auch sonst sekundär wiederverwendete Wendung aus Da 7,13 (mit der den dortigen Sinn verändernden Beziehung der μετὰ τῶν νεφελῶν τοῦ οὐρανοῦ nur auf ἐρχόμενον) ist hier noch nicht angefügt.' Colpe finds significant the coherence of Lk 22.69 with the overall picture presented by the genuine Son of man material, i.e. purely heavenly judicial activity in which the Son of man is appointed judge (rather than advocate).

[4] Similarly, Colpe art.cit. 438.

[5] Die lukanische Sonderquelle, Tübingen, 1959.

[6] J. Wellhausen, Das Evangelium Lucae, Berlin 1904, 130. It is because of a totally eschatological context, unconnected with the immediate audience, that the Parousia reference in Lk 21.27f remains unmodified. Hence the latter is not quite 'geradezu konträre' (Bammel, art.cit. 24).

[7] E. Fascher, Theologische Beobachtungen zu δεῖ, in Neutestamentliche Studien für Rudolf Bultmann, Berlin 1954, 238-240; G. W. H. Lampe, The Lucan Portrait of Christ, NTS 2 (1956), 166f; H. Conzelmann, Luke, 153. It is difficult

this saying, the words τοῦ θεοῦ are certainly Lukan redaction,[1] but the periphrasis τῆς δυνάμεως is too strong an overlap with Mk 14.62 to be coincidental. Finally, Rehkopf (and Schürmann) have indeed demonstrated the independence and antiquity of the Lukan narrative, but within this narrative there occurs occasionally the superimposition of Markan detail.[2] This would seem to be the case in Mk 14.62 = Lk 22.69.

The relationship between Acts 7.56 and the synoptic sayings belongs, strictly speaking, to the area of Traditionsgeschichte rather than source criticism. However it is noteworthy that although Acts 7.56 and Lk 22.69 agree against Mk 14.62 in having no Parousia reference,[3] yet Lk 22.69 and Mk 14.62 agree against Acts 7.56 in the words τῆς δυνάμεως and the καθήμενος reference. Lk 22.69 also appears closer to, and in the light of the argumentation above, more recent than Mk 14.62 when the probable meaning of Acts 7.56 is exposed. The latter could be influenced by Dan 7.13 LXX καὶ οἱ παρεστηκότες παρῆσαν αὐτῷ,[4] but this falls short of proof. The formulation as we have it is most probably a description of the Son of man acting as witness for the defence,[5] precisely on the Lk 12.8 pattern.[6] It is not possible, unfortunately, to prove whether Acts 7.56 owes its form to Luke or to source material. Very probably Luke is using a source, as Haenchen[7]

---

to agree with E. Ruckstuhl, Die Chronologie des letzten Mahles und des Leidens Jesu, Zurich 1963, 41, that Luke's form with ἀπο τοῦ νῦν is more difficult to understand, and therefore more primitive.

[1] A typical Lukan editorial emphasis, cf. Lk 4.43, 5.26, 6.12, 8.11,39, 9.20, 18.43.   [2] Rehkopf, op.cit. 84.

[3] Contra H. P. Owen, Stephen's vision in Acts vii. 55-56, NTS 1 (1955),224-226. See on this Tödt, Son of man, 304.

[4] Lampe, art. cit. 172; Tödt, Son of man, 303 f.

[5] O. Cullmann, The Christology of the New Testament, 2nd ed. London 1963, 157 f; A. J. B. Higgins, Jesus and the Son of man, London 1964, 144-146; Bammel, art. cit. 25 f; C. F. D. Moule, The Phenomenon of the New Testament, London 1967, 90 f.

[6] The legal bearing of Lk 12.8 is widely accepted, whatever the view of its authenticity; cf. P. Vielhauer, Aufsätze zum Neuen Testament, München 1965, 102.

[7] E. Haenchen, Die Apostelgeschichte, 14th ed. Göttingen 1965, 243, points out the plural οἱ οὐρανοί which may go back to 'shamayim', contrasts with the singular in 7.55, and is not typical of Luke. Similarly, H. Traub, art. οὐρανός TDNT 5 (1967), 530. There is only one other plural in Acts:οὐ γὰρ Δαυὶδ ἀνέβη εἰς τοὺς οὐρανούς, 2.34. The logic of the argument at this place is paralleled in Acts 13.36f which may well, in terms of content and form, depend on traditional material, too. See M. Wilcox, The Semitisms of Acts, Oxford 1965, 178, and, with modifications, J. W. Bowker, Speeches in Acts: a Study in Proem and Yellamedenu Form, NTS 14 (1967), 101-105. By extension therefore, Acts 2.34 probably uses tradition.

and Colpe [1] have argued. But this does not preclude editorial activity in connection with the function of the Son of man, and since this has happened at Lk 12.8 [2] the Acts 7.56 presentation of the 'advocate Son of man' may be a Lukan assimilation to that pattern.[3] In contrast, neither Mk 14.62 nor Lk 22.69 give the Son of man this defensive role. Hence Lk 22.69 is best taken as a redaction of Mk 14.62 by Luke, edited and interpolated according to his own design.

If then Lohse is correct that Lk 22.69 is dependent on Mk 14.62, it by no means follows that this verse takes its context with it. In fact it causes dislocation in its context,[4] the δέ in 22.69 being too weak to bind it to what precedes in 22.67b,68. The narrative reads quite smoothly once this logion and possibly οὖν ,22.70,[5] are removed.

(c) Lohse also argues that dependence on Mk explains the loosening of the connection between the trial and Peter's denial, as well as the shortening of the account of the hearing.[6] It is difficult to understand why this is so, since it is equally possible that the evolution of the tradition should tighten the connection between the two events, and expand or remould the earlier form. That this is indeed the case is supported by the fact that the 'sandwich structure' whereby the trial is

---

[1] Colpe, art.cit. 465, adds also the replacement of ἰδεῖν by θεωρεῖν (cf. 7.55), and the addition of δόξα θεοῦ in the introduction, implying that Luke is giving his own introduction to a traditional saying.

[2] See J. Jeremias, Die älteste Schicht der Menschensohn-Logien, ZNW 58 (1967), 159-172.

[3] This is perhaps more likely than the suggestion of C. K. Barrett that this is an individual parousia of the Son of man to the Christian at the moment of his death. Stephen and the Son of man, in Apophoreta, Festschrift E. Haenchen, Berlin 1964, 32-38. If Tödt is right, op.cit. 303-305, that synoptic material intends to relate advocacy of the Son of man to the parousia or judgment, then Acts 7.56 is a case of realised eschatology, cf. Lk 23.43. C. F. D. Moule writes of the Son of man title in Acts 7.56 having been 'subtly and convincingly adapted to a distinctly post-resurrection martyr-situation'. The Christology of Acts, in Studies in Luke-Acts, ed. L. E. Keck—J. L. Martyn, London 1968, 164. This would further support the link with Lk 12.8 upon which Conzelmann (who does not accept the authenticity of any Son of man sayings) accurately comments, that the distinction is not between two people but between two epochs in the work of the same person: An Outline of the Theology of the New Testament, London 1969, 136.

[4] H. Flender, St Luke: Theologian of Redemptive History, London 1967, 45, rightly remarks that 'the transition from v.68 to v.69 is abrupt'. He does not however go on to ask why this abruptness should have been tolerated in a narrative which is, ex hypothesei, being editorially moulded according to a highly christological pattern.

[5] See p. 197.

[6] Prozeß, 27; Geschichte, 72.

inserted into the version of the denial is typically Markan,[1] and there are countless examples within the gospels of expansion of an earlier more summary form. Both the features in question may well therefore mark out the Lukan Sonderquelle from Mk.

It is now possible to compare in detail the three incidents which make up Lk 22.54-71 with the corresponding parallels in Mk 14.53-72.

B. PETER'S DENIAL: LK 22.54b-61 = MK 14.54,66-72.

Many scholars who favour some degree of Lukan independence of Mk in the Passion narrative as a whole have yet questioned the independence of the account of Peter's denial.[2] On the other hand F. Rehkopf has urged that Luke does give us a second independent account by reason of its coherence with the pre-Lukan passage Lk 22.33f.[3] Now concerning Rehkopf's suggestion: 1. If he is right, on Lk 22.34 at least, then the Sonderquelle must have had an account of Peter's denial, or the story would have left a word of Jesus unfulfilled.[4] 2. If he is wrong about 22.34,[5] an account of the denial is not thereby excluded from the Sonderquelle, provided 22.61b is pruned away. There are however small traces of pre-Lukan usage in 22.61b, and so Rehkopf's

---

[1] See pp. 177-179.

[2] B. H. Streeter, The Four Gospels, London 1961, 217; V. Taylor, Behind the third Gospel, Oxford 1926, 48f; P. Winter, The Treatment of his Sources by the third Evangelist in Lk 21-24, StTh 7 (1953), 138-172, esp. 161f; H. Schürmann, Jesu Abschiedsrede, Münster 1957, 34, but contrast p.140 where Lk 22.61 is included in non-Markan material, and resistance raised against the suggestion that this, together with 22.43,51, 23.2, 24.10f, is artistic invention by Luke.

[3] Sonderquelle, 84. Rehkopf argues this on the following grounds: (a) The consistent introduction of direct speech, 22.33f, with ὁ δὲ εἶπεν (αὐτῷ). (b) The addresses κύριε, 22.33 = Jn 13.37, and Πέτρε, 22.34. (c) The translation variants πρὶν ἤ (Mk-Mt)/ ἕως (Lk-Jn). (d) The readiness to die, cf. Jn 13.37. (e) Extensive agreement of form and content with Jn 13.37f. (f) The literary reminiscence of 2 Sam 15.23. (g) The different setting, as compared with Mk, of Lk 22.31-34 and 22.33.

[4] It is not possible to argue on the basis of Lk 24.6-8 that the fulfilment of Jesus' words is the concern of the Sonderquelle as much as it is of Luke (cf. 18.34), since 24.6-8, like 17.25 and Acts 3.18, must be taken as Lukan editorial work. Cf. C. F. Evans, The Kerygma, JTS 7 (1956), 37f. J. A. T. Robinson, Twelve New Testament Studies, London 1962, 146; E. Schweizer, Zu den Reden der Apostelgeschichte, in Neotestamentica, Zürich 1963, 419; otherwise, Colpe, art.cit. 462. It is however inconceivable that any narrative or source would mention the prediction of such an event as Peter's denial without describing the event itself: A. Schlatter, Das Evangelium des Lukas, Stuttgart 1931, 436.

[5] A. M. Perry, op.cit. 41, and P. Winter, Treatment, 159, both think 22.34 is drawn from Mk 14.30; more powerfully, H. Schürmann, Abschiedsrede, 27-35.

conclusion is strengthened at this point.[1] On a broader front the evidence can be set out as follows.

1. *The common vocabulary*

Streeter cited Hawkins' list of material drawn from Mk and noted that 'it includes nearly all the passages which deal with Peter's denial'.[2] Hawkins had however spoken with certainty about only vv.54b,61 (where dependence on Mk had not caused any embarrassment to earlier advocates of the Sonderquelle![3]) and with hesitation about vv.55f,59f. It will be noted that vv.57f are omitted, though it is evident that these two verses could not exist in isolation. Streeter's view has been maintained by V. Taylor, who states that 'this passage has no less than half its words in common with Mark', and he continues by arguing, rather surprisingly: 'If we ask why, in this case, the percentage is not even greater than it is, an important part of the answer lies in the fact that the narrative includes three very similar questions addressed to Peter, and three similar answers. It is hardly to be wondered at that in reproducing the story there should be a considerable amount of variation in the wording of these questions and answers.'[4] But this is to beg the question. For the differences cannot of themselves suggest redaction of Mk, and may equally be due to a separate tradition, as will indeed be argued. Yet overall, Taylor's claim has been widely echoed,[5] and particular attention has been drawn to the points of overlap he proposed: (a) Peter following from afar, v.54b; (b) πρὸς τὸ φῶς, v.56; (c) καὶ γὰρ Γαλιλαῖός ἐστιν, v.59; (d) καὶ ὑπεμνήσθη ὁ Πέτρος τοῦ ῥήματος . . . . ὡς εἶπεν αὐτῷ ὅτι Πρὶν ἀλέκτορα φωνῆσαι . . . ἀπαρνήσῃ με τρίς.[6] To these, Bailey added: (e) παιδίσκη, v.56; (f) the close similarity of v.57 and Mk 14.70; (g) ἐπ' ἀληθείας, v.59.[7]

Not all of these will be examined in the present section, but the following points are here appropriate:

First, πρὸς τὸ φῶς, v.56, is parallel to Mk 14.54. φῶς is too unusual a

---

[1] Contra H. Schürmann, Abschiedsrede, 22-27.

[2] op.cit. 217. J. C. Hawkins, in Oxford Studies in the Synoptic Problem, Oxford 1911, 77.

[3] e.g. B. Weiss, Die Quellen des Lukas-Evangeliums, Berlin 1907, 154f.

[4] Behind the Third Gospel, Oxford 1926, 48.

[5] Winter, Treatment, 162: 'The verbal agreement with Mark is so great that we must assume that the Third Evangelist knew this account from the Second Gospel—though he could have had access to other information.' Cf. J. A. Bailey, The Traditions common to the Gospels of Luke and John, Leiden 1963, 55.

[6] Behind the Third Gospel, 48.

[7] Traditions, 56.

word for fire for the two instances of πρὸς τὸ φῶς to be independent
But the sentence is positively improved if the words καθήμενον πρὸς
τὸ φῶς are removed, since (a) this is the third reference in two sentences to Peter's sitting; and (b) Luke has already described the fire as πῦρ
in v.55; and (c) as it stands the subject of the sentence, παιδίσκη τις
divides the two members of the object, αὐτὸν .... καθήμενον. If Luke
has constructed the whole sentence in v.56 he has departed from his
normal practice of changing order for the better,[1] whereas if all but
καθήμενον πρὸς τὸ φῶς were pre-Lukan he has merely introduced an
extra phrase rather clumsily. On the other hand, B. Weiss[2] argues too
far when he wishes to exclude from the special source (=S) everything from ἰδοῦσα δὲ αὐτόν to ἀτενίσασα αὐτῷ εἶπεν and to replace it
with εἶπεν δὲ εἷς. For (a) his appeal to the εἷς/ἕτερος pairing as in Lk
18.10, 23.40 is to texts which are not actually parallel, for in these cases
a pair has been specifically described, with first one and then the other
being singled out—whereas in 22.56-58 the first challengers are part of
a trio and not contrasted with one another. Also the definite article
ὁ εἷς/ὁ ἕτερος is used in 18.10, 23.40 but not here. (b) The address
γύναι, v.57, coheres with the reference, and is a pre-Lukan characteristic.[3] (c) Although the σὺν αὐτῷ reference would recall Jesus (αὐτόν,
v.54) very neatly if v.56 αὐτόν (=Peter), ... αὐτῷ were not present,
yet the apparent interruption of a reference to Peter in no way weakens
the unmistakable reference to Jesus in the challenger's words. (d) The
objection that Peter is not addressed in καὶ οὗτος σὺν αὐτῷ ἦν is value-
less because v.56a, the introduction, does not imply that the girl spoke
to Peter (N.B. ἀτενίσασα αὐτῷ εἶπεν, not εἶπεν αὐτῷ). Hence the intruding material is probably limited to καθήμενον πρὸς τὸ φῶς.

Second, καὶ γὰρ Γαλιλαῖός ἐστιν, v.59. This fits less than smoothly
with the preceding statement ἐπ' ἀληθείας καὶ οὗτος μετ' αὐτοῦ ἦν, where
as it was appropriate as evidence for ἀληθῶς ἐξ αὐτῶν εἶ, Mk 14.70.
(a) Mk's assertion refers to membership of the band of disciples, and
uses the present tense; Luke refers to association with Jesus in the past.
(b) The μετ' αὐτοῦ, referring to a specific accompaniment of Jesus
corresponds to Jn 18.26 both in wording and meaning: οὐκ ἐγώ σε
εἶδον ἐν τῷ κήπῳ μετ' αὐτοῦ. (c) If Luke has drawn καὶ γὰρ Γαλιλαῖός
ἐστιν from Mk, and redacted ἐξ αὐτῶν εἶ into μετ' αὐτοῦ ἦν he has not

---

[1] H. J. Cadbury, The Style and literary Method of Luke, Cambridge, Mass.
1920, 152.
[2] op.cit. 155.
[3] Rehkopf, op.cit. 98.

clarified but rather disturbed the Markan version, and has made a change which, on the theory of Markan redaction, he did not bother to do in Mk 14.69/Lk 22.58.

Third, when the two glosses above are removed, the statistics of common vocabulary are as follows: Mk has 151 words and Lk 119; there are 38 words which are exactly parallel, and 6 more in common though syntactically different. This means that the precise overlap with Mk in Lk's account is 31.9%. According to Taylor [1] problems arise when the figure is lower than 50%. Moreover Taylor's claim that there is an even distribution of common words [2] is not adequate because, firstly, he himself singles out 22.61, and if this were excluded the overlap becomes very thin, and secondly, the words concerned are, with the exception of παιδίσκη, μακρόθεν, ἰδοῦσα and the statement of v.61, such that the story of Peter's denial could hardly be told without them.[3] Words such as καί, δέ, ὁ Πέτρος, ἠρνήσατο, αὐτῷ/αὐτόν scarcely prove dependence and yet they account for 17 of the overlap words, whereas in the crucial and characteristic features of each narrative there is virtually no overlap.

Fourth, it is convenient to deal with the other two major parallelisms here. The first of these is ὁ δὲ Πέτρος ἠκολούθει μακρόθεν, v.54b. This is probably not a Markan element intruded into S.[4] (a) Some explanation of Peter's presence in the αὐλή, v.55, is required, and it is not convincing to suggest that this statement is superfluous because the S version of the arrest did not explicitly record the flight of the disciples.[5] (b) The change from aorist ἠκολούθησεν to imperfect ἠκολούθει is not in line with Luke's normal tendency.[6] ἠκολούθει is also a point of contact between Lukan and Johannine material (Jn 18.15). (c) The removal of the object αὐτῷ would be contrary to Luke's usual preference for completing sentences where lack of subject or object causes obscurity.[7] All this makes use of a separate source here very probable [8] though it cannot be affirmed with certainty.

Fifth, Lk 22.61: ὡς εἶπεν αὐτῷ ὅτι πρὶν ἀλέκτορα φωνῆσαι σήμερον

---

[1] ET 71 (1959), 69.
[2] Behind the Third Gospel, 48.
[3] This is a consideration to which Taylor himself on occasion appeals, ET 71 (1959), 70.
[4] Contra Perry, op.cit. 41; B. Weiss, op.cit. 154.
[5] B. Weiss, op.cit. 155.
[6] Cadbury, Style, 149-152.
[7] Cadbury, op.cit. 149-152.
[8] Contra Taylor, Behind the Third Gospel, 48.

ἀπαρνήσῃ με τρίς. It is surprising that Taylor should attach so much weight to the overlap with Mk 14.72, for in other places, e.g. Mk 14.62 = Lk 22.69, such verbal parallelism does not deter him from suggesting an alternative source. There are a number of supporting parallels within the gospels, where the wording is remarkably similar and yet where there are two traditions present, e.g. Mk and Q.[1] In the case of Lk 22.61 the overlap is probably of this sort for the following reasons. (a) The word σήμερον occurs in Lk but not in Mk. It belongs to a Jewish time-reckoning. But Luke can hardly have inserted it since he normally changes away from Jewish time notes,[2] as part of a general de-Judaizing tendency.[3] And it is not sufficient to argue that 22.61 depends on the σήμερον in 22.34 because on that showing Luke has quite without reason modified the word-order.[4] Moreover, the word cannot be regarded as inserted in the interests of the salvation-historical view of Luke: not only are the other 'today' references of that sort very clearly theological, but they also occur within Q-L sections, with the single redactional exception of Lk 5.26 (=Mk2.12).[5] If then

---

[1] The following are examples of close verbal parallelism coexisting with independence of sources: 1. The Beelzebub controversy in Mk 3.23-30 and Q: Mt 12.35-37 = Lk 11.17-23. Cf. F. G. Downing, Towards the Rehabilitation of Q, NTS 11 (1965), 169-176. 2. The parable of the mustard seed in Mk 4.30-32 and Q: Mt 13.31f = Lk 13.18f. Cf. G. D. Kilpatrick, The Origins of the Gospel according to St. Matthew, Oxford 1946, 10; E. Haenchen, Weg, 172. 3. The christological preaching of John the baptist in Mk 1.7f and Q: Mt 3.11 = Lk 3.16. That Q material is involved here is shown by the agreement of Mt and Lk in ἐν πνεύματι ἁγίῳ as against the lack of preposition in Mk, the word order ὑμᾶς βαπτίσει as against βαπτίσει ὑμᾶς, the scheme in which the 'stronger one' saying is inserted within the two halves of the saying contrasting the baptisms, and finally the agreement in the words καὶ πυρί which proves that a saying about the coming baptizer must have been in Q.

[2] See W. Grundmann, Das Evangelium nach Lukas, 192, on Mk 9.2 = Lk9.28. To this can be added the healing of the epileptic child (Lk 9.37-43 = Mk 9.14-29) which is placed by Luke on the day following (τῇ ἑξῆς ἡμέρᾳ) the transfiguration, which was itself placed in the night by Luke, Conzelmann, Luke, 58, Grundmann, Lk, 192. But on a Jewish time-reckoning it would not have been the next day, but the same day.

[3] Thus cf. the change in ἐξουσία, Lk 4.31-37, so that it no longer has the rabbinic sense but is parallel with δύναμις; the change from ῥαββί to ἐπιστάτα Lk 9.33, or to κύριε Lk18.41; the change of sense for εὐλόγησεν, Lk 9.16; the dropping of ἀρχὴ ὠδίνων in Mk 13.8 (Lk 21.11).

[4] An indication of Luke's mathematical precision in such repetitions is provided by the exact reproduction of the wording of sayings quoted earlier: Lk 7.20(19), Lk 19.34(31), cf. the parallelism in Lk 15.18,21(L).

[5] Lk 4.16-30 is not dependent on Mk 6.1-6. B. Violet, Zum rechten Verständnis der Nazareth-Perikope Lc 4.16-30, ZNW 37 (1938), 251-261; J. Jeremias, Jesus' Promise to the Nations, London 1958, 41-46.

σήμερον, v.61, is not redactional, the sentence in which it is embedded cannot be Markan. (b) The introduction to the saying ὑπεμνήσθη ὁ Πέτρος τοῦ λόγου τοῦ κυρίου would stand awkwardly without a citation of the saying itself,[1] and this introduction shows signs of pre-Lukan traits. The use of κύριος in the narrative points this way, even though Rehkopf[2] states a statistic '18mal Lk = 16mal L'. In fact it occurs six times in Q passages,[3] in Lk but not in Mt, and since Matthew would be unlikely to remove it once it was in, these six Lukan examples must be regarded as redactional at some stage. But Caird's judgment is correct in this case: 'The usage is clearly editorial, for it occurs in both Q and L passages; but, as it never occurs when Luke is editing Mark, it cannot be regarded as characteristic of the final redaction of the Gospel.'[4] It is quite true that Luke never redacts it into Mk:[5] in 19.31 he draws it from Mk 11.3, and 19.34 is a repetition of 19.31. Hence it is very unlikely that he is responsible for a redaction at Lk 22.61. Indebtedness to S here would cohere with seven clear cases in L[6] and another in the Passion narrative at a point where there is clear dependence on early tradition, 24.34 (cf. 1 Cor 15.5).[7] Further indications of dependence on S in Lk 22.61 emerge from the parallel τὸ ῥῆμα, Mk 14.72/τοῦ λόγου,[8] Lk 22.61. In such a context we would expect Luke to tend towards ῥῆμα rather than λόγος. Firstly, he uses ῥῆμα in redaction at 9.45b (Mk 9.32), 18.34 (18.13 = Mk 10.34), 20.26 (Mk 12.17) and 24.8. The example 20.26 shows how Luke's instincts are towards ῥῆμα, for the incident uses λόγος earlier (Mk 12.13 = Lk 20.20); in this case Luke's tendency has overcome the urge towards consistency of style. Moreover, whereas λόγος has a general reference, the redactional uses of ῥῆμα refer to a specific saying rendered at that point. Since 22.61 would fit this, it is the more surprising that ῥῆμα does not occur, if, that is, Luke is using Mk. Secondly, Luke retains

---

[1] Contra B. Weiss, op.cit. 156; A. M. Perry, Sources, 44,190.
[2] Sonderquelle, 95.
[3] Lk 7.19, 10.1, 11.39, 12.42, 17.5f.
[4] Saint Luke, London 1963, 26.
[5] Similarly, W. E. Bundy, Jesus and the first three Gospels, 522; W. Bussmann, Synoptische Studien III, Halle 1931, 110 also accepts κύριος as evidence of an earlier source. Yet in III.125 he does not include 22.61 in the Sonderquelle and confines the Denial narrative in S to vv.55,59a.
[6] Lk 7.13, 10.39,41, 13.15, 16.8, 18.6, 19.8.
[7] Cf. Jeremias, Eucharistic Words, 101-103; Haenchen, Weg, 366.
[8] This reading is accepted by Nestle-Aland and Kilpatrick; the variant ῥήματος is probably an assimilation to the text of Mt or Mk.

λόγος in Markan sentences 9 times but discards it 6 times.[1] Three of these examples are explicable in terms of the overloading of the Markan context with λόγος instances [2] and in another case the whole introduction has been remoulded (Lk 5.17 = Mk 2.2). In Mk 5.36 (Lk 8.50) and 10.22 (Lk 18.23), λόγος has the ordinary meaning 'saying' and Luke drops it in line with his tendency to use the word λόγος for more kerygmatic/didactic material. The insertion of λόγος at this point would be inconsistent with normal Lukan redaction, but its original occurrence here would be consistent with other instances in the Passion narrative, 23.9, 24.17,19, as well as its varied use in the L strand, 4.22, 5.1, 7.17, 10.39, 11.28, 16.2.

From this evidence it appears that the verbal parallelism of Lk and Mk in the Denial narrative is not so suggestive of literary dependence as Taylor and others have claimed. All the instances cited by Taylor and most of those mentioned by Bailey have already been examined; the rest will be covered in other sections.

2. *The time scheme*

Mk and Lk give seriously divergent time schemes [3] as the following chart makes plain:

	*	Denial 1: Lk 22.56f	
		Short gap (μετὰ βραχύ)	
	*	Denial 2: Lk 22.58	
		1 hour (ὡσεὶ ὥρας μιᾶς)	
Denial 1: Mk 14.67f	*	Denial 3: Lk 22.59f	

COCKCROW

?

Denial 2: Mk 14.69f   *

Small gap (μικρόν)

Denial 3: Mk 14.70f   *

COCKCROW

Linguistic grounds alone are incapable of establishing the literary background of this scheme. (a) For μετὰ βραχύ, v.58, there are only two other instances of βραχύς in the Lukan writings: Acts 5.34, where a source may be involved, and Acts 27.28, part of a we-passage. (b)

---

[1] There are also 7 Markan cases where Lk contains no parallel sentence or incident.

[2] See Mk 4.17-19.

[3] For the precise chronological data, see Blinzler, Prozeß, 416: ἀλεκτοροφωνία = 3.a.m.

ὡσεί ὥρας μιᾶς, v.59, cf. μετὰ μικρόν, Mk 14.70. ὡσεί appears redactionally at Lk 9.14 (twice),28, and also in L passages, Lk 3.23, 22.41,44, 23.44, 24.11, thus including the Passion narrative. It would be possible to take these instances of ὡσεί as Luke's own work, reacting against unlikely mathematical precision,[1] but for the fact that Luke himself would be responsible for the inclusion of a more specific interval at v.59. The examples in Lk 9.14,24 show that even when ὡσέι is redactional this does not make the whole time-note Lukan, and the L cases make it equally coherent with an origin in the Sonderquelle. (c) διαστάσης, v.59. διστημι appears in Lk 24.51 and also in Acts 27.28 (we-passage). Again nothing emerges for either literary hypothesis. (d) παραχρῆμα, v.60, cf. εὐθύς, Mk 14.72. Luke plainly has no love for εὐθύς[2] and on 4 occasions changes it into παραχρῆμα,[3] which he also inserts twice where there is no Markan time-note.[4] Yet this word also occurs in L, and therefore it is not possible to conclude that Mk is the source here.

What literary considerations fail to achieve is indicated on other grounds. (a) There is absolutely no circumstantial, theological or literary reason for Luke to make the changes from Mk's scheme, if changes they be.[5] Although the change made by Matthew from two cockcrows to one [6] means that we cannot claim that the single cockcrow *must* be more original, yet it is likely that Mk's double cockcrow is in fact an elaboration,[7] and the agreement between Lk and Jn 18.27 supports this. Note also that the pushing back in time of the denials in Lk, as compared with Mk, is by no means demanded by the timing of the subsequent hearing. There is still room for Mk's timing before the event timed ὡς ἐγένετο ἡμέρα, Lk 22.66. (b) Attempts to provide a motivation tend to suggest an interest peculiar to Lk which is however present already in Mk, or to provide a fanciful reconstruction. Thus

---

[1] Blinzler, op.cit. 416: 'Es liegt auf der Hand, daß hier ein künstliches Zeitschema vorliegt; das wirkliche Leben spielt sich nicht in gleichmäßig abgezirkelten Intervallen ab.'

[2] Cadbury, Style, 199.

[3] Lk 5.25, 8.44,55, 18.43.

[4] Lk 4.39, 8.47.

[5] B. Weiss, Die Quellen der synoptischen Überlieferung, Leipzig 1908, 155; F. Spitta, Die synoptische Grundschrift, Leipzig 1912, 403. Bussmann, Studien III, 110 sees in 22.59a one piece of evidence for a non-Markan source.

[6] The words καὶ ἀλέκτωρ ἐφώνησεν, Mk 14.68 are to be accepted as original, since (a) their omission stems from attempts to harmonize with Mt and Lk, and (b) a number of texts which do not have this wording still have δίς in Mk 14.30, and vice versa.

[7] Spitta, Grundschrift, 403.

Bailey[1] argues that μετὰ μικρόν (as Mk 14.70) would not, after μετὰ βραχύ (Lk 22.58) produce the great climax at the third denial which Lk is aiming for, and so διαστάσης ὡσεὶ ὥρας μιᾶς (22.59) is Luke's creation instead. But this is by no means self-evident, any more than the necessity to insert μετὰ βραχύ itself.[2] Moreover the final denial, with the immediate fulfilment of Jesus' prediction attached, is climactic in both Mk and Lk, not to mention Mt and Jn. It cannot be otherwise, for only then is Jesus' warning attached. Again, it is hard to see why Taylor thinks the interval of about an hour before the final challenge is an inference from Mk,[3] for the latter is quite imprecise. In view of the different chronological pattern, and the lack of explanation for it in terms of redaction of Mk, the use of a non-Markan tradition gains in probability.

3. The geographical structure

The setting of the denials is different in Mk and Lk.[4] Both speak of ἡ αὐλή (Mk 14.54, Lk 22.55) in ἡ οἰκία τοῦ ἀρχιερέως (Mk 14.53 πρὸς τὸν ἀρχιερέα + 14.54 ἡ αὐλὴ τοῦ ἀρχιερέως; Lk 22.54). But Mk has two features which demand attention: first, Peter leaves the αὐλή for the προαύλιον after the first denial, Mk 14.68, and secondly, the αὐλή is, in relation to where Jesus is, κάτω (Mk 14.66). Lk, by contrast, has no change of setting, and Jesus is present in the same place. The latter is clear not only from 22.61 but also from the first challenge καὶ οὗτος σὺν αὐτῷ ἦν, 22.56—a statement which is natural if Jesus is there (and could be indicated by a gesture accompanying the word) while αὐτῷ would not be so specific (cf. the clearer reference in Mk 14.67, μετὰ τοῦ Ναζαρηνοῦ τοῦ Ἰησοῦ). Much depends for a literary evaluation on (a) whether the tradition of Jesus' promixity to Peter is a Lukan contrivance or not; (b) whether there is any motive for the omission of Peter's exit after the first denial; (c) where Luke envisages the whole action as taking place.

Firstly, the tradition of Jesus' promixity to Peter, expressed particularly in 22.61a, is not a Lukan contrivance.[5] (a) στραφείς is almost cer-

---

[1] Traditions, 55.
[2] Cf. A. M. Perry, Sources, 132. Luke tends to use fewer details of this sort than his Markan source.
[3] Behind the Third Gospel, 48.
[4] Cf. Spitta, Grundschrift, 403.
[5] Contra Bultmann, Synoptic Tradition, 283; Bailey, Traditions, 55; Haenchen, Weg, 506.

tainly pre-Lukan.[1] In Lk 7.9, 10.23 it is not wholly clear whether it is Q or redaction of Q, but it is certainly L in Lk 7.44, 9.55, 14.25, 23.28. (b) As argued above, κύριος is unlikely to be Lukan redaction. (c) Although Lk does introduce ἐμβλέψας αὐτοῖς at 20.17 (=Mk 12.10), in other places he shows himself not particularly interested in this sort of detail, e.g. the vivid ὁ δὲ Ἰησοῦς ἐμβλέψας αὐτῷ ἠγάπησεν αὐτόν (Mk 10.12a) is replaced by the colourless ἀκούσας (Lk 18.22) and ἐμβλέψας αὐτοῖς (the disciples, Mk 10.27) is omitted in Lk 18.27. Although the pattern is not uniform in view of Lk 20.17, it can still be stated with assurance that to change a location by means of such a phrase would be quite unparalleled in Lk.

Secondly, the omission of Peter's exit into the προαύλιον (Mk 14.68) is regarded by Taylor as an editorial modification.[2] On the other hand, Winter admits that Lk's unity of place suggests prima facie the use of a non-Markan record. But he draws back from this: 'It should not be overlooked that in the Third Gospel Peter also leaves the place of his interrogation—even though only after his third denial.'[3] But (a) Lk 22.62 and Mk 14.68 are in no sense parallel, and (b) Lk 22.62 is doubtful textually and should be excluded.[4] Not only is there lacking all rationalizing and theological ground for changing the scheme, but the very change of locale coheres in Mk with the first and second challenges coming from the same person, Mk 14.66,69. The corresponding difference in Lk (ἕτερος, 22.58) would be part of the same modification but, as will be argued below, is unlikely to be redactional. Further evidence of independence is provided by Jn's agreement that all took place in the αὐλή, Jn 18.16-27, and his silence about the exit of Peter even after the third denial.

Thirdly, Jesus and Peter are both in the οἰκία τοῦ ἀρχιερέως. Now who is the high priest? Wellhausen, Loisy, Bultmann and Bailey[5] have all argued for Annas. The grounds for this must be examined. (a) Lk 3.2 apparently speaks of a double high priesthood: ἐπὶ ἀρχιερέως Ἄννα καὶ Καϊαφᾶ. Since Ἄννα καὶ would certainly not be an insertion,

---

[1] Rehkopf, Sonderquelle, 69.

[2] Behind the Third Gospel, 49.

[3] Treatment, 162.

[4] Streeter, Gospels, 323; Creed, Luke, 277; E. Klostermann, Das Lukasevangelium, 2nd ed. Tübingen 1929, 219; Haenchen, Weg, 506.

[5] J. Wellhausen, Kritische Analyse der Apostelgeschichte, Berlin 1914, 8-10; A. Loisy, Les Actes des Apôtres, Paris 1920, 242f,275f; R.Bultmann, Das Evangelium nach Johannes, 11th ed. Göttingen 1950, 497; J. A. Bailey, Traditions, 59.

καὶ Καϊαφᾶ may be,[1] and the singular ἀρχιερέως strongly suggests this. But even if the text originally included both, (but so much the more, of course, if Annas alone is original), Annas is given priority—and that in L. (b) Acts 4.6. Here again Annas is given primacy in order and in the designation as high priest: καὶ "Αννας ὁ ἀρχιερεὺς καὶ Καιαρᾶς καὶ 'Ιωάννης. Bailey is correct in stating that there is no evidence that the reference to Caiaphas is an intrusion,[2] though it still could be in view of Lk 3.2, but at the very least Acts 4.6 supports Lk 3.2 in giving prominence to Annas in the high priestly role.[3] (c) In Acts 5.17 it is thought that ἀναστὰς δέ is a corruption of "Αννας δέ.[4] In spite of the alleged grammatical difficulty of ἀναστάς it cannot be regarded as proven that "Αννας is original here. Certainly Dibelius argues too narrowly when he understands that 'the high priest in the general description of 5.17 must 'rise' in order to initiate a persecution of the Christians'. For ἀναστάς is a literary device and not a literal one as its usage, so frequent and typical in Luke-Acts shows.[5] This frequency favours ἀναστάς as the original reading, as well as the fact that a change from "Αννας to ἀναστάς is hard to explain, and finally, the slender textual support [6] in p probably represents an assimilation to the leading role assigned to Annas in Acts 4.6. If however Acts 5.17 cannot be used in support of Lk 3.2 and Acts 4.6, these two verses are themselves sufficient to show firstly, that Annas is the dominant high priest in the Lukan writings [7] (from the stage of the pre-Lukan material onwards) and is given prominence over Caiaphas in matters relating to Christianity, and secondly, he is the person singled out as ὁ ἀρχιερεύς. A consistent

---

[1] There is no evidence, however, to support Winter's conjecture that it is a post-Lukan adaption.

[2] Traditions, 59; contra Winter, On the Trial, 32.

[3] Bailey goes too far in claiming, op.cit. 59, that Luke regarded Annas as the incumbent high priest. This would certainly not be the case if he introduced καὶ Καϊαφᾶ at Lk 3.2. Even less likely is the suggestion of Winter, On the Trial, 33, that Annas II is in mind. So rightly in reviews of Winter: J. E. Bruns, CBQ 23 (1961), 360-363; P. Benoit, RB 68 (1961), 593; contra J. Isaac, Rev Hist 85 (1961), 122, and J. Parkes, JJS 4 (1962), 130f.

[4] M. Dibelius, Studies in the Acts of the Apostles, London 1956, 91, following J. Wellhausen, Kritische Analyse, 10.

[5] Used in L at Lk 1.39, 4.29, 11.7f, 15.18,30 17.19, 22.45f and 24.12,33; used in redaction of Mk at Lk 4.38f, 5.25,28, 6.8; also 19 times in Acts. Its originality at Acts 5.17 is favoured by E. Haenchen, Apostelgeschichte, 203.

[6] Noted favourably by Winter, On the Trial, 167; regarded as an early corruption by F. F. Bruce, The Acts of the Apostles, London 1952, 140.

[7] J. Schniewind, Die Parallelperikopen bei Lukas und Johannes, 2nd ed. Darmstadt 1958, 38; E. Ruckstuhl, Chronologie, 42.

deduction is therefore that 22.54 refers to the house of Annas. Consequently, Luke's narrative is in striking accord with the tradition reproduced in Jn, for (a) in Jn 18.19-24 Annas plays a primary role in dealing with Jesus; (b) Peter's denials, according to Jn 18.15, occured in
the αὐλὴ τοῦ ἀρχιερέως, who is Annas; (c) Jesus is taken first to Annas
and then to another place, Jn 18.24,28, for some subsequent proceedings.[1] The Lukan and Johannine traditions thus fit neatly into one
another at this point, and suggest that the geographical situation of the
Lukan account stands on its own feet and is not a redaction of Mk.

Three further points relating to Peter's situation reinforce this view.
Firstly, he sat μέσος αὐτῶν, v.55 (Mk 14.54: μετὰ τῶν ὑπηρετῶν). But
(a) μέσος + G is not typical of Lukan redaction, and occurs in the
N. T. only at Mk 14.24, Lk 22.55, Jn 1.26 and Phil 2.15. μετ' αὐτῶν

---

[1] J. Wellhausen argued that the Caiaphas references in Jn 18.13f,24 were
redactions added to the Vorlage because (a) the change of scene in 18.24 fits ill
with the lack of movement by Peter in 18.25; (b) Caiaphas appears in 18.24 and
has nothing to do; (c) Jn 18.13f hardly provides sufficient motivation for the
conveyance of Jesus to Annas. Das Evangelium des Johannes, Berlin 1908, 81;
Erweiterungen und Änderungen im vierten Evangelium, Berlin 1907, 24-26.
Hence 18.13f from πρῶτον onwards, and ἀπο τοῦ Καϊαφᾶ, 18.28, are removed;
similarly, R. Bultmann, Jn, 497f, adding the disruption caused by taking the
ἀρχιερεύς as Caiaphas in 18.13,19,22 but finding it impossible at 18.24; Bailey,
Traditions, 57, takes 18.12-13a, 15-23, 25b-27 as the earliest tradition, to which
vv.13b-14,24-25a were later and awkwardly added.

But against this argumentation: (a) The position of 18.24 is not meant to
indicate a corresponding change for Peter, but stems from a theological intention using literary means to achieve a contrast between Jesus and a disciple. The literary method is similar to Mk's, though different in that the
three denials are split in Jn 18.18,25-27. (b) The absence of content for the Caiaphas scene is no longer surprising when it is realised that material belonging
here in the tradition has already been used in Jn 10.24-36. 19.7 indeed suggests
earlier legal proceedings. See later, pp. 195f.

The theory of H. Strathmann that a gap is left because the scene is presumed known from the synoptics founders on the fact that on this reasoning there
would be no place for Peter's denial. A similar view is adopted by J. Blinzler,
Johannes und die Synoptiker, Stuttgart 1965,53; H. Strathmann, Das Evangelium nach Johannes. 9th ed. Göttingen 1959, 238.) (c) The reason for sending
Jesus to Annas is not quite so empty, since without the stated kinship—which
fits well with the known fact that the high priesthood was monopolized by a few
families—Annas clearly could not have been a participant. (d) ἀρχιερεύς is well-
attested as a title for former high priests: J. Jeremias, Jerusalem in the Time of
Jesus, London 1969, 157. (Bailey, op.cit. 59, is scarcely convincing in that case
when he argues that at the final stage Caiaphas was intended by Jn at 18.19: for
18.24 was certainly in the final edition of Jn.)

The underlying tradition can therefore be found by removing 18.13b,14
possibly (not including πρῶτον) as editorial parenthesis, and allowing the other
references to Caiaphas to stand.

would have served just as well. (b) The αὐτοί are spoken of vaguely, instead of precisely as in Mk 14.54. Clearly the Sanhedrin members, who were the last people mentioned in Luke's narrative (22.52) are not in mind, and the arrest party should be understood. But Luke does not normally move from clarity to vagueness [1] and so indebtedness to Mk is again unlikely.[2] Secondly, ἐν μέσῳ + G, v.55, is also authenticated in the Lukan source.[3] Thirdly, Luke, if here using Mk, has refused his periphrastic imperfect ἦν συγκαθήμενος (Mk 14.54; cf. συγκαθισάντων ἐκάθητο, Lk 22.55). Yet Luke both retains periphrastic tenses in L many times [4] and, more importantly, uses it redactionally 9 times.[5] Indeed, there is only one instance of a periphrastic form being dropped by Luke from his source—at Mk 9.4, but this passage shows Luke undertaking a *total* remodelling of the formulation. There is therefore at 22.55 a strong suggestion of Lukan independence of Mk.

4. *The challengers*

In Mk the only personnel involved are the maid, 14.66,69, and οἱ παρεστῶτες, those who stand by in the προαύλιον, 14.69f. The challenges have the following form:

Denial 1. Maid:	to Peter directly.
Denial 2. Maid:	about Peter to the bystanders.
Denial 3. Bystanders:	to Peter directly.

In Lk the scheme is quite different:

Denial 1. Maid:	about Peter (audience unspeci- fied).
Denial 2. A man (ἕτερος):	to Peter.
Denial 3. Another man (ἄλλος):	about Peter.

The first striking fact about these two schemes is that the direction of each challenging remark (i.e. to Peter or to others) is different in each case. No streamlining purpose has been achieved if Luke has redacted Mk, and indeed there is a complete absence of motivation for such a change. Secondly, the only overlap in personnel is in Denial 1, where Mk 14.66 reads μία τῶν παιδισκῶν τοῦ ἀρχιερέως, while Lk

---

[1] H. Schürmann, Der Paschamahlbericht, Münster 1953, 84f.

[2] Bussmann already placed 22.55a in S, op.cit.III, 110.

[3] Schürmann, Abschiedsrede, 88.

[4] 1.10,21f, 2.8,33,51, 3.23, 4.20, 9.53, 11.14, 13.10f, 14.1, 15.1 and in the Passion narrative: 23.8,51; 24.13,32,53.

[5] 4.38,44, 5.16f,29, 6.12, 8.40, 19.47, 21.37.

22.56 has παιδίσκη τις. Here the question of dependence or otherwise can be quickly settled: (a) παιδίσκη τις could be redaction of Mk,[1] but it is also heavily consistent with the style of L to have τις after a supporting noun.[2] (b) γύναι, 22.57, is certainly pre-Lukan[3] and this requires an earlier reference to a female questioner. Therefore the παιδίσκη, the solitary point of contact between Mk and Lk, is in fact only the coincidence of divergent traditions.

Certain features of the introductions to the challenges suggest a Sonderquelle. (a) ἕτερος, Lk 22.58. This occurs 16 times in pre-Lukan material, and 10 times redactionally.[4] There are 3 cases which could be L or Q.[5] It occurs 4 times in the Passion narrative (Lk 22.58,65, 23.32,40). But when ἕτερος is introduced redactionally there is never lacking in the source the idea of otherness/distinctness from something mentioned previously. Therefore if 22.58 is redactionally using Mk, it is a unique phenomenon, which in turn suggests the contrary hypothesis. (b) ἔφη, v.58. ἔφη is attested in the Passion narrative at 22.58,70, 23.3,40. All other Lukan examples belong to L (Lk 7.40,44, 15.17). Hence, although it is frequent in Acts, the evidence within the gospel favours S. (c) ἄλλος, v.59, is consistent with either theory (since there is but a single case of redaction of Mk, Lk 5.29) but is better attested as a word taken over by Luke when his sources contained it. 4 examples in Markan passages (Lk 9.8,19 twice, 20.16), 2 in Q (Lk 6.29, 7.8), 2 in the Passion narrative (22.59, 23.35) and 5 in Acts of which none occur in we-passages (Acts 2.12, 4.12, 15.2, 19.32, 21.34) suggest a balance of probability—though it cannot be put more strongly than this—against redaction.

In the specific wording of the challenges to Peter there are two further suggestions of a Sonderquelle. (a) Rehkopf has shown in a study of Luke's prepositional usage[6] that whereas a change from μετά to σύν would be characteristic (1st denial), a change from ἐξ αὐτῶν to μετ' αὐτοῦ would be strange. (b) Bailey[7] argued that ἐπ' ἀληθείας, v.59, depended on ἀληθῶς, Mk 14.70. But against this is not only the fact that the former can be literally translated back whereas the latter can-

---

[1] Cadbury, Style, 193; cf. Lk 8.27, 9.8,19, 18.35.
[2] 21 examples in L material in the body of the gospel; 4 examples in the Passion narrative: 22.56,59, 23.26, 24.22. Cf. Rehkopf, op.cit. 91.
[3] Rehkopf, op.cit. 98f.
[4] Lk 4.43, 6.6, 8.6,7,8, 9.29, 10.1, 11.16, 20.11.
[5] Lk 16.18, 17.34f.
[6] op.cit. 74f.
[7] Traditions, 56.

not, but also the evidence that ἀληθῶς is the word Luke uses in redaction (Lk 9.27, 21.3, and possibly 12.44). ἐπ᾽ ἀληθείας is therefore not only evidence of S but also a minor indication of the superiority of Luke's version over that of Mark. Finally, Peter's replies are all prefaced with the vocative γύναι/ἄνθρωπε. This has been shown by Rehkopf to be a pre-Lukan characteristic.[1]

5. αὐτόν (Lk 22.63)

Taylor has argued that the αὐτόν in 22.63 implies that the Denial narrative in Lk is a later insertion.[2] For Lk to read smoothly ᾽Ιησοῦν would be needed, but in the non-Markan source ᾽Ιησοῦν was not necessary, since 22.63 followed immediately after 22.54a. But (a) since 22.62 is a copyist's insertion [3] we can read from v.61 to v.63, and the double κύριος reference is sufficient to give content to the αὐτόν, and (b) when reading 22.63 after 22.54a the words οἱ ἄνδρες οἱ συνέχοντες αὐτόν are redundant, since these people are clearly envisaged as having arrested Jesus.

Our conclusion therefore on the literary origin of Lk 22.54b-61 is that the evidence points firmly towards the Sonderquelle.[4] As with all passages drawn from any source, Luke himself is probably responsible for some features, but the crucial and distinctive elements are not his work but rather come from his non-Markan source.

C. The Mockery of Jesus: Lk 22.63-65 = Mk 14.65

Winter has pointed out that Lk 22.63-65 diverges from Mk 14.65 in setting, timing and vocabulary, and he concludes: 'The differences are too prominent to be fortuitous and they cannot be attributed to a Lucan redrafting of the Marcan account.'[5] This has also been argued by

---

[1] op.cit. 98.

[2] Behind the Third Gospel, 40; similarly, A. Schalit, Kritische Randbemerkungen zu Paul Winters On the Trial of Jesus, ASTI 2 (1963), 90.

[3] Allowed by Winter, Treatment, 165. It is not to be taken as an agreement of Mt and Lk suggesting a Passion narrative in Q, since the number of such agreements is trivial in comparison with the number in passages normally assigned to Q: contra E. Hirsch, Frühgeschichte des Evangeliums, 2nd ed. Tübingen 1951, 244.

[4] Spitta, Grundschrift, 404, also concludes: 'Wie man diese Darstellung auf Grund der in Markus-Matthäus hatte herstellen können, ist nicht einzusehen.' Similarly, Ruckstuhl, Chronologie, 41.

[5] On the Trial, 21. Cf. Treatment, 162, where Lk 22.63-65 is taken as the source of Mk 14.65, the latter having been rewritten according to a theological purpose.

W. Bussmann, W. Grundmann and V. Taylor [1] among others, but is doubted by J. A. Bailey and J. Blinzler.[2] Criteria of literary criticism strongly favour Winter's view, especially when the establishing of the original text of Mk reveals how limited is the verbal overlap with Lk. Good reasons have been presented for accepting the reading of Daf sy^sin at Mk 14.65,[3] and on this basis the two parallel versions read:

Mk 14.65	Lk 22.63-65
καὶ ἤρξαντό τινες ἐμπτύειν τῷ προσώπῳ αὐτοῦ καὶ κολαφίζειν αὐτὸν καὶ λέγειν αὐτῷ προφήτευσον καὶ οἱ ὑπηρέται ῥαπίσμασιν αὐτὸν ἔλαβον [4]	καὶ οἱ ἄνδρες οἱ συνέχοντες αὐτὸν ἐνέπαιζον αὐτῷ δέροντες καὶ περικαλύψαντες αὐτὸν ἐπηρώτων λέγοντες προφήτευσον τίς ἐστιν ὁ παίσας σε; καὶ ἕτερα πολλὰ βλασφημοῦντες ἔλεγον εἰς αὐτόν

The verbal overlap is thus confined to the words καί and αὐτῷ (cf. Mk: αὐτοῦ) in 22.63, λέγοντες (cf. Mk: λέγειν) and προφήτευσον in 22.64, and καί, 22.65. The two instances of καί and αὐτῷ can be dismissed speedily, and λέγοντες introducing a quotation is commonplace. All then that remains to support derivation from Mk is the word προφήτευσον, upon which Bailey relies heavily. Yet this reliance is undermined not only by the loneliness of this single word binding the two accounts together, but also by the fact that the sense is rather different in each case. In Mk the idea is, 'Function as a prophet!'; in Lk it is, 'Exercise the gift of second sight!'[5] And the context is all-important: in Lk the narrative shows the same test being applied to

---

[1] W. Bussmann, Synoptische Studien III, 110 attributing 22.63f to the Sonder-quelle: W. Grundmann, Lukas, 417; V. Taylor, Behind the Third Gospel, 49f.

[2] Bailey, Traditions, 56; Blinzler, Prozeß, 4th ed., 165.

[3] Cf. R. H. Gundry, 1QIsaiah a 50.6 and Mark 14,65, Revue de Qumran 2 (1960), 559-567; P. Benoit, Les Outrages à Jésus Prophète, in Neotestamentica et Patristica, O. Cullmann Festschrift, Leiden 1962, 98f. The reasons for accepting this reading are: (i) Its support in both the Western and Caesarean—Θ 565—recensions. (ii) The explanation of what is otherwise a surprising omission by Matthew. (iii) Its presentation of a coherent event in Mk 14.65. Benoit, art.cit 97f, argues that the presence of (ἡμῖν χριστέ) τίς ἐστιν ὁ παίσας σε is due to an assimilation to Mt within the Markan text.

[4] The underlined words are reminiscences of Is 50.6 LXX: τὸ νῶτόν μου ἔδω-κα εἰς μάστιγας, τὰς δὲ σιαγόνας μου εἰς ῥαπίσματα τὸ δὲ πρόσωπόν μου οὐκ ἀπέσ-τρεψα ἀπὸ ἐμπτυσμάτων.

[5] So rightly, Taylor, op.cit.49; W. C. van Unnik, Jesu Verhöhnung vor dem Synedrium (Mc 14.65 par), ZNW 29 (1930), 310f; D. E. Nineham, Saint Mark, London 1963, 409.

Jesus as was used in the case of Bar Kochba, b.Sanh. 93b, whereby a messianic candidate was required to show his ability to work without the aid of sight or hearing and so to satisfy Is 11.3.[1] Within this technical Jewish procedure the word προφήτευσον does not have more than a popular sense as describing the required act of the person being tested. Now it will be noticed that this technical procedure is detailed in Lk, but not in Mk. If Luke was using Mk, he has introduced something Jewish and technical, which has already been shown to be against his instincts.[2] It is therefore all the more likely that Mk's tradition is a later one in which the original sense has been almost completely lost.

1. *The agents of mockery*

The mockers in Mk are in two groups: τινές, who, by virtue of the continuity of the narrative are some of the πάντες (=Sanhedrin members) 14.64, and later the ὑπηρέται.[3] In Lk however only one group is mentioned: οἱ ἄνδρες οἱ συνέχοντες αὐτόν, 22.63.

The following points may be made: (a) The scheme suggests a more primitive form in Lk.[4] The doubling of maltreatment is more elaborate, and the involvement of Sanhedrin members in the physical attack on Jesus is highly unlikely. Moreover, the mockery centring on προφήτευσον is better placed before the Sanhedrin hearing than after it.[5] The dialogue in Mk 14.61f gives no ground for the inference that Jesus is a prophet, for, in E. Haenchen's words, 'der Messias ist kein Prophet';[6] also, the time after a legal verdict has been pronounced is no time for the testing of the accused. The opposite scheme of Lk is extremely neat here: Jesus is first tested and then directly questioned

---

[1] J. D. M. Derrett, An Oriental Lawyer looks at the Trial of Jesus, London 1966, 20. Only at one point does Derrett's treatment need modification, i.e. where he remarks that 'it is of great interest that only Mark preserves the Haggadic idea undamaged'. In fact only Luke does that. The shorter text of Mk is to be accepted; but already in Mk's longer text the ritual is no longer understood and is interrupted by κολαφίζειν; the blindfolding thus becomes part of the physical maltreatment, which is again not the case in Lk.

[2] See p. 164.

[3] Blinzler, op.cit. 163f, argues that v.65a and v.65b are doublets, in that the second mockery does not exceed the first in content: consequently the τινές = the servants. However, this is doubtful because one would expect the ὑπηρέται to be mentioned before the vaguer τινές in this case; and also v.65a and v.65b are bound together by Is 50.6 allusions.

[4] So rightly, Bultmann, Synoptic Tradition, 269; Grundmann, Lukas, 418.

[5] Otherwise, Blinzler, op.cit. 163.

[6] Weg, 515.

about messiahship, and it is entirely logical then that the first question in the Sanhedrin hearing should be about this very topic. (b) The involvement of Sanhedrin members in Mk 14.65 is not solely the product of Markan ordering. The τινές are distinguished from the ὑπηρέται, and yet must be persons present at a trial; further, the testing procedure as in Lk must have at least official authorization. Hence the connection between Mk 14.65 and 14.55-64 is indestructible. For literary analysis of the Markan form of the narrative this means that decisions on the two blocks of material cannot be separated, and for the history of the tradition it becomes difficult to accept the suggestion of Winter [1] that an earlier form of the tradition can be reached by omitting Mk 14.53b, 55-64; this latter passage is required for Mk 14.65 to lean on, at least in the Markan version. This conclusion is established by the 'sandwich structure', so frequently used as an interpretative device by Mark,[2] in which mockery and the earlier trial hang together within the two sections of Peter's denial.[3] Consequently, Winter's use of arguments about interpolation is open to serious objection. He admits that, after removal of the Sanhedrin trial, the mockery and denial are differently ordered in Mk and Lk. But he then uses Jn 18.22 to establish the primitive order, which turns out to agree with Mk.[4] But (a) the evidence concerning order boils down to a Markan construction in which mockery precedes denial, a Lukan scheme in which denial precedes mockery (Winter accepts the independence of the

---

[1] On the Trial, 21f.

[2] Definitively, E. von Dobschütz, Zur Erzählerkunst des Markus, ZNW 27 (1928), 193-198; similarly, W. G. Kümmel, Introduction to the New Testament, London 1965, 64; E. Schweizer, Mk, 185. This means that Winter is excessively literal when he states in Markus 14.53b,55-64 ein Gebilde des Evangelisten, ZNW 53 (1962), 262, that Mk requires us to believe that a Sanhedrin trial took place between two cockcrows (this is not even forced upon us if Mark is taken as a chronologically consecutive narrative). Mk's purpose is theological, not chronological. T. A. Burkill, whose work is used by Winter, acknowledges and expounds this editorial technique, The Trial of Jesus, VC 12 (1958), 1f.

[3] It is surprising that Bultmann, Synoptic Tradition, 269, should speak of the insertion of Mk 14.55-64, rather than of Mk 14.55-65, into the story of Peter. Ditto, P. Vielhauer, Gottesreich und Menschensohn, in Neutestamentliche Aufsätze, München 1965, 72. Awareness of this fact is clearly suggested in two references by Winter to the insertion of Mk 14.53b,55-64(65), in The Marcan Account of Jesus' Trial by the Sanhedrin, JTS 14 (1963), 97.

[4] On the Trial, 161: 'If we may be allowed to consult the Fourth Gospel (Jn 18.22) in an endeavour to reconstruct an earlier form of the tradition, it would appear that at this point Mark stands closer to a more primitive form. Intended to be related as more or less simultaneous happenings, the mockery of Jesus might nonetheless have been recorded before the account of Peter's denial.'

narrative), and a Johannine scheme which is ambivalent. In the last case the denial is divided more decisively than in Mk, there being one denial before and two after the hearing and mockery. (b) Winter's reason for allowing himself the use of Jn 18.22 f consists of the reminiscence of Mk 14.65 and Lk 22.63 provided by ἔδωκεν ῥάπισμα and τί με δέρεις; But it is difficult to see why that is reason for suggesting a more primitive *scheme*, or that such a scheme is more authenticated in Mk. Winter has in fact preserved the traditional argument against Mk 14.53b,55-64, namely that it appears within the two parts of Peter's denial,[1] without allowing for the unity of Mk 14.65 with the former passage or for Mark's editorial responsibility for the arrangement. (c) The speed with which Mk 53b, 55-64 is extrapolated here receives a setback. At times one has the impression that the removal of this passage, which is meant to be the thing to be proved, is being made part of the process of proof. For instance, Winter writes: 'Lk 22.54-66 is from a historical point of view better than Mk 14.53a-15.1a'.[2] But in the previous argument up to that point the following pairings have been made: Lk 22.54/Mk 14.53a; Lk 22.55-62/Mk 14.54,66-72; Lk 22.63-65/Mk 14.65; Lk 22.66/ Mk 15.1a. Thus Mk 14.53b, 55-64 is hurriedly included in the block to be dismissed as less trustworthy. But to date, the only intrinsic difficulties raised against it have been: first, that the blasphemy clashes with Sanh. 7.5, and second, that no action is taken to put the death sentence into effect.[3] And the familiar argument 'interpolation implies total unhistoricity' must cope with three facts: (a) It is widely agreed that Mk 14.58 reflects a genuine saying of Jesus, yet this is part of the interpolation. (b) Other interpolated passages are not thereby discredited, e.g. the cleansing of the temple, Mk 11.15-19. (c) Another group of interpolated passages consists of those which are supported by either or both of a separate tradition within the gospels (e.g. the anointing, Mk 14.3-9, cf. Lk 7.36-50 in L) or by non-Christian documentation (e.g. the imprisonment of John the baptist, Mk 6.14-29, cf. Lk 3.19-20 from L, and Josephus, Ant. 18.116-119;

---

[1] Cf. Lietzmann, Prozeß, 253f.

[2] On the Trial, 23.

[3] Winter argues: 'It is impossible to understand—from Mark—why Jesus should stand trial before Pilate if he had already been tried and sentence had been passed.' op.cit. 23. But what does 'from Mark' mean? Certainly there is no statement like Jn 18.31 in Mk, but he, like Mt and Lk, proceeds on exactly such an assumption.

the exorcisms, Mk 3.22-30, cf. Lk 11.17-23 from Q and b.Sanh. 43a). The mockery belongs to this group in view of the likelihood, which can be strengthened still further, that Lk 22.63-65 represents a separate tradition. All this is not to prejudge the question of historicity, (and the examples cited show considerable fluidity and divergence actually within the tradition) but only to call in question the argument that a phenomenon, stemming from Mark's editorially-achieved theological purpose, requires the rejection of the material in respect of historical criticism. Rather is it necessary always to enquire into the tradition behind such material. In the present case, we have already seen reason to believe that behind the Markan account there stands a Lukan version which is not only independent but better from the point of view of historical basis.

In terms of wording, Lk's description of those who mocked Jesus provides no evidence in favour of either theory about the literary origin of the passage. ἀνήρ occurs in passages taken straightforwardly from Mk, and is also introduced redactionally into Luke's version of Mk, and is present both in L and the Passion narrative. συνέχω occurs three times redactionally and twice in L. The failure to use Mk's τινές provides no material for argument: Luke omits it 9 times in passages with a Markan parallel, and retains it 5 times. This omission, like the other divergences, is more important for its coherence with a general pattern which is markedly different and apparently better than Mk 14.65.

2. *The action of mockery*

Again vocabulary statistics are not compelling, mainly because of the rarity of the words used. But the balance of probability favours a Sonderquelle. Thus κολαφίζειν is used only at Mk 14.63 = Mt 26.67 in the gospel material, but if Luke found it in a source he was using it is unlikely he would drop it, in view of its use in the early Christian traditions for the corporate sufferings of the apostle or the Christian in Christ (cf.1 Cor 4.11, 2 Cor 12.7 and 1 Pet 2.20).[1] ἐμπαίζω occcurs in Lk 3 times in the Passion narrative (22.63, 23.11,36), once in L (Lk 14.29) and once from Mk (Lk 18.32 = Mk 10.34).[2] There are therefore

---

[1] K. L. Schmidt, art. κολαφίζω, TDNT 3 (1965), 818-821.

[2] It is possible that the change from active to passive, ἐμπαίξουσιν Mk 10.34 to ἐμπαιχθήσεται Lk 18.32, is intended to broaden the reference so that the maltreatment expressed in this and the two following verbs is not confined to τὰ ἔθνη. It is certainly striking that the ἐμπαίζειν treatment is symmetrically positioned in

no cases of Lukan redaction using this word, and this, together with its presence in the Sonderquelle, points towards the latter in 22.63. The omission of ἤρξαντο could be due either to absence from S or to redaction of Mk, for although ἄρχομαι is retained twice in Mk-Lk parallels, it is dropped 12 times. However δέροντες [1] joins the evidence in favour of S, for there is no case of Luke's redactional use of δέρω, whereas it occurs twice in L (Lk 12.47f). When Luke finds it in Mk, he retains it twice (Lk 20.10f = Mk 12.3,5) and omits once (Lk 21.12, cf. Mk 13.9). Its occurrence in Jn 18.23 strengthens the case for its inclusion in an earlier form of the tradition.

It is however considerations other than literary ones which establish the non-Markan provenance of Lk 22.63. It has already been noted that Mk 14.65 carries unmistakable echoes of Is 50.6 LXX.[2] In sharp contrast Lk lacks all allusion to the Servant here, and this must suggest another tradition for the following reasons:

(a) Luke lays particular emphasis on the fulfilment of the O.T. in the Passion.[3] This is plain not only from the redactional καὶ τελεσθήσεται πάντα τὰ γεγραμμένα διὰ τῶν προφητῶν (Lk 18.31 = Mk 10.33) but also the broader conjunction of τέλος words for both the fulfilment of the O.T.[4] and the Passion,[5] and finally the destruction by Jesus of the veil of secrecy and hiddenness which lay across the scripture.[6] It is therefore scarcely likely that Luke would obliterate an O.T. allusion.

(b) The plain Servant allusions in Mk 10.34 καὶ ἐμπαίξουσιν αὐτῷ καὶ ἐμπτύσουσιν αὐτῷ καὶ μαστιγώσουσιν αὐτόν are taken over quite straightforwardly in Lk 18.32f. Indeed the crucial allusions to Is 50.6 are retained in spite of deviation in two important respects from the

---

Lk's passion narrative: 22.63 by the Jewish guards, 23.11 by Herodians, 23.36 by Roman soldiers. But this may be coincidental, and Lk 18.32 cannot be brought too close to the passion narrative in view of differences at other points.

[1] It is just possible that δέροντες is not original, being omitted by D it 69 1071. But it is more likely to have figured in 22.63 in view of its slightly awkward position and the possibility that it was omitted for reverential reasons.

[2] See p. 175. Cf. Grundmann, Lk, 418; M. D. Hooker, Jesus and the Servant, London 1959, 90; D. E. Nineham, Mk, 408; Haenchen, Weg, 515; Lohse, Prozeß, 37.

[3] E. Lohse, Lukas als Theologe der Heilsgeschichte, EvTh 14 (1954), 256-275. esp.261-264; K. H. Rengstorf, Das Evangelium nach Lukas, 11th ed.Göttingen 1966, 211.

[4] e.g. 22.37. H. Schürmann argues that this is a pre-Lukan tradition subsequently redacted by Luke, Jesu Abschiedsrede, 124-129.

[5] e.g. 12.50, 13.32. Cf. W. Grundmann, Lk, 355: 'Die Passion ist Durchgang zur Vollendung.'

[6] e.g. Lk 9.45, 18.34, contrast 24.25-27,44f. Flender, Luke, 31.

Lukan passion narrative: first, that Jesus is not spat upon by anyone, and second, that whereas scourging is the preliminary to execution and will actually be carried out according to Mk 10.34=Lk 18.33, in the passion narrative it is the preliminary to release, is described in different words, and is not carried out.[1] This is a salutary corrective to the suggestion that Luke modified the passion predictions to conform to the events of the passion narrative. But at this point the important point is Luke's retention of Servant allusions when he finds them in Mk.

(c) Luke is positively attracted to the Servant concept, and especially to its suffering aspect, in the account of the Transfiguration.[2] Firstly, the redactional μετὰ τοὺς λόγους τούτους, Lk 9.28, connects the event, even more closely than the Markan account had done, with the sayings about Jesus' way of suffering, Lk 9.23-27.[3] Secondly, the change from ἀγαπητός, Mk 9.7, to ἐκλελεγμένος, Lk 9.35,cf.23.35, makes more explicit the allusion to Is 42.1, cf.Is 49.2. The occurrence of the latter word in only the two places, at the transfiguration and at the passion, is itself important as part of the scheme connecting the two theologically.[4] Thirdly, the insertion of an explicit topic of conversation, the exodus, Lk 9.31, means that suffering and the second exodus of the Servant provide the key to this pericope.[5] Fourthly, the repetition, although in reverse order, of ἀκούετε αὐτοῦ, probably reflecting Dt 18.15,[6] coheres with the portrait of Jesus as a second Moses like the Servant. But as such he is not the lawgiver as in Mt[7] but the sufferer. Grundmann rightly remarks, apropos of αὐτοῦ ἀκούετε: 'Das gilt in diesem Zusammenhang für die Ankündigung seines Leidens.'[8] Therefore, faced with the theme of the Servant in his Markan source, Luke has retained and exploited it.

(d) Possibly, though less certainly, there is a redactional introduction

---

[1] Jn too fails to mention scourging. For the procedural background, cf. A. N. Sherwin White, Roman Society and Roman Law in the New Testament, Oxford 1963, 27. Luke at this point is technically correct, op.cit. 32.

[2] R. H. Fuller, Foundations, 172.

[3] Compare the common theme of sufferings, culminating in Lk 9.26,32.

[4] In parallel with this, the connection between transfiguration and the Mount of Olives (Lk 22.40-46) has been noted: Grundmann, Lk, 192; Conzelmann, Lk, 59; Flender, Luke, 31.

[5] Caird, Luke, 132.

[6] Fuller, Foundations, 172.

[7] Cf. W. D. Davies, The Setting of the Sermon on the Mount, Cambridge 1964, 50-56.

[8] Das Evangelium nach Lukas, 193.

of Servant language in Lk 11.22, drawn from Is 53.12 (cf. Is 49.25)[1]. If so, it is notable that, as in the transfiguration, the themes of the Servant (Lk 11.22), the exodus (ἐν δακτύλῳ θεοῦ, 11.20, cf. Ex 8.19),[2] the realised presence of the kingdom (11.20, cf.9.27), and discipleship (11.23) come together. An exodus pattern with implications for discipleship is initiated by Jesus in both cases.

The evidence gathered in the above points shows that Luke's theological structure predisposes him towards Servant theology; consequently, an eradication of this theme from Mk 14.65 would be quite foreign to his view. Hence the provenance of Lk 22.63 from a non-Markan tradition is clear.

3. *The verbal taunts*

It is now necessary to consider whether the details of verbal opposition to Jesus help the source-critical inquiry forward in any way.

(a) 22.64. It has already been shown that the verse as a whole reflects a technical procedure which Luke would not have inserted. The only question remaining is therefore a word-study of ἐπηρώτων, which, it will be noticed, does not imply hostility. Luke takes ἐπερωτάω from Mk 5 times (Lk 8.30, 9.18, 18.18, 20.27, 21.7) and 3 times omits it from Markan contexts (Lk 9.20,45, 20.3). There are 3 L examples, not counting 2.46, i.e. 3.10,14, 17.20, and 5 cases of Lukan redaction (Lk 6.9, 8.9, 18.40, 20.21,40), together with 3 instances in the passion narrative (22.64, 23.6,9). On word statistics alone, therefore, the case is evenly balanced. But in 22.64, the formulation ἐπηρώτων λέγοντες is exactly as at 3.10,14 (L). It is not likely that Luke would introduce the imperfect tense—the only other case of redactional ἐπηρώτων is at Mk 4.10 = Lk 8.9, where Luke at least has a Markan imperfect to begin with—but it has to remain possible, unless 3.10,14 and 22.64 were once in an equivalent layer of tradition (unless of course the contact is pure coincidence). However this raises the whole problem of Proto-Luke, which it is not appropriate to investigate here.[3] It is

---

[1] So, tentatively, J. Jeremias, art. παῖς, TDNT 5 (1967), 713; W. Grundmann, art. ἰσχύω, TDNT 3 (1965), 399-401. It is not sufficient to emphasize Is 49.25 and then argue that 'there is no indication in the N.T. passage that this verse (Is 53.12) was in Jesus' mind', as does M. D. Hooker, Jesus and the Servant, 73f. For there is just as much in common with Is 53.12 as with Is 49.25. God acts directly in the latter passage, and he acts through the Servant in the former passage.

[2] R. H. Fuller, The Mission and Achievement of Jesus, London 1963, 37. It is probable that both δακτύλῳ and πνεύματι, Mt 12.28, are to be taken as redactional, perhaps replacing an original δυνάμει.

[3] In favour, B. H. Streeter, Gospels, 201-222; against, W. G. Kümmel, Introduction, 91-95.

therefore necessary to leave in abeyance the significance of ἐπηρώτων, while noting that the material to which it is attached is pre-Lukan.

(b) 22.65. This verse deals only with words directed against Jesus. It is clearly intended as a summary of what has gone before [1] and yet that is precisely what, in terms of content, it cannot be! For the hostility mentioned in 22.63f has been physical but not verbal. This means in turn that 22.65 represents a misunderstanding of the technical procedure used in 22.64, and therefore that 22.64 belongs to an earlier layer of tradition than 22.65. But who is responsible for this verse? It could be Luke, or it could be some one before Luke. This can only be decided by study of the wording here and in the parallel passage, Lk 3.18. In Lk 3.18, the word εὐηγγελίζετο is to be given its full technical sense, for Conzelmann is hardly successful in devaluing it to mean merely 'preach'.[2] If it were established that εὐαγγελίζεσθαι is a word which can only be used in Luke's own scheme for the period of Jesus and exclusive of John the Baptist, then 3.18 would have to be pre-Lukan. This however cannot be so,[3] and therefore Lk 3.18 cannot be separated from Luke on these grounds. In Lk 22.65 there is unfortunately rather a small amount of material upon which to base a decision. The use of the imperfect ἔλεγον is possible as Lukan writing, though against 4 times when this is redacted in by Luke (Lk 5.36, 9.23,31, 21.10) there are 24 occasions when Luke omits or alters Mark's use of it. Similarly, εἰς + A is regarded by Rehkopf as a feature of pre-Lukan style, though it is not a case of all examples being in L. Lk 15.18,21 certainly are, but in Lk 12.10 the two instances were probably in Q (Mt 12.32 has κατά, but there is no reason to think Luke would change from κατά to εἰς). But overall, firm conclusions cannot be formed about 22.65. What is secure is that in the account of the mockery, Lk 22.63f depend on a non-Markan source which is historically the better version.

D. The Sanhedrin hearing:
Lk 22.66-71 = Mk 14.53b,55-64, 15.1a.

The most crucial question for Prozessforschung is the value of Lk 22.66-71. Lietzmann gave no attention to its distinctive features be-

---

[1] Cf. J. K. Chamblin, Gospel and Judgment in the Preaching of John the Baptist, Tyndale House Bulletin 13 (1963), 7-15, on the similar case, 3.18.

[2] Luke, 23. In any case, κηρύσσω is used in parallel with εὐαγγελίζομαι by Luke, 8.1, 9.2,6.

[3] W. Wink, John the Baptist in the Gospel Tradition, Cambridge 1968, 51-57.

cause he regarded it as a redaction of Mk.[1] While Winter depends to a considerable extent on Lietzmann generally, he diverges from him at this point and takes Lk's passion narrative as basically independent of Mk. However, he excludes 22.67-71, regarding it as a post-Lukan insertion. It will be apparent that if, to the contrary, this passage is pre-Markan, then clearly the hypotheses of Lietzmann and Winter are seriously jeopardized. The evidence is as follows.

1. *The setting in Luke's overall presentation*

There are two items which have been used to support a negative evaluation of Lk 22.66-71.

The first is Acts 13.27f. Winter writes: 'The absence of a report of a death sentence passed by the Sanhedrin must have been deliberately intended. This comes out in Ac 13.27,28 where the author of Luke-Acts allows Paul to say: "The inhabitants of Jerusalem and their rulers . . . . finding no cause of death (μηδεμίαν αἰτίαν θανάτου εὑρόντες) in Jesus, asked Pilate that he should be killed." Allowing for the apologetic colouring of the formulation in the second half of this statement,we find here a definite assertion that the rulers (= the Sanhedrin) had neither found Jesus guilty nor passed sentence upon him.'[2]

Unfortunately for Winter's proposal, this is not accurate. Firstly, there is no definite assertion here of the sort Winter claims, and the apologetic colouring which he locates in the request of the rulers to Pilate would suggest a Tendenz precisely opposite to the first half when that is interpreted as a denial of Sanhedrin involvement.[3] Even in the words cited by Winter, an examination of Jesus by the rulers is implied. Secondly, Winter simply omits the crucial words which undermine his view: 'because they did not recognize him nor understand the utterances of the prophets which are read every sabbath, they fulfilled these by condemning him'. The word κρίναντες is specially crucial and its meaning leaves no room whatever for doubt. κρίνω sometimes has the sense of 'make a decision' but even here there is often involved the formal decision of authorities and assemblies.[4] The meanings 'decide' and 'pass judgment' often merge into one another, and this judicial background impregnates popular usage (cf. Mt 7.1 =

---

[1] See above, pp. 153-155.
[2] On the Trial, 28, cf.48.
[3] Acts 13.27 is a statement of guilt. H. Conzelmann, Luke, 91,146, rightly distinguishes this from anti-Semitism.
[4] Acts 3.13, 15.19, 21.25.

Lk 6.37; Lk 19.22).[1] This basic judicial sense of passing judgment and declaring a verdict is clearly definitive. In Acts 13.27 there is therefore a plain statement that the Sanhedrin, against the evidence (implying that what they regarded as a crime was in fact the truth) passed sentence on Jesus.[2] Consequently Winter cannot be followed when he declares: 'We have in Ac 13.27,28 the explanation why the Third Gospel nowhere mentions that the Sanhedrin sentenced Jesus to death.'[3]

The second item is the complex of Passion predictions. The first two, Mk 8.31, 9.31 = Lk 9.22,44 can be considered together. In the second of these, Luke drastically abbreviates, omitting 'and they will kill him; and when he is killed, after three days he will rise'. The saying does not identify the ἄνθρωποι who will kill Jesus, but the redaction at this point is sufficient to show that Luke makes omissions because of emphasis and not because he believes that the words omitted describe events which did not happen: hence argument from silence is inadmissible. It must also be noticed that the first prediction does nothing to lessen the Sanhedrin's involvement, and indeed fails to mention the Romans at all. Moreover Lk 9.22 takes over the word ἀποδοκιμασθῆναι from Mk 8.31, and W. Grundmann has convincingly demonstrated that δοκιμάζω means 'to test/try' often in an official context, and that ἀποδοκιμάζω means to throw out as the result of such a test. The context always implies a judgement.[4] A further point demonstrating the weakness of correcting the Passion narrative in the light of the predictions, is contained in the πρεσβύτεροι reference, Mk 8.31 = Lk 9.22: these officials only appear in the story of the arrest, Lk 22.52, which certainly does not fill out the ἀποδοκιμασθῆναι reference.

The argument about the Passion predictions is of considerable importance to Winter, for he inserts a paragraph into On the Trial of Jesus which did not occur in the previously published article,[5] of which the chapter in question is otherwise an almost exact reproduction. The argument in this paragraph claims that there is a contrast between Luke's redaction of Mk 8.31, 9.31 and of Mk 10.33, including the statement that 'in Lk 9.44b there is no substantial alteration of the words presented in Mk 9.31a'. The first two sayings show acceptance

1 See F. Büchsel, art. κρίνω, TDNT 3 (1965), 922f.
2 Cf. Blinzler, Prozeß, 433-435.
3 On the Trial, 28.
4 art. δοκιμάζω, TDNT 2 (1964), 256.
5 Marginal Notes on the Trial of Jesus II, ZNW 50 (1959), 221-251.

of the Markan tradition, therefore, whereas the omission of part of the third saying is made to be very significant. Winter also argues that 'the Markan wording (that is, 8.31) does not imply here that the Sanhedrin would pass a death sentence upon Jesus, and the Third Evangelist could easily have understood that the "rejection" came to expression in the Council's decision to hand Jesus over for trial to Pilate'.[1] But against these assertions it is necessary to stress that this is not at all in line with the meaning of ἀποδοκιμάζω, that the treatment of the first two Passion predictions counts against this argument from the third, and Winter is only able to construct such a contrast by speaking of Mk 9.31a and Lk 9.44b. As already mentioned, the omission of Mk 9.31b gives a quite different perspective, and makes for more caution in drawing conclusions from the modification of Mk 10.33 in Lk 18.32f.

So the omission of the role of the Sanhedrin in Lk 18.32f [2] is not so striking, and cannot be used to suggest that Luke thought they had not condemned Jesus.[3] To this omission can be added a list of divergences from the Passion predictions in Luke's version of the Passion itself. 1. Jesus is not spat upon (pace Mk 10.34 = Lk 18.32). 2. The scourging is proposed but not carried out, and is preliminary to release not execution (pace Mk 10.34 = Lk 18.33). 3. The Romans play a crucial role (pace Mk 8.31 = Lk 9.22). 4. The elders are not involved in the rejection (pace Mk8.31 = Lk 9.22). 5. The resurrection followed (pace Mk 9.31 = Lk 9.44). Arguments from silence having proved inadequate, it is clear that, if we confine ourselves to statements made or accepted by Luke in Acts 13.27f and the Passion predictions, it is clear that he does think that the Sanhedrin judged and condemned Jesus.

2. *The time note:* ὡς ἐγένετο ἡμέρα, *Lk 22.66*

This has often been regarded as the most striking feature of the Lukan narrative. Many have felt it rests on better tradition than Mk's nocturnal session.[4] Tyson, for instance, argues that it stems from no apologetic purpose, and although it would make the Sanhedrin trial more legal, nevertheless does not remove other illegalities such as the

---

[1] On the Trial, 28.

[2] On this already, H. Danby, The Bearing of the Rabbinical Criminal Code on the Jewish Trial Narratives in the Gospels, JTS 21 (1920), 51-76, esp. 62; E. Klostermann, Das Lukasevangelium, 2nd ed. Tübingen 1929, ad loc.

[3] Note in passing that Winter uses Mk 10.34 as evidence of the earliest tradition of the mockery, in spite of the κατακρινοῦσιν αὐτόν reference, op.cit. 106.

[4] V. Taylor, Behind the Third Gospel, 51; J. B. Tyson, The Lukan Version of the Trial of Jesus, NovT 3 (1959), 252.

occurrence of a trial on a feast day or the lack of a second session.[1] Blinzler on the other hand argues that no independent tradition comes to light here, because (a) Lk's narrative has 'filled up' the night time, so the Sanhedrin session *had* to be placed in the morning; (b) Luke may be historicizing to remove the difficulty of the Great Council's assembling in the middle of the night; (c) from a literary-critical angle Lk 22.66 is a combination of Mk 14.53b and 15.1a, and therefore on methodological grounds the Lukan time note must be discarded; (d) Lk records only the final phase of the hearing, having omitted the interrogation of witnesses, and doubtless this did take place towards daybreak.[2] A further objection is raised by A. N. Sherwin White, namely that Luke's version is not so good as Mark's because, on this scheme, the Jewish officials would have been late for the early beginning of the procurator's judicial day.[3]

Apart from the third of these arguments, which requires an extended examination in the next major section, these arguments will be taken in turn now. First, has Luke's narrative 'filled up' the night time? The pre-dawn events in Lk consist of Peter's denial (also in Mk) and the mockery of Jesus (also in Mk), and no trial (which is in Mk.) So there is *less* in this period in Lk than is in Mk; and moreover, the timing of Peter's denials has all three over before cockcrow, whereas only the first had occurred in Mk up to that time. If Luke was redacting Mk there, as Blinzler believes, he has moved the denial back in time with the result that the gap between 3 a.m. and dawn is to be filled with Lk 22.63-65 alone. This does not suggest that Luke had no alternative but to time the Sanhedrin session in the morning because he had filled up the night.

Secondly, is Luke historicizing? It is true that Luke does on occasion alter time-notes in Mk. 1. Mk 1.35 πρωΐ ἔννυχα λίαν becomes γενομένης δὲ ἡμέρας in Lk 4.42. To the extent that Luke is avoiding the incongruity of the crowds seeking Jesus before dawn (Mk has only ('Simon and those who were with him'), it is appropriate to take this as a rationalization by Luke. But it must be noticed that the redaction of this block is aimed at broadening and expanding the group who confront Jesus, partly in line with Luke's stress on the extraordinary effect Jesus

---

[1] art.cit. 253.
[2] Prozeß, 172.
[3] Roman Society, 45; also, The Trial of Christ, in Historicity and Chronology in the Gospels, S.P.C.K. Theological Collection 6, London 1965, 97-116, esp. 114f.

had at this stage and partly to stress the all-compelling pressure of the divine δεῖ (cf. ἀπεστάλην Lk 4.43, as against ἐξῆλθον, Mk 1.38) when Jesus resists popular pressure. Consequently, Luke can only be regarded as rationalizing in the service of a theological purpose.   2. Mk 4.35 ὀψίας γενομένης becomes in Lk 8.22 ἐγένετο δὲ ἐν μιᾷ τῶν ἡμερῶν. Mk, but not Lk, makes the stilling of the storm take place on the evening of the day when Jesus gave the parable of the sower. Mk, but this time Lk as well, closely associates the stilling of the storm with the cure of the Gadarene demoniac (Mk 5.2; Lk 8.27). Luke has apparently rationalized the time-scheme of Mk, according to which they crossed the lake in the evening and so met the demoniac at night, for an appeal by the swineherds to a large group of people at night is odd. However, the time-change must here again be interpreted with reference to a personnel change: those from the city are not for Lk, as in Mk, the owners. Rather they are 'all the people of the surrounding country of the Gerasenes', Lk 8.37. Once again a widening has occurred in line with Luke's stress on the massive effect of Jesus' activity. Therefore, as in the first example, such rationalizing as has occured is within a theological perspective.   3. According to Lk 9.37 the healing of the epileptic child occurred on the day following the transfiguration, whereas Mk conveys the impression that the two events occured on the same day. Luke's motive for the change here is theological: the transfiguration is at night (cf. βεβαρημένοι ὕπνῳ, 9.32), thus heightening the glory and assimilating the incident to the scene on the Mount of Olives.[1] There is therefore no choice but to time the healing on the next day.   4. According to Mk, Jesus cleansed the temple on the day following the entry to the city (Mk 11.12); Luke changes this and makes Jesus proceed directly to the temple. Again the reason is theological: Jesus makes the temple the scene of his own characteristic activity.[2]

Thus we have four time changes. Since Lk 22.66 shows no theological scheme being presented by means of the chronological datum, the four examples above would only present a partial parallel for a rationalizing method. To this rather tenuous evidence must be added the Mk 3.13 = Lk 6.13 case,[3] which does not involve a change of time but which shows Luke redacting in a closely parallel linguistic formation: καὶ ὅτε ἐγένετο ἡμέρα, (cf. Acts 27.39—in a we-passage). This draws

---

[1] Flender, op.cit. 31.
[2] See pp. 130f.
[3] Cf. E. Klostermann, Lk, 220.

attention to the word ὡς, by which alone 22.66 is distinguished. Neither of the 2 Markan instances of the conjuction ὡς have parallel passages in Lk (Mk 9.21, 14.72). Luke uses ὡς redactionally in Markan passages 4 times (Lk 6.4, 8.47, 19.29, 20.37), but of these only 19.29 is a temporal case. (The others have a sense equivalent to the Markan πῶς). Temporal examples of ὡς in L are plentiful, 8 in all, not counting the infancy narratives (4.25, 5.4, 7.12, 11.1, 12.58, 15.25, 19.5,41). The fact that two texts, 1.44 and 4.25, have the even closer parallel ὡς ἐγένετο may suggest that all three cases are editorial. The decision at this point must however take account of the fact that 1.44 belongs to material which is not Luke's own creation, and 4.25 belongs to a pericope which is not a redacted Markan block and draws on a Jewish tradition which Luke would not have inserted.[1] These two instances would suggest therefore that even if ὡς ἐγένετο ἡμέρα is Lukan at 22.66 this does not mean that the material to which it is added is redactional or originally Markan, and 6.13, otherwise the closest parallel, suggests that there is not necessarily a change of time in such a case. But for 19.29 it would be possible to claim that ὡς as a temporal conjunction is never used by Luke when redacting Mk, but in view of this instance the possibility remains open. There are two other factors which must be borne in mind. The first is that the different timings of the denials in Lk as against Mk are a warning against regarding such divergences as redactional, for Luke was neither theologizing not historicizing there. Secondly, the relative order of the denial, mockery, and trial in Lk as against Mk, would show two transpositions, which we have already seen to be against Luke's disposition. It is within such a structure that Lk 22.66 belongs, and therefore although Lukan redaction cannot be ruled out in the actual phrasing of ὡς ἐγένετο ἡμέρα the underlying source is not thereby shown to be Mk, nor is the time-implication in the underlying source likely to have been different.

Thirdly, is it correct to take Luke's account as a record of only the last phase of the hearing? This is certainly not how anyone who had not read Mk would interpret Lk, and the suggestion falls under suspicion as a harmonization in consequence. Luke does not intend his narrative to be taken in this way, for the time-note is connected not with the interrogation but with the entry into the council-chamber where the proceedings were to take place.

Fourthly, is Sherwin White's criticism of Lk such as to support a

---

[1] P. Feine, Eine vorlukanische Überlieferung des Lukas, Gotha 1891, 44.

preference for Mk at this point? It is plainly an overstatement of the case to argue that 'on Luke's timetable the reference to Pilate cannot take place until several hours after dawn',[1] for no indication is given of the length of time taken by the Sanhedrin hearing. In fact Lk is no worse than Mk here, for the latter also has a morning meeting, though of a different kind. The argument from the normal working routine of the Roman official is not entirely conclusive for Passover time when in any case that routine had been changed to bring the procurator to Jerusalem during a period of exceptional restlessness. Finally, the matter is not clinched by the argument that 'the quite inessential detail of the fire . . . . supports the Marcan version'.[2] The fire merely indicates that the whole sequence included a nocturnal period, but not that during that particular period Jesus must have been on trial. And even if Jesus was at that time being examined it does not have to be the Mk 14.55-64 event: in view of the close relationship of the Lukan and Johannine traditions, Jn 18.19-21 is a better candidate for filling the gap.

3. *Lk* 22.66 *in relation to Mk* 14.53b, 15.1a

Blinzler has written: 'Jedenfalls stellt sich Lk 22.66 literarkritisch als eine Verbindung von Mk 14.53b und 15.1a dar.'[3] In order to test this view it will be helpful to set out the Markan and Lukan data, and from the comparison of the texts it emerges that there are just three details in Mk 15.1a which are not in 14.53b, i.e. (a) καὶ εὐθὺς πρωί, (b) συμβούλιον ἑτοιμάσαντες and (c) ὅλον τὸ συνέδριον.

Mk 14.53b	Mk 14.55a	Mk 15.1a	Lk 22.66
καὶ συνέρχονται πάντες		καὶ εὐθὺς πρωί συμβούλιον ἑτοιμασάντες	καὶ ὡς ἐγένετο ἡμέρα συνήχθη τὸ πρεσβυτέριον τοῦ λαοῦ
οἱ ἀρχιερεῖς καὶ οἱ πρεσβύτεροι καὶ οἱ γραμματεῖς	οἱ δὲ ἀρχιερεῖς	οἱ ἀρχιερεῖς μετὰ τῶν πρεσβυτέρων καὶ γραμματέων	ἀρχιερεῖς τε
	καὶ ὅλον τὸ συνέδριον	καὶ γραμματεῖς καὶ ὅλον τὸ συνέδριον	καὶ γραμματεῖς . . . εἰς τὸ συνέδριον αὐτῶν

The question of the time note in Lk which might correspond to καὶ εὐθὺς πρωί has been dealt with, and dependence would only be assured

---

[1] Roman Society, 45.

[2] op.cit. 45.

[3] Prozeß, 172.

if all the surrounding data showed signs of a Markan origin; there are already good reasons for doubting this.

As regards (b), the contents of Lk 22.66-71 do not fit the meaning of Mk 15.1, which they would have to do if dependence were to be a secure conclusion. The word συμβούλιον in its only other occurrence in Mk, that is 3.6,[1] describes the planning of strategy, the holding of a consultation,[2] but certainly not the interrogation of the accused or the examination of testimony. Mk 15.1 can hardly have meant anything else to Mark than the planning of the case against Jesus with a view to carrying the day before Pilate.[3] Moreover it cannot be argued that Luke might have understood Mk 15.1 differently, inferring perhaps something like the session of Lk 22.66-71, because (a) he certainly understood the meaning of Mk 3.6 correctly, and paraphrased, 'they discussed with one another what they might do to Jesus', a sense which fits Mk 15.1 exactly and only makes plainer the divergence from Lk 22.66; (b) the phrase was not so ambiguous in itself that Matthew misunderstood it, since his uses of the term apart from 12.14(=Mk 3.6) and 27.1(=Mk 15.1) are at 22.15 where a plan of campaign is hatched which issues in the debate about tribute, 27.7 where the decision to buy the potter's field is debated, and 28.12 which describes an Easter morning conference. In every case the private process of agreement on a plan is in mind. (c) By inserting the redacted form of Mk 14.62 at Lk 22.69 Luke also shows that he regards 22.66-71 as equivalent to Mk 14.55-64 and therefore Lk 22.66 as parallel to Mk 14.53b, with no necessity to refer to Mk 15.1 at all. (d) The four instances of συμβουλεύω in the N.T. (Mt 26.4, Jn 18.14, Acts 9.23, Rev 3.18) fit precisely the sense of conferring. So Luke's account does not conform to this word as far as the actual contents of Lk 22.67-71 are concerned, nor is a process of taking counsel afterwards required. For Lk 20.20,26 makes clear by redaction that the issue was a search for some self-incriminating saying of Jesus which, once found, would be sufficient to cause him to be passed on to the governor. In view of all this, element (b) does not provide any contact between Mk 15.1a and Lk 22.66.

It is necessary in the case of (c) to begin by determining the meaning

---

[1] For our purpose it does not matter whether ἐδίδουν or ἐποίησαν is the original reading.

[2] W. F. Arndt—F. W. Gingrich, A Greek-English Lexicon of the New Testament, Cambridge 1957, 785.

[3] Thus, J. Finegan, Leidensgeschichte, 73: 'Sie fertigten einen Plan, d.h. sie machten eine Vorbereitung, wie sie die Sache Pilatus vorführen sollten.' Similarly, Sherwin White, Roman Society, 44f.

of εἰς τὸ συνέδριον αὐτῶν. It could mean either 'into their council-chamber' [1] or 'into their assembly'.[2] The evidence in favour of the first interpretation is, firstly, the fact that the assembly has already been named, τὸ πρεσβυτέριον,[3] and to do it a second time would be tautologous. Secondly, συνέδριον is used in this local sense, according to Winter,[4] at Acts 6.12 and possibly at Acts 4.15, 23.6,20,28. Thirdly, the preposition εἰς does not mean 'before' (the council).[5] Fourthly, a change of setting from ἡ οἰκία τοῦ ἀρχιερέως is implied by the verb ἀπήγαγον.

The only modifications needed to these arguments are minor ones. The Acts references are not all unequivocal: [6] Acts 23.6,20,28 are unclear and their closeness to Acts 23.1,15 counts, if anything, against the topographical sense. But Acts 6.12, where the formulation is very similar to Lk 22.66, is geographical, and very probably Acts 4.15 too.[7] Further a change of venue is certainly intended, as in the Johannine tradition,[8] and it is even possible that A. Merx is correct that ἀνήγαγον is the original reading.[9] The significance of the reference for our present purpose is that the Lk 22.66 sense is different from that in Mk 15.1: it is both reduced from an official title by the addition of αὐτῶν and also denotes a place.

Hence at the three points of apparent overlap between Lk 22.66 and Mk 15.1, we find in fact independence. This is only what we would expect from what is known about Luke's editorial method: he does not conflate material from various sources, preferring to work with blocks, nor does he ever merge two separate events into one. We can now go on to accept Winter's suggestion [10] that Lk 22.66 preserves a non-Markan tradition, provided Mk 14.53a and Lk 22.66 are similarly

---

[1] E. Hirsch, Frühgeschichte, 266; P. Winter, On the Trial, 20; E. G. Kraeling, The Four Gospels, London 1964, 255; E. Lohse, TWNT 7 (1964), 868; Blinzler, Prozeß, 167.

[2] Grundmann, Lk, 419; Klostermann, Lk, 220; Rengstorf, Lk, 259; F. E. Meyer, NTS 14 (1968), 548.

[3] On this, cf. J. Jeremias, ΠΡΕΣΒΥΤΕΡΙΟΝ ausserchristlich bezeugt, ZNW 48 (1957), 127-132; G. Bornkamm, art. πρεσβυτέριον, TDNT 6 (1968), 654.

[4] On the Trial, 160.

[5] On the Trial, 160.

[6] Acts 5.21,27,34,41, 22.30, 24.20 are almost certainly personal.

[7] Arndt-Gingrich, Lexicon, 794; E. Lohse, TWNT 7 (1964), 868.

[8] J. Schniewind, Parallelperikopen, 40.

[9] Die Evangelien des Markus und Lukas, Berlin 1905, 473f. He argues that this stems from 'eine wirklich alte Quelle'. It fits the facts, namely the necessity of going up the Temple mount to the place of the assembly of the Sanhedrin, cf. Lk 18.10.

[10] On the Trial, 21,160.

unrelated. But there is nothing to suggest any relationship except the common ἀρχιερεῖς .... καὶ γραμματεῖς and, possibly, the verb ἀπήγαγον. The former phrase is commonplace in any context dealing with the Sanhedrin, and the latter, even if original, is an obvious word to use for a change of scene. Independence is therefore the result.

4. *The connection between Lk 22.66 and 22.67*

This, it has been argued by Winter,[1] is so strained that the two verses cannot belong to the same source. He claims that the subject of ἀπήγαγον is the guards of 22.63-65 whereas λέγοντες refers to the Council.[2] But this is not so because (a) the αὐτοί of the phrase εἰς τὸ συνέδριον αὐτῶν are the subjects of ἀπήγαγον, i.e. the Sanhedrin members, not the guards, and (b) the actions ἀπήγαγον/ἀνήγαγον and λέγοντες are not meant to be contemporaneous.[3] The attempt to attribute 22.67-71 to a post-Lukan editor is part of Winter's aim at this point, and this will be dealt with later, but here it is sufficient to note that the signs of Lukan redaction in 22.69 prevent the context of that verse from being post-Lukan.

5. *The interrogation, Lk 22.67f,70*

Reasons have already been given [4] for the view that 22.69 is an interruption in its present context. H. Flender has rightly seen 22.67b,68 as an answer complete in itself.[5] An examination of the material surrounding 22.69 strongly suggests an independent tradition.

A word must first be said about the interrogators of Jesus. Blinzler has quite rightly remarked that even if the Lukan narrative were independent (and he himself does not believe it is), it still has to be asked whether it is better historically than Mk.[6] He then argues that Mk is better because it gives prominence to the high priest, whose role Luke ignores. While as a historical argument this is not quite convincing—for Luke scarcely expects his statement to be interpreted with the utmost literalness as meaning that the whole body spoke in chorus—it raises a point of importance for source-criticism. If Luke changed from Mk's specific reference to the one high priestly ques-

---

[1] Treatment, 163.
[2] Similarly, Merx, op.cit. 473.
[3] C. F. D. Moule, Idiom Book, 101, cites as parallels for this: Lk 2.42, 23.49, Acts 14.21, 19.9, 24.10, 27.7, 28.6.
[4] See pp. 157-159.
[5] Luke, 45.
[6] Prozeß, 171.

tioner to the more general reference, he would have been acting out of character. (a) He continually shows an inclination to make general references more specific, rather than the other way round. This happens in various ways: Capernaum is defined more carefully (4.31, cf. Mk 1.21), unnecessary and additional disciples are dropped (4.38, cf. Mk 1.29), Jesus is questioned about fasting by only the disciples of John (5.33, cf. Mk 2.18), only one boat is mentioned instead of a group (8.22, cf. Mk 4.36), the epileptic child is μονογενής (9.38, cf. Mk 9.17), a vaguely described accompanying group is defined as disciples (19.37, cf. Mk 11.9), general references to many servants are dropped (20.12, cf. Mk 12.5), two disciples are named Peter and John (21.8, cf. Mk 14.13). It is something of an exception when Luke drops the name of Bartimaeus (18.35, cf. Mk 10.46). (b) A probably historicizing tendency leads him to modify references to Jewish leaders en bloc by the qualification τίνες (6.1, 20.27, cf. Mk 2.23, 12.18). (c) At the same time as he makes reference to the Sanhedrin as a body, Luke's Acts references do not hesitate to single out the high priest(s) individually (Acts 4.6, 5.17,21,27, 7.1, 23.2). It cannot therefore be argued that the Sanhedrin as a body replaces a reference to the high priest in Luke's view in order to give corporate solidarity to the opposition to the Christian cause. Also, in the Lukan narrative the solidarity of the Sanhedrin is modified as much as in Mk by the dissent of Joseph of Arimathea (23.51, cf. Mk 15.43). (d) Changes in group references have already been noticed [1] but the reasons in those cases cannot be paralleled at 22.66.

It appears therefore that the difference between the two accounts is indicative of separateness, but how are they related in the history of tradition? In the same way as Matthew made Mk's reference more specific by naming the high priest at the Mk 14.53 = Mt 26.57 parallel, so the more general reference at Lk 22.66 would seem to be earlier than the specific one in Mk. The reason which Blinzler urges as an historical judgment turns out to be significant as a traditio-historical one.

It is now possible to turn to the content of the interrogation. Many scholars have noticed the closeness of Lk 22.67f to the Johannine tradition.[2] Lk 22.67a recalls Jn 10.24 εἰ σὺ εἶ ὁ χριστός εἰπὸν ἡμῖν παρρησία

---

[1] See pp. 187f.

[2] W. Bussmann, Synoptische Studien III, Halle 1931, 143; J. Schniewind, Die Parallelperikopen bei Lukas und Johannes, 2nd ed. Darmstadt 1958, 34; J. A. Bailey, Traditions, 60f; K. H. Rengstorf, Lk, 259; E. Ruckstuhl, Chronologie,

and similarly Lk 22.67b is close to Jn 10.25 ἀπεκρίθη αὐτοῖς ὁ Ἰησοῦς. Εἶπον ὑμῖν καὶ οὐ πιστεύετε. The separation of messiah and Son of God discussions in each passage led Blinzler to speak of 'zwei selbständige Fragen .... (johanneische Tradition?)',[1] though he then turned from this possibility to the view of Conzelmann that Luke is redacting Mk.[2] The literary parallelism between Lk and Jn is however too close to be overlooked, and the more so as it occurs in a passion narrative with so many signs of relationship with Johannine material.[3] The only necessity is to determine which is the dependent version.

Winter opposes the view that John used Lk 22.67-71 for the construction of Jn 10, on the grounds that the fourth evangelist intended to give—and gave—a very full version of the trial of Jesus, and since he had set his mind on stressing the responsibility of the Jewish authorities for Jesus' death, he would not have tampered with Lk in this way.[4] But: (a) Jn's account does show signs of transposition in that Jesus had not up to that point (contra 10.25) affirmed his messiahship before the Jews. (b) His overall presentation of the career of Jesus as a trial, with witnesses, cross-examinations and confessions throughout, makes it thoroughly feasible that passion material should be scattered through the gospel. Parallels for such a retrojection of passion material are the presence of the temple cleansing at Jn 2.13-17 (cf. Mk 11.15-17), the question about authority at Jn 2.18 (cf. Mk 11.27-33), the saying about temple destruction at Jn 2.19 (cf. Mk 14.58), the eucharistic saying at Jn 6.51 (cf. Lk 22.19, 1 Cor 11.24),[5] and the

---

41; E. Haenchen, Weg, 510. Contra F. Spitta, Die synoptische Grundschrift, Leipzig 1912, 397, who thinks of an amalgamation of Matthaean and Markan traits as in Lk 9.20 (cf. Mt 16.16, Mk 8.29). The weight of evidence for Lukan θεός/τοῦ θεοῦ redactions makes it overwhelmingly probable that Lk 9.20 and Mt 16.16 are totally unrelated redactions of Mk 8.29.

[1] Prozeß, 173. Compare the reticence combined with uncertainty on the part of W. Bussmann, Synoptische Studien III, Halle 1931, 110,126, who allows the existence of a special Lukan passion narrative but confines traces of it in the block 22.66-71 to 22.67b,68. Cf. op.cit.I,200: '67-68 könnte aus der Sonderquelle stammen' and op.cit. III, 110: 'vielleicht auch 67-69'. Bussmann's uncertainty at this point is paralleled by some discrepancy in his references to 22.55a, and yet the reproduction of all of 22.55 in the text of the Sonderquelle, op.cit. III, 125. Similarly, the mockery appears in S by way of 22.63,65, op.cit.III, 125, but through 22.63-64, op.cit.III, 110.

[2] Luke, 84.

[3] Schniewind, Parallelperikopen, 37-62; Bussmann, op.cit.III, 142-144; S. I. Buse, St. John and the Passion Narratives of St. Matthew and St. Luke, NTS 7 (1960), 65-76.

[4] Lk XXII.66-71, StTh 9 (1955), 112-115.

[5] P. Borgen, Bread from Heaven, 89-92; Jeremias, Eucharistic Words, 107f.

Gethsemane agony at Jn 12.27f (cf. Mk 14.33-35). (c) If this material were the product of Lukan redaction we should expect not εἶπεν δὲ αὐτοῖς, 22.67, but πρὸς αὐτούς for which Luke has a predilection.[1] (d) The intensive negative οὐ μή, here repeated in 22.67b,68, is untypical of Luke.[2] (e) The parallelism of structure in Jesus' reply is not Lukan. Heinz Schürmann has remarked: 'Es kann kein Beispiel beigebracht werden, daß Luk einen Satz-parallelismus von sich aus schafft'.[3] (f) Luke's version is in small details less elaborate than that in Jn. Firstly, Jesus does not state in Lk that he has already declared his messiahship, even though the wording is related to Jn 10.25. Secondly, υἱὸς τοῦ θεοῦ εἰμι Jn 10.36, lacks the small qualification[4] inherent in ὑμεῖς λέγετε, Lk 22.70. (g) Jn's passion narrative has a curious gap left by its totally vacant references to the encounter with Caiaphas, Jn 18.24,28. Therefore we cannot see a direct indebtedness on the part of either Lukan or Johannine versions to the other. Lk's tradition is an independent one relying on neither Jn nor Mk. And Bailey is right at this point to conclude that Jn derived his picture 'neither from his imagination nor from Luke, but from the same non-Johannine source from which Luke derived it'.[5]

Still more considerations stemming from a further comparison with Mk support this view. A change from the decisive ἐγώ εἰμι, Mk 14.62, to the non-committal reply of Lk 22.67b,68 is inconceivable.[6] Moreover, Luke does not tend to lengthen Mk's dialogues, but he has done so here if he uses Mk.[7] The second reply ὑμεῖς λέγετε ὅτι ἐγώ εἰμι is tautologous [8] and this suggests that ὅτι ἐγώ εἰμι is drawn from Mk 14.62. But mutatis mutandis, this means that ὑμεῖς λέγετε was drawn from another source, which indeed is proved by (a) the Semitic idiom;[9] (b) the change from the utterly clear affirmation of divine Sonship in Mk 14.62; (c) Luke's normal dislike of the present tense [10] which, if he

---

[1] H. Schürmann, Der Paschamahlbericht, Münster 1953, 4f; Jeremias, Eucharistic Words, 185.

[2] Schürmann, op.cit. 17f.

[3] op.cit. 2.

[4] Cf. D. R. Catchpole, The Answer of Jesus to Caiaphas, NTS 17 (1971), 226.

[5] Traditions, 60.

[6] Caird, Luke, 245; Grundmann, Lk, 420; Ruckstuhl, Chronologie, 41; Colpe, art. ὁ υἱὸς τοῦ ἀνθρώπου, 438; H. Flender, Luke, 45: 'Jesus gives an "evasive" answer, thus exposing the insincerity of the question and leaving the problem still in the air.'

[7] Schürmann, Paschamahlbericht, 3.

[8] B. Weiss, Die Quellen der synoptischen Überlieferung, 1908, 157.

[9] Cf. Mt 26.64.

[10] Cadbury, Style, 158-164, 168-171; Schürmann, Paschamahlbericht, 83;

was determined to introduce a ὑμεῖς form, would have made ὑμεῖς εἴ-πατε more likely.

At this point the question of οὖν, 22.70, arises. It has to be decided whether this is Lukan or pre-Lukan, and this in turn hinges on whether it takes up 22.68 or 22.69. When the pericope is relieved of v.69, it is immediately apparent that οὖν does not fit if understood in a logically consecutive sense, though it could be original if understood simply as a connective. For this last sense there are parallels: Lk 3.7,18, 7.31 (note the parallel δέ in Mt 11.16), 14.34, 20.17,29,44, 21.7. This is more likely to be the case than the alternative theory of Lukan insertion of οὖν, though that is possible. In the latter case, it would be part of the Lukan scheme's acceptance of material (drawn from sources) linking christological titles with the resurrection and exaltation, Acts 2.36, 13.32-37, and his own connection of sonship with resurrection existence, Lk 20.27-40, esp.36.

It is necessary now to examine H. E. Tödt's treatment of the christology of Lk 22.67-71. He has rightly questioned Conzelmann's theory that these verses are intended to set out explicitly the fundamental identity of the current Christological titles.[1] Against this Tödt points out that (a) the questions about messiah and Son of God are separated; (b) Son of God comes as a climax; (c) the titles themselves are not interchangeable.[2] His conclusion is therefore to be preferred: 'The titles complement one another. This complementary relationship is established by Luke's attributing all the designations to the one Jesus but each with a meaning of its own.' Even so Tödt's evaluation is to be questioned in some respects. (a) He argues that Luke has a different conception of the christological titles mentioned in Mk 14.61f.[3] But this is not so, for Luke's own view emerges from the redactional activity at Lk 4.41 as well as from Acts 9.20-22, and it is exactly that of Mk 14.61f. In Lk 4.41, Luke is redacting Mk 1.34, and he inserts the cry of the demons: σὺ εἶ ὁ υἱὸς τοῦ θεοῦ and then adds his own commentary ᾔδεισαν τὸν χριστὸν αὐτὸν εἶναι. This shows irrefutably the equivalence of the titles in Luke's own mind;[4] the demons know Jesus

---

Jeremias, Eucharistic Words, 150. For this reason all suggestion of indebtedness to Mt 26.64 must be resisted.

[1] Conzelmann, Luke, 84,171.

[2] The Son of Man in the Synoptic Tradition, London 1965, 101-103.

[3] op.cit. 101.

[4] Blinzler, Prozeß, 150, writes: 'Im NT finden sich zwei Stellen, wo die Ausdrücke "Gottessohn" und "Christus" offensichtlich synonym gebraucht sind: Lk 4,41a.b; Apg 9.20,22. Sie allein schon verwehren es, unter Berufung auf das

is the messiah and express it in the declaration that he is Son of God. The same result follows from Acts 9.20,22, where there are set in parallel two statements: οὗτός ἐστον ὁ υἱὸς τοῦ θεοῦ and οὗτός ἐστιν ὁ χριστός. (b) Tödt suggests that Jesus' answer to the first question reveals his lowliness, and the judges' unbelief covers up the validity of his claim to be messiah, 22.67b. But this is not quite the thrust of Jesus' reply, for vv.67b,68 fail altogether to respond to the content of the question. Tödt is pushing the evidence too far in finding at this precise point a contrast between 'utmost humiliation' and 'heavenly sovereignty',[1] however much Luke himself may contrast and correlate suffering and glory elsewhere. What we are able to deduce at this point is:—(a) The evasion concerning messiahship is so untypical of Luke that he cannot be responsible for it. (b) The separation of 'messiah, Son of God' which is expressed in the distinct questions, is continued by the various replies, provokes different legal consequences, and also contradicts Luke's theology [2] as seen in Lk 4.41, Acts 9.20-22, and so again redaction of Mk cannot be defended.

Helmut Flender has expounded Lk 22.66-23.1 as an example of Luke's use of two-stage christology (Zweistufenschema).[3] He argues that in the two questions two levels of evaluating the person of Jesus emerge, expressing respectively two spheres of existence. His conclusions, which are regarded as typical of Luke, are summed up as follows:[4] 1. The two modes of Jesus' existence are differentiated and stand related to one another in terms of climactic parallelism. The Sanhedrin sees only the messiah according to Jewish understanding, whereas confession of the (exalted) Son of God is required. 2. To this the two-stage christology corresponds. The question, 'Are you the Christ? ', in the Jewish sense of David's son, remains on the level of

---

Fehlen sicherer jüdischer Zeugnisse die messianische Bedeutung des Ausdrucks "Sohn des Hochgelobten" in Mk 14,61 für unmöglich zu erklären.' But in both these cases it is *Luke* who is responsible, and since the background is that of Hellenistic Christianity it does nothing to support Mk 14.61. Rather does Lk 22.67-70 stand out as all the more clearly divergent from Mk and as the more Jewish and non-Lukan conception. It is certainly not possible to regard the two terms as 'Wechselbegriffe', Blinzler, op.cit. 189.

[1] op.cit. 102.
[2] A. J. B. Higgins, Jesus and the Son of Man, London 1964, 68, is wrong to say that in spite of the separation the net result is the same. Son of God is not an inference from the discussion of messiahship, and the former, unlike the latter, brings the trial to a climax.
[3] Luke, 44-46.
[4] op.cit. 46.

popular opinion which holds Jesus to be a prophet (Lk 7.16,39, 9.8,19).
The question about divine Sonship aims, according to heavenly reality,
at faith which takes directly what Jesus says, 'from his own lips'.
3. The section as such shows a tripartite scheme: in contrast with the
human ambiguity level stands that of heavenly consummation which
in turn becomes present on earth through faith.

Although this proposed exegesis by Flender contains some valuable
insights, it is still weak in places. (a) He has not made a clear decision
on source-analysis. He cites Conzelmann who treats the whole as
redaction of Mk and indeed speaks of the omission of the temple
saying,[1] yet also asks whether the passage owes its form to an older
tradition[2] and suggests that there may be an underlying older tradition—indeed a Johannine tradition on which Luke is dependent. Failure
to decide on the exact source-critical situation means that the theolo-
gies of Luke and of his sources are not separately exposed. (b) The
parallel two-layer scheme in Lk 20.41-44 (=Mk 12.35-37) is not quite
so exact. Here it is a matter of two definitions of messiahship corresponding to the earthly and heavenly levels.[3] But Lk 22.67-70 is different, for in v.69 it is not that 'Lord' is set over against 'Son of David'
but that 'Son of man + Lord' is set against nothing at all. Not only
does Lk 20.41-44 accept Davidic messiahship, but it is also differentiated from the trial scene by the omission of the reference to the scribes,
20.41. (c) Similarly there is nothing in v.67 which Luke brands as
political and contrasts with what follows, and a contrast between
opinion and faith, v.67 as against v.70, is vitiated by the fact that the
same people ask and are answered in each case. πάντες is quite unable
to broaden the questions beyond the Sanhedrin.[4] (d) In order to bring
in the theme of popular opinion Flender has to recall the view that
Jesus is a prophet. But prophet is not the same as messiah, and Luke
reproduces sources in which Jesus himself, and not just the people,
adopts the title of prophet (4.24-27, 13.33).

The distinctive features of Lk 22.67-70 remain: in the questions the
two titles are separate and in the answers an evasion of one title and a
confession of the other is made.[5] Hence this is not Luke's view of the

---

[1] op.cit. 44.

[2] Similarly, E. E. Ellis, The Gospel of Luke, London 1966, 260.

[3] See D. Daube, New Testament and Rabbinic Judaism, 158-169; H. Conzelmann, Outline, 74.

[4] op.cit. 45.

[5] The same argumentation applies against F. Spitta, Grundschrift, 397-400.
Spitta thinks vv.66-69 come from a pre-Lukan source and vv. 70f from redaction

equivalence of messiah and Son of God. Nor is it a post-Lukan construction as Winter would suggest,[1] for the presence of v.69 pins the passage down to either the Lukan or the pre-Lukan stage.[2]

Still more can be said. Lk 22.66-70 depicts a scheme in which the identification of messiah and Son of God has not yet taken place. It has been shown to be a non-Markan and Semitically-coloured account. Even Mark's version showed Semitic traces.[3] So too does Luke's, and the latter has to be pushed back even further in time. Although the equivalence of messiah and Son of God in pre-Christian Judaism has been disputed,[4] it yet seems probable that the equation of the two was being established in Qumran at the time.[5] Lk 22.67-70 belongs to circles where the equation is not yet current, and where divine Sonship is a repugnant concept sealing the doom of the claimant. By contrast with this passage Mk 14.61f emerges as secondary theologically, and influenced kerygmatically in a way which Lk is not. It is with the latter version that historical authenticity corresponds.

6. *The end of the hearing*

There are three elements which need consideration. (a) πάντες, 22.70. Winter regards the involvement of all the Sanhedrin as both the hasty work of an adaptor intent on blaming all official Jewry and also

of Mk 14.61f and Mt 26.63f. This means: 'Es schliesst also die aus ihm erkennbare Grundschrift die Synedriumsitzung so ab, daß Jesus jede Antwort verweigert und sich seiner Erhöhung zum Vater getröstet.' Spitta's argumentation proceeds from two questions: 1. How can Jesus be asked about Son of God when he had previously spoken only of Son of man? 2. How can Jesus answer ὑμεῖς λέγετε ὅτι ἐγώ εἰμι when he had previously refused to answer the question about messiahship? But in answer to this, question 1 is misconceived in view of the dependence of v.69 on Mk 14.62, and question 2 fails to allow for the inconsistency it raises within the Lukan editorial process in view of the clear equivalence for Luke of the two terms messiah and Son of God.

The differentiation applies against C. K. Barrett's suggestion that 'You say that I am' is the reply to the messianic question, parallel to Mt 26.64 (Mk 14.62), Jesus and the Gospel Tradition, London 1967, 23.

[1] Treatment, 163: 'The term 'Son of God' is opposed to the connotation of Messiahhood, but in no way explained in any specific non-Messianic meaning . . . .; it belongs to the period when the term 'Son of God' in Christian usage had already become dissociated from its Messianic foundation.'

[2] In all points other than the statement that 22.67-70 is typically Lukan, Conzelmann's criticisms of Winter hold good: Luke, 85.

[3] G. Dalman, Die Worte Jesu, 2nd ed. Leipzig 1930, 163-165; F. Hahn, Hoheitstitel, 181.

[4] E. Lohse, Geschichte, 85.

[5] O. Michel—O. Betz, Von Gott gezeugt, in: Judentum Christentum Urkirche, Festschrift J. Jeremias, Berlin 1960, 3-23; R. H. Fuller, Foundations, 32.

a sign that vv.66-71 do not originate with Luke. The pivot of the argument is 23.51, where Luke hastens to clarify that Joseph of Arimathea had not consented to their counsel and deed.[1] If this stems from Luke, the argument is that πάντες and ἅπαν τὸ πλῆθος αὐτῶν cannot do so. But this is too literalist, for πάντες does not always have to be interpreted in a mathematical sense. Thus in Lk 8.45 πάντες = all except the woman who confessed, in 8.52 πάντες = all except the parents, and in 21.29 πάντες = all except the fig tree. Therefore again, a post-Lukan adaption at vv.66-71 is quite improbable. Whether πάντες is Lukan or pre-Lukan cannot be determined. Certainly Luke does often use it redactionally [2] and this may be the case here. (b) τί ἔτι ἔχομεν μαρτυρίας χρείαν; Whereas the Lukan form is smoother than the Markan through not bisecting χρείαν μαρτυρίας by ἔχομεν, and this would be consistent with redaction of Mk, yet there seems no reason for the movement of χρείαν to the end of the question. It is true that v.71b could stand without v.71a, and therefore the possibility remains open that the latter is an insertion drawn from Mk.[3] (c) ἀπὸ τοῦ στόματος αὐτοῦ. This is the climax of the trial and has three parallels in Lk, all in L material (4.22, 11.53f, 19.22). All three passages bear on 22.71. In 4.22 the word ἐμαρτύρουν is used in the same sentence; in 11.53f the context is a plot to get rid of Jesus, and a dangerous word would be enough. In 19.22 the intensified condemnation of the slothful servant is expressed in ἐκ τοῦ στόματός σου κρινῶ σε. 22.71 therefore uses a phrase which is unusual in itself, confined to L and in all contexts legal in its bearing. Probably this is a mark of the Sonderquelle.

Lk 22.71 also contributes to the exact evaluation of the whole hearing in 22.66-71. It is important to know whether this is a formal trial or

---

[1] Winter argues that βουλευτής does not imply membership of the Sanhedrin, Treatment, 165. But it certainly means membership of the council (βουλή), and since Luke takes steps to dissociate Joseph, the implication is that membership of the Sanhedrin is intended.

Winter states: 'The account which the Third Evangelist gives of the proceedings by the πρεσβυτέριον τοῦ λαοῦ excludes all possibility of identifying "their counsel and deed" with the condemnation of Jesus.' On the Trial, 48. This is a completely unprovable assertion. Lk 22.66-71 fits perfectly well with what Winter rejects. And if he were correct about the post-Lukan origin of this, and if in consequence only v.66 were original, there is too little said for a claim to be made in either direction, but a condemnation is not at all excluded. It is with conscious hesitation that Winter identifies the counsel and deed with approval of the charge sheet and the despatch to Pilate.

[2] Lk 4.37, 5.28, 6.10,17,19, 8.40,45,47,52,9.1,7,13,23,43, 18.22,31,43, 20.18,38, 21.12,29.

[3] So B. Weiss, op.cit. 157; R. Bultmann, Synoptic Tradition, 271.

only a preliminary hearing.[1] The argument for the latter is based chiefly on the silence of Luke about a verdict, as well as the problems arising from a trial being held on a feast day. Undoubtedly the comparison with Mk has exerted a heavy influence on the first reason. But such a silence is not conclusive, especially when Luke's account is in any case so short. As for the second reason, it begs legal questions. Moreover there are arguments on the other side, suggesting that a formal session is intended: 1. The change of place and subsequent assembling in το συνέδριον αὐτῶν, v. 66. 2. The formal title το πρεσβυτέριον τοῦ λαοῦ, v.66, which suggests a formal hearing. 3. The words τι ἔτι ἔχομεν μαρτυρίας χρείαν; imply a legal session in the view of the Sonderquelle (if these words are original) or of Luke (if they are redactional). 4. βουλή and πρᾶξις, 23.51, fit a trial better than a preliminary examination and decision to hand Jesus over to Pilate. 5. Acts. 13.27 κρίναντες plainly shows that Luke believed that a verdict had been passed on Jesus.

7. The origin of Lk 22.54a

The record of the arrest and delivery of Jesus to the house of the high priest must first be seen in the wide scheme of Luke's structure. (a) 22.54a is dependent on vv.47-53, for there is no mention of the actual arrest in that passage, which is certainly drawn from the Sonderquelle.[2] (b) There is a schematic agreement with Jn 18.12, where the arrest itself occurs at the beginning of the next block of material and is part of the transference from the garden to the high priest's house.[3] (c) There is a transposition of order in comparison with Mk: Lk-Jn have the sword incident before the arrest.[4] (d) There is an agreement in terminology, both Lk 22.54 and Jn 18.12 using συλλαβόντες. This use of συλλαμβάνω itself bears further investigation. Firstly, συλλαμβάνω in the sense of 'seize' is attested in L (Lk 5.7,9) but also occurs in Acts four times, with Acts 1.16 echoing Lk 22.54. This means it could well be redactional. On the other hand, it is not easy to think of Luke avoiding the terminology of Mk 14.46 (οἱ δὲ ἐπέβαλαν

---

[1] Thus A. Merx, Die Evangelien des Markus und Lukas, Berlin 1905, 479; E. Klostermann, Lk, 231; A. M. Perry, Sources, 45; J. B. Tyson, NovT 3 (1959), 254; G. B. Caird, Luke, 245.

[2] Rehkopf, op.cit. 31-82.

[3] Cf. Schniewind, Parallelperikopen, 34.

[4] Rehkopf, op.cit. 65, also points out correctly that in Lk-Jn the attack with the sword is defensive, not offensive as in Mk.

τὰς χεῖρας αὐτῷ), for the latter phrase occurs twice in Lk, both times redactionally, 20.19, 21.12. In support of this, there are other words Luke could have used, e.g. ἐπιλαμβάνομαι, which appears three times in redaction of Mk (Lk 9.47, 20.20,26) or possibly even συναρπάζω (redactional at Lk 8.29). The evidence is therefore evenly poised: the word could be either Lukan or pre-Lukan, but whatever its derivation the scheme behind it is pre-Lukan.

In the remainder of 22.54a the only verbal overlap with Mk is τὸν ἀρχιερέα/τοῦ ἀρχιερέως, and such an allusion, commonplace in all traditions, is quite insufficient to demonstrate dependence. However, some reference to the transfer of Jesus from the Mount of Olives to the house of the high priest is necessary in order to connect the independent accounts of the arrest and Peter's denial. We are therefore once again in contact with Luke's special source.

If we now return to the issues sketched in the introduction to this chapter, we find that the movement towards acceptance of an independent Lukan tradition, which has gained ground in recent years, does in fact open up a new view of the trial of Jesus. Here is a narrative which is not only unrelated to Mk in almost all respects, but also historically a better source with widespread agreement with the contemporary setting in matters of law and theology.

E. JEWISH USE OF LUKAN TRADITION

From a survey of the approach of Jewish authors to Luke, it emerges that Paul Winter has very few predecessors in the use of a literary-critical method which isolates the Lukan version as a separate source. During the 200 years which span our study, Luke is used occasionally, but when he is it is usually as a witness, details of whose testimony can be set over against what is recorded by other witnesses. He stands as one of the earliest critics of the Markan narrative, and yet often not himself a particularly accurate one. It is not frequent for Jewish writers to investigate his narrative first of all from the angle of source analysis.

The first time Lk 22.66-71 received any attention was in 1861 when Cohen[1] assimilated the dialogue about messiahship and divine Sonship to the material in Mk 14.56,59. Clearly Luke's account, with its climax in the declaration about 'Son of God' is particularly easy to harmonize with a fundamentally Johannine scheme, which in fact Cohen's is. It

---

[1] La Vérité Israélite 3 (1861), 11. See above, p. 89.

must be noticed that Cohen does not use Lk because it is legally preferable; he assumes the work of Salvador on the illegality question, and so shows that it is the content rather than the context of the Sanhedrin trial which interests him. In the end his approach is dislocated and a mixture of non-interlocking schemes. For instance, he projects into the career of Jesus a view of the theological development of the gospels from Mk-Mt through Lk to Jn which was used in contemporary criticism of the gospels in order to locate them historically.

The legality question emerged swiftly after Cohen, briefly with Graetz's preference for Luke's timing,[1] but more significantly with Samuel Hirsch's argument that no Sanhedrin trial took place.[2] He cites the agreement of Luke and John that there was no nocturnal session. The use of this argument, with the later addition of Luke's lack of witnesses and verdict, sets a trend which was followed to the same conclusion by I. M. Wise,[3] J. Lehmann,[4] C. H. Levy[5] and H. E. Goldin.[6] The distinctive features of Luke are also serviceable to those who propose a preliminary hearing. In this case Luke is not simply a witness against one view but also a positive proponent of a different one. This line is taken by J. Hamburger, J. Klausner, I. Mattuck and J. Isaac.[7] For Klausner, the chief appeal of the Lukan tradition was the morning timing in 22.66, but in 1932 he came out more strongly in favour of the view that Luke's account of the arrest and trial is generally better.[8] Nevertheless the contents of the Sanhedrin hearing are still drawn from Mark. Klausner's tendency, such as it is, towards Luke is partly due to the influence of R. W. Husband.[9] With this group Edersheim may most conveniently be classed. His method is essentially harmonistic and he accepts that Luke's session is the equivalent of

---

[1] Geschichte, 2nd ed. 243.

[2] Archives Israélites 26 (1965), 388.

[3] Martyrdom, 63-67: 'We think Luke and John were so much nearer to the time of Mark than we are, that their mere denial should suffice all critical minds to reject the nightly trial of Mark as a piece of fiction.'

[4] REJ 37 (1898), 16: 'On peut donc affirmer sans hésitation, en se fondant, à la fois, sur une vraisemblance qui approche de la certitude et sur le témoignage de Luc, qu'avant de comparaître devant Pilate, Jésus n'a pas été jugé par le Sanhedrin dans le sens exact du mot.'

[5] New World 8 (1899), 497-506.

[6] The Case of the Nazarene reopened, New York 1948, 201,445.

[7] J. Hamburger, art. Jesus von Nazaret, 49; J. Klausner, Jesus, 334,340f; I. Mattuck, The Trial of Jesus, London 1929, 4,11; J. Isaac, Jésus et Israel, 438-443.

[8] EJ 9 (1932), 65.

[9] The Prosecution of Jesus, Princeton 1916.

Mk 14.55-64, and that Luke has changed the order of events in order to unite the two parts of the story of Peter's denial. 'At the same time I confess myself in no wise anxious about an accord of details and circumstances when, admittedly, the facts agree.'[1] This is simply to evade the issue. There is, however, one feature of Luke which remains an embarrassment to Edersheim, namely the συνέδριον reference in 22.66. Having stated, 'There is truly not a trifle of evidence for the assumption of commentators that Christ was led from the palace of Caiaphas into the Council Chamber', he declares it strange that 22.66 should be understood as alluding to that Council Chamber. All the proceedings, he urges, took place in the high priest's house.

This συνέδριον reference is either a difficulty or an opportunity for other Jewish writers. According to E. Grünebaum,[2] Jesus was not examined by the religious authorities (who would be described by συνέδριον) but by a political gathering. Hence Lk 22.66 is explained as redaction of Mk 14.54. For Zeitlin later, συνέδριον is the term which confirms his theory of a political Sanhedrin's having judged Jesus.[3] He mentions the peculiar characteristics of the Lukan version (i.e. the morning timing, no mention of the elders assembling in the house of the high priest, no mention of blasphemy and no verdict) as discrepancies and confusions among the evangelists.[4] So for the contents of the hearing Zeitlin reverts to Mark. It is the συνέδριον reference and the lack of verdict which are most useful to him.

Recently, F. E. Meyer has put forward a distinctive variation on this theme.[5] He takes Luke's version with its daytime hearing to be an alteration, indeed a misguided alteration, of Mark. Luke, thinking Mark's version improbable, was yet unaware that the Sadducean 'Kronrat' could meet in their own room (the Parhedrin = τὸ συνέδριον αὐτῶν, 22.66) during the night. Jesus never stood before the Beth Din ha-Gadol but only before this private body which corresponds to the Acts 4 part of the trial of the apostles. In respect of this approach: (a) Meyer accepts the involvement of Annas, but leaves no room for the Annas hearing, Jn 18.13-24. (b) He appeals to the absence of Pharisaic involvement and urges that the Jesus v. Pharisees conflicts

---

[1] Life and Times, 559.
[2] Sittenlehre, 2nd ed. 263f.
[3] JQR 31 (1941), 359; JQR 55 (1964), 10.
[4] Who crucified Jesus? 151-154.
[5] Einige Bemerkungen zur Bedeutung des Terminus Synhedrion in den Schriften des Neuen Testaments, NTS 14 (1968), 545-551.

belong to the final third ot the first century; yet he appeals to Jn 11.49 which includes the Pharisees, and he is certainly wrong about the controversy stories.[1] (c) He has not brought evidence to establish the validity of the parallel between Jewish hearing + Roman hearing and Acts 4 + Acts 5. (d) The application of his claim that Synhedrion can mean either 'session' or Beth Din does properly fit into Acts 4-5 because firstly, Luke does not interpret them in a different sense (5.28 alludes back to 4.18); secondly, Acts 5.25f may imply that the authorities are not on the temple site; and thirdly, Acts 4.15, the best parallel to Lk 22.66, uses συνέδριον in a local sense.

The tendency to treat the evangelists as separate witnesses has already been noticed. It reappears in the book of H. E. Goldin in a very extreme form, but before that more moderately in the work of M. Radin. He regards Luke as a free follower of Mark [2] but one who draws on material which has the ring of authenticity.[3] Radin notes in particular the reference to the στρατηγοί,[4] the change of time,[5] the different description of the place of the trial [6] and the absence of the high priest.[7] He sees Luke as recording an event which can scarcely be a trial: no witnesses are examined, an indefinite number of the council interrogate Jesus, no accusation about the temple is raised and no formal condemnation follows. 'There is what is apparently an informal questioning by a certain number of persons, followed by the determination to take him to Pilate.' Yet all this is dismissed: 'Whether when Luke differs from Mark or Matthew he is entitled to greater credibility must be determined by other considerations. The balance of probability is against him in some matters, if for no other reason than the avowed religious and didactic purpose of the book'.[8] In detail the following points are made in criticism of Luke: (a) His picture of the organization of the Jewish community is inferior to Mark's, especially in respect of the plural high priests and στρατηγοί. (b) His difference in timing reflects a rationalizing tendency. (c) Mark's account is lucid whereas Luke's is vague, manifests the tendency in developing tradi-

---

[1] See pp. 107-109.
[2] The Trial of Jesus of Nazareth, Chicago 1931, 100.
[3] op.cit. 102.
[4] op.cit. 107.
[5] op.cit. 104.
[6] op.cit. 107.
[7] op.cit. 109.
[8] op.cit. 125.

tion to split one entity into two, and reflects the time when the religious charge could be dropped! [1]

Apart from Klausner's tentative change of mind, the only Jewish writer to tend towards a use of Luke which takes seriously and on reasonable literary grounds the possibility of a separate tradition in Luke is C. G. Montefiore. Montefiore himself is strongly influenced by Husband in his 2nd edition, and Husband had used Luke in a striking way. For him the striking features of the Lukan account were the lack of a night session or formal trial,[2] and this version provided a starting-point for the attempt to find a via media between the view of the trial as manifestly illegal and the alternative of radical criticism of the gospels. The proceedings are accordingly reconstructed as follows: Lk 22.66, Mk 14.56, Mt 26.60b,61, Mk 14.60a,61b, Lk 22.67b-69, Mk 15.1. For the crucial events he takes Luke and Mark as parallel but substantially prefers Luke. Yet while details in which Luke is preferable are stated, there is no adequate explanation of why it is permissible to use them. Husband's rejection of arguments from silence over illegalities is in some tension with his use of silence concerning the verdict. Further there is some ambiguity over the relationship of Lk 22.66 to Mk 15.1: in one place they are regarded as parallel but in the reconstruction they are not.[3] The important fact is however that Luke is used as a source of information (and this is broadly what Klausner gains from Husband) but there is no suggestion of a separate Lukan literary source. It is in this latter question that Montefiore had been moving towards a more distinctive position in 1909,[4] and his second edition, powerfully influenced by Husband, continued this tendency. His original reference to a possible separate Lukan tradition was in dependence on J. and B. Weiss, and based on 'the marked divergence of Luke'.[5] Here however there reappears Montefiore's characteristic hesitancy in forming final conclusions, which makes him state alternatives objectively without taking a decision between them. For instance, he remarks rather obviously that the Denial narrative is due either to redaction of Mk (Loisy) or to a special source (B. Weiss).[6] He does

---

[1] op.cit. 123-125.
[2] The Prosecution of Jesus, 205.   [3] op.cit. 126, 207f.
[4] Gospels I, 337,352; II, 1048.
[5] I(1927), 361.
[6] II (1909), 1069. Compare the fact that although he tends towards a separate Lukan account, he yet accepts Loisy's arguments for the omission of the Temple saying, which are directed against Wellhausen and proceed from the view that Luke depends on Mark.

however regard Lk 22.66-71 as separate tradition[1] and a preferable one
in that it omits the verdict, and does not describe a formal trial.[2]
Separate tradition does not as such imply better tradition, and Montefiore singles out 22.66 with its confusion of πρεσβυτέριον and συνέδριον
as an example of clumsiness—all this in spite of having written earlier[3]
that πρεσβυτέριον stands for the court and συνέδριον for the court-
house.

Against this background it is apparent what a marked step forward
is taken by Paul Winter within the development of Jewish Prozeßforschung, in using to such an extent the Lukan tradition and putting
forward literary-critical reasons for doing so. There was no Jewish
writer whose work in this area he could use.

F.   WINTER ON THE LUKAN TRADITION

During the discussion of Lk 22.54-71 an evaluation of Winter's
arguments was included on some of the crucial points. It was suggested that while he is correct in arguing for a non-Markan Passion narrative and for a role for Annas in Luke,[4] there are yet grounds for questioning his use of the Markan formation of a 'sandwich structure' at
Mk 14.54-72, of the evidence of Acts 13.27f and the Passion predictions, and, in connection with Lk 22.67-71, of his suggestions about its
relation to 22.66 and Jn 10.24-36. To this must now be added a further survey of his views on Lukan material.

1. *Winter's general view of Luke's method*

(a) The interference of Luke with his sources is regarded as minimal.[5]
He gives examples of typical redaction: Luke might change Mark's
λιμοί to λοιμοί καὶ λιμοί, and he was prepared to add 'supplementary
or accessory points of a descriptive or explanatory character if such
addition suggested itself plausible from the Evangelist's own environment and his own experience'.[6] From this Luke emerges as a collector
of data, almost an annalist. All that he did was done with care.[7]

---

[1] II(1909), 1071.

[2] II(1909), 1072; II(1927), 612.

[3] II(1909), 1070.

[4] This does not require the identification with Annas II.

[5] The Treatment of his Sources by the Third Evangelist in Luke XXI-XXIV,
StTh 8 (1955), 138-172, esp. 170f.

[6] Treatment, 171. This accords with Winter's source analysis of Lk 21, op.cit.
141-155.

[7] On the Trial, 28.

However hard it is to defend this, particularly in view of the Mk-Lk parallels, its bearing is clear. Firstly, points where Luke diverges from Mark become evidence for a separate source of information. Such is exemplified in the following statement: 'The Third Evangelist could not have drawn the information that Jesus was led away from the house of the high priest to be confronted by the πρεσβυτέριον τοῦ λαοῦ from Mark—in all likelihood Lc 22.66 is based on a non-Markan record.' [1] Secondly, there is significant deviation from Lietzmann at this point, for the latter thought Luke had used Mark and had modified him considerably. Similarly there is little room for Conzelmann and Redaktionsgeschichte.[2]

Nevertheless this position is too tight to be maintained. Firstly, in the chapter on 'The Enemies of Jesus' [3] Luke is also shown to manipulate the data on Jesus' opponents. Secondly, extensive manipulation must have occurred if Winter is right that Lk 24.1-11 is derived from Mark.[4] Thirdly, in the Passion narrative Winter is at times prepared to allow Luke a significant part in moulding the material. Thus: 'There is no mistaking *his editorial intention*, namely to stress Pilate's friendly disposition towards Jesus; dramatically he repeats three times the protestation of his innocence.' [5] Similarly: 'In the Third Gospel (Lk 23.16,22) Pilate offers to have Jesus scourged and then to set him free. The version of the Third Evangelist is obviously editorial. The repetition of the offer is an indication of the fact that the writer wished to drive home his point; it betrays the Evangelist's eagerness to convince the

---

[1] On the Trial, 21.

[2] Winter cites Conzelmann in On the Trial, 179,193, but not on significant passages where Luke has modified Mark. For Winter's view of Conzelmann, Die Mitte der Zeit, Tübingen 1954, and powerful criticisms in the area of source criticism, see ThLZ 81 (1956), 36-39.

[3] On the Trial, 111-135, esp. 114,118,121. 'The remarkable fact is that even in rendering Marcan matter, the later evangelists often enough unhesitatingly altered the designations in question for the sake of casting in a hostile role such Jewish groups as were prominent at the time when the evangelists were engaged in their work.' Yet Winter argues in Treatment, 164, that a tendency to blame all official Jewry for Jesus' execution was definitely not characteristic of Luke.

[4] Treatment, 166.

[5] On the Trial, 56 (Winter's own italics). This is said in spite of the fact that the three verses concerned, i.e. 23.4,14,22, are traced to the post-Lukan interpolator, Sx(?), and the interpolator respectively, Treatment, 165f. In a section which does not figure in ZNW 50 (1959), 234-249, Winter comments on the confused character of 23.13-25, singling out vv.4,14-16 and 22, and implying that these belonged to a draft known to the evangelist, On the Trial, 178. Clearly the analysis into sources is not consistent.

reader that the governor was anxious to avoid a death sentence.' [1]
This clearly allows for a considerable intrusion of activity by the evangelist.

(b) Winter draws a distinction between Luke's treatment of sources
in 21.5-23.49 and his earlier procedure. He suggests that he abandoned
the block method and adopted the procedure of conflation. This was
because incidents could not be told twice and so Luke had to weld
various different accounts into one.[2] This has important consequences
for two literary phenomena. The first of these is connections. Winter
writes: 'When he intermingled different sources, he did so with such
fidelity to the original records that, after he had combined them, the
result appears occasionally clumsy.'[3] This necessarily implies that
abrupt connections are quite in line with Luke's own method and are
not in themselves evidence of post-Lukan interpolation. Yet this does
not fit well with the argumentation on Lk 22.66f where Winter comments on ἀπήγαγον .... λέγοντες and the alleged awkwardness there:
'The Third Evangelist did not write in such a manner.... The
interpolated passage is connected with the first half of v.66 in such a
slipshod manner that we cannot ascribe it to the Evangelist who was a
stylist.'[4] The second phenomenon to be affected by Winter's view of
editorial activity in the Passion narrative is transpositions. Because
Winter's view of Luke's method in the Passion narrative is so different
from Lietzmann's, he has no need to begin by discussing Luke's attitude to transpositions.[5] However transpositions in the Passion narrative cannot always be explained by amalgamation of sources, e.g. Lk
23.44-47 is the product of 'merely editorial mutations' of Mk
15.33,38,34,39, and Lk 23.50-56 is a redraft of Mk 15.42-47 involving
additions and minor transpositions but no other source. Moreover.
Winter's own argument that Luke dismembered the account which he
found and displaced its parts [6] destroys the claim that the sequence of
events itself imposed an order on the material or on Luke's use of it.
It still seems logical to suggest that Luke's treatment of the order of
his source material was uniform. In other places, however, Winter's
argument depends on some degree of faithfulness to the order of the

[1] On the Trial, 102.
[2] Treatment, 140f.
[3] Treatment, 171.
[4] Treatment, 163.
[5] Winter here follows a path different from most protagonists of Proto-Luke—
the existence of which he himself accepts, Treatment, 139,171.
[6] Treatment, 166.

sources as Luke found them. He suggests [1] that if Mk 14.53b,55-64 is removed, it will be seen that the Lukan order approximates to the Markan sequence of events with which at present it conflicts irreconcilably. The resulting order is:

1. Jesus is brought to the house of the highpriest, Mk 14.53a, Lk 22.54.
2. Mockery, Mk 14.65, Lk 22.63-65.
3. Denial, Mk 14.(54)66-72, Lk 22.55-62.
4. Assembly of Sanhedrin, Mk 15.1a, Lk 22.66a.

Winter argues that this order, in which Luke only deviates in the order of items 2 and 3, is probably original. This is claimed on the basis of the Johannine structure (Jn 18.22). But (a) Winter fails to recognize the Markan technique in 14.65 as well as 14.55-64. The mockery is still interpolated, and while this is no criterion of historicity,[2] it certainly prohibits any deduction about original order. Mark himself puts it there. (b) Whereas Winter stresses the interpolation as an argument against the Sanhedrin trial, he plays it down here by bracketing the first part of the Petrine section, Mk 14.54.[3] (c) John's evidence is quite ambiguous. For he has, even more than Mark, a sandwich structure: Jn 18.17f the first denial, Jn 18.19-24 the interrogation, and Jn 18.25-27 the second and third denials. It is the more surprising that Winter can argue from Jn since he himself writes: 'The interrogation by Annas (Jn 18.12-14,19-24) is intercalated into the story of Peter's denial as is the case with the nocturnal trial in Mark.' [4] Winter here damages his own argument severely, and capsizes it totally when he states that Jn 18.19-24, which includes the mockery, is 'an editorial introduction, in default of tradition, due to the Fourth Evangelist'.[5] (d) Winter has already argued that Mk 14.65 is dependent on Lk 22.63-65.[6] (e) Luke's order is therefore the only one which shows no signs of secondary editorial activity, and so must be rated a more reliable starting-point than Mark's or John's.

---

[1] On the Trial, 22f.
[2] Winter allows that Mk 14.65 depends on an earlier tradition even though in the end that tradition is traced to the Mk 15.16-20 position.
[3] On the Trial, 22; similarly, Treatment, 161, referring to the insertion of Mk 14.(53),55-64(65).
[4] On the Trial, 30.
[5] On the Trial, 136. Contrast op.cit. 30, where a tradition, possibly primitive, is discerned behind Jn 18.19-24.
[6] Treatment, 162; On the Trial, 100.

2. *Winter's analysis of the Passion narrative*

(a) The first category is L. This consists of:

22.14-19a	The meal
22.23	Prediction of betrayal
22.24-30	Dispute about rank
22.31-33	Prediction of denial
22.35-38	The two swords
22.47-53	Arrest (elements probably)
22.54b-62	Denial (possibly)
22.63-65	Mockery [1]
22.66	Entry to συνέδριον
23.1b-3	Accusation (including variants on washings) and Jesus' answer to Pilate's question

After that 'we are in the dark about the contents of the L account besides vv.1-3'.[2] Winter stresses that the L account is very Jewish,[3] non-Markan and old. The Semitic colouring is stressed in 22.15f ('strongly Semitic'[4]), 22.24-30 ('the L version is Palestinian'[5]), and the earliness and pre-Markan origin[6] are highlighted in 22.14-19a ('The description of the Last Supper in L seems to preserve a tradition from very early days—prior to the shaping of that material by the hand of the Second Evangelist'[7]), 22.24-30 ('undoubtedly non-Marcan and undoubtedly early'[8]), 22.38 ('The tradition on which 22.38 is based is undoubtedly old'[9]), the arrest ('an old pre-Marcan tradition'[10]), the mockery ('belongs to an account of Jesus' Passion that is independent of the Second Gospel and to all appearances older than it'[11]) and 23.1b-3 ('part of an old Trial account'[12]). These emphatic statements are in sharp contrast with comments on Sx material, e.g. 22.39-46 is said to be full of late elements.[13]

---

[1] Originally placed in L before the Denial, according to Winter, On the Trial, 22.

[2] Treatment, 165.

[3] On the Trial, 212: 'Traditions from the Lukan "Special Source" have, generally speaking, preserved their Palestinian timbre whilst "Markan" tradition underwent a process of editorial redrafting in Rome.' So already, P. Feine, Eine vorlukanische Überlieferung des Lukas, Gotha 1891, passim.

[4] Treatment, 156.

[5] art.cit. 159.

[6] Winter rightly compares the form of Lk 10.25-27, 22.24-27 with Mk 12.28-34, 10.35-37,42-45, and argues for the greater age of the Lukan version, On the Trial, 215.

[7] Treatment, 156.

[8] art.cit. 159.

[9] art.cit. 159.

[10] art.cit. 160.

[11] art.cit. 162.

[12] art.cit. 165.

[13] art.cit. 161.

(b) A further division of material consists of the non-editorial and post-Markan blocks. [1] These are:

22.39-46	On the Mount of Olives
23.6-16	Christ before Herod; subsequent dialogue between Pilate and rulers [2]
23.27-31	Weeping women of Jerusalem [3]
23.39-43	Conversation with the penitent thief.

There are however hints of non-Markan derivation in

23.34,35a	Prayer, parting of garments, people watching [4]
23.36-38	Mockery of soldiers, superscription [5]
23.48-49	Grief of multitudes and acquaintances. [6]

But here there is no indication of L or Sx as the specific origin.

It is at this point that some criticisms of Winter's analysis are appropriate: (a) He claims: 'Most of the non-Marcan material in the last four chapters of the Third Gospel formed a coherent account when separated from the Marcan portions.' [7] This is of a piece with the assertion that 'Luke has a literary record with qualities and characteristics of its own' which was subsequently combined with Mark.[8] But this is far from the truth in the L +Sx material. Thus, the narrative for Lk 23 consisted of vv.1b-3,6-16,27-31, tradition behind vv.34-35a, tradition behind vv.36-38, vv.39-43,48-49. This means that we move from Jesus' reply σὺ λέγεις to Pilate's question whether Jesus is a Galilean, which is (i) quite disconnected, and (ii) in sequence dependent on 23.5, a verse which is assigned to the interpolator [9]; we then jump from Pilate's proposal to chastise [10] and *release* Jesus, v.16, to the mournful procession, v.27, so that a total blank is left with no expla-

---

[1] Treatment, 139.

[2] Cf. On the Trial, 137, which labels 23.4,13-16,20-24 as 'editorial embellishments'. On the Trial, 202 states that 23.6-12 could have been introduced either by Luke or by the interpolator. But the tradition is later than that underlying Mk, op.cit. 137,213.

[3] This with 19.39-44, while preserving a Palestinian stamp, reflects a situation after A.D.73 and when favourable relations existed between Jewish Christianity and Pharisaism, On the Trial, 212,215.

[4] Treatment, 166: '*in the main* Lucan modification of the Marcan theme'.

[5] Treatment, 166: 'a non-Marcan undercurrent'.

[6] Treatment, 166: 'non-Marcan'.

[7] Treatment, 170.

[8] Treatment, 171.

[9] art.cit. 166.

[10] Evidence for the accuracy of Luke's terminology in A. N. Sherwin White, op.cit. 27f; contra Winter, On the Trial, 178.

nation given of the reason for Pilate's change of mind,[1] no record of
the sentence being finally pronounced, and later no record of the crucifixion itself before the conversation on the cross, and no mention
of Jesus' death. Hence it is altogether fanciful to claim that this is a
coherent account. (b) Winter allows that the old account included in
the charge-sheet an allegation that Jesus dissuaded people from ritual
washings.[2] This means that the Roman procurator had a religious
issue placed before him[3] whereas Winter elsewhere insists that Romans
fastidiously refrained from all matters of religion.[4] (c) The difficulties
are in many cases solved if more material than Winter allows did
in fact belong to the L narrative.

(c) The following material is drawn from Mark:

Lk	22.1-6	Plot against Jesus
	22.7-13	Preparation of supper
	22.19a	'This is my body'
	22.21-22	Prediction of betrayal
	22.34	Prediction of denial
	22.47-54a	Arrest
	22.54b-62	Denial
	23.26	Simon bears the cross
	23.32	Two criminals crucified
	23.33	Arrival at Golgotha and crucifixion
	23.35	Division of clothing, mockery of Jewish leaders
	23.44	Darkness over the land
	23.45	Damage to the Temple
	23.46	Cry from the cross
	23.47	Centurion's confession

However, firstly, Jeremias has shown that considerations of order
favour the view that more of this comes from L than Winter allows.[5]
And it is, on the conflation theory, quite inexplicable that the mention
of the two criminals should be dissected, that the titulus should be
transferred to a later position,[6] and that the damage to the temple

---

[1] Blinzler has shown that the record of the Burial, which Bultmann allows to
be historical in Mk 15.42f,46 (Synoptic Tradition, 274), suggests that Pilate acted
under pressure. 'Nur wenn es zutrifft, daß Pilatus in Jesus keinen wirklichen
Staatsverbrecher gesehen und das Todesurteil nur ungern ausgesprochen hatte,
wird es verständlich, daß er dem Antrag auf Ausfolgung der Leiche ohne jede
Bedingung oder Auflage stattgegeben hat.' Prozeß, 394. Hence the material
dealing with Jewish pressure on Pilate, assigned to a late date by Winter, has
historical support.

[2] Treatment, 165; against this, Blinzler, op.cit. 280.

[3] Cf. A. N. Sherwin White, op.cit. 35.

[4] On the Trial, 11.

[5] Perikopen-Umstellungen bei Lukas? NTS 4 (1957), 118.

[6] It is not sufficient to say that v.38 depends on v.37, for its introduction ἦν δὲ
καί (not ἦν γάρ) makes a break with the preceding verse.

should be moved away from the position after Jesus' death. Secondly, in several cases the literary dependence on Mark is by no means substantial, e.g. the crucifixion of the two thieves (Mk 15.27/Lk 23.32,33b), especially the cries from the cross which are quite unrelated (Mk 15.34/Lk 23.46), and the eyewitnesses (Mk 15.40f/Lk 23.49).

3. *Winter on Lk* 22.66-71

It has already been noticed that Winter regards v.66 as the vestige of an old tradition and vv.67-71 as a post-Lukan adaption.[1] The division occurs after εἰς τὸ συνέδριον αὐτῶν, and of the interpolated passage it may be said that 'the writer of Lk XXII:66-71 knew of a narration essentially identical with Jn X:24-36, and that it was he who drew on that narrative whilst conflating it with the Matthaean wording of the account of Jesus' investigation or trial by the Sanhedrin. The wording of Lk XXII.67,70 where it departs from the other synoptic reports is strangely reminiscent of Jn X:25,36 and . . . . . we have to suppose that there is an inner connection between these two accounts.'[2]

In his first article Winter sets out the Matthaean parallels [3] and in the second the Johannine ones. Here both will be set out together and followed by some examination.

Mt	Lk	Jn
27.1 οἱ πρεσβύτεροι τοῦ λαοῦ	22.66 τὸ πρεσβυτέριον τοῦ λαοῦ	
26.63 εἰ σὺ εἶ ὁ χριστὸς ἐξορκίζω σε ἵνα ἡμῖν εἴπῃς	22.67 εἰ σὺ εἶ ὁ χριστός εἰπὸν ἡμῖν	10.24 εἰ σὺ εἶ ὁ χριστὸς εἰπὸν ἡμῖν παρρησίᾳ
	22.67 εἶπεν δὲ αὐτοῖς	10.25 ἀπεκρίθη αὐτοῖς ὁ Ἰησοῦς
	ἐὰν ὑμῖν εἴπω οὐ μὴ πιστεύσητε	εἶπον ὑμῖν καὶ οὐ πιστεύετε Jn 10.31-33 omitted and '(comp Jn V. 18)' added
	22.70 εἶπαν δὲ πάντες	10.34 ἀπεκρίθη αὐτοῖς ὁ Ἰησοῦς

---

[1] On the Trial, 21,160: 'Only the words from καὶ ὡς ἐγένετο ἡμέρα to εἰς τὸ συνέδριον αὐτων can be considered as derived from an old pre-Marcan record or tradition.' Similarly, Treatment, 164.

[2] Luke XXII 66b-71, StTh 9 (1955), 112-115.

[3] Winter insists that Mt and not Mk is the source, Treatment, 164. Though see later, JTS 14 (1963), 98: 'As Luke xxii.67-71 merely reproduces Mark xiv.61b-64a or Matthew xxvi.63b-65 in an elaborated form . . . .' But if it were conceded that Mk was the source Lk 22.67ff would not necessarily have to be post-Lukan.

Mt	Lk	Jn
26.63 ὁ υἱὸς τοῦ θεοῦ	σὺ οὖν εἶ ὁ υἱὸς τοῦ θεοῦ; ὁ δὲ πρὸς αὐτοὺς ἔφη	10.36 ὃν ὁ πατὴρ ἡγίασεν καὶ ἀπέστειλεν εἰς τὸν κόσμον
26.64 σὺ εἶπας	ὑμεῖς λέγετε ὅτι ἐγώ εἰμι	ὑμεῖς λέγετε ὅτι βλασφημεῖς ὅτι εἶπον υἱὸς
ἀπ' ἄρτι ὄψεσθε τὸν υἱὸν τοῦ ἀνθρώπου καθήμενον	22.69 ἀπὸ τοῦ νῦν ἔσται ὁ υἱὸς τοῦ ἀνθρώπου καθήμενος	τοῦ θεοῦ εἰμι
	23.1 καὶ ἀναστὰν ἅπαν τὸ πλῆθος αὐτῶν ἤγαγον αὐτὸν ἐπὶ τὸν Πειλᾶτον	10.39 ἐζήτουν οὖν αὐτὸν πάλιν πιάσαι. καὶ ἐξῆλθεν ἐκ τῆς χειρὸς αὐτῶν

(a) The first parallel between Mt and Lk must be dismissed because firstly, οἱ πρεσβύτεροι figure in Mk 15.1 as well as in Mt 27.1, and so τοῦ λαοῦ is all that is distinctively common to Mt and Lk. But λαός-references are too widespread in Lukan redaction for there to be any need to resort to a Lukan imitator here. Secondly, πρεσβυτέριον occurs elsewhere in Luke-Acts, i.e. Acts 22.5, and so also does not need to be post-Lukan. Thirdly, τὸ πρεσβυτέριον τοῦ λαοῦ belongs to v.66 which Winter himself separates off from vv.67-71 and places in L. Hence it should never have been included in the list of parallels.

(b) The last parallel of Lk and Jn (Lk 23.1/Jn 10.39) is also void, for there is neither verbal parallelism nor schematic overlap. Moreover, Winter himself makes the very necessary statement that 23.1 belongs to L: were it not so, there would be no record of the transference from the συνέδριον to the confrontation with Pilate.

(c) The parallelism of the Son of man saying in each is again forced. Firstly, τῆς δυνάμεως which is common to Mk and Lk (though not cited here by Winter) is sufficient to show Mk as the source. Secondly, ἀπὸ τοῦ νῦν and ἀπ' ἄρτι, although identical in meaning, are in not any dependence relationship. For ἀπὸ τοῦ νῦν occurs elsewhere in Lk without any suggestion of dependence on Mt, and here belongs with ἔσται as part of the localisation of eschatology achieved by redaction of Mk.[1] The suggestion that it was drawn from Mt and was also an imitation of Lukan language[2] is awkward and improbable.

---

[1] See above, p. 157.
[2] Treatment, 165.

(d) ὑμεῖς λέγετε has nothing to do with σὺ εἶπας. The meaning is the same, but not the wording, and the choice, on this hypothesis, of λέγετε as against εἴπατε destroys any relationship.[1]

(e) All that remains of the Matthaean parallel is now reduced to 26.63. But here the Johannine and Matthaean parallels are mutually exclusive. Every one which was claimed in Winter's first article as an assimilation to Mt is, in his second article, drawn from Jn. One theory or the other may be right: both cannot be. It is therefore impermissible to say that 'the author of Lk XXII.66-71 knew of a narration essentially identical with Jn X.24-36, and that it was he who drew on that narrative whilst conflating it with the Matthaean wording'. [2] At this point there is no conflating to be done, unless it is the addition of ὁ to υἱὸς τοῦ θεοῦ. Winter himself seems to be aware of this difficulty, for he continues: 'The wording of Lk XXII.67,70 where it departs from the other synoptic reports is strangely reminiscent of Jn X.25,36 . . . .' Why does he omit Jn 10.24? It not only figures in his list of parallels, and indeed rightly, but is actually the most exact of them all.

(f) By inserting Jn 10.31-33, and comparing with Jn 5.18, Winter recalls a traditional Jewish scheme for the condemnation of Jesus, one which can be traced back even to Salvador. Winter uses the christology to argue for a non-Palestinian, non-Jewish background, although in fact the theology and terminology suggest a Semitic background.[3]

(g) If 22.67-71 is omitted from L, we have yet another example of incoherence and discontinuity in a narrative which Winter claims as mostly consecutive. Having led Jesus into their συνέδριον, they all lead him to Pilate: a yawning gap replaces the required details of what happened before the Council. Winter claims that 'the meeting mentioned in Lk 22.66a Mk 15.1a seems to have dealt with an administrative question within the Council's competence, namely the delivery of a person suspected of sedition to the procurator.' [4] Also he says: 'The Supreme Court would hardly have met to decide whether there was a prima facie case to answer, and whether an indictment should be drawn up.' [5] These two statements are significant. Firstly, we can see why το πρεσβυτέριον τοῦ λαοῦ was excised as Matthaean adaptation, for this clearly implies 'the Supreme Court'; in the same

---

[1] See above, pp. 196f.
[2] Lk XXII 66b-71, 113 f.
[3] See above, pp. 199f.
[4] On the Trial, 27.
[5] op. cit. 26.

way, Winter suggested that καὶ ὅλον τὸ συνέδριον, Mk 15.1, was Markan redaction. Yet, in fact, εἰς τὸ συνέδριον αὐτῶν which Winter interprets geographically, implies the same thing, for why, if there was no
question of the Supreme Court's involvement, did they go to the
required place? Winter himself acknowledges this in a later article.[1]
This συνέδριον reference, like other similar ones in Acts, is strongly
suggestive of a full Council meeting. Secondly, whatever Mk 15.1
may say, there is nothing in Lk 22.66, when that is deprived of what
follows, to permit any guess as to the purpose of the meeting.[2]

(h) Winter is quite correct to suggest a connection between Lk
22.67-71 and Jn 10.24f, but reasons have been adduced above in favour of the view that John drew on the tradition which Luke also
used, rather than the theory that Luke used John.

4. *Winter on the mockery*

Firstly, Winter quite rightly regards Lk 22.63-65 as independent of,
and prior to, Mk 14.65. He notes the differences of setting, timing and
vocabulary;[3] indeed, he continues, Mark knew the older account and
rewrote it in accordance with his purpose.[4]

Secondly, his account of the origin of the tradition is more open to
question. He notes the echoes of Is 50.6 (LXX) in Mk 14.65, and argues
that the tradition must therefore have originated in a Greek-speaking
community. Its source is 'testimony from scriptural prophecy' (following Lietzmann), and four facts suggest that the whole tradition is
secondary as compared with Mk 15.16-20. First, 'the scene takes place
within enclosing walls—and in fact in surroundings less accessible to
the public than the barrack-ground of the legionaries. Eyewitnesses'
reports are not to be assumed.'[5] Second, 'the oldest report manifestly

---

[1] JTS 14 (1963), 99: 'Some critics find it puzzling that Jesus should have been
taken to the high priest's house, and kept there for the rest of the night. The
reason appears to be that the entire complex of buildings on the Temple Mount
was locked up at night. The Council Chamber was apparently located on the
Temple Mount. Only in the morning when access could be gained, was it possible
to take Jesus to the Council Chamber.' On the inaccuracy of this theory, see p. 154.
[2] The same applies to the statement in On the Trial, 48: 'The account which
the Third Evangelist gives of the proceedings by the πρεσβυτέριον τοῦ λαοῦ
(sic !) excludes all possibility of identifying 'their counsel and deed' with the condemnation of Jesus.' But the Lukan account, as it stands, *does* suggest this, and
without 22. 67-71 it tells us nothing at all of the actual proceedings.
[3] On the Trial, 21, 104.
[4] Treatment, 162.
[5] On the Trial, 104.

recorded one instance of Jesus' mockery',[1] and the oldest tradition, Mk 15.16-20, has been shifted around. Third, its attachment to the arrest is explained by the involvement of Roman soldiers in arresting Jesus.[2] Fourth, the primary tradition, i.e. Mk 10.34, reported the actions of mocking, spitting and scourging in connection with killing—and all at the hands of the Gentiles.[3]

But against this: (a) It is illogical to argue from the language of Mk 14.65 when Lk 22.63-65, repeatedly acknowledged by Winter as older,[4] does not contain the Septuagintal words. If Mark reshaped the tradition and used language borrowed from the Septuagint, that tells us nothing whatever about Mark's source. (b) Even if there were echoes of prophecy, this would not itself ipso facto suggest the creation of the incident out of scriptural testimony.[5] This important principle is in fact allowed by Winter in another place, Lk 22.35-38. Lk 22.38 is, of course, serviceable for Winter's theory, but he writes of vv.35-38: 'First came the story; prophecy was discovered later.'[6] (c) The citation of Lietzmann in support is in fact inexact. Lietzmann argued that the scene, in describing which Luke is dependent on Mark, was 'unwahrscheinlich' because of the impossibility of thinking the Sanhedrin members would do this. He thought it lacked motivation: if Jesus had been condemned as a false prophet, the invitation to him to prophesy would be understandable, but not otherwise. Yet Winter does not think that Luke depends on Mark. So one must notice that the Lukan account does not involve Sanhedrin members, the mockery precedes condemnation, and the term 'prophesy' is not itself technical as a term even though its context is technical. (d) Although it is misguided to rely heavily on eyewitnesses in evaluating the gospel tradition, it is by no means clear that eyewitness reports of the incident are excluded. There must have been many people present. (e) While it is quite clear that traditions of incidents in the Passion have floated, there is no reason at all to make the categorical statement that the oldest tradition

---

[1] On the Trial, 101.
[2] On the Trial, 104.
[3] On the Trial, 106.
[4] On the Trial, 21f; Treatment, 162.
[5] So rightly, P. Benoit, Les outrages à Jésus prophète, in: Neotestamentica et Patristica, Festschrift O. Cullmann, Leiden 1962, 96f. Winter indeed notices the ἐμπαίζω in Lk 23.11, Mk 15.19f, and thinks the pre-synoptic record included the word. 'If so, the originality of Lk 22.63-65 would be apparent.' On the Trial, 161. Here then the oldest tradition and scriptural allusion are allowed to co-exist.
[6] Treatment, 160.

manifestly recorded *one* instance of Jesus' mockery.[1] Jn 19.2f certainly is the same as Mk 15.16-20 with its position changed, but Lk 23.11 is markedly divergent from this passage,[2] and Lk 22.63-65 is quite credible as an incident.[3] (f) It is not certain that Roman soldiers figured in the arrest.[4] (g) The use of Mk 10.34 assumes that this saying is indeed a primary tradition [5]—which needs proof—, allows that the Passion narratives can be controlled by the predictions, and rests on an argument from silence.[6]

The Lukan Passion narrative is of crucial importance for the assessment of the history of the tradition. It represents a different channel for the formation of the story of Jesus' last hours. Negatively, it shows that the Markan account has been subject to greater modification during the passage of time and under the pressure of the belief of the communities. Positively, it provides a check on too hasty dismissal of Mark by failing to enquire whether there are traditions behind the Markan account which may be more primitive. In its own right the Lukan Sonderquelle appears to have a high level of historical reliability. Only by a patient study of the relationship of this tradition to Mark can we erect the apparatus for a reconstruction of events, and prevent the very necessary use of the tools of Formgeschichte from succumbing to the pitfalls of undisciplined a priori presuppositions. The variants in the narratives are sufficient to demonstrate that Formgeschichte is, with appropriate modifications and safeguards, a proper method of approach, but alongside this, source analysis and the historical evaluation of each strand as a whole and in its separate parts must be rigorously practised.

---

[1] Winter has already allowed that Lk 22.63-65 belonged to 'the early tradition of Jesus' Passion', On the Trial, 22.

[2] R. Delbrueck, Antiquarisches zu den Verspottungen Jesu, ZNW 41 (1942), 124-145; J. Jeremias, Eucharistic Words, 79.

[3] W. Grundmann, Lk, 418.

[4] See pp. 149f.

[5] Cf. On the Trial, 148: 'There is no evidence that he equated himself with . . . . the Son of man.'

[6] Benoit, Outrages, 109, questions whether the maltreatment in Mk 10.34 is to be confined to the Romans. 'Ils peuvent valoir de toutes les autorités hostiles du v. 33.'

CHAPTER FOUR

THE LEGAL SETTING OF THE TRIAL OF JESUS

A. From Mendelssohn to Geiger

During the period 1770-1870 the high point of the discussion of illegalities occured in the debate between Salvador and the French lawyer A. M. J. J. Dupin.[1] This is so in spite of the fact that Salvador only examined two possible infringements, namely the false witnesses and the bypassing of the two-session rule. But the following features are sufficient to establish the character and place in history of this debate.

(a) The legal approach of Salvador is adopted as an alternative to the confrontation of two religions.[2] Jesus must be treated as a plain citizen, and his examination as such assessed, and moreover without value-judgements being passed on the law itself. This means that the controversy about Jesus' divinity, the stock Jewish/Christian controversy of the past, is set aside though not in fact forgotten wholly.[3] One is immediately impressed by the methodological divergence from Mendelssohn who asked that examinations of justice and legality should be forgotten for the sake of burying old dissensions.[4] Salvador cannot adopt that line because agnosticism about christology cannot be maintained, and because he feels a political pressure, and because the Emancipation brings with it an urge on the Jewish side to investigate Jesus.[5] In the act of pleading neutrality he is forced away from it.

(b) For both Salvador and his opponent Dupin, the contemporary political setting is formative. The thrust of Salvador's argument is: Jesus, viewed as an ordinary citizen, turns out to be a bad citizen. He

---

[1] See G. Lindeskog, Jesusfrage, 96, 278f.

[2] Histoire, 80.

[3] Histoire, 80: 'Qu'on puisse s'étonner qu'un Dieu en personne qui aurait voulu se faire comprendre n'ait pas été compris' is mentioned as a natural reaction but professedly set aside. However the point has been made.

[4] Letter of 15.1.1771, Schriften, 103: 'It is the duty of all good men to promote forgetfulness of old dissension. It is exactly the same with the guilt of the Pharisees and Sadducees concerning Jesus. What do I know about what moved my ancestors 17-1800 years ago in Jerusalem to a just or unjust verdict ?'

[5] Lindeskog, op. cit. 29 ff. Compare also Salvador's parentage: his mother a Roman Catholic and his father a Jew.

is at odds with the law from birth,[1] and brings political dissension;
but the Jews acted justly, wisely and legally, as well as out of concern
for the well-being of the nation. Here is thinly-veiled pro-Jewish apologetic for the French situation[2] —Salvador is a nineteenth-century
Jewish Luke. On the other side, Dupin not only exposes illegalities
but adds positively the concern Jesus felt for his people's wellbeing,
and negatively, the infringement by the Jews of Roman laws as well,
i.e. the laws of the ruling power. In so doing, he cuts at the roots of
the Jewish consciousness of being a law-governed and law-abiding
people. Thus the debate about Jesus is a debate about Jewish citizenship.

(c) The spirit of the Hebrew legislation is the starting-point. This
complements the thin discussion of procedure and gives a positive
thrust. Jesus' career is outlined within a framework of three fundamental principles: publicity of debate, liberty for the accused and
protection from hostile witnesses.[3] In stressing the spirit of the legislation Salvador has to examine Jesus' life first, and for the same reason
gives a primary place to the discussion of witnesses in the trial. Again
for political reasons, although he says the goodness or otherwise of
the laws can be left out of the discussion, there is here a clear attempt
to ground Jewish laws in principles acceptable to non-Jews.

Three topics are introduced into the debate because of this emphasis. The first is the arrest. Salvador simply states that this was effected by
'les gardes autorisés'.[4] Dupin's retort that these were in fact a ruffian
band and that 'if in the crowd there were any Roman soldiers they
were there as spectators and without having been legally called on
duty' is not aimed simply at the spirit of the law. He is in fact alleging
an infringement of Roman regulations in their having arrested Jesus
at all—and note how he thus introduces a crux of interpretation which
in the history of Prozessforschung would turn against him. Salvador
in reply misses the first point, uses Lk 22.52 as an ad hominem argument against the 'ruffian band' charge, but adds more potently that

---

[1] Dt 22.23, 23.2, introduced by 'Jésus naquit d'une famille peu fortunée'.
Histoire, 81.
[2] Cf. Lindeskog, op. cit. 96. The Jews obtained full citizenship in France in
1791 in the new post-revolutionary situation. Not till 1871 did this occur in
Germany. Therefore, although Salvador is in France a post-Emancipation Jew,
the situation was yet so new and so unconsolidated by similar freedom in surrounding countries that some influence of this must be taken into account.
[3] Histoire, 84f.
[4] op. cit. 86.

Jn 18.12 gives the best answer: a Roman cohort and tribune were there.[1]

The second topic is Jn 11.47-53. Salvador states that this meeting was convened in the face of the political menace of Jesus, that Caiaphas appointed himself Jesus' accuser, and that the subsequent arrest-warrant was issued publicly and without prejudice.[2] In spite of Jn 11.57, Dupin replied that the decree was not mentioned, that Jn 11.53 (=Mt 26.5) implies a plot to put Jesus to death, and that the chief priests and Pharisees did not constitute a judicial tribunal among the Jews. But again pressure from Dupin causes the apologetic case for the trial to crumble. For the charge of malice brings Salvador's response that they were moved by fear of Rome, thus again introducing a political theme; the whole case makes him claim that we must distinguish John as historian from John as theologian, which is at least a change from the profession of arguing uncritically from the Christian documents;[3] and thirdly, although Salvador misses the point about the Council and replies weakly that the verb 'assemble' proves that it was such, together with the demonstrable fact that the Sanhedrin existed from Maccabean times,[4] yet Dupin has again raised a question of the Sanhedrin's rights, this time to assemble on its own initiative.[5] Here as in the first point, the capital powers controversy is prepared for by Dupin's argumentation.

The third topic is the mockery. Here Salvador's conservative stand on the text disintegrated and he dismissed the incident as unhistorical because of lack of eyewitnesses,[6] the contradiction against not only the Hebrew law but also 'l'ordre de la nature' and the law-abiding instincts of a respectable court,[7] and finally the evangelist's anti-Jewish Tendenz.[8] The combination of Hebrew and natural law is again

---

[1] Jésus-Christ II (1838), 537-539; op. cit. II (1865), 191.

[2] Histoire, 85f.

[3] op. cit. 81.

[4] II (1838), 534-536.

[5] II (1838), 525-528.

[6] Histoire, 88. That the same presumably applies to the preceding trial is not mentioned.

[7] Most Jews follow the presupposition that the Jews, with the possible exception of the Sadducees, would not have acted illegally. In Salvador's case this also lies behind the statement that agreement of the narratives with the laws would tend to support the veracity of the former. I(1838), viii.

[8] Salvador writes in II(1838), 524f, that he reserves the right to compare versions and to discriminate against Tendenz. Cf. the treatment of witnesses, and Jn 2.19 set against Mk 14.58.

significant, taking the weight off the former and suggesting a harmony between the two. It is remarkable that this line, so characteristic of early 19th century reformers should be taken by one who was not himself a reformer. Dupin in reply fixes on some circularity of argument, agreeing that it contradicts the spirit of the law but still breaks the letter.[1] Moreover Peter and the young man of Mk 14.51 were present as witnesses. Again he stresses that no verdict (i.e. no Roman one) had yet been passed, and hence violation is established. Clearly, Dupin the lawyer begins his argument, as is natural for him, from the position in Roman law, an impression further strengthened by his use of the discontinuity between Jewish and Roman proceedings to prove a hostile Jewish spirit.

(d) Both sides show a community-consciousness. This may seem so commonplace as to be not worth comment, but the illegality shows it with particular clarity. The centuries of experience which moulded Salvador's approach had been reflected earlier through Mendelssohn: 'What do I know about what moved my ancestors 17-1800 years ago to a just or unjust condemnation? I would be very embarrassed to be held responsible for what happens in a court of my own time. And on our side we have no admissible accounts of that great incident, no legal annals, no reports which we can oppose to yours.' [2] Here is expressed the Jewish dilemma and unhappy sense of history. The comment on the sources proceeds from a community-consciousness which the remark about legal procedures attempts to dispel. Mendelssohn's retreat into agnosticism is less aggressive than Salvador's approach and even less so than J. R. Peynado's uncomplicated acceptance of identification with those who judged Jesus.[3] Mendelssohn represents agnosticism, distaste for the legal discussion, pleading no viable *Jewish* sources and severance from his ancestors; Salvador in the same Jewish apologetic cause stands for bold declaration, adoption of the legality discussion, use of the Christian sources, and unity with his ancestors—all of which are to a degree concessions to the Christian viewpoint.

The discussion of specific contraventions of Jewish law was marked

---

[1] He uses both Luke's pre-hearing mockery, Matthew's after the hearing, and Jn 18.22 (during the hearing !).

[2] Letter of 15.1.1771: Schriften, 103.

[3] Letter to the Rev. A. M'Caul, D.D., in The Occident 7 (1849), 26: 'The Jews, as in duty bound at that time, received the decision of the existing Sanhedrin; they now individually come at the same conclusion by reference to the same evidence that convinced their judges — the holy scriptures.'

by almost total disengagement. Salvador began by dealing with: 1.
The witnesses. 'Les deux témoins que saint Matthieu et saint Marc
accusent de fausseté, rapportent un discours que saint Jean déclare
vrai, sous le rapport de la puissance que Jésus s'attribue.' [1] Here
Salvador fails to note the division between Mt 26.60a and v.60b (which
actually ranges Matthew with John), but his point is firstly to take
only the rebuilding claim [2]—about which there is less disagreement
between the gospels—which tends towards Divine pretensions, and
secondly that no one could blame the Jews for failing to grasp any
esoteric meaning, as in fact the disciples did too.[3] When Dupin in
answer saw the falsity of Mk 14.58/Mt 26.61 in the assertion that Jesus
said he personally would destroy the temple, and dismissed the Jewish
misunderstanding on the grounds that Jesus spoke of the new build-
ing as 'not made with hands' (Mk, not Mt), Salvador was able to
maintain his view that the rebuilding was the essential element, and
that an invitation to the Jews of all people to destroy the temple was
nonsense.[4] Therefore John could still be used to refute Matthew.[5]
2. The double-session rule. Salvador here wrote: 'Le conseil se ras-
sembla de nouveau dans la matinée du lendemain ou du surlendemain,
comme le veut la jurisprudence.' [6] The inclusion of 'le surlendemain'
clouds the issue, and betrays an uneasiness which is underlined by the
defence in 1865 [7] that the imminence of the Passover [8] necessitated

---

[1] Histoire, 87. Note that he mentions the *two* witnesses but fails to deduce the
legal significance of it, a significance he did not miss in commenting on Mt 18.16,
II(1865), 194.

[2] Similarly, II(1838), 541; II(1865), 196.

[3] Histoire, 434. This argument that Jesus' sayings were either incomprehensible
or evasive (cf. above, p. 221, footnote 3) is a subsidiary part of Salvador's defence
with which Dupin cannot cope. The lack of clarity, which is a material argument
only if the teaching is considered secret, also lies behind the conclusion of the essay
with Mt 27.42f (Histoire, 90) and the comment: 'Un miracle à cette heure même
n'eût-il pas été décisif ?' Here is the 'testing of the Messiah' theme, ultimately
sealed by the death of the person in question as was the case with Bar-Kochba.
Compare Maimonides: 'If he does not meet with full success, or is slain, it is
obvious that he is not the Messiah promised in the Torah.' More recently J. Jocz
stresses that a messianic claim was no offence but needed to be substantiated,
Christians and Jews: Encounter and Mission, London 1966, 41. Cf. J. C. O'Neill,
The Silence of Jesus, NTS 15 (1969), 153-167.

[4] II (1838), 540-542; II (1865), 194-196.

[5] Support for John is also drawn from Mt. 24.2.

[6] Histoire, 88.

[7] II (1865), 161f; no comment was made on this in 1838.

[8] There is no mention made of the law against legal proceedings on the eve of
Passover.

shortening the interval between sessions. The disengagement of the Salvador/Dupin controversy is plain in that Dupin totally ignores this illegality, which could have been very useful to his cause.

The remaining illegalities covered by the debate are all raised by Dupin, and all ignored by Salvador: 1. Proceedings at night. 2. Trial on a feast day. 3. Condemnation on the accused's confession. 4. Judgment pronounced by Caiaphas first. Salvador does not even defend by claiming that the laws were not yet in existence.[1]

It has already been indicated that Dupin rests even more on infringement of Roman provincial law than on the relationship with Mishnaic procedure. If disengagement marked the debate about Jewish law it certainly did not in respect of Roman law, as has already been shown in the discussion of Salvador's treatment of the arrest. On the larger issue he argued simply in 1828: 'Ils avaient conservé la faculté de juger selon leurs lois, mais dans les mains du procurateur seul résidait le pouvoir exécutif.'[2] Dupin retorted that the Sanhedrin had power neither to execute nor to pass a sentence of death; they were permitted only to hold a preliminary hearing. Against the Jews he argues that (a) Pilate does not ask for their verdict, but begins a new hearing; (b) the religious charge was abandoned and a political one substituted; (c) they falsely alleged that Jesus had discouraged payment of tribute and made himself king of the Jews; (d) Pilate acted unjustly, but only because he was pressed by the Jews; (e) 'The proof that Jesus was not, as M. Salvador maintained, put to death for the crime of blasphemy or sacrilege, and for having preached a new religious worship in contravention of the Mosaic law, results from the very sentence pronounced by Pilate, a sentence in pursuance of which he was led to execution by Roman soldiers .... Jesus was the victim of a political accusation.'

So Dupin brings the jus gladii controversy in by way of the illegality debate. His claims prepare the way for five typical Jewish defences: 1. The Jews did not have the right to execute (and pass sentence)[3] and therefore only a Roman trial occurred. 2. The discrepancy between the charges in the Jewish and Roman courts and general discontinuity suggests that there was no preceding Sanhedrin trial.[4] 3. Pilate's char-

---

[1] II (1865), 117f: 'Le code de la jurisprudence hébraïque, dont les principales règles étaient en rigueur à l'époque de Jésus-Christ.'   [2] Histoire, 88.

[3] The problem of whether the removal of the jus gladii prevented legal hearings as well as executions becomes an integral part of the debate about capital powers.

[4] Samuel Hirsch, Religionsphilosophie, 685, was the first to adopt this argument.

acter as depicted in the gospels is tendentiously unrealistic. 4. Crucifixion proves that the case was political. 5. Roman initiative is proved by Jn 11.48 and the Roman arrest. The way leads through points 1-5 to Philippson, and through points 2-5 to Juster and Paul Winter.

Salvador's own reaction is a vigorous defence of Jewish rights in which he first argues that the Jews did have capital powers but voluntarily relinquished them in Jesus' case,[1] and later that the Jews did not have power to execute but could certainly try capital cases. At stage one, the evidence cited is as follows: (a) Acts shows the Sanhedrin using publicly their right to pronounce the death sentence.[2] (b) Acts 23ff proves that the Romans accepted this, provided essential interests were safeguarded.[3] Hence Jn 18.31 proves the opposite of what Dupin asserts: 'Il se rapporte aux conditions locales de son usage. Si d'une part, la jurisprudence des Juifs n'autorisait aucune suspension de la peine capitale dès qu'un arrêt définitif était prononcé, d'autre part, la solennité actuelle de pâques défendait à la nation d'accomplir un arrêt de ce genre.'[4] Parallel to their action in Jn 18.28, they told Pilate: 'Il ne nous est pas permis de faire mourir quelqu'un . . . . aujourd'hui.'[5] At stage two, the only extra point added is that the Jewish law was left untouched by the invading power,[6] but the conclusion is more restrained: 'Du droit, si l'on passe au fait, il est incontestable que le sénat juif rendait des jugements, après comme avant Pilate. Mais aux jours de Jésus il n'en avait pas l'exécution.'[7] Hence the 1828 view is reinstated and backed by parallel capital cases.

The Salvador-Dupin debate does not come to grips with the issues raised inside itself as regards things Jewish, though it opens up issues for subsequent controversy by its treatment of Roman regulations. Salvador avoids the real Jewish legal problem; Dupin's claims, when set in the long-term development, backfired.

In the period between Salvador and Geiger, four approaches to the illegality problem emerge:

(a) To accept the illegalities and blame Caiaphas. Without scientific

[1] II (1838), 171-177.
[2] e.g. the three judgments on Peter, as well as the execution of Stephen in accordance with 'la loi inexorable de rebellion nationale et de blasphème religieux'. II(1838) 227 f, 245.
[3] II (1838), 173f.
[4] II (1838), 175f.
[5] II (1838), 176.
[6] II (1865), 120.
[7] II (1865), 121.

basis and with forceful and slightly tactless ad hominem arguments, Joseph Parkes had already blamed the priests for destroying Jesus.[1] As with Salvador political circumstances provided the guiding force, in this case the appeal for equal rights. But the same theory, based on evidence, is proposed by I. M. Jost and M. M. Noah.[2] Jost in 1820 ignored the Sanhedrin trial, perhaps under Mendelssohn's influence, but in 1832 spoke of a trial convened by Pilate: 'das übereilte, durch die Form der Procedur nicht gerechtfertigte Verfahren'.[3] No details beyond haste are specified, but the connection of the procedure with the growth of the Christian church (for he says it gave the disciples power and unity) again presupposes a close connection between this issue and religious confrontation.

In 1857 Jost denounced all attempts to deny illegality, whether by the statements in b.Sanh. 43a or by Salvador.[4] As regards specific contraventions, he cites false witnesses and the night session [5] but, as in the Salvador-Dupin debate, the meaning is greater than the issues explicitly cited. (a) Haste is several times mentioned.[6] This can only be the discarding of apologetic for the two-session irregularity, since there is no textual suggestion of haste (except perhaps the disregard of the decision recorded in Mk 14.2—but Jost does not mention this), and otherwise the defence by Salvador passes unnoticed. (b) Dupin's arguments seem to have impinged, above all in that he moves from an authorization by Pilate (1832) to a lack of any sort of authorization (1857).[7] Again there are no textual grounds for commenting on Pilate's authorization or the lack of it: it can only be that Dupin's interpretation of the jus gladii has been adopted. This indebtedness to Dupin is further suggested by the acknowledgement of shameful behaviour in Pilate's hall,[8] and of the change to a more convincing charge for the Roman proceedings.[9] The change to the view that this was not a full-

---

[1] An Epistle from a High Priest of the Jews to the Chief Priest of Canterbury on the Extension of Catholic Emancipation to the Jews, London 1821, 10-12: 'They behaved themselves as priests generally behave, wickedly, ambitiously, cruelly and impiously . . . . this act of cruelty and tyranny.'

[2] Discourse on the Restoration of the Jews, New York 1845, 19-21. Noah's view is that everything was done in panic, but judgments on this or any attempt to blame contemporary Jews are equally out of place.

[3] Geschichte, 68.

[4] Geschichte des Judenthums und seiner Secten, Leipzig 1857, 403.

[5] op.cit. 407.

[6] op.cit. 406, 408.   [7] op.cit. 404.

[8] op.cit. 408.

[9] op.cit. 406. He does however accept a Roman arrest, stemming from collusion between Caiaphas and Pilate.

blown trial (thus Mt 26.59 is devalued [1]) is not made under pressure of the illegalities, for these are not thereby regarded as removed. Also, by speaking of an ad hoc assembly in Caiaphas's house another illegality appears. (c) Jost writes: 'Nur die verblendetste Einseitigkeit (Salvador) kann es versuchen, die Hinrichtung Jesus unter solchen Formen rechtfertigen zu wollen, und die That eines Kaiapha und hasserfüllter Genossen, dem ganzen Volke oder seinen gesetzmässigen Vertretern von neuem aufzubürden.' [2] This means that a division is being made between Caiaphas and both law-keeping and contemporary Jews. This gives additional point to the attempt to exonerate the Great Sanhedrin and to absent Gamaliel from the proceedings. Continuity there is between 1st and 19th century Judaism, but this does not mean the whole of 1st century Judaism. Jost ranges his 19th century co-religionists on the side of Gamaliel who cannot have approved. And Prozeßforschung keeps pace with Judentumforschung and its newly developed differentiation of the legal role of the Sadducees.

The picture is therefore of an illegal gathering perpetrating a 'Privat-mord',[3] in which infringements of the daytime, double session, witnesses and location laws are freely acknowledged. The Christian position is basically acknowledged [4] but the Jews of later generations dissociated.

(b) To accept the illegalities and dismiss the Sanhedrin trial. In 1842 Samuel Hirsch drew from Salvador the view that the gospels generally, and the description of Pilate in particular, were dramatic and not historical writings.[5] He dismissed the Sanhedrin trial but without comment on legality and without denying 'den Haß des Synedriums'.[6] In the account of the trial he acknowledges that the high priest should have sought clarification of the term Son of God, and not condemned Jesus hastily and without defence. Here then is deviation from Salvador, but in a different direction from Jost, under the influence of makeshift literary criticism.

In 1865 a fuller treatment is given, and previous conclusions supported by discussion of illegality, but it must be noticed that neither

---

[1] op.cit. 404.

[2] op.cit. 409.

[3] op.cit. 408.

[4] Philippson, Haben die Juden, 15f, is therefore not quite correct in claiming that Dupin's pamphlet had little influence.

[5] Religionsphilosophie, 685.

[6] Religionsphilosophie, 680. The character of the documents, together with the impossible christology, justify the rejection of the narratives.

Hirsch nor Jost [1] modified their assessment of the Sanhedrin trial in the first place because of the illegalities.[2] In both cases these are secondary. Further it must be noticed that the full validity of the Mishnaic procedure in Jesus' time is accepted by Hirsch.[3] Three illegalities are cited: the two-session rule, the eve of feast and day-time rules. Only the exception allowed for a mesith in Tos. Sanh. 10 is excluded as inherently suspect and inapplicable to Jesus.[4]

(c) To deny the illegalities. Already it is clear that Jews were among those not convinced by Salvador, and that a movement away from his position was gathering pace. This movement overtook J. Cohen, who had originally followed Salvador [5] (though even then he was behind the development of Jewish research) but who later modified his position under the influence of the new research on Sadducees and Pharisees.[6] His final view approximated to that of Jost in 1857, with the exception that the Sadducees were singled out and the Shammaites regarded as possible allies. Importantly, it was again an ad hoc tribunal and one which met in the wrong place—a 'lamentable procès' at which R. Simeon b. Hillel could not have been present.

If the tide was flowing against Salvador he was not left to resist it on his own. Rabbinowicz and Philippson were convinced,[7] and Saalschütz not only agreed but attempted to strengthen Salvador's argument at crucial points: (a) The two-session rule is satisfied by a new time-scheme in which the arrest and mockery occur on Nisan 15 but the crucifixion a week later.[8] (b) He says that Jesus made a claim and not a confession ('eine gravirende Behauptung') and therefore he was not an accused person condemned on his own confession. (c) The argument about the witnesses is tightened. 'Wer falsch Zeugniss sucht, hat es mit den falschen Zeugen offenbar gefunden', and there-

---

[1] Thus, for instance, Jost has a preliminary hearing and yet does not use it to make all question of irregularity irrelevant.

[2] With this correlates Philippson's acceptance of Salvador if the text were to be acceptable — but since on other grounds it cannot be, the Sanhedrin trial must be rejected in toto.

[3] Archives Israélites 26 (1865), 387.

[4] art.cit. 387f.

[5] art.cit. (1860), 223, 246; (1861), 11, 28.

[6] Les Pharisiens, Paris 1877, 54.

[7] Rabbinowicz, Rôle, 134; Philippson, Haben die Juden, 18f. The latter is Straussian on the gospels (his only criticism is that Strauss does not go far enough) but pre-Geigerian on things Jewish in the trial. It is later on in his book that he objects to trial and execution on a feast day, op.cit. 58.

[8] Das Mosaische Recht, 413. He cites Mt 26.5, Mk 14.2: 'not at the feast'. Or was the delay suggested subconsciously by b.Sanh. 43a?

fore Mt 26.60 contradicts Mt 26.59; so Mk 14.55, the 'einleuchtender' version, is to be preferred with its implied omission of κατὰ τοῦ 'Ιησοῦ. A defence of the procedure follows: each witness separately and in the presence of the accused. He then deviates from Salvador as to the legal bearing of the temple claim so that Mk 14.59 is accepted: he remarks that even the pretension of rebuilding 'erschien als von keinem Belang'.

Thus apart from the rather tenuous statement (b), Saalschütz confines himself to the only two legality problems covered by Salvador.

(d) To ignore the illegality problem. This can be done by explicit dismissal (Graetz [1]) or simple disregard (Geiger). Graetz's treatment is noteworthy in that, firstly, he assumes a daytime trial without argument;[2] secondly, he argues for a Sanhedrin of 23, since Caiaphas and not a rabbi was presiding; thirdly, the false witnesses are defended in precisely Salvadorian terms (i.e. Jn 2.19 proves the truth of the assertion); fourthly, the framework of thought is Talmudic,[3] and into this relevant gospel material is inserted, so a problem arising from gospel sources alone is necessarily marginal. Graetz, by ignoring the illegalities and constructing a 'mesith' trial, is at precisely the opposite pole from Samuel Hirsch. Geiger, the other example of the tendency to by-pass the illegalities, does so in spite of having provided the material on Sadducees and Pharisees which was to enable Jewish scholars later on to accept these infringements without personal involvement. Such conclusions are not yet drawn by him.

The main features of the illegality discussion during this period can be quickly summarized. The 'just trial' theory concentrates on repulsing illegality at only two points: the witnesses and the two-session rule. Infringements put forward by opponents are the night hearing, its setting in the house of Caiaphas, and the timing on a feast or its eve. Modification of the Sanhedrin trial, either in terms of a reinterpretation as an ad hoc preliminary gathering or the abandonment of it as totally unhistorical, become associated with the illegality argument, but the latter's role is not primary. Christian apologetic, by statement or over-statement, provides an impulse for Jewish modifi-

---

[1] Geschichte III, 2nd ed. 244: 'Aus der Erzählung der christlichen Grundquellen läßt es sich nicht entnehmen, ob die Richter nach den damals gültigen peinlichen Gesetzen ihn ungerechter Weise verurtheilt hätten.'

[2] This is without reference to Luke. Geschichte, 2nd ed. 243, 3rd ed. 324.

[3] This is so in spite of his dismissal of b.Sanh. 43a because of the unhistorical 'forty days'.

cation, as does Jewish movement towards a new assessment of the Sadducees and the political evaluation of Jesus' downfall.

B. FROM GEIGER TO JUSTER

During this period scholars who mention the illegality question divide into two groups: those who, following Hirsch, use the illegallities as evidence against any Sanhedrin hearing,[1] and those who follow the path laid down by Jost.[2] Concerning the first group it may be said immediately that two logical possibilities remain undiscussed, namely (a) the inapplicability of the topic if less than a full formal trial took place, and (b) the warning eventually voiced by C. G. Montefiore that illegal procedure could still be historical.[3] As regards the second group it is clear how powerful is the trend towards some modification of the nature of the trial, i.e. either to a preliminary hearing or to an informal priestly court or political Sanhedrin. Proponents of a full religious trial are few in number.[4]

A general pattern of argument emerges: (a) Caiaphas was merely Pilate's tool,[5] and the two acted together in Jesus' case. Caiaphas's action was repugnant to all Pharisees, as is shown by Acts 5.33-39, Josephus, Ant.20.200 and sometimes Makk. 1.10.[5] (b) In spite of pressure from Christian writers [6] it is generally assumed and occasionally asserted that the Mishnaic rules were valid at the time Jesus was tried. It is clear that this objection is more naturally a Christian than a Jewish one (Edersheim the convert does in fact raise it [7]), and the only concrete investigation from the Jewish side during this period concerns the special case of the mesith (Tos. Sanh. 11.7). (c) Certain stock illegalities recur regularly: the night trial, the timing on the feast or

---

[1] J. Krauskopf, I. M. Wise, S. Schindler, E. G. Hirsch, K. Kohler, J. Eschelbacher and C. H. Levy.

[2] He is several times explicitly cited: e.g. M. Duschak, Strafrecht, 56; A. Edersheim, Life and Times, 553.

[3] Gospels I (1909), 345: 'It does not follow because the trial of Jesus before the Sanhedrin or high priest violates Jewish law in many important points, that therefore the account given of it cannot be true. There have been illegal trials at all times, and even the flimsiest legal forms have sufficed to get rid of an enemy.'

[4] e.g. Derenbourg, Chwolson and Jelski.

[5] Derenbourg, Essai, 200, 471; Grünebaum, Sittenlehre, 167, 2nd ed. 287; Rodrigues, Roi, 68, 217; Hamburger, Jesus, 52; cf. I. M. Wise, History, 266, Martyrdom, 15.

[6] e.g. E. Schürer, Lehrbuch der neutestamentlichen Zeitgeschichte, Leipzig 1874, 415. Later, in Geschichte des jüdischen Volkes im Zeitalter Jesu Christi II, 3rd ed. Leipzig 1898, 197.

[7] Life and Times, 553f.

its eve, and the non-observance of the two-session rule.[1] (d) Special
attention is paid to the discrepancy between Sanh. 7.5 and anything
Jesus said,[2] clearly because here is a ruling which does not seem far
from the Mosaic law (Lev 24.16), and also because here is focussed
the problem of the continuity between Jewish accusation and sentence
on the one hand and Roman execution on the other. (e) A special
problem is the setting in the high priest's house. This can be just
another infringement [3] or it can be entirely normal within the framework of Derenbourg's 'booths of the house of Annas' theory,[4] but
it can also play a decisive part in proving that the court was informal
or priestly or both,[5] or (later) a political Sanhedrin.[6] When the informal-
ity or priestly character is stressed, Jost's attempt to weaken ὅλον τὸ
συνέδριον references is followed.[7] (f) Always there is the assertion close
by that the Sanhedrin no longer possessed capital powers.[8]

---

[1] Rodrigues, Roi, 234; Grünebaum, Sittenlehre, 2nd ed. 263; Schlesinger,
Jesus, 77; Wise, Martyrdom, 67f; Edersheim, Life and Times, 556; Hamburger,
Jesus, 50; Chwolson, Passamahl, 119 and Blutanklage, 40; Fluegel, Messiah-Ideal
I, 89; C. H. Levy, Progressive Judaism, 544; Krauskopf, Impressions, 99;
Danziger, Forerunners, 46; Montefiore, Gospels I(1909), 347. Jacobs, As others
saw him, 175, thinks the two-session rule was waived because of the political
pressure and the impending Roman trial, though he also writes, op.cit. 184, that
there was a second session next morning to confirm the sentence; against this,
Montefiore, op.cit. 300.
[2] e.g. Krauskopf, R. Jeshua, Chwolson, Hamburger and E. G. Hirsch, but
especially M. Joel, Blicke II, 64-72. Montefiore, op.cit. 347, is an exception in
arguing that the definition of blasphemy may have been stretched.
[3] Thus Fluegel, Messiah-Ideal I, 103; Danziger, Forerunners, 57; Krauskopf,
Impressions, 98; Wise, Martyrdom, 67, is unusual in that he allows this as an
illegality in spite of the non-existence of the Sanhedrin at the time Jesus was crucified.
[4] Derenbourg, Essai, 201; Edersheim, Life and Times, 546, 553-555; Lehmann,
art.cit. 18; Chwolson, Passamahl, 123; Jacobs, As others, 168.
[5] Grünebaum, Sittenlehre, 162; Rodrigues, Roi, 228; Hamburger, Jesus, 50; J.
Jacobs, op.cit. 168, 183; Franz, Buch der Religionen, 109f.
[6] Ziegler, Kampf, 6; Lehmann, art. cit. 13; criticized by Chwolson, Blutanklage, 36.
[7] e.g. an interpolation according to E. Grünebaum, Sittenlehre, 162; in his
2nd ed. 263f, he regards Lk 22.66 as stemming from Mk 14.54. Pace Lk 22.66,
Edersheim writes, Life and Times, 555: 'There is not a tittle of evidence for the
assumption of commentators that Christ was led from the palace of Caiaphas into
the council chamber.'
[8] Derenbourg, Essai, 203; Grünebaum, 2nd ed, 273; Wise, Martyrdom, 67;
Schlesinger, Jesus, 78; Joel, Blicke II, 65f; L. Weiss, Burning Questions, 68;
Jelski, op. cit, 47; Magnus, Outlines, 48f; Edersheim, op.cit. 540; Fluegel,
Messiah-Ideal I, 97: 'Jn 18.31 decides the whole of our discussion'; Soloweyczyk,
Kol Kore (1868), 102; T. Reinach, art.cit. 15; Lehmann, Dates, 17, who defends
the 'forty years' of b.A.Z. 8b, and regards the Sanhedrin's exile as voluntary;
E. G. Hirsch, My Religion, 374; Danziger, Forerunners, 48; Duschak, Strafrecht,

This then is the structure of an established pattern of argument. Variations within it are rare, and it only remains for us to discuss some special features.

(a) The applicability of the laws. As mentioned above, this is not a live issue for Jewish scholars, at least when they write about the trial.[1] Eschelbacher, for instance, is content to state without argument their applicability.[2] For Grünebaum any thought of idealized legal procedure is not a live option: the argument is simply that later on no cases were tried.[3] But in any case, the illegalities are for him not a primary element in the proof that politics permeated Jesus' trial, for his first edition ignores them. Chwolson, whose book is largely centred on a reconstruction of halakhic development, uses this to enforce the current validity of these laws, e.g. tight rules about feast and sabbath cannot be later in date since in later times the attitudes on these points softened.[4] Edersheim stands out as an exception, and he merges the Jewish and Christian tendencies in so doing. In a faintly polemical remark he declares that this legislation may be 'the ideal rather than the real', i.e. what the rabbis imagined should be, rather than what was, or else it may date from later times.[5] Yet he does not specify which rules this might affect, nor does he hold back from using the assumed illegalities as proof of the non-involvement of the Great Sanhedrin.[6]

The one loophole, which several scholars realize, is the case of the mesith. Edersheim mentioned it guardedly and inclined towards its relevance to the case of Jesus, but he did not need to apply it since he thought the mesith charge apparently broke down. Earlier, when Samuel Hirsch treated this he adduced against it that Jesus was not a seducer but was later regarded by the rabbis as such, and since it was

---

7; S. Mendelssohn, art. Capital Punishment, JE 3 (1902), 557. Montefiore, I(1909), lxix, 345 maintains that although the Jews had been deprived of this right they were eager to regain it, and illegal executions were not unknown.

[1] Cf. J. Derenbourg, Une stèle du temple d'Hérode, Journal Asiatique 20 (1872), 192, who allows that the cultic regulations are later and theoretical but does not draw a parallel in the case of the criminal legislation.

[2] Vorlesungen, 418.

[3] Sittenlehre, 2nd ed. 263. Cf. Samuel Hirsch, art. cit. (1865), 387, who argued that the rabbis did not legislate for ideal messianic days. This is a case of proving one case by simply overstating the opposite.

[4] Passamahl, 7.

[5] Life and Times, 553f. He also asks how possible it would be to carry out these rules under Herod and the procurators.

[6] op.cit. 552, 555.

known by them that he had died at Passover time a legal exception was deduced; further, he asks, why relax the laws for more serious crimes? [1] M. Joel follows the pattern of the second of these arguments: Akiba based his ruling on synoptic chronology which was known to him through Matthew (Mt 5.17, b. Shabb. 116a).[2]

(b) The problem of Sanh. 7.5. The riddle of Jesus' trial is defined by Joel as follows: 'die oftgefühlte Schwierigkeit, den Prozeß Jesu sich zu denken unter Mitwirkung eines auch nur den Schein mosaisch-talmudischen Rechts wahrenden Synedriums'.[3] Jesus' trial is unique (those of Stephen and James are not analogous) for having a Jewish sentence and a Roman execution,[4] and this cannot be explained simply by the jus gladii complication. Since 'Gidduf ist immer wirkliche Gotteslästerung' and since Sanh. 7.5 represents a correct interpretation of Lev 24.16, nothing Jesus said will qualify, and the Talmud confirms this by omitting all reference to blasphemy in the charge.[5] Joel comes to a position of general agnosticism (cf. Mendelssohn) but tentatively accepts a mock trial by the priests in collusion with Pilate.[6] This presentation of the problem indicates how deep is the impression that limitation of the jus gladii involves forfeiture of the right to hold trials as well.

In spite of the tendency to blame the Sadducees there is still some uneasiness at the lack of correspondence between Sanh. 7.5 and what Jesus said. It therefore constantly invites a solution and it is for this reason that both the heavenly session theory of Chwolson [7] and the Ani Hu theory in 'Rabbi Jeshua' arose—but in both cases a malicious twisting of what Jesus meant is said to have taken place.[8]

To sum up: the denial of illegalities fades away during this period, and Jewish writers now accept them and incorporate them into a scheme in which either no Jews at all, or at most an unrepresentative group are implicated. Pharisees and the uninvolved Great Sanhedrin embody the true nation with which contemporary Jews feel their

---

[1] art.cit. 387f.
[2] Blicke II, 62.
[3] op. cit. 64.
[4] Cf. later Juster, Les Juifs, 135f, and Lietzmann, Prozeß, 257.
[5] Blicke II, 65.
[6] op.cit. 68f. Execution by Pilate is the fundamental datum.
[7] Beiträge, 47.
[8] p. 140. This writer is influenced by the Tol'doth Yeshu, op.cit. 84. Similarly, G. Klein, Katechismus, 55-59, and Ist Jesus eine historische Persönlichkeit? 40-42 although this time without any blame being attached to the high priest.

oneness. The applicability of the laws is accepted throughout with very little question, as is the truth of Jn 18.31. Since the latter is interpreted in the light of b.A.Z. 8b, the limitation extends beyond the execution of a capital sentence to the right to meet formally and pass one.[1]

C.   JUSTER AND HUSBAND ONWARDS

There has probably never been a more influential book by a Jewish writer on the trial of Jesus than Jean Juster's Les Juifs dans l'Empire Romain[2]. By way of Hans Lietzmann, Juster's theory that the Jews did have capital powers has not only provoked a debate which cannot yet be regarded as finished,[3] but also dictated the starting point for many scholars engaged in research into the trial. Although doubt about the Sanhedrin's loss of powers had occasionally been raised before,[4] the normal view had certainly been that curtailment had occurred.[5] Indeed for many Jewish scholars after Juster as well as before him, this remained the accepted view. This is in some ways surprising but the persis-

---

[1] It is interesting to see a reproduction in miniature of the features of the pre-1914 debate, in the controversy between the lawyer E. Gottschling (Die rechtliche Seite der Verurteilung Jesu Christi, in Leipziger Neueste Nachrichten 20.6.1928), F. Lipsius (Der Prozeß Jesu — eine Erwiderung, in the same paper for 24.6.1928), and H. Laible (Der Prozeß Jesu, in Allgemeine Evangelisch-Lutherische Kirchenzeitung for 13.7.1928). Gottschling in effect harmonizes the gospels, relies on Jn for the Pilate hearing and uses Mommsen's work for the legal data. Lipsius, against this, raises against the Markan (N.B) Sanhedrin sessions a list of illegalities — nocturnal session, only one hearing, clash with Sanh 7.5 — and dismisses the suggestion that the laws were not then valid. Finally, Laible urges in defence of the Sanhedrin hearing, that the laws were wider in Jesus' time and were later narrowed on an anti-Sadducean principle, for the Sadducees had judged by their own harsh laws. In this debate there is no argument about Jn 18.31, nor any mention of the preliminary hearing theory as a serious solution: Gottschling blandly discounts it by citing Mk 14.64, Mt 26.66.

[2] Published in Paris 1914.

[3] H. Lietzmann, Der Prozeß Jesu, published in Sitzungsberichte der Preussischen Akademie der Wissenschaften, phil.-hist. Klasse 1931, XIV Berlin 1934, 313-322, and reprinted in Kleine Schriften II, Berlin 1958, 251-263; also in the same volume, Bemerkungen zum Prozeß Jesu I, II. pp. 264-268, 269-276. For recent treatments of the problem, see P. Winter, On the Trial of Jesus, Berlin 1961; E. Lohse, art. συνέδριον, TWNT 7 (1964), 863-869; A. N. Sherwin White, Roman Society and Roman Law in the New Testament, Oxford 1963; J. Blinzler, Der Prozeß Jesu, 4th ed. Regensburg 1969, 229-244.

[4] On the Jewish side, J. Salvador; on the Christian side, I. Döllinger.

[5] Cf. T. Mommsen, Römisches Strafrecht I, Leipzig 1899, 240-244; E. Schürer, Lehrbuch der neutestamentlichen Zeitgeschichte, Leipzig 1874, 415f. Geschichte des jüdischen Volkes im Zeitalter Jesu Christi II. 3rd ed. Leipzig 1898, 208-210.

tence in retaining this view is impressive,[1] and indeed it is still made the outstanding argument against the charge that the Jews crucified Jesus.[2] Undoubtedly this is largely due to the direct influence of R. W. Husband, whose book [3] followed Juster's so quickly. The attraction of Husband's work is understandable in that (a) his theory of a preliminary examination preceding Roman trial was in line with the growing tendency in Jewish research towards a modified hearing; (b) his attitude to the gospels was markedly more positive than Juster's,[4] and Jewish scholars have often tended to deal less radically with Christian documents than Christian scholars themselves; (c) his avoidance of either extreme, belittling the documents or blaming the Jewish authorities, and a conscious effort to be fair all round were attractive features; (d) he was influenced by the Jewish tradition about Jesus. Hence Juster's book was immediately overshadowed, partly also no doubt because of its publication at the beginning of the war (in which Juster himself was killed). It was left to Lietzmann to project Juster's work into the scholarly debate, but by that time Husband's theory had been in the field for fifteen years and had gained such influential adherents as J. Klausner and C. G. Montefiore. In spite of this retarded beginning, Juster's influence did make itself felt. For Lietzmann's article made an impact on some Jewish writers,[5] and the arguments of Juster were used not only by those who were concerned with the Great

---

[1] Thus T. Reinach, reviewing Juster in REJ 70 (1920), 94f: 'J'aurais d'expresses réserves à faire sur son interprétation de la jurisdiction pénale laissée aux Juifs sous le régime des procurateurs et notamment sur l'étendue des pouvoirs qu'il attribue au Sanhédrin, même en matière capitale, au mépris de textes explicites, qu'il torture ou écarte arbitrairement. On sait l'importance de cette question pour l'appréciation de la valeur historique du récit des Évangiles; ici l'exposé de M. J. me paraît marquer une régression de la critique.' Similarly Hyamson, JQR 11 (1920), 96; Klausner, Jesus, 345; G. Brandes, Jesus: a Myth, London 1927, 27; Montefiore, I(1927), 347; M. Joseph, Jesus von Nazareth, JL 3 (1929), 240; Sachar, History, 132; E. Jacob, EJ 5 (1930), 528; Trattner, op.cit. 132; Radin, Trial, 57, 253; S. W. Baron, History, 70; Rosenblatt, Crucifixion, 316; C. Raddock, Portrait of a People, New York 1965, 183; E. L. Ehrlich, A Concise History of Israel, London 1962, 135; A. Schalit, Zu AG 25, 9 ASTI 6 (1968), 112. J. Isaac, Jesus, 409f originally took this view, but retracted it in The Teaching of Contempt, New York 1964, 141f, following P. Winter. Zucker, op.cit. 86, takes a mediating position arguing that the Sanhedrin had powers but chose not to use them in order to avoid responsibility.

[2] G. G. Fox, The Jews Jesus and Christ, Chicago 1953, 49f, where an unjust Sadducean hearing is not disputed.

[3] The Prosecution of Jesus, Princeton 1916.

[4] See Juster, op. cit. 135.

[5] M. Guttmann, Schlußwort, 43; Zucker, Studien, 86; Buber, op.cit. 108; S. W. Baron, History, 70.

Sanhedrin's role [1] but in a modified form by those who accept the Jn 18.31 limitation for political affairs conducted by a political Sanhedrin (or a priestly court), but who stress that complete autonomy in religious affairs still belonged to the Great Sanhedrin.[2]

Juster's arguments centre on a series of examples of capital procedure, and his treatment will be outlined in the light of issues raised then and subsequently.

1. j.Sanh. 1.1, 7.2. Four factors emerged in Juster's discussion of this passage. (a) Its age. Juster discounted the text on the grounds that the tradition originated 150 years after the event [3] through the father of R. Ishmael b. Jose. On the other hand opponents of Juster have supported it by drawing attention to its Tannaitic origin.[4] (b) The 'forty years'. Almost everyone agrees that this is unhistorical. Juster himself argued against it, firstly because any constitutional change would have occurred in A.D. 6, and secondly because it fits the pattern of associating preliminary woes with the destruction of the temple.[5] Whereas Juster and others [6] argue that the apparently wrong date proves the total untrustworthiness of the tradition, others [7] take the statement as true and referring to A.D. 6, while several advocates of the 'political Sanhedrin' theory take 'forty' as a corruption of 'four'.[8] (c) The evolution of the tradition. Juster argued that the tradition that the Sanhedrin moved from the Hall of Hewn Stones forty years before A.D. 70 [9] (a movement which he regards as historically doubtful but which, if true, would not mean forfeiture of capital powers) has been merged with the ruling, post-dating A.D. 70,[10] that capital

---

[1] e.g. Zucker and Winter.

[2] Hyamson, JQR 11 (1920), 94-96; S. Zeitlin, Who crucified Jesus ?, 75f; Polack, Jesus, 63, 103; Mantel, Studies, 285, 315; S. B. Hoenig, The Great Sanhedrin, New York 1953, 88.

[3] Juster, op.cit. 133, cf. Lietzmann, Prozeß, 258; T. A. Burkill, The Competence of the Sanhedrin, VC 10 (1956), 84f; C. K. Barrett, John, 445.

[4] U. Holzmeister, Zur Frage der Blutgerichtsbarkeit des Synedriums, Bib 19 (1938), 43-59, 151-174, esp. 169; J. Jeremias, Zur Geschichtlichkeit des Verhörs Jesu vor dem hohen Rat, ZNW 43 (1951), 145-150, esp. 147; Blinzler, Prozeß, 241f.

[5] Josephus, B. J. 6.288-309; b. Yoma 39b; b. A.Z. 8b; b. Gitt. 56a.

[6] Burkill, art.cit. 85.

[7] Husband, op.cit. 161; Jeremias, art.cit. 147; Lohse, art. cit. 863; Blinzler, Prozeß, 242; also Rosenblatt, Crucifixion, 316.

[8] Hoenig, op.cit. 211; Mantel, Studies, 285.

[9] Thus b. R. H. 31a; b.Sanh. 41a. However the assumption that b.Sanh. 41a represents an earlier form is not to be accepted uncritically.

[10] Juster, Juifs, 133f. Burkill even argues that it cannot be earlier than A.D. 150.

cases could only be judged in that Hall. It has also been suggested that the tradition is a defensive attempt to avoid responsibility for the death of Jesus.[1] (d) Contradictions with known cases and principles. Juster argued that capital powers were covered by the B.J. 2.220 statement of preservation of national customs—a view rightly criticized by A. N. Sherwin White.[2] Further, he argues that the Mishnah presupposes that cases were tried until A.D. 70, and indeed in the Hall of Hewn Stones.[3]

Since attempts to explain the evolution of the tradition fail to carry conviction, it seems best to accept the existence of an historical kernel. The movement of the Sanhedrin is different in kind from the portents of disaster; and although Jewish tradition does put forward apologetic concerning the death of Jesus (e.g. the 'forty days' of b.Sanh. 43a), the thrust concerns the manner and not the fact of Jewish action—indeed involvement is exaggerated (again b.Sanh. 43a).

2. Sanh. 7.2: the execution of the priest's daughter.

> R. Eliezer b. Zadok said: It happened once that a priest's daughter committed adultery, and they encompassed her with branches and burnt her.

This case was produced triumphantly by Juster,[4] and since the source is R. Eliezer the attempt of Husband to discount its historicity entirely has rightly been rejected by Mantel.[5]

The date of the incident is the one key issue here. Jeremias [6] in particular has investigated this and drawn together three strands of evidence: Firstly, R. Eliezer must have been very young when he saw the incident for he was held on his father's shoulders (Tos. Sanh. 9.11). Secondly, he studied Torah under R. Joshua the Horonite during the drought years, A.D. 47-49 (b.Yeb. 15b), and so was young then. Thirdly, there is the text of b.Ber. 19b: 'R. Eliezer b. Zadok said: We used to leap over coffins with bodies in, to see the Israelite kings.'

---

[1] Winter, On the Trial, 191. For refutation of this argument, cf. Blinzler Prozeß, 235.

[2] Roman Society, 37.

[3] Sanh. 7.2; b.Sanh. 37b, 52b; b.Sota 8b; b.Keth. 30a-b. Similarly, Winter, op.cit. 191.

[4] Juifs, 138; Lietzmann, Prozeß, 259.

[5] Studies, 285.

[6] In a letter published by Lietzmann, and Jeremias's article, p. 146. Also, F. Büchsel, Die Blutgerichtsbarkeit des Synedrions, ZNW 30 (1931), 202-210, esp. 205; Holzmeister, art. cit. 173; Lohse, Geschichte, 78; Blinzler, Prozeß, 243.

This clearly reflects childhood activity. So Sanh. 7.2 decribes an incident during the reign of Agrippa, A.D. 41-44.[1]

Lietzmann's decision on this was: 'Beweisen läßt sich somit nach keiner Seite etwas; wir bleiben bei Möglichkeiten.' [2] Zadok worked before A.D. 70 and knew rabbis in the time of Trajan, so was probably born about A.D. 20-30. So Eliezer was born at the earliest A.D. 39-49. Studying Torah at 7-9 years old is certainly possible and being carried at 4-5 years old equally so—but 6-10 years old is also possible. Burkill [3] makes a very similar attempt to extend the age-range. But, firstly, Lietzmann's calculation of dates has too wide a margin of error to provide concrete evidence, and secondly, Burkill's criticism of Jeremias's arguments takes up the letter cited by Lietzmann but not the later article, so that when he suggests A.D. 42 for R. Eliezer's birth he neglects the evidence of b.Ber. 19b. This source in fact refutes Burkill, for kings (plural) are mentioned, i.e. Agrippa I and Herod II,[4] and so the text envisages a situation before A.D. 44. This would make Eliezer at most two years old, and it is not very likely that a two-year old would jump the coffins. By comparison, Jeremias's arguments are much the more convincing. It is surprising that Sanh. 7.2 is quoted by some Jewish scholars favouring Jewish rights, but without examination of this crucial issue of the date.[5]

3. The temple inscription: Josephus, B.J. 6.124-126, Ant. 15.417, Philo, Leg. ad Gaium 307.[6] Everyone agrees that this is an exception but the question is: to which rule is it an exception? Two theories are proposed. (a) The a minori ad majus theory: 'Wenn in einem Ausnahmefall die Kompetenz des Synedrions zur Aburteilung von Religionsverbrechen sich sogar auf römische Bürger erstreckte, so wird sie in normalen Fällen für Juden wohl sicher in Geltung gewesen

---

[1] So already A. Büchler, Die Todesstrafen der Bibel und der jüdisch-nachbiblischen Zeit, MGWJ 50 (1906), 559. Winter, op.cit. 15, 156, declares that the representation of execution examples as irregularities or occurrences in the reign of Agrippa is special pleading, and he relies on Burkill in treating these cases.

[2] art.cit. 274.

[3] art.cit. 94.

[4] W. Bacher, Die Agada der Tannaiten, Straßburg 1884, 51.

[5] Zeitlin, Who crucified Jesus? 75; Zucker, op.cit. 82; Goldin, Case of the Nazarene, 340. An inconsistency in Zeitlin's theory is that he takes the Sanh. 7.2 case as one for the religious Sanhedrin, but Mariamne's adultery as the concern of the political Sanhedrin, Ant. 15.218-231. op.cit. 79.

[6] Juster, Juifs, 142; H. J. Ebeling, Zur Frage nach der Kompetenz des Synedrions, ZNW 35 (1936), 290-295, esp. 294; Mantel, Studies, 315.

sein.' So writes Lietzmann.[1] (b) The view that this represents a concession, i.e. permission to execute anyone, including a Roman, though neither was normally permitted.[2] The formulation κἂν 'Ρωμαῖός τις ᾖ definitely favours this interpretation.

As regards the Philonic parallel Juster, followed by Lietzmann and Burkill,[3] argued that this demonstrates that executions did not depend on the procurator. That this is not compelling appears from the explanations, i.e. that this is 'ein Sonderrecht, das eine besondere Konzession der Römer darstellte',[4] or that this is a general formulation of Jewish law (Lev 16.2), regarded by Jews as unaffected by the reluctantly-accepted limitation on their powers.[5]

4. Josephus, Ant. 18.81. Juster [6] and Burkill [7] both use this case of the man who fled, in order to prove Jewish autonomy in religious affairs. This assumes that Jewish law is involved; Husband [8] and Holzmeister [9] reject this, and there is too little detail in this case to permit its use in the debate.

5. Josephus, Ant. 20.200-203: the death of James. The following issues are involved in interpreting the text. (a) The original version. Those who follow Juster on the Sanhedrin's powers have generally not accepted his amendment of the text,[10] which involved retouching

---

[1] art.cit. 273, followed exactly by Burkill, art.cit. 96; cf. Hoenig, The Great Sanhedrin, 88; Goldin, Case of the Nazarene, 341; Winter, op.cit. 155f also argues from this source for full Jewish powers, but slightly twists the matter by stating: 'It is unbelievable that Jewish magistrates had less authority in respect of Jewish offenders than in respect of Roman.' No exegete envisages this.
J. Derenbourg, Une stèle du temple d'Hérode, Journal Asiatique 20 (1872), 178-195, thinks that from Herod's time the threat was impossible, and that punishment came from heaven (perhaps with human assistance!) and not through a capital sentence. Similarly, E. Bickermann, The Warning Inscription of Herod's Temple, JQR 37 (1947), 387-403; S. W. Baron, History I, 239. For the contrary views, S. Zeitlin, The Warning Inscription of the Temple, JQR 38 (1947), 111-116.
[2] Büchsel, art.cit. 206; Jeremias, art.cit. 146; G. D. Kilpatrick, The Trial of Jesus, 18; Blinzler, Prozeß, 238f; Sherwin White, Roman Society, 38, though the latter argues too far, undervaluing the special case of the Roman citizen, when he claims that this rule would be irrelevant if the Sanhedrin had full powers.
[3] Lietzmann, Prozess, 259; Burkill, art.cit. 95.
[4] Jeremias, art.cit. 146.
[5] Büchsel, art.cit. 206; Holzmeister, art.cit. 57f.
[6] Juifs, 140.
[7] art.cit. 89.
[8] Prosecution, 113.
[9] art.cit. 165.
[10] There are exceptions, e.g. S. Zeitlin, The Christ Passage in Josephus, JQR 18 (1928), 231-255, esp. 233-235.

§ 200 and omitting most of §§ 201-2.[1] Attention is drawn to the role of
Agrippa of Chalcis during the period,[2] against the arguments of Juster
that Josephus makes the Pharisees, not the procurator, restrain Sadducean severity; that Josephus certainly did not mention Christ; that the
ideas of informing the procurator of his rights, together with the
absence of any deputy during an interregnum [3] are so suspect that
they must be a Christian interpretation of the same sort as Jn 18.31.
(b) The actual offence of Annas. Juster's argument was weakened by
inattention to this and it has correctly been pointed out against him
that the use of the interregnum [4] and the subsequent deposition [5]
must dictate the text's interpretation.

The interpretation of πρῶτον (§ 201) is crucial, and it is appropriate
to outline some approaches to the problem of this word before making
an alternative suggestion. It could refer to the convening of the Sanhedrin (καθίζει),[6] as opposed to the next act (παρέδωκεν) though
difficulty has often been felt in accepting that the Sanhedrin required
procuratorial permission to meet.[7] Lietzmann was not impressed by
this difficulty [8] and was also prepared to belittle the delegation to
Albinus. As a result he understood Annas' offence to be the convening
of a Sanhedrin to deal with a political case—which James's is assumed
to be. Following a different approach H.J.Ebeling argued that πρῶτον
stands for the first act of Annas as high priest (cf. τοιαῦτα πράσσειν).
The protests of the strict group were roused because they regarded
this as the cruel slaughter of an innocent man. For Ebeling therefore
the content of πρῶτον is not just an execution as such but an unjust
one. His conclusion on capital powers is like Lietzmann's.

(c) A religious or political case? The political aspect was stressed
by Lietzmann and Burkill, and again recently by Winter [9] and Brandon.[10] The views put forward by the latter two are most important
for our purpose. According to Winter, Annas offended by convening
the Sanhedrin without the necessary authorization which had to be

---

[1] Juster, Juifs, 140; Lietzmann, art.cit. 270; Burkill, art.cit. 91.

[2] Josephus, Ant. 20.222f.

[3] Sherwin White stresses that capital jurisdiction was precisely what a governor
could not delegate, least of all when he had left his province.

[4] M. J. Lagrange, reviewing Juster in RB 15 (1918), 264.

[5] Büchsel, art.cit. 172.

[6] Büchsel, art.cit. 85.

[7] Cf. Holzmeister, art.cit. 160; Blinzler, Prozeß, 242f.

[8] Prozeß, 271.

[9] On the Trial, 156.

[10] Jesus and the Zealots, 116-126, 168f.

renewed by each procurator. This and not the execution, which would have brought proceedings against him for murder if the Romans had disapproved, was the sole issue.[1] Brandon appeals to the version of Hegesippus as well as to Josephus, and assimilates the case of James to a dispute between the lower orders of priesthood and the sacerdotal aristocracy. The vital link is achieved by an appeal to the fact of involvement of many priests and others zealous for the law in the Christian community.[2] Although proceedings before the Sanhedrin and the penalty of stoning are slightly embarrassing to this view that the case was political rather than religious, Brandon evidently regards the rest of his argument as sufficiently strong to disregard these points.[3]

These arguments can now be assessed. Firstly, the alleged political complexion cannot be accepted. (a) If political reasons had precipitated the action there would have been no need to use the interregnum between procurators, for Festus, the predecessor of Albinus, had been rigorous and ruthless in putting down anything smacking of Zealotism.[4] (b) There is no evidence for any implication of James within the priestly dispute upon which Brandon relies so heavily. (c) The version of Hegesippus can and should be discounted.[5] (d) The accusation of having transgressed the law ($\pi\alpha\rho\alpha\nu o\mu\eta\sigma\acute{\alpha}\nu\tau\omega\nu$) within the context of Pharisee-Sadducee divergence—which is how Josephus frames the incident—indicates a religious affair. (e) Stoning proves the religious character of the case. (f) As Brandon sensed, the involvement of the Sanhedrin counts against the political interpretation.

Secondly, the interpretation of $\pi\rho\tilde{\omega}\tau o\nu$ is of great importance and clinches the accumulating evidence for limitation of Jewish powers. Ebeling's view that this word refers to Annas' first action in office is weakened by the vagueness which this gives to the account, whereas we would expect such a reference, unnecessary in itself, to be specific. Also $\tau o\iota\alpha\tilde{\upsilon}\tau\alpha$ in the sentence in question merely means that pressure was to be brought on the high priest to prevent any repetition. In

---

[1] On the Trial, 18.

[2] Jesus and the Zealots, 118.

[3] Brandon had earlier in his argument appealed to the use of the sword *as against stoning* to prove the political complexion of the case of James the son of Zebedee, op.cit. 97.

[4] Josephus, B.J. 2.271, Ant. 20.185. So rightly, M Hengel, Die Zeloten, Leiden 1961, 359. By contrast Albinus was to prove more lenient, but of course this could not be known in advance.

[5] See J. Blinzler, The Jewish Punishment of Stoning in the New Testament Period, in E. Bammel ed. The Trial of Jesus, C. F. D. Moule Festschrift, London 1970, 157-159.

order to set πρῶτον in its context it is worth citing the relevant part
of the text in full:

> Those of the inhabitants of the city who were considered the most
> fair-minded and who were strict in observance of the law were offend-
> ed at this. They therefore secretly sent to king Agrippa urging him,
> for Ananus had not even been correct in his first step (μηδὲ γὰρ τὸ
> πρῶτον ὀρθῶς αὐτὸν πεποιηκέναι), to order him to desist from any fur-
> ther such actions. Certain of them even went to meet Albinus, who
> was on his way from Alexandria, and informed him that Ananus had
> no authority to convene the Sanhedrin without his consent.

Within the complex of this incident were apparently two offences,
for both the word πρῶτον and the two-fold delegation, with their complaints to Agrippa and Albinus, suggest this. To what then does
πρῶτον refer? There are three logical possibilities: 1. The convening
of the Sanhedrin. 2. An unjust trial. 3. Execution without procuratorial
permission. Now πρῶτον cannot refer to 1. because this cannot be
regarded as offending the 'strict according to the law' group, who in
any case were not the defenders of Roman interests, and also because
it is in respect of πρῶτον that complaint is made not to the Roman but
to Agrippa. πρῶτον cannot, for logical reasons refer to 3. Therefore,
the only option remaining open is 2.—and this fits extremely well
with Josephus's introductory opening about the judicial harshness of
the Sadducees, for the incident that follows must surely be intended
as an instance of this. Again we are not to suppose that a remark like
this is made and then left hanging in the air. Hence πρῶτον is 2. and the
implicit δεύτερον is 3. The situation was accordingly that complaints
were made to Agrippa in view of the injustice of the proceedings, and
to Albinus in view of the infringement of the laws of the occupying
power. Roman ire was such that Annas paid for his temerity with his
office, and the lesson was emphatically taught that the Jewish authorities would only at their peril execute a capital sentence without permission.

6. Josephus, B.J. 2.145: Essene practice. Juster argued, again followed by Lietzmann,[1] that by the a minori ad maius principle, the Essene practice of killing for blasphemy even against Moses means that
the capital competence of the Sanhedrin must have been an established
fact. This has in fact exercised little influence on the debate. Holzmeister mentioned it but understood the penalty as actually the exclusion

---

[1] Prozeß, 260.

from the order alone, an exclusion which might well lead to death.[1] Whether or not this is correct Kilpatrick's objection that it is scarcely permissible to argue a general case from the practices of a secret society [2] holds good and is in no way weakened by the argument of Burkill that no record exists of proceedings against them for contravening an imperial decree.[3]

7. Josephus, B.J. 6.300-309: the case of Jesus ben Ananios. The offence of this man has often been interpreted as political, e.g. by Juster and Zeitlin.[4] However the claim that this was not a religious matter is as unlikely as the assertion that no capital crime was involved.[5] It is scarcely possible that Stephen's case was religious and this man's not so. The most likely conclusion is therefore that threats against the temple constituted a religious crime, and that with the delivery of the man to Albinus the Jews acknowledged their inability to execute.[6]

8. Megh. Taan. 6. Here is a statement about the regaining of the right to execute criminals, connected with the 22nd of the month; this follows immediately on the 17th, the commemoration of the Roman departure after the siege (Josephus, B.J. 2.440). This has rightly been proposed by Jeremias[7] as a formidable objection to Juster's view. The latter cannot be salvaged by the unsupported theory of Burkill that the criminals in question were specifically those who had given support to Rome.[8]

9. The penalty of strangulation. Strictly speaking this belongs outside a discussion of the issues raised by Juster, but for the sake of

---

[1] art.cit. 155.

[2] The Trial of Jesus, 19.

[3] art.cit. 89.

[4] Juster, Juifs, 148: 'Il est évident que nous sommes, ici aussi, en présence d'un cas pouvant être interprété comme rébellion; car la ruine prédite devait sûrement être la peine méritée pour la tolérance du joug étranger.' S. Zeitlin, Who crucified Jesus ? 158, argues that the man was handed over to the procurator under suspicion of being δαιμονιώτερος, i.e. an apocalyptist and therefore a rebel. Against the latter, it is surprising that apocalyptic tendencies should be equated with rebellion: there had been plenty of apocalyptic thinkers who had not been regarded as politically menacing.

[5] Contra Ebeling, art.cit. 293.

[6] Büchsel, art.cit. 87; Holzmeister, art.cit. 162; Jeremias, art.cit. 147; Blinzler, Prozeß, 243.

[7] art.cit. 150: 'Hängen die beiden Ereignisse, wie kaum zu bezweifeln ist, zusammen, dann ist uns durch Megh. Taan. 6 urkundlich bestätigt, daß die Juden — wie überall im römischen Reich die Provinzialen — kein Exekutionsrecht besaßen.' Similarly, Lohse, art.cit. 864; Blinzler, Prozeß, 237.

[8] art.cit. 88.

completeness it is important to cover it. This is in fact one of the two distinctively fresh arguments brought by Paul Winter,[1] the other being a new treatment of the case of Paul. Winter is of the opinion that the main lines of the arguments of Juster and Lietzmann may still be followed and that throughout the pre-A.D. 70 period there remained intact the Jewish right to pass and execute death sentences for all but political offences. This point was in fact singled out for criticism by reviewers more than any other apart from the 'Pharisaic Jesus' theory.[2]

Winter argues that strangling was a relatively new procedure when the Mishnah was compiled.[3] It was not an O.T. method. Certainly it was used by Herod, but no deductions can be drawn from his behaviour.[4] It was not introduced as a more humane method than the others since it ranked above decapitation.[5] The conclusion must be that it was introduced as a secret method after the right to inflict death sentences publicly had been lost, and this happened in A.D. 70.[6] Winter bases his view that death sentences continued to be passed on b.Sota 8b and b.Sanh. 37b,[7] and argues further that there is no recorded case of strangling before A.D. 70. Hence, prior to A.D. 70 the situation did not require a method of execution adaptable for secret use.[8] and so: 'Before the year 70 C.E. the Sanhedrin had full jurisdiction over Jews charged with offences against Jewish religious laws, and had the authority openly to pronounce and carry out sentences of death where such penalty was provided in Jewish legislation.'

This reconstruction is open to the following objections: (a) The logic depends on there being no examples of strangling before A.D. 70 and some known examples immediately afterwards. But these are lacking, and so a change in A.D. 70 cannot be substantiated. Even if Winter's reconstruction of the motives for its introduction were correct, the conclusion would no more relate to A.D. 70 than to A.D. 6 without these required examples. (b) b.Sota 8b and b.Sanh. 37b do

---

[1] On the Trial, 67-74.

[2] Explicitly favourable to Winter here: O. E. Evans, LQHR 187 (1962), 70; F. C. Grant, JR 44 (1964), 231. Critical: W. Michaelis, ThZ 17 (1961), 227; P. Benoit, RB 68 (1961), 595; O. Betz, JR 44 (1964), 182; E. Lohse, Gnomon 33 (1961), 625; P. Mikat, BZ 6 (1962), 306; I. de la Potterie, Bib 43 (1962), 93. A. Schalit, Randbemerkungen, 96, thinks the issue unimportant.

[3] op.cit. 71.

[4] op.cit. 188.

[5] op.cit. 71, 189. Cf. j.Sanh. 7.2; b.Sanh. 50b.

[6] op.cit. 73.

[7] op.cit. 190.

[8] op.cit. 74.

not help Winter's view any more than they support the view that capital powers had been lost. For the implication is that strangulation was inflicted before A.D. 70 and then replaced (N.B.) by an equivalent heaven-sent death. (c) Strangling does not stand over against the other three methods as a private rather than public method. For beheading could equally be inflicted privately. (d) Winter's argument has already been severely criticized by Blinzler,[1] who points out that strangling in fact ranked fourth among the methods used [2] and was grounded in the principle of humanizing justice. An additional reason is pointed out by D. Daube,[3] who while allowing that strangling might have the additional attraction of drawing less attention to itself, argues for a movement between 100 B.C. and A.D. 100 based on the bodily resurrection of the dead.

10. Jn 18.31: ἡμῖν οὐκ ἔξεστιν ἀποκτεῖναι οὐδένα. This statement has often been included in a general devaluation of John. We have in recent years learnt not to be so hasty in dismissing Johannine data, however,[4] and deviations of the Fourth Gospel from the Synoptics are by no means necessarily unhistorical. Here we do not have even such a divergence, for the Synoptics assume precisely such a legal situation.[5] Various objections have been raised against this statement. Firstly, a Jewish reminder to the procurator about the limitation of powers is thought to be unlikely.[6] But this argument neglects the excellent sense of Jn 18.31a: Pilate receives a sufficiently inadequate charge to make him mistake the case for a non-capital one, which ex hypothesei the Jews could judge. The Jews reply in effect that this is indeed a capital

---

[1] Prozeß, 233f. This is one example of the unfortunate neglect by Winter of scholars who disagree with him, especially Blinzler. This was noted in the reviews of W. Michaelis, ThZ 17 (1961), 227; E. Stauffer, ThLZ 88 (1963); I. de la Potterie, Bib 43 (1962), 93; P. Mikat, BZ 6 (1962), 300. Winter attempted to defend himself in CommViat 6 (1963), 303-307, but could still only adduce two citations of Blinzler.

[2] Cf. S. Mendelssohn, art. Capital Punishment, JE 3 (1902), 556-558.

[3] The New Testament and Rabbinic Judaism, 304-308.

[4] Cf. C. H. Dodd, Historical Tradition in the Fourth Gospel, Cambridge 1963; R. E. Brown, The Gospel according to John, New York 1966.

[5] A. N. Sherwin White, The Trial of Christ, in S.P.C.K. Theological Collections 6, London 1965, 107. Winter, On the Trial, 10, argues altogether too narrowly when he says that Mark knew no such regulation as Jn 18.31 and that his account lacks coherence. For it is precisely such an assumption which gives Mark coherence, and it is an unnecessary modern presumption that if Mark knew such a regulation he would have mentioned it.

[6] Burkill, art.cit. 83; R. H. Lightfoot, History and Interpretation in the Gospels, London 1935, 147; Zeitlin, Who crucified Jesus ? 154; Goldin, Case of the Nazarene, 285.

affair. Secondly, Brandon thinks this legal statement is an ex eventu explanation of how Jesus was executed by the Romans in spite of the responsibility of the Jews.[1] This is akin to the argument that v.31b is invalidated by v.32 in that the 'fulfilment' motif has led to the creation of the regulation stated by John. However, against this stands the fact that the only other example of the 'fulfilment' motif in connection with Jesus' words in the Passion narrative is at Jn 18.8f and there is no reason to doubt the historicity of the disciples' flight. Indeed, here again Synoptic support is ready to hand in Mk 14.50. In Jn 18.31 we have an unpolemical statement which it is hard to believe would have been created ex nihilo, and which has every appearance of legal authenticity.[2] John gives it a theological significance, but the fulfilment he finds in it could have been demonstrated without it and certainly without the dramatic boldness which would have been needed to motivate its creation.

11. The death of Stephen. In spite of trenchant criticism of the historical value of Acts, Juster argued that there is at least discernible

---

[1] Jesus and the Zealots, 6.

[2] E. Schweizer, Mk, 187; Blinzler, Prozeß, 229f. A different approach to Jn 18.31b has recently been proposed by J. E. Allen, Why̦ Pilate? in: The Trial of Jesus, C. F. D. Moule Festschrift, London 1970, 78-83. Allen argues that a re-examination of Jn 18.31 reopens the possibility that the Jews failed to convict Jesus because of lack of evidence rather than lack of jurisdiction. The case is built up around the following points: 1. Acts 13.28 says that 'the Jews failed to condemn Jesus to death, so asked Pilate to have him killed'. 2. The word ἔξεστιν at Jn 5.10 and throughout the Synoptics refers to Jewish law only. 3. While οὐδένα is without objection textually, αὐτόν would make better sense and has probably 'floated' from v. 31b to v. 31a. 4. Whereas Jn 19.7 would contradict this rewriting of 18.31, support would be found in the threats against Jesus' life in 5.18f, 8.57f and 10.30-36 which are closer to the O.T. legislation than is the Mishnaic ruling on the blasphemer and which are also without any suggestion of being ultra vires. 5. The Synoptics do not say that the Sanhedrin passed sentence, and ἔνοχος means 'liable to' as in Mt 5.21. 6. j.Sanh. 1.1, 7.2 provide the one solitary corroboration of Jn 18.31 in its present form.
This ingenious theory fails to carry conviction because:
1. Acts 13.28 does not say what is alleged: see p. 184 on κρίναντες.
2. Since the setting of Jesus' ministry was Jewish, and the content of his teaching largely concerned with Jewish legal matters, it is not surprising that ἔξεστιν only expresses Jewish legality. Not until the Passion was any other content logically possible. 3. The text of Jn 18.31b is too secure to permit conjectural rewriting. 4. Jn 19.7 is not so easily dismissed since it belongs to the pre-Johannine tradition. 5. The use of the word ἔνοχος, leaving aside all question of formal sentence, is scarcely consistent with any statement that they had failed to find evidence. But in any case ἔνοχος is preceded by κατέκριναν, and ἔνοχος θανάτου is not a phrase which belongs to the same stage of legal proceedings as ἔνοχος κρίσει in Mt 5.21. 6. As has already been seen in the texts dealt with above, Jn 18.31 has far more legal support than the tradition in j.Sanh. 1.1, 7.2 alone.

here a judgement and execution by the Sanhedrin.[1] The alternative opinions, that this was lynch law [2] or that there are two literary strands [3] have always left some uneasiness even among critics of Juster because of the conformity to law of some aspects of the procedure reported. Juster himself noted the observance of Dt 17.7 in Acts 7.58.[4] Similarly, Jeremias has since drawn attention to the cry of the hearers aimed at drowning the blasphemy, the stopping of ears to prevent incurring guilt by hearing it, and their throwing themselves on Stephen to prevent any more blasphemy from him.[5] However Jeremias's argument that a legal trial was carried out, based on an understanding between Caiaphas and Pilate,[6] is not convincing, for the long overlap of their respective official tenures of office is not necessarily to be attributed to complete agreement, but more probably to Caiaphas's ability to pay for the office; [7] moreover, incidents like the introduction of the standards are unlikely to have been palatable even to Caiaphas, and Pilate's policy was one of continual provocation of the Jews.[8] Rather is Blinzler's argument to be preferred in that (a) the trial was interrupted and ended without sentence, and (b) the lamentation (Sanh. 6.6, Josephus, Ant. 4.202), forbidden for those legally executed by both Jewish and Roman law, is provided for Stephen, thus indicating an illegal act.[9] As regards Jeremias's arguments, an illegal execu-

---

[1] Juster, Juifs, 139; Lietzmann, Prozeß, 258; Goldin, Case of the Nazarene, 341; Burkill, art.cit. 92f; Mantel, Studies, 316; Winter, On the Trial, 156, and The Trial of Jesus as a Rebel against Rome, JQ 16 (1968), 34f.

[2] Büchsel, art.cit.205; Lohse, art.cit.863,869; Sherwin White, Roman Society,40, who thinks however that the limitation of capital powers may have been modified in cases affecting the temple. Against this is the case of Jesus ben Ananios. Zeitlin, Who crucified Jesus ? 188-192, takes Stephen as a beguiler, stoned perhaps by some zealous people who did not wait for a verdict, but tried by a regular religious Sanhedrin.

[3] So, F. Spitta, Die Apostelgeschichte, Halle 1891, 97.

[4] Juifs, 139; similarly, Winter, On the Trial, 193.

[5] G. Stählin, Die Apostelgeschichte, 11th ed. Göttingen 1966, 114, adds the execution outside the city (Lev 24.14). Stählin accepts the analysis into two strands and prefers the formal legal execution as historical. For the opposing view, H. Conzelmann, Die Apostelgeschichte, Tübingen 1963, 53.

[6] Similarly, F. F. Bruce, Acts, 179; Stählin, op.cit. 115.

[7] Cf. Philo, Leg. ad. Gaium 302; b.Yoma 8b; b.Yeb. 61a; Sifr. Num. 25.12. On this theme, see Blinzler, Prozeß, 139f.

[8] Philo, Leg. ad Gaium 303.

[9] On this custom, cf. E. Bammel, Galater 1.23, ZNW 59 (1968), 108-112. In Josephus, Ant. 17.206 (cf. 153) the lament is provided for martyrs who have died for the law, but whose execution by Herod is vigorously rejected. Stephen, on the other hand, is treated as a martyr in spite of an apparently opposite view of the law (Acts 6.11-13).

tion and instinctive regard for some legal forms are not mutually exclusive.

It is appropriate to mention at this point Acts 26.10. Winter lays great stress on this verse as indicating that at the time Acts was written the Sanhedrin was known to have had capital powers.[1] This is however pressing the text further than is permissible. Acts 26.10 certainly attests Jewish right to pass a death sentence but it does not prove that the execution was carried out by the Jews.[2]

12. The proceedings against Paul. Juster attached little weight to this evidence because of the unreliability of Acts, but with that reservation he interpreted the story, as did Winter later, as showing an insistent claim by the Jewish leaders to jurisdiction over Paul: hence the tribune's sending Paul to the Sanhedrin (21.31-38) when he realised the case was not political, and hence the reiterated requests for jurisdiction (24.6-8, 25.3,9,11).[3] Consequently Paul's case, suitably interpreted, raises no objection to Juster's theory of full Jewish powers.

It is notable that the case of Paul played almost no part in the debate stirred up by the articles of Lietzmann,[4] and apart from a distinct and unrelated treatment by Solomon Zeitlin, it is left to Paul Winter to make this the second notable personal contribution to the argument about Jewish rights in the pre-A.D. 70 period. Before giving an extended coverage of his view, the points put by Zeitlin must be considered.

Zeitlin's approach is very different from Juster's. He almost obliterates any idea of transference to the Jewish authorities, and throughout the case the religious side is played down. Only in Acts 25 does any Jewish trial on a theological charge, i.e. the resurrection, appear.[5] The religious issue of leading the Nazarenes is not pursued,[6] and

---

[1] JQ 16 (1968), 35.
[2] Cf. J. Blinzler, Prozeß, 244. Contra P. Winter, On the Trial, 173; Conzelmann, Apostelgeschichte, 138.
[3] Juifs, 144: 'On pourrait dire, en style moderne, que Paul va jusque devant l'instance supérieure pour une question de compétence, de conflit de jurisdiction, et cela seulement parce qu'il était citoyen romain.'
[4] M. Goguel gives only a footnote to it, A propos du procès de Jésus, ZNW 31 (1932), 301. He agrees with Juster thus far that the Jews pleaded for jurisdiction over Paul. Lietzmann, Büchsel, Dibelius, Ebeling, Kilpatrick, Jeremias and Burkill all ignore it.
[5] Who crucified Jesus? 203f.
[6] op.cit. 201.

earlier still Zeitlin writes: 'Paul could not have been brought before the religious Sanhedrin as he did not commit a religious transgression.'[1] Now here, as can easily be seen, is an interpretation radically different from Juster's. (a) Even the charge of defiling the temple is regarded as political 'since the Roman authorities prohibited any pagan, even a Roman citizen, from entering the court'.[2] Here Zeitlin cuts the ground from not only Juster's feet (arguing Josephus, B.J. 6.126 for the Sanhedrin's competence in religious matters) but also his own, for the offence against the temple is earlier regarded as within the competence of the Great Sanhedrin [3] and indeed a proof of that body's competence.[4] (b) The pre-Festus hearings are understood without any reference at all to the discussion of competence. (c) When Zeitlin deals with the possible transference of the accused, he very noticeably omits the words 'before me'.[5] (d) Whereas Juster declared that Lysias sent Paul to the Sanhedrin because he realised no political crime was involved, Zeitlin claims that the crime was political and that Paul went before the political Sanhedrin.[6] Zeitlin's imprecision about the distinction between political and religious matters sometimes confuses the argument, as e.g. when the Jewish law (Acts 25.8) is included under a political heading.[7]

It is now time to turn to an analysis of what Winter says about Paul's trial. His conclusions are summed up as follows: '(1) The Sanhedrin demanded that Paul should be tried before a Jewish court; (2) the Roman authorities seriously considered this demand, and at one point were inclined to accede to it.' [8] Hence, if the matter of juri-

---

[1] op.cit. 199f.

[2] op.cit. 200f; cf. Mantel, Studies, 298.

[3] op.cit. 70.

[4] op.cit. 75. Similarly Zeitlin is only able to maintain that Stephen was sentenced as a beguiler by the religious Sanhedrin by ignoring the charge that he criticized the temple, op.cit. 188-192. (In fact, note how similar Paul's crime is to Stephen's, Acts 21.28, including teaching against the law.) Moreover, Zeitlin argues, op.cit. 199, that a religious Sanhedrin logically could not include both Pharisees and Sadducees, and that it was presided over by the high priest. But in Acts 6-7 both γραμματεῖς (6.12) and ὁ ἀρχιερεύς (7.1) are present, and the latter presides.

[5] op.cit. 204. This is the more important since Mantel, Studies, 290, 294, (who agrees with Zeitlin about two Sanhedrins) argues that a Roman's presence means it could not be the Great Sanhedrin in Acts 22.30, 23.10. The same would therefore apply if ἐπ' ἐμοῦ were taken in the lower sense of 'in my presence'.

[6] op.cit. 199; similarly, Mantel, Studies, 57, 70.

[7] op.cit. 202.

[8] op.cit. 86. Several reviewers expressed doubts as to the appropriateness of the trial of Paul to the problem in hand: I. de la Potterie, Bib 43 (1962), 93; E.

dical competence hung in the balance for so long in Paul's case 'the deduction is that if Jesus had been tried by the Sanhedrin for an offence against Jewish law and had been sentenced to death by the Sanhedrin, there would have been no legal objection on the part of the Roman authorities to the Sanhedrin's carrying out its sentence.' [1]

The events connected with Lysias claim attention first (Acts 22.24-23.32). Winter claims that Luke has obscured the basic question of competence. The Sanhedrin demanded from Lysias that Paul be tried by them, assumed jurisdiction (22.30-23.1) but subsequently adjourned and then demanded a re-session (23.15-20). Because he had no precedent Lysias avoided a decision and sent Paul on to Felix. But against this, if it is true that Lysias realised that Paul, although possibly innocent of any crime in Roman law, might still have infringed Jewish law and so would be answerable to the Jewish authorities, it is difficult to see why Lysias subsequently sent Paul to Felix. It is not possible to obliterate *both* intrusions of Lysias, i.e. his extradition of Paul from the Council, and his sending him to Felix. Therefore a Roman interference with and supervision of Jewish legal proceedings remains, on Winter's theory, unexplained. If Acts 23.1-10 represents a legal trial, which is suggested only by κρίνων/κρίνομαι, 23.3-6, and the variant 24,6c-7,[2] as against the context 22.30 and the total lack of evidence of legal procedure, the Jewish right to execute a sentence already passed is not thereby proved. Indeed the intrusion itself, in view of the oft-quoted Roman respect for subject religions, together with the deflection of the issue by Paul, suggest that it is not even a trial.[3]

When Winter turns to the events involving Felix (Acts 23.33-24.27) he declares that the whole matter was exclusively concerned with the question of competence,[4] and in no way with Paul's innocence or guilt. Yet Stählin is certainly correct when he describes this as 'die erste Verhandlung im Prozeß des Paulus vor dem Statthalter' [5] and Winter is guilty of some circularity of argument, for instance when

---

Lohse, Gnomon 33 (1961), 625; D. E. Nineham, JTS 13 (1962), 389; A Schalit, ASTI 2 (1963), 100.

[1] op.cit. 87f.

[2] On this, see Haenchen, Apostelgeschichte, 581.

[3] A hearing at which information on a charge was, as Acts suggests, being sought, coheres with the earlier interruption of the inquisitorial beating. Cf. the reconstruction of H. J. Cadbury, Roman Law and the Trial of Paul, in: The Beginnings of Christianity, London 1933, 305.

[4] op.cit. 80-82; similarly in: The Trial of Jesus and the Competence of the Sanhedrin, NTS 10 (1964), 497.

[5] Apostelgeschichte, 294.

he states: 'As if the hearing before Felix were not concerned exclusively with the question of competence but with a discussion in merito, Paul comments on the absence of "certain Jews from Asia" who have laid unsubstantiated charges against him (24.18b,19).'[1] But against this view, a trial is indicated not only by the form of the hearing—charges preferred followed by the accused's defence—and the context in which accusers are expected to appear before a judge (23.30,35, 24.2 and 24.8 v.l. if original [2]) and in fact do so (24.8f [3]), but also by the indications of Roman legal procedure: the enquiry about Paul's origin (23.34), the hostility of Roman law to accusers who abandon their charges (24.19[4]), the appearance of an advocate (24.1f [5]), and, possibly, the examination of Lysias as a witness (24.8b, if v.8a is original; cf. v.22). It is therefore surprising and without textual basis when Winter declares: 'He (Felix) is not convinced of Paul's innocence—innocence or guilt have not been discussed so far; only the problem of judicial competence has been discussed.' [6] It is difficult to find the request that the prisoner should be handed back for trial to the Sanhedrin, and it is no more compelling when Winter includes the right to carry out a sentence in the potential verdict.[7]

The final episode involves Festus and is again interpreted by Winter as a debate about the demand that Paul be handed back to the Sanhedrin's jurisdiction, even though this ignores the fact of accusations (25.5,11,18), the procurator's sitting ἐπὶ τοῦ βήματος (25.10,17),[8] Paul's consciousness of being judged (25.10) and Festus' consultation with his συμβούλιον.[9] Whereas Winter plays down Paul's speech to Felix (24.10-21)[10], Paul's remarks in 25.10f are made the pivot of an interpretation which is neither the only possible one nor a deduction

---

[1] op.cit. 81.
[2] Winter insists on the originality of the variant 24. 6c-8a, On the Trial, 81.
[3] Sherwin White, Roman Society, 48: 'the narrative insists on formal prosecution'.
[4] Sherwin White, op.cit. 52.
[5] Sherwin White, op.cit. 49.
[6] On the Trial, 82.
[7] op.cit. 81.
[8] Haenchen, Apostelgeschichte, 598: 'damit, daß sich Festus auf den erhöhten Richterstuhl setzt, ist die Gerichtsverhandlung eröffnet.'
[9] Sherwin White, op.cit. 49. H. Conzelmann, Apostelgeschichte, 137, while leaving aside the question of what actually happened, affirms that according to Luke it was certainly intended to be a 'Gerichtsverhandlung'.
[10] op.cit. 81: 'The speech is a clever one but certainly not Paul's.' Luke seems to be accused of obscuring the real issues except where he supports Winter's theory.

from the most likely understanding of 25.9. For against Winter's
view that in 25.8 Festus proposes that Paul should submit to the jurisdiction of the Sanhedrin at Jerusalem while he personally would attend
the trial,[1] it is necessary to maintain that there is no other case in Acts
of ἐπί + G meaning 'in the presence of'; that in legal contexts it
always means 'before a judge',[2] that it is highly improbable that the
Sanhedrin leaders (who had already appeared as accusers in a Roman
court) would be trusted to carry out their own trial impartially, especially in view of 23.10; that there is a parallel for the transference of a
court to a more favourable neighbourhood;[3] and finally that the presence of a Roman, and he indeed the procurator, at a Sanhedrin session
is extremely improbable and encounters all the difficulties raised by
Mantel[4] and others against the presence of Lysias at the earlier hearing.

This concludes our survey of the texts bearing on the problem of
Jewish capital powers during the period before A.D. 70. The distinction asserted by Blinzler between the right to pass a sentence and the
right to execute it turns out to be entirely justified.[5] The conclusion
which seems most in accord with the evidence is that the Sanhedrin
could pass sentence but that the execution could not be in their hands
but was restricted by and to the Romans.

It has been necessary in the preceding discussion to anticipate later
discussion in order to assess fairly and fully the issues raised by Juster.
It is now necessary to return to a more chronological survey and to
take up once more the developments which stemmed from the inter-
action of the approaches of Juster and Husband.

The setting for the publication of Husband's book has already been
sketched. His thesis is that Jesus was given a Grand Jury type of prelimi-

---

[1] op.cit. 83. Winter is here criticized by A. Schalit, Randbemerkungen, 97-100,
who thinks that there was an offer of a transfer of Festus' court for an examination
of both religious and political charges—and if the political one broke down, the
Sanhedrin could then have taken Paul and judged him.

[2] Cf. Mt 28.14, Mk 13.9, Acts 23.30, 24.20, 25.10, 1 Cor 6.1, 1 Tim 6.13.
Cadbury, Style, 304, 309. Of particular importance for the clear-cut establishment
of this result is the article of A. Schalit, Zu AG 25,9 in ASTI 6 (1968), 106-113.

[3] Sherwin White, op.cit. 68, cites the transference of the trial of the philosopher
Dion by Pliny from Prusa to Nicaea.

[4] Studies, 290-294.

[5] Blinzler, Prozeß, 246f. Winter's amalgamation of the two is unjustified. Cf.
On the Trial, 85: 'It would indeed be strange for a Roman procurator to have
proposed to Paul to submit to the Sanhedrin's jurisdiction in a case involving
the death penalty, if the Sanhedrin had no jurisdiction to pass death sentences and
no power to ensure that its judgments were carried out (Jn 18.31b).'

nary examination,[1] rather than a full Sanhedrin trial, and he cites in
support the practice of the Roman provincial government in Egypt.[2]
The numerous illegalities [3] clash not only with the necessary presumption that the court acted justly,[4] but also with the evidence we have
of the interrogation of witnesses.[5] Husband allows that the 'Talmudic'
rules may not yet have been formulated,[6] but his approach is more
through Roman than through Jewish law, and he emphasizes strongly
the dictum 'ne bis in idem'.[7] In the Jewish area, however, his treatment is interesting for the view that the religious charge against Jesus
was false prophecy (Lk 23.2,5, b.Sanh. 67a,107b), and that both religious and political charges were presented in the Roman trial.[8]

Husband's preliminary hearing idea has had a wide influence on
Jewish scholars over fifty years, most notably C. G. Montefiore,
J. Klausner and H. Mantel among others.[9] Yet often tension between
argumentation from Jewish and from Roman law makes itself felt,
and introduces inconsistencies within the total scheme. Two examples
may be cited: (a) Hyamson argues that Jesus was examined by a high
priestly council (whose purpose was to ascertain whether Jesus should
be handed over to the Romans as a revolutionary) and is critical of
Husband, declaring that the Grand Jury idea is a novel idea unknown
in Jewish law, an idea for which Husband allegedly offers no support.[10]
Furthermore, he argues, to act as an informer is repugnant to the
Jewish conscience.[11] But the argument that Husband offered no

---

[1] Prosecution, 14f, 281.
[2] op.cit. 9, 138-150.
[3] op.cit. 107-114.
[4] op.cit. 10.
[5] op.cit. 117.
[6] op.cit. 7, 151.
[7] op.cit. 9; cf. Mantel, Studies, 254.
[8] op.cit. 223-230.
[9] C. G. Montefiore, Gospels I(1927), 351-357. Montefiore had changed his
view of the trial under Husband's influence. He did not however discard illegalities, but mentioned the possible justification in terms of 'the demand of the
hour', op.cit. 314. J. Klausner, Jesus, 333; Mantel, Studies, 282; Hyamson, art.cit.
90-96, is very critical of Husband, but reaches a very similar conclusion; Sachar,
History, 132; Trattner, As a Jew sees Jesus, 131f; J. Isaac, Jésus, 409f (his earlier
view); Hoenig, Great Sanhedrin, 210; Schalit, Randbemerkungen, 93, takes the
view that Jesus was examined at night, in line with Sanh. 5.5, to see if there was
any indictable offence.
[10] art.cit. 91. Similar opposition was later voiced by Dienemann, Zur Leben-
Jesu-Forschung, Der Morgen 6 (1930), 373-382, esp. 379; Goldin, Case of the
Nazarene, 766.
[11] op.cit. 91.

evidence, and that Jewish law never envisaged a preliminary hearing
shows the total otherness of the approach. For Jewish law is no more
relevant to this point, in Husband's reconstruction, than to the limitation of capital competence, which Hyamson accepts.[1] Hyamson's
centre of gravity is totally within Jewish law, and so the main thrust
is still that the illegalities prove that the assembly was not the Sanhedrin; [2] like Jost and his followers, Hyamson has to interpret ὅλον τὸ
συνέδριον (Mk 15.1) as either incorrect or a reference to a special
priestly Beth Din, and to lay stress on the setting in the high priest's
house, away from the Hall of Hewn Stones.[3] (b) Klausner also incor-
porates Husband's findings,[4] but has rightly been criticized by Zeitlin
for confusing them with other approaches and failing to realise the
differing presuppositions of the scholars he cites.[5] Three separate
theses intertwine in Klausner's book: first, Chwolson's view that the
Sadducees were responsible and broke the laws; [6] second, Husband's
view that it was a preliminary hearing, and so the laws were not applicable; third, the view that the laws did not exist at the time anyway.[7]
The first and second of these are used in dealing with the trial at night,[8]
all three in treating the eve of feast ruling,[9] and the first and third in
discussing the Sanh. 7.5. problem.[10]

During this period the movement parallel to Husband, envisaging
a political/priestly Sanhedrin, gains ground. Like Hyamson these
scholars tend to argue that the illegalities reflect not the moral character [11] but the constitutional status of the court—thus S. Zeitlin who

---

[1] op.cit. 96.   [2] op.cit. 96.

[3] Schalit, art.cit. 94 argues that these words were not in the original text.
Hyamson's view is in art.cit. 94, 96.

[4] Jesus, 334f.

[5] Zeitlin, JQR 14 (1923), 138.

[6] op.cit. 336. Contrast with this, p. 334: 'Thus we see why the procedure of the
"trial" as conducted by the Sanhedrin does not conform with the details of
procedure laid down in the Mishna; it was *not* a trial but only a preliminary
judicial investigation and, as such, was altogether fair and legal.' The same tensions
are apparent in Trattner, op.cit. 131f, 146, who follows Klausner.

[7] op.cit. 334f.

[8] op.cit. 340. Sanh. 4.1 is presumed to exist, but Lk 22.66 used to avoid the
problem.

[9] op.cit. 341.

[10] op.cit. 343.

[11] There are exceptions. G. G. Fox, The Jews Jesus and Christ, Chicago 1953,
49, works from the view that Jesus was condemned by a 'Sadduceean court'
and delivered to Pilate. In the corresponding sentence of Jesus Pilate and Paul,
Chicago 1955, 94, he adds the adjective 'illegal': he cites Zeitlin at this point, yet
appears not to adopt Zeitlin's dismissal of illegalities.

stresses that the political Sanhedrin was untrammelled by the laws binding on the Great Sanhedrin,[1] Mattuck, Zucker, Asch, Polack, Hoenig and Mantel.[2] The other solution to the illegality problem is to acknowledge them in full and so eliminate a Jewish hearing of any sort. Thus the wheel comes full circle from Salvador's remark that the agreement of the narratives with Jewish law tended to confirm their trustworthiness. The list of those who stress disagreement, and consequent inaccuracy or falsity of the narratives, is long: Enelow, Hunterberg, E. Jacob, L. I. Edgar, Rosenberg, Dimont, Umen, Baer,[3] but especially H. E. Goldin.[4] Methodologically, Goldin follows the approach of I. M. Wise,[5] arguing from contradiction or inconsistency within or between the documents, i.e. an essentially legal and not literary approach. He gathers a list of illegalities so extensive that the party-spirited attempts of some Christian writers, whether based on arguments from silence or explicit statements, are recalled: 1. Moving a body after sunset or on a sabbath. 2. Simon of Cyrene working on a feast day. 3. Not in the Hall of Hewn Stones. 4. Night time (for Luke cannot be trusted either). 5. On a feast or its eve. 6. The writing by court clerks on a sabbath or feast. 7. Asking the accused for defence or explanation of witness testimony. 8. Adjuration of the accused. 9. The President's passing verdict first. 10. The unanimous verdict. 11. Not two sessions. 12. Bearing arms on a feast.[6] Goldin is also emphatically opposed to the Chwolson-Klausner solution which would blame the Sadducees, because firstly, Jn 18.3 involves the Pharisees;[7] secondly, the Sadducees had to follow the legal rulings of

---

[1] Who crucified Jesus ?, 55, 72, 74, 156, 163. Zeitlin draws particular attention to the rules requiring trials by day in the Hall of Hewn Stones and not on the eves of feasts, and also the definition of blasphemy.

[2] Mattuck, Trial, 10; Zucker, Studien, 77; S. Asch, The Guilty Ones, Atlantic Monthly 166 (1940), 713-723, esp. 719. Although Asch argues that the illegalities mean that the court was not the Great Sanhedrin, he adds quite unnecessarily that the Sadducees bear the blame. Thus patterns of approach overlap. Polack, Jesus, 63, 101f: he also blames the Sadducees and the influence of Zeitlin is plain in this book. Hoenig, Great Sanhedrin, 209f; Mantel, Studies, 254f.

[3] Enelow, Jewish View, 487; Hunterberg, Crucified Jew, 42-44; E. Jacob, art.cit. 528; Edgar, Jewish View, 14; Rosenblatt, art.cit. 316-318; S. E. Rosenberg, Bridge to Brotherhood: Judaism's Dialogue with Christianity, New York 1961, 14; Dimont, op.cit. 141; Umen, Pharisaism, 129-131; Y. Baer, Some Aspects of Judaism as presented in the Synoptic Gospels, Zion 31 (1966), IIf.

[4] The Case of the Nazarene reopened, New York 1948.

[5] Martyrdom, 67-78.

[6] op.cit. (1) 35; (2) 140; (3) 408; (4) 408, 445; (5) 405, 452; (6) 408; (7) 415; (8) 416; (9) 419; (10) 443; (11) 443; (12) 35.

[7] op.cit. 267, 779.

the Pharisees (Josephus, Ant.18.17; b.Nidd. 33b, b.Yom. 19b); thirdly, the Sadducean attitude to law was more strict; fourthly, none of
the points in dispute between the parties was raised by the trial of
Jesus.[1]

Both the groups of scholars outlined above, who accept that illegalities are implied, work from the belief (or tacit assumption) that
some at least of the Mishnaic rules were operative at the time. A denial
of this has never become characteristic of Jewish research on the trial.
On the contrary, efforts have been made periodically to prove that
certain of the rules were indeed valid, centring on the following three
cases:

(a) The 'eve of sabbath or feast' rule. Zeitlin argues for the existence
of this rule by appealing to Josephus, Ant. 16.163.[2] Here is certainly a
case where the anti-Sadducean solution will not hold, since the Sadducees were in power at the time of this edict. However, Josephus's
formulation ἀπὸ ὥρας ἐνάτης suggests that the rule only affected the
period of the preparation day from 3 p.m. onwards. To this consideration must be added the evidence of Josephus's technique, projecting
data from his own time or consonant with his own view of suitability
into earlier settings.[3] It is likely therefore that the earlier ruling was,
at the time of Josephus, one which only touched eves of sabbaths and
that feasts should not be included. Only later was the ruling extended
to the form it has in Sanh. 4.1 so that the prohibition operating from
3 p.m. on the eve of a sabbath was extended to cover the whole of
that eve and with it the corresponding period for a feast.[4]

(b) The 'two session' rule. Zeitlin cites the case of Herod (Josephus,
Ant. 14.165-184, B.J. 1.210f) to prove the earlier existence of this
rule.[5] However, the adjournment by Hyrcanus does not seem to have
been prompted by such a law but rather by reasons of expediency (cf.
especially Ant. 14.170,177,182), and Ant. 14.178 shows that there was
no question of a session being fixed for the following day. Not only
does Ant. 16.163 suggest that this rule was not in use [6] (for a first

---

[1] op. cit. 409.

[2] Who crucified Jesus?, 74, 156; similarly, Mantel, Studies, 255.

[3] M. Dibelius, Studies in the Acts of the Apostles, London 1956, 139.

[4] Contra E. Lohse, art. συνέδριον, 867.

[5] Zeitlin, op.cit. 72f; Mantel, op.cit. 255.

[6] Winter, On the Trial, 156, in a context dealing with examples of executions,
notes that this rule is not implied in the Ben Stada text (Tos. Sanh. 10.11). He
remarks that the evidence of this text is disputable, and does not draw conclusions.

session may begin there up until mid-afternoon on a sabbath eve, but clearly could not continue next day), but other cases, e.g. Mariamne, Ant.15.229, suggest that a verdict was reached on the same day. Consequently, Lohse is correct that the humanizing tendency has been at work [1] and that this rule may only go back to the later rabbis.

(c) The definition of blasphemy. Many Jewish scholars take Sanh. 7.5 as the current definition of blasphemy [2] though some differ.[3] This cannot however be claimed with confidence in view of Tos. Sanh. 1.2 and b.Sanh. 38b; and the debate between R. Meir and the sages in b.Sanh. 56a implies that the tight form of Sanh. 7.5 had not yet been formulated. Also Mantel himself notes that the rending of garments does not narrow the definition to a precise legal use of the term 'blasphemy', and Winter's attempt to discredit a looser sense of the word is not convincing. He argues that 'to attempt to determine the meaning of Markan words from the use of the same vocabulary in the writings of pagan authors is a questionable enterprise'.[4] But this is not only strange methodologically[5] but difficult to maintain in the light of Mk 2.7 (cf. Acts 6.11).[6] It is necessary therefore to admit the possibility that, firstly, blasphemy was more widely defined at the time of Jesus than later in Sanh. 7.5,[7] and secondly, that βλασφημία in Mk 14.64 does not necessarily reveal the precise legal definition of Jesus' crime.

These three illegalities figure in the attempt to defend the applicability of certain individual laws. The most notable defence of the Mishnah's applicability in general terms was made by I. Abrahams,[8] who has been closely followed by Hoenig.[9] The basis of the argument is the dependence of the legal tradition on the cautious R. Jose b.

---

[1] art.cit. 866. Cf. J. Blinzler, Das Synedrium von Jerusalem und die Strafprozessordnung der Mischna, ZNW 52 (1961), 54-65, esp. 60.

[2] Goldin, op.cit. 421-423; Edgar, op.cit. 7; Zeitlin, Who crucified Jesus ?, 153; Winter, On the Trial, 162; Mantel, Studies, 274.

[3] C. G. Montefiore, I(1909), 350. Schalit, Randbemerkungen, 101, allows a *formal* deviation from Sanh. 7.5, but regards Jesus' answer as 'wenn nicht der Form, so doch dem Sinne nach, etwas was vom Hohenpriester als Gotteslästerung ausgelegt werden konnte'.

[4] op.cit. 26, against E. Bickermann, Utilitas Crucis, RHR 112 (1935), 169-241.

[5] Winter immediately proceeds to gather parallels within the New Testament for ἔνοχος, rather than confining himself to Mk.

[6] See Kilpatrick, Trial, 10f.

[7] So, Lohse, art.cit. 866.

[8] Studies in Pharisaism and the Gospels II, Cambridge 1924, 129-137, contra H. Danby, The Bearing of the Rabbinical Code on the Jewish Trial Narratives in the Gospels, JTS 21 (1919), 51-76.

[9] Great Sanhedrin, 209.

Halafta, as well as earlier precedents for strangling,[1] the court of 23, Pharisaic mildness demonstrated a century before the Christian era, and the punishment of 39 stripes. Similarly, Hoenig cites in support the deadening potion and the rending of garments; Goldin argues from the existence of earlier Mishnaic collections [2] like R. Akiba's, and the method of handing on rather than developing tradition which the rabbis followed.[3] Against this attempt to construct an essentially a priori position, Klausner noted the divergence between the Mishnah and the procedure for executing the priest's daughter (Sanh. 7.2),[4] and Abrahams's thesis has been demonstrably refuted by Blinzler.[5]

The threads can now be drawn together. When viewed from the angle of its legal aspects, the trial of Jesus in Jewish historiography has given rise to two characteristic assertions. Firstly, the limitation of the capital powers of the Sanhedrin has usually been accepted—and this is probably correct. The uniformity of the tendency serves to highlight the important contribution of Juster and Winter. They are not completely alone in this conclusion, but no one matches them in intensity of argument. Secondly, the rules of legal procedure as codified in the Mishnah are normally assumed to have been applicable to the case of Jesus. This is much more questionable. It has been seen how the theme of illegality stood in the centre at the beginning of the period, and has over a span of 200 years given rise to solutions, of which all but the first have persisted to the present day: (a) They can be denied. (b) They can be accepted, and the Sadducees blamed. (c) They can be used against the historicity of the narratives. (d) Their existence can be used in favour of the view that the session was either merely preliminary, or before a priestly court, or before a political Sanhedrin.

In conclusion, it is clear that of the five illegalities cited by Lohse, three are inapplicable to Luke even if it were proved that the laws in question were extant at the time, and the remaining two—the 'eve of feast or feast day itself' rule and the 'two session' rule—are lacking in all support as contemporary legislation. Within the new source-critical situation, therefore, the illegality debate must be regarded as having burnt itself out.

---

[1] Abrahams, op.cit. 130. Note that Winter and Abrahams diverge here over the value of Josephus' evidence.

[2] On this problem, cf. G. Hölscher, Sanhedrin und Makkoth, Tübingen 1910, 5-15.   [3] op.cit. 411.   [4] Klausner, Jesus, 343.   [5] Prozeß, 216-229.

CHAPTER FIVE

CONCLUSION

It has often become plain in the preceding discussion that Jewish research into the Trial of Jesus cannot be understood apart from its setting in debate. This is at once a strength, in that the matter is lifted from the area of cold theoretical analysis, and also a weakness, in that apologetic considerations sometimes exert an overwhelming pressure to cut critical corners.[1] Indeed, as Lindeskog has remarked: 'Hier geht es um mehr als einen wissenschaftlichen Dialog.'[2]

Only the setting in debate can explain some of the typical Jewish trends. Thus, for instance, there is a diverse attitude to the Christian sources, which is often unable to keep pace with current scientific method on the Christian side.[3] Samuel Sandmel often remarks that Jewish writers accept too much in the gospels,[4] and this, while it is a common Jewish unease, still represents the attempt to establish a position and convince Christian readers at a popular level by working on Christian territory.[5] One has only to think of Salvador's early

---

[1] On occasion Jewish scholars themselves point this out. For example, Jost charges Salvador with 'verblendetste Einseitigkeit': Geschichte des Judenthums, Leipzig 1857, 409. K. Magnus writes that 'many critics, especially Jews, have altogether rejected the idea of Jesus ever having been tried before the Sanhedrin': About the Jews, London 1881, 77. S. Zeitlin accuses D. Chwolson 'whose book is not scientific but apologetic with the object of disproving the responsibility of the Jews for the death of Jesus and placing it simply on the Sadducees'. JQR 14 (1923), 136. Similar criticism of Chwolson comes from S. Dubnow: 'In dem Bestreben, seine ehemalige Glaubensgenossen von der Schuld des Gottesmordes reinzuwaschen, versucht der apostatische Apologet Daniel Chwolson . . . . den Beweis zu führen, daß Christus ein orthodoxer Pharisäer gewesen sei . . . .' Weltgeschichte II, 581.

[2] Der Prozeß Jesu im jüdisch-christlichen Religionsgespräch, in Abraham unser Vater, Festschrift O. Michel, Leiden 1963, 328.

[3] In parallel with this it must be noticed that literary criticism of the Jewish sources has not been developed to the same extent. Jewish scholars have therefore not always been at ease methodologically. Also Christian scholars who were interested in rabbinic sources in the early period tended to be conservative themselves, e.g. H. Laible, Jesus Christus im Talmud, Berlin 1891; R. T. Herford, Christianity in Talmud and Midrash, London 1903.

[4] We Jews and Jesus, London 1965, 66.

[5] Cf. J. Cohen, Les Déicides, Paris 1864, xix. Such a problem lies behind the rather mournful remark of Rabbi J. Litvin in his review of Paul Winter's book, in Gates of Zion 17 (1963), 19. Having summarized the book,[1] applauded it and

position, later abandoned, or Klausner's heavily criticized reconstruction, or even the use of Troki to this day. Yet alongside this there is the tendency to be more negative than contemporary New Testament criticism, even at its most severe, will allow. This is represented in Sandmel's experience by 'the question often put to me by Jews, to the effect that perhaps there never was a Jesus',[1] and his own words: 'Perhaps we might be willing to say to ourselves that it is not at all impossible that some Jews, even leading Jews, recommended the death of Jesus to Pilate. We are averse to saying this to ourselves, for so total has been the charge against us that we have been constrained to make a total denial.'[2] This is the honest and objective reflection of a great and fair-minded Jewish scholar.

This same tendency to treat gospel material with very harsh scepticism, and to exceed contemporary trends on the Christian side, is also apparent in Paul Winter's notable book. One has only to recall the total dismissal of debates between Jesus and the Pharisees, and the rejection of material which Bultmann, for one, accepts as genuine. But more than this: Winter even goes further than almost all Jewish scholars by denying the limitation of capital powers (as Jn 18.31)[3] and the messianic claim of Jesus.[4] An instinct here comes to the surface, an instinct which explains how a book published in 1961 can yet belong critically to a period perhaps three decades earlier. This, I would stress, is not said in a negative spirit, but only because one is impressed by the predominance of references to Dibelius, Lietzmann, Goguel, etc., and the markedly limited amount of allusion to the pupils of Bultmann, or to Jeremias (especially for the bearing of the parables on the original message of Jesus) or, within the compass of Prozessforschung, to Kilpatrick or Blinzler.[5]

Another feature of Jewish assessment of the Trial of Jesus, which finds its rationale in the situation of confrontation, is the way in which Christian writers have at times supplied their Jewish opponents

---

remarked that Chwolson and many mediaeval rabbis proved this theory long ago (!), Litvin concludes that the book is unlikely to help in the struggle against anti-Semitism because unbelieving Christians do not care, and believing Christians would not believe that the New Testament contains any falsification.

[1] We Jews and Jesus, ix.
[2] op.cit, 141
[3] See above, pp. 236ff.
[4] On the Trial, 148: 'Jesus was a normal person—he was the norm of normality—and he neither identified nor equated himself with anyone except Jesus of Nazareth.'
[5] This criticism is also voiced by E. Schweizer, EvTh 21 (1961), 239.

with ammunition. This takes place in a variety of ways. Perhaps the
locus classicus was the scheme of Dupin, which originated in polemic
against Salvador, and which foreshadowed precisely the pattern of
argument which would be turned fiercely against the historicity of
the Sanhedrin trial.[1] Centuries before, it had happened in a different
way when Troki was supplied with anti-Trinitarian material stemming
from an inter-Christian dispute.[2] But it is the overall trend of a total
movement which is more impressive than the isolated examples.
During this period of 200 years, roughly coincident with critical
studies, Christians have been engaged in the introspective process of
retreat from the positions of their forbears. Viewed from the Jewish
side this is indeed a defensive movement of retreat. It is a movement
which gathers pace, and Jews are able to profit from its momentum.
And here it is noticeable that though the materials and methods may be
supplied from the Christian side, yet the contours of the resulting
structure often remain essentially Jewish. New argumentative forms
are used, but older schemes are preserved. Thus in the first chapter
it was shown how often there appear and vanish and reappear themes
which derive ultimately from the Talmudic sources. The pendulum
swings back and forth almost inexorably. One need only mention here
the impression that 'leading astray' is a much more natural category
than blasphemy as the description of Jesus' crime. Again, the famous
book of Klausner attempts in places to bind together divergent schemes,
and it is the existence of the traditional orthodox disapproval of
Jesus within a book whose overall attitude to Jesus is sympathetic,
which attracts attention.

   It is the setting in a tragically polemical confrontation with Christianity which underlies the great attraction towards Tendenzkritik.
Jews have been persecuted as killers of Jesus, and they find in the
Christian documents themselves, and especially in the Passion narratives, a stance critical of Judaism.[3] This leads to the attempt to reverse
the Tendenz and so determine 'wie es *eigentlich* gewesen ist'. This

---

[1] See above, p. 226.
[2] See above, p. 73.
[3] Lindeskog, Prozeß, 325, 327f. Cf. Sandmel, op.cit. 119: 'So frequently are
the passages (in the gospels), especially in connection with the death of Jesus,
anti-Jewish, that it can be very difficult for us Jews merely to read them.' This
also troubles G. Baum for dogmatic reasons: The Jews and the Gospel, London
1961, 4f. For an important corrective, see P. Richardson, The Israel-idea in the
Passion Narratives, in The Trial of Jesus, Festschrift C. F. D. Moule, London
1970, 1-10.

process is not however without anomalies and inconsistencies. For instance, the process of blackening the Jews has often been said to develop from Mark through Matthew and Luke to John. Moreover the accounts of the Sanhedrin trial are said to be product of this Tendenz. Yet here is a paradox. For frequently during this period Jewish scholars have stressed that two pieces of data are to be noted: first, that Luke has only a preliminary hearing,[1] and second, that John has no trial at all.[2] This means that the development at the place where the Tendenz is located is contrary to the direction of the Tendenz itself.

Nevertheless it remains true that one of the most difficult aspects of the debate from the point of view of scientific critical scholarship develops from the insistence that the gospels show an anti-Jewish trend in their Trial narratives. Of course, it is necessary to define in what sense these presentations are anti-Jewish, for to blame the Jews for the death of Jesus is not the same as being anti-Semitic. (Thus Matthew certainly blames the Jews, but he is not anti-Semitic). Nevertheless this sense that the gospels have such a Tendenz sometimes causes Jewish scholars to exert pressure on Christian scholars to deny the Sanhedrin's involvement in legal proceedings or be branded with anti-Semitism. This means that Christians are put heavily on the defensive. Such a situation quite clearly lies behind a recent article by Krister Stendahl, who records the disappointing results of a Jewish/Christian Colloquium at Harvard.[3] Some examples will make clear the effective influence of pressure from the Jewish side.

1. The description of the whole proceedings begins with the following objective statement: 'It could be argued .... that the beneficial contribution of Christianity to Western culture was exactly its function as the vehicle for the Jewish component in Christianity, while some of the less attractive elements of Christian ideology are the properly "Christian" ones. Or—as is often done in Christian circle—such an

---

[1] Winter stands apart from this approach in its simple form by his theory of a pre-Markan tradition in Luke, which has no Sanhedrin hearing and is therefore in this respect more reliable. But the point still applies to the use of John.

[2] Thus it is part of the proposed memorandum submitted by Jules Isaac to the Seelisberg Conference. See The Christian Roots of Anti-Semitism, repr. London 1965, 20. Cf. earlier, L. Philippson, Haben die Juden, 55; I. M. Wise, Martyrdom, 65; Enelow, Jewish View, 488; P. Winter, CommViat 6 (1963), 303.

[3] Judaism and Christianity II—after a Colloquium and a War, Harvard Divinity Bulletin 1 (1967), 2-9.

argument could be put forward in its exactly opposite form.'[1] The first thesis is very evidently indebted to the Formstecher theory.

2. Stendahl accepts that a distinction cannot ultimately be pressed between Christianity and the Nazi massacres.[2] This is a thesis put forward repeatedly and with tragic pathos throughout the writings of Jules Isaac, e.g. 'Hitlerian racialism appeared on ground which previous centuries had prepared for it.'[3] Thus solidarity on the Christian side is accepted, whereas the corresponding solidarity on the Jewish side between those of the 1st and of the 20th centuries is disputed. Now Jews, persecuted for an event 19 centuries earlier may have a prime facie right to such a position, but a satisfactory solution can never be to accept total Christian solidarity in this way and deny Jewish solidarity. Rather must both parties involved in the 1st century be distinguished totally from their counterparts in the 20th—this applies to both Jewish and Christian attitudes—and in consequence, neither generalizations made about attitudes in this century nor a matter for historical study be clouded by questions about guilt. For this reason it is difficult to accept Stendahl's comment that 'it is a fine point, immensely difficult to retain in the future development' when Cardinal Bea urges that 'the gospels often confine the responsibility for the death of Jesus to the Sanhedrin or to the inhabitants of Jerusalem; hence it is not tied to all "the Jews" of that time, let alone of later generations'.[4] The ultimate question is how far a proved Tendenz within gospels is binding upon Christian scholars. The answer must, of course, be No, particularly, where Mt 27.25-type sayings are concerned,[5] and a renewed insistence that a narrative in which such a Tendenz may be located is not thereby proved to be unhistorical in toto.[6]

[1] op.cit. 2.

[2] op.cit. 3.

[3] Christian Roots of Anti-Semitism, 12. It must certainly be recorded that nothing less than the deepest sympathy is evoked by the bereavements recorded by e.g. H. J. Schoeps, The Jewish-Christian Argument, London 1963, xiv, and P. Winter in the dedication of On the Trial of Jesus.

[4] Stendahl, op.cit. 4. The reference is to Cardinal Bea's book, The Church and the Jewish People, New York 1966. The same view as Cardinal Bea takes is vigorously championed throughout Jewish literature on Jesus, and emphatically by J. Isaac in draft resolutions nos. 7, 12, 13, 15, 16 and 17 for the Seelisberg Conference: Christian Roots, 18-20.

[5] On this saying, cf. K. H. Schelkle, Die "Selbstverfluchung" Israels nach Matthäus 27, 23-25, in Antijudaismus im Neuen Testament? ed. W. P. Eckert. München 1967, 148-156.

[6] The Pilate episode, in which the same Tendenz is located, provides a good analogy. Even if we are unable to reconstruct precisely what Pilate said and did.

3. A totally deferential attitude is adopted towards the Jewish faith, rather more indeed than a right and proper sensitivity and respect. Stendahl says: 'We are not primarily anxious to impart our views as they impart theirs. We need to ask in spite of it all, whether they are willing to let us become again part of their family, a peculiar part to be true, but, even so, relatives who believe themselves to be a peculiar kind of Jews, and it is up to 'Judaism' to see if that is possible.' [1] In line with this, Stendahl accepts the Jewish attitude of repugnance towards Christian evangelism, in spite of the admission that the church is 'by definition set on mission and conversion'.[2] Yet here the issue is not so much the extent to which the New Testament is or is not binding on Christians, as the bearing for Christians of the attitude of Jesus. Firstly, if 'the compassionate sorrow of Jesus (Mt 23.37-39)' is accepted, then also the reason for it must be accomodated. Jesus clearly asked for and expected some response in Jerusalem and did not find it. Secondly, it is not possible to solve all problems by getting back into Jewish territory, in the same way as stressing that remarks critical of Judaism must operate 'within the framework of Jewish self-criticism',[3] for it was within Jewish territory that Jesus made remarks such as Mt 10.5f and 15.24,[4] which imply a mission to Israel (cf. Lk 10.1-16). The point at which Stendahl must be most directly questioned, and which is the presupposition of all such argumentation, is his use of the idea of identification: 'The Christian church has no "right" to the use of these prophetic statements, once it has lost its identification with Judaism.' Much though the use of denunciatory passages may be avoided, it is still necessary to ask: In what sense is 'identification' a right and apt

---

it is not possible to deny that he did condemn Jesus. On the whole topic there is a remarkable statement in a review of Winter's book by J. Finegan: 'In a monograph by the present reviewer which is cited in the notes, some of the same methods were applied to the same records. The reviewer recalls how at one point Hans Lietzmann remarked: 'Jetzt schneidet das Messer zu fein', and one can only say that one wonders more often rather than less often whether that is not the case. And one wonders if our own Tendenzen are not as influential on our results as we think those of the Gospel writers were upon what they wrote.' A Quest for the History of the Passion, Interpretation 16 (1962), 102-104. Cf. criticisms of Winter in a similar way by P. Benoit, RB 68 (1961), 599.

[1] op.cit. 5f.
[2] Mentioned as a Jewish attitude, op.cit. 2. Cf. att.cit. 9, footnote 15.
[3] op.cit. 5.
[4] These are verses used continually from the days of Samuel Hirsch onwards to express the Jewishness of Jesus. Religionsphilosophie, 666: 'Es liegt in diesen Worten nur der treue Ausdruck der wahrhaft tiefen und ächt jisraelitischen Anschauungen Jesu.' Clearly they say even more than that !

word? It can mean something either historical or theological, but it easily slips from one to the other.

At this point the wheel comes full circle, for a rapprochement between Judaism and Christianity cannot be forged without the guiding and controlling consideration of Jesus' own personal position with regard to Judaism. This is precisely the point which Lindeskog has stressed in relation to the problems of the Trial of Jesus, too.[1] Those cannot be solved without reference to Jesus' own theological stance, and so Winter's unanswered questions about the pre-history of the event [2] press themselves upon us with relentless insistence. As far as the contemporaty dialogue is concerned, Stendahl's problem may be set out in terms of an historical analogy from the pre-schism situation. If Christians are to be regarded as a peculiar kind of Jews, they clearly cannot be in the position of the Pauline Christian Jews, since Paul's position on the law is intolerable to Judaism.[3] The other possibility is that they might be in a position analogous to the Jerusalem church: Judaism + a certain belief in Jesus. But here is a remarkable paradox: a certain unity between Jews and Christians may be found in a re-Judaized Jesus. But this attempt to bring Christians and Jews together, focussing as is necessary on the two points of Jesus and the law, breaks down on one basic fact: *Jesus stood in a position of tension with Judaism.*[4] To quote Lindeskog again, there is an 'innere Notwendigkeit des Bruches Jesu mit der maßgebenden Richtung des damaligen Judentums'.[5] Similarly this has to be remembered in the study of the Trial of Jesus: 'Man kann nicht die Leidensgeschichte von dem Wirken Jesu isolieren.' [6]

---

[1] Prozeß, 334f.

[2] Similarly, E. Lohse, Gnomon 33 (1961), 626 and H. van Oyen, Neue Forschungen über den Prozeß Jesu, Christlich-jüdisches Forum 26 (1961), 1-3. In a sympathetic review of Winter's book, J. B. Soucek poses the fundamental problem: 'Es bleibt die Frage, ob dies (the post-Passion messianic belief of the community) im historischen Leben und Verhalten Jesu so ganz unvorbereitet wurde, ob in seinem faktischen Autoritätsanspruch faktisch nicht eine begrifflich wohl nicht festgesetzte und metaphysisch nicht ausgeführte "Christologie" impliziert war . . . .' Zum Prozeß Jesu, CommViat 6 (1963), 197-202. Cf. W. D. Davies in Commentary 33 (1962), 540f.

[3] Sandmel, op.cit. 138; Schoeps, Jewish-Christian Argument, 19.

[4] Isaac, Christian Roots, 6, declares that the schism stemmed from the rejection of law, faithfulness to which is of the essence of Judaism. But he is certainly one-sided in stating that of this faithfulness 'Jesus himself gave an example up to his last hour.'

[5] Prozeß, 334.

[6] Prozeß, 334.

There is one further feature of the Jewish approach to Jesus in this period, which must be mentioned before turning to the issues raised by their approach to the Trial. That is the effect of controversy within Judaism. It is easier for some Jews than for others to adopt a favourable attitude towards Jesus, which is the overall tendency. One need only recall Montefiore and Enelow on the one side and Ginzberg on the other.[1] The reason is that whereas Jesus is a Jew to all, he is more than that to some: he is a Reform Jew as well.[2] Hence, although in book after book Mt 23-type polemic is neutralized by b.Sota 22b[3] and made a dialogue within Judaism, the controversies with contemporaries can be turned to a positive end: here Jesus fights the battles of the liberal wing. He is bone of their bone and flesh of their flesh. He can even be a prophet—and here again it is noticeable against such a background in Jewish historiography that Stendahl sets the denunciations of Jesus in this very tradition, calling it 'prophetic language'.[4] On the other side, however, the orthodox see only the tendency of Reform Judaism to follow Jesus into non-Judaism. There is another element here, of which the present dialogue must take account. For the more Christians are regarded as a peculiar kind of Jews, and so Christianity and Judaism approach one another, the more Judaism is faced with the problem of explaining its own separate existence, and where therefore Christianity is wrong in Jewish eyes. One is reminded of the Pauline speeches in Acts, which represent Paul as attempting to make the *Jewish* hope his Christian position [5]—but when this happens some idea of fulfilment and, hence, evangelistic pressure inexorably occur, so that what is intolerable to Jews is rekindled.

What then are the issues raised by the Jewish approach to the Trial of Jesus, and what bearing do these have for the future? Firstly, the

---

[1] See above, pp. 54-56.

[2] O. J. Simon, The Mission of Judaism: a Reply, JQR 9 (1897), 413; K. Kohler, in a letter of 23.8.1899, published in G. Croly, Tarry thou till I come, New York 1901, 553f; C. G. Montefiore, Gospels I(1909), xcix: 'His teaching is a revival of prophetic Judaism, and in some respects points forward to the liberal Judaism of today.' Similarly, H. G. Enelow, Jewish View, 440; Edgar, Jewish View, 9-12.

[3] S. Hirsch, Religionsphilosophie, 639; J. L. Saalschütz, Versöhnung, 55-57; M. J. Raphall, Post-Biblical History, 373; J. Cohen, in La Verité Israélite 3 (1861), 148; Grünebaum, Sittenlehre, 136f; A. Benisch, Judaism surveyed, 72; Schreiber, Prinzipien, 123; Chwolson, Blutanklage, 29f; Jacobs, As others saw him, 103; Kohler, Origins, 226; Ackermann, Judentum, 17; Elbogen, Religionsanschauungen, 33; Ziegler, Kampf, 13; Trattner, As a Jew sees Jesus, 101.

[4] op.cit. 4.

[5] e.g. Acts 24.14f. E. Haenchen, Apostelgeschichte, 586; Dibelius, Studies, 170; Flender, St. Luke, 117; Conzelmann, Apostelgeschichte, 129.

debate about illegalities should be regarded as at a dead end,[1] and at most able to make only a minor contribution. It is a merit of Paul Winter's book that he makes very little use of this argument. Methodologically, it is necessary to insist that a certain looseness must be corrected. It was mentioned above that most Jewish scholars accept that the laws in question existed.[2] It must be remembered that in other contexts scholars would criticize the use of sources of uncertain date for the purposes of theological interpretation, yet here the defensive pressure seems to have set such rigour aside all too often. It must be proved in each case that a given law existed, and that it applies to any given account.

Secondly, the Passion narratives raise in a particularly clear way the phenomenon of the gospel material. Jewish scholars have been in the habit of starting their discussion of the Trial of Jesus with the observation that the gospels are 'Glaubensbücher' and this is of course entirely correct. But it has been rare before the book of Winter for Jewish scholars to apply rigorously the tools of Formgeschichte. On the basis of the source-critical solution proposed in this book, tests can be made to check how the evidence of the divergent, and almost entirely unrelated from a literary angle, traditions [3] provide evidence for a realistic critical procedure. 1. The argument that the use of O.T. material implies unhistoricity must be questioned in the light of the Mk 14.65/Lk 22.63-65 parallel.[4] The former passage, which is probably the later of the two, uses Is 50.6, but the latter passage shows that there may lie behind such a version a tradition having high claim to historical credibility. The framework used for the interpretation of an event has, therefore, to be distinguished from the event itself and its historicity. 2. Comparison of Mk 14.55-64 and Lk 22.66-71 shows clearly the inroads made by theology into history. It would be idle and methodologically improper to try to assimilate the traditions to one another. The contrast of the Markan version with the Lukan account shows that the later insights of faith have modified the tradition, but also that behind such a process there can still exist a not totally unrelated tradition untrammelled with the same difficulties. A parallel observation about Tendenzkritik can also be made here:

---

[1] Similarly, J. Blinzler, Zum Prozeß Jesu, Lebendiges Zeugnis 1 (1966), 15.
[2] See above, p. 258.
[3] See above, pp. 161f. for the limited extent of dependence.
[4] Cf. Blinzler, Prozeß, 59-62; and earlier, P. Feine, Eine vorlukanische Überlieferung des Lukas, Gotha 1891, 60.

firstly, Matthew has a Tendenz which overreaches itself in the redaction of the false-witness incident (Mk 14.55f = Mt 26.59f),[1] but the Markan tradition exists behind his account and involves no such contradiction. Secondly, when the narrative of the Sanhedrin trial is alleged to be born of a Tendenz, it must be noticed that in one narrative there co-exist an account of this event and material presupposing a favourable attitude on the part of some Pharisees towards Jesus (Lk 7.2-4,36f, 14.1).[2] 3. Arguments relying on eye-witnesses for the safeguarding of the gospel tradition have been questioned by D. E. Nineham.[3] Though his case is pushed through too far at some points, his assertion against some conservative scholars that some, if not all, of Mk 8.14-21, 8.27ff and 14.66-72 have passed through a stage of community tradition,[4] can be supported with further evidence in the case of the last example. Vividness, such as is often associated with eye-witnesses,[5] could be ascribed to both Mk 14.66-72 and Lk 22.55-61. Yet they are independent and cannot be harmonized. The process of tradition is conservative in the matter of three challenges with similar content, and three denials, but it is extremely fluid in details of place, timing, personnel, and setting in tradition. There is probably no stronger example for the advocates of eye-witness influence than Mk 14.66-72, yet this apparently strong case crumbles under the weight of the divergent tradition.[6] 4. The editorial method of each evangelist emerges as something not always sufficiently taken into account. The objection that Mk 14.55-64 is presented within the story of Peter's denial should never again be raised.[7]

Thirdly, the relationship between Jesus' career and his downfall continually requires re-examination. Lindeskog rightly declares that the 'political Jesus' theory is a failure,[8] and although there are few

---

[1] See D. R. Catchpole, Answer of Jesus, 223.

[2] Blinzler, Prozeß, 295, convincingly argues, against the traditional addition of Lk 13.31-33 to the pro-Pharisaic verses, that in fact the role and attitude of the Pharisees mentioned here is not favourable.

[3] Eyewitness Testimony and the Gospel Tradition, JTS 9 (1958), 13-25, 243-252; JTS 11 (1960), 253-264.

[4] op.cit. 20; cf. M. Dibelius, From Tradition to Gospel, London 1934, 183.

[5] Cf. C. E. B. Cranfield, Saint Mark, Cambridge 1963, 12; D. Guthrie, New Testament Introduction: Gospels and Acts, London 1965, 189-192.

[6] Nineham's argument from the change made from Mk 10.45, 16.7 in Lk 22.27, 24.6, art.cit.19, is less secure as an editorial one than as a divergence in the pre-Markan stage, since the two traditions are independent, certainly at Lk 22.27 and possibly at Lk 24.6.

[7] See above, pp. 177-179.

[8] Prozeß, 332f.

Jewish writers who would go as far as to echo the words of one recent author, that 'the Christian message is one of mercy; but its bearer, Christ, was a passionate revolutionary, his words an inflammatory denial of both Roman and Judaic law',[1] yet we have seen continually the trend away from religious to political issues. However, the more the Trial of Jesus is limited to a political issue, the more pressing does the need become to explain the long- and short-term causes of his end. Winter's tentative answer that it may have been the politically exciting effect of Jesus' itinerant preaching, is not really enough.[2] The one place where Jesus can be shown to have caused offence is in matters religious.[3] It is here that he was both different and dangerous, and it would be surprising if his end should take up something he had not done and completely bypass something he had done.

Fourthly and lastly, the old dominance of the traditions of Mark and Matthew can no longer, after the work of Winter as well as of non-Jewish writers, persist. In this book it has been suggested that a new attention must be paid to the tradition preserved in Luke, and related to John, which deserves the greatest respect from the point of view of historical reconstruction. If this is so, the events unfolded in the following way. Jesus was taken after his arrest by Jewish officials to the house of Annas, where he was examined, tested and treated unofficially with some violence. The following morning he was conducted before a meeting of the Sanhedrin in its customary place on the Temple Mount, and his case decided on the basis of a claim to Divine Sonship. Thereafter the case passed to, and remained in the hands of, Pilate.

---

[1] Theodore H. White, The Making of the President 1964, London 1965, 164.

[2] On the Trial, 148.

[3] See above, pp. 107-112.

APPENDIX

Since the foregoing material went to the press there has become available the important and illuminating book of Gerhard Schneider: Verleugnung, Verspottung und Verhör Jesu nach Lukas 22, 54-71. Studien zur lukanischen Darstellung der Passion.[1] Unfortunately it is not possible at this stage to make more than a preliminary examination of the points of difference between his work and mine, and to reserve fuller treatment and documentation for a later publication. What is certainly significant is the widespread agreement which exists between two entirely independent examinations of the source-critical problems posed by the Lukan account of these events, an agreement which can fairly be claimed as substantially vindicating the conclusions. Where our paths diverge is basically over the extent of the special Lukan material, which Schneider confines to 22.63-64, 66-68. In what follows a preliminary investigation is made of the two most important points at issue.

According to Schneider, the whole of Peter's denial (Lk 22.54-61) stems from Mk or free Lukan redaction, with the hypothetically possible exception of vv. 55 bc, 60 d. (op. cit. 134). A dominant redactional motive is a concern to shield Peter and to mitigate his shame (op. cit. 166). While acknowledging the weight of many arguments to the contrary, I remain unconvinced of the Markan derivation of this passage. (a) It is certainly true that vv. 54-61, following vv. 33-34, conform to the prediction-fulfilment theme in which Luke is so interested, but the very insertion of these passages ex hypothesei is inconsistent with the intention to shield Peter.[2] Their account of Peter's fall is of damning intensity. (b) A tendency to

---

[1] München 1969. Cf. also, Gab es eine vorsynoptische Szene 'Jesus vor dem Synedrium'? NovT 12 (1970), 22-39.

[2] It is equally doubtful whether Matthew's redaction includes any tendency to shield Peter (contra Schneider 45). Peter does not come into the high priest's court in Mk 'um sich zu warmen' — the warming is merely incidental scene-setting—so any contrast with ἰδεῖν τό τέλος is unnecessary. On the other hand the additions of ἔμπροσθεν πάντων and μετὰ ὅρκου scarcely favour Peter. Indeed, in the absence from Mt of the καὶ τῷ Πέτρῳ (Mk 16.7), the Matthaean narrative ends with Peter disappearing with the burden of the Mt 10.33 threat upon him, and any rehabilitation is only such as can be inferred from the reference to the eleven in 28.16. The Matthaean Passion narrative therefore deals more harshly with Peter than do any of the other accounts.

soften any reproach against the disciples is not a consistent concern
in the body of Lk. Passages like 8.25, 9.49-50 and 18.15 show no
tendency to deal gently with the disciples in general and, as regards
Peter in particular, the selection of 5.1-11 (which shows Peter in a
confessedly gloomy light) rather than Mk 1.16-20, and the redactionally inserted Petrine reference in 8.45 show that any thought of protecting
Peter is far from Luke's mind. This throws in doubt any appeal to
this sort of concern as a motive for individual deviations of Lk from
Mk in 22.54-61.[1] Such an appeal can only be maintained by abandoning
consistency of Lukan method between the main body of the gospel
and the Passion narrative. (c) Schneider argues on the basis of Lk 22.34
(Mk 14.30) that the point of interest in the denials is Peter's knowledge
of Jesus (op.cit. 82). Yet if this is so, the interest is not consistently
maintained, for the οὐκ οἶδα theme with Jesus as object is in the 1st
Lukan denial (as against Mk 14.68), in neither version of the 2nd
denial, nor in the Lukan 3rd denial (as against Mk 14.71). Such an
interest can therefore be seen no more in Lk than in Mk, and is in
fact of minor significance in both. This in turn raises the question of
the μὴ εἰδέναι in 22.34. Schürmann and Schneider both take this
passage as a redacted form of Mk 14.30, and they may well be right.
On the other hand, it may be possible here to follow up Rehkopf's
arguments for independent Lukan material in the light of Merkel's
suggestion that οὐκ οἶδα at Mk 14.71 recalls the rabbinic ban language.[2]
If Lk 22.34 reflects this circle of ideas it has a more primitive ring
than Mk 14.30. (d) In Mk 14.70 Peter's 2nd denial is recorded in
summary form ὁ δὲ πάλιν ἠρνεῖτο, whereas in Lk 22.58 direct speech
is used. Schneider explains this direct form as 'entsprechend einer
allgemeinen Tendenz in der synoptischen Überlieferungsgeschichte'
(op. cit. 52). However this tendency, which is certainly established
for Mt, is supported by only 2 parallels in Lk (20.40, 22.8)[3]; against
it stand no less than 15 cases where Luke drops direct speech from
Mk and prefers summary form (8.24, 29, 32, 41, 42, 44, 9.10, 13, 14,
42, 46, 18.40 twice, 20.7, 21.5, 22.2). Consequently, the change to direct

[1] Schneider makes this appeal at vv. 54c, 55a, 56b, 57bc, 58abd, 59b
and 60a. Equally open to doubt is the suggestion (op. cit. 69) that the omission
of βλασφημία from Mk 14.64 aims at shielding Jesus: Luke has no compunction
about retaining the same allegation in 5.21 (Mk 2.7) or recording accusations which
were, according to his narrative, blatantly false in 23.2 (cf. 20.20-26).

[2] Peter's Curse, in E. Bammel, The Trial of Jesus, 69.

[3] 19.34 is a partial example, as compared with Mk 11.6, but is probably caused
simply by avoidance of the repetition of καθὼς εἶπεν (already Lk 19.32).

speech at Lk 22.58 emerges as extremely unusual and all the more
striking when the content of the wording οὐκ εἰμί is precisely parallel-
led at Jn 18.25 and, on Schneider's own admission, 'kann allerdings
nicht als lukR erwiesen werden' (op. cit. 86).[1]At the same place it is
not quite certain that ἄνθρωπε is a Lukan peculiarity. Schneider
appeals to Lk 5.20 (Mk 2.5), but there the vocative is prepared for by
Mk's τέκνον, and Luke has already previously changed the description
of the παραλυτικόν to ἄνθρωπον ὃς ἦν παραλελυμένος, so this is
plainly not a case of ἄνθρωπε created ex nihilo. No certain support can
be gained from Lk 12.14 (L or Q). (e) Schneider argues that material
from Mk's 3rd denial is used in Lk's 2nd (pp. 82-83) and that this is
motivated by the need to replace the servant-girl by a man, thus
sparing Peter. But, even if this were the motive (which is not convincingly plain), the person could be changed without this semi-
transposition, and there is no overlap between οἱ παρεστῶτες and
ἕτερος. Moreover, Luke shows by the use of καὶ γὰρ Γαλιλαῖός ἐστιν
(see above, p. 162) that for him the two versions of the 3rd denial
correspond. Finally, the introductory καί, used once by Mk and twice
by Jn but 3 times by Lk, shows once again that the Lk-Jn relationship
is closer than that between Lk and Mk.[2]

The second and rather more important point of divergence between
Schneider and me is over the origin of Lk 22.70. Issues of far greater
historical moment hang on the decision here than at 22.54-61, and
I believe the case is in fact stronger here for the extension of the
special Lukan material to include at least this verse. Schneider on the
other hand argues that 22.67-68 is in line with all gospel tradition
(cf. Jn 10.31) in making messiahship the decisive issue (op. cit. 114).
This is, he believes, a tradition using the prophetic model of Jer 38.15,
originally belonging to the same complex as the non-Markan version
of 'The Question about Authority' lying behind Lk 20.1-8 (op. cit.
33-35, 117).[3] It has been inserted in Lk 22 under the influence of the
'prophetic' answer ὑμεῖς λέγετε, which in turn is formulated under
the influence of Mk 15.2/Lk 23.3 (op. cit. 126). The basic material
of Lk 22.70 is drawn from Mk 14. 61-62, which is a Markan construction (op. cit. 57). Here Schneider appeals to the uniqueness of the

[1] It must also be noted that Schneider (p. 66) is willing to allow that ἕτερος
(22.58) may reflect a non-Markan tradition known to both Luke and John.

[2] On καὶ σύ, Schneider 85.

[3] Schneider raises at this point the possibility of Q having contained a Passion
narrative (he was more critical of this on p. 56), and draws a connecting thread
from the Q Temptation narrative to the Sanhedrin hearing.

Son of God title without messianic addition in a human confession and in a question introduced by σὺ εἶ. The real issues underlying the discussion here are firstly, how pivotal in Traditionsgeschichte the Son of God formulation in Mk is, and secondly, whether the complex inter-linkings of tradition proposed by Schneider can in fact be firmly established.

Firstly, ὁ υἱὸς τοῦ εὐλογητοῦ is not a Markan construction in view of the periphrasis, and therefore it follows that a Semitic stage of the tradition contained the term, and that the most which can be attributed to Mark is the assimilation of the two titles. Both titles were accordingly present in the tradition before his work upon it. Moreover, Schneider's appeal to the unanimity of the tradition, including Jn 10.31, that messiahship was the crucial issue, founders not only on the evidence of pre-Markan Son of God involvement, but also on Jn 19.7 (to which, I believe, Schneider makes no reference). Incidentally, Jn 10.31 itself occurs at a point where the discussion has moved beyond messiahship (Jn 10.24) to Divine Sonship, and is commented on in this sense in Jn 10.33, 36. The schematic agreement with Lk 22.67-70 is striking. The doubling of christological titles raises in turn the doubling of replies. There are good reasons for believing that ὑμεῖς λέγετε is neither Markan in origin nor Lukan in position. Luke is emphatically not prone to introduce Semitisms, and Schneider himself quite rightly in another place (p. 125) accepts that 'Die vor- und neben-mk Tr hat offenbar die Antwort Jesu in der mt/lk Weise geboten'.[1] In fact σὺ εἶπας can be regarded as a witness to the earlier occurrence of ὑμεῖς λέγετε as the answer to the Son of God question, in terms of the influence of oral tradition on Mt (cf. the parallel oral tradition which may have operated behind Lk 22.64/Mt 26.67). Moreover, any cross-influence between Lk 22.67b,68 and ὑμεῖς λέγετε in terms of 'prophetic character' can be ruled out in view of the essential divergence between the two (one 'ausweichend', the other 'bejahend'),[2] and the fact that there is no case among the σὺ εἶπας family of statements where there is any prophetic flavour.[3]

Thus we have evidence that early Trial tradition contained two answers which do not overlap, and also the two issues of messiahship

---

[1] This uncertainty is also present in Schneider's conclusions about 22.70 so that he qualifies 'luk R der mk-Vorlage wahrscheinlich' by 'dabei ist eine Anlehnung an eine nicht-mk Tr möglich'.

[2] Schneider 57.

[3] Cf. my article, The Answer of Jesus to Caiaphas (Matt. xxvi. 64), NTS 17(1971), 213-226.

and divine Sonship. The only remaining obstacle to correlating the two is the possible connection between Lk 22.67 b, 68 and tradition behind 20.1-8. Is this tradition a reality? When Schneider first alludes to a connection, the two common factors to which he appeals are Jesus' reduction of his opponents to silence and his refusal of an answer (p. 35, similarly p. 118). But the Lukan presentation of these features is quite remarkably dependent on Mk, so we are here dealing with nothing specifically Lukan. If there is any connection between Mk 11.33 and Lk 22.67 b, 68 that connection must be defined either in some layer of the tradition or in the events concerning the historical Jesus, but not with any reference to Lk 20.1-8 in terms of the evidence so far presented. The same reasoning applies against Schneider's subsequent reference to the inability of the leaders to stand up to Jesus: 'das wird besonders hervorgehoben von Luk (diff Mt/Mk), ähnlich aber auch von Matth (Mt 22.46)'. Mt 22.46 is drawn from the less immediate parallel Mk 12.34 (= Lk 20.40) and is surely not germane here.

What is at first sight a more cogent argument is the appeal to agreements between Mt and Lk against Mk in Lk 20.1-8.[1] For the sake of completeness these must be dealt with alongside the features which occur only in Lk.

In the latter group, elements which can plainly be written off as typical of Lukan redaction are ἐγένετο ἐν μιᾷ τῶν ἡμερῶν, εὐαγγελιζομέ-νου, ἐπέστησαν, σύν, πρός + A after a speech verb, τίς ἐστιν, ὅτι, πεπεισμένος, εἶπεν. The same applies to ὁ λαὸς ἅπας καταλιθάσει ἡμᾶς: although the mention of stoning recalls Jn 10.31,33, there is here the difference that the object of the threat is not Jesus, and the formulation is so close to Acts 5.26 that this must be a Lukan stylistic intervention. There remains only εἰπὸν ἡμῖν (Lk 20.2). This is a rare form in the N.T.[2] as well as in Lk, other occurrences being Lk 10.10 (Q), 10.40, 13.32 (L), 20.3, 22.67, Acts 24.20, 28.26 (citation). It cannot be ruled out that here in Lk 20.2 there is a non-Markan tradition but such can only be established if other indications point in the same direction. It they do not, this occurrence must be regarded as either insignificant, or a verbal anticipation ot Mk 13.4 (along the lines ot the reminiscences discussed by Schürmann [3]), or a thematic connection with 22.67. In the last case this would mean that Luke regarded the

[1] op. cit. 103, 117.
[2] Rightly, Schneider 56-57.
[3] Traditionsgeschichtliche Untersuchungen, 111-125.

two incidents as having a bearing on each other, but not that he had other source-material.

When we turn to the list of features common to Mt and Lk, these are 1. διδάσκοντος (Mt: διδάσκοντι). 2. αὐτοῦ 3. τὸν λαόν (Mt: τοῦ λαοῦ) 4. λέγοντες 5. Omission of ἵνα ταῦτα ποιῇς, Mk 11.28. 6. ἀποκριθείς 7. ἐρωτήσω 8. κἀγώ 9. εἴπατε (cf. Mt: εἴπητε) 10. Omission of ἀποκριθητέ μοί, Mk 11.30. 11. οἱ δέ 12. ἐὰν δέ 13. προφήτην 14. πόθεν (cf. Mt 21.25). It is immediately apparent that this list contains none of the decisive elements of the narrative, while these decisive elements are repeatedly found in the common Mk-Lk material. In detail: 1. Both Matthew and Luke repeatedly emphasize the teaching theme. 2. αὐτοῦ appears in a Genitive absolute construction in each case, but with a different verb. It is therefore not significant. 3. The λαός reference is not only common in the redactional work of both evangelists, but is also joined here with a different qualification. 4. λέγοντες. The λέγων (λέγοντες) introduction to direct speech is extremely common in both Matthaean and Lukan redaction and, not surprisingly therefore, is a frequent point of Mt-Lk agreement against Mk in passages where there is not the slightest hint of non-Markan tradition. Similarly, parallels are available for the redactional doubling of a speech verb. 5. This is a rough and unnecessary repetition eliminated by both Matthew and Luke in the interests of stylistic improvement. 6. ἀποκριθείς is again a common feature of the editorial activity of both later evangelists. 7. ἐρωτήσω. Matthew changes from ἐπερωτᾶν to ἐρωτᾶν at Mt 16.13 (Mk 8.27) and Mt 19.17 (Mk 10.17) and he introduces redactionally at 15.23. Luke uses the word redactionally at 4.38. 8.37, 9.45, 19.31, and changes from ἐπερωτᾶν to ἐρωτᾶν at 9.45 (Mk 9.32). Once again there is no reason to regard the wording here as significant. 8. κἀγώ is a rare form, though certainly redactional at Mt 26.15 (Mk 14.10), In Luke-Acts it is spread across Infancy narrative, Q, L and Acts and therefore is probably to be attributed to independent Lukan redaction at 20.3. 9. εἴπατε (cf. Mt: εἴπητε) cannot be treated independently of εἰπόν (20.2), for there is clearly a parallelism and rounding off which is being achieved. The replacement in Mt and Lk of Mk's ἀποκρίνομαι is frequent, and agreement between Mt and Lk paralleled at Mk 6.37, 9.17, 10.51 and 12.35. 10. ἀποκριθητέ μοί is clearly redundant and its absence in Mt and Lk can certainly not be treated as significant. 11. οἱ δέ/ὁ δέ introductions are frequent in Matthaean and Lukan redaction. 12. ἐὰν δέ. Schneider is quite correct when he remarks: 'Gegen ἐάν hat Luk eine merkliche Abneigung' (p. 115). There is no case where Luke uses ἐάν in the gospel where it has not been provided by a source. This is in fact the case here, where the occurrence has been provoked by Mk 11.31. 13. The Matthaean formulation πάντες γὰρ ὡς προφήτην ἔχουσιν τὸν Ἰωάννην is shown by Mt 14.5 (Mk 6.20) to be Matthew's own construction. In Lk the accusative as part of an infinitive construction is a common phenomenon. 14. πόθεν is rare in the N.T. outside Jn. Of the 4 Mt occurrences apart from Mt 21.25, one is M (13.27) and 3 are drawn from Mk. Acts has no instance of it; Lk has 1 in the Infancy narrative, 1.43, and 2 in Q (13.25, 27). In the latter case, however, the Q form is probably more faithfully preserved in Mt, with the result that πόθεν is attested in Lukan redaction, although weakly.

The result is that the only cases where Lukan redaction is in doubt are εἰπὸν ἡμῖν, καγώ, and πόθεν. There is no coherence between these and only one of them overlaps with Lk 22.67-68. Consequently it is difficult to be convinced of any traditional link between Lk 20.1-8 and 22.67-68 on the level of pre-Lukan non-Markan strata.

In sum, therefore, the combination of two questions and two answers in Lk 22.67-68,70 emerges as pre-Lukan and non-Markan on the grounds of the unrelatedness and primitiveness of the answers, the independent Johannine material, the pre-Markan character of the divine Sonship reference, and the divergence of the whole from known characteristics of Lukan redaction. At this point the enquiry moves beyond the study of source-critical evolution to questions of theological milieu (see above, p. 200) with, I believe, the result that this record of the interrogation by the Sanhedrin plays a vital role in the historical reconstruction of the trial of Jesus.

JEWISH BIBLIOGRAPHY

Abrahams, I.
(1858-1925; lecturer at Jews' College, London, and later Reader in Rabbinics, University of Cambridge).
Studies in Pharisaism and the Gospels I-II. London 1917-1924.

Ackermann, A.,
Judentum und Christentum. Leipzig 1903.

Agus, J. B.,
The Evolution of Jewish Thought. London 1959.
The Meaning of Jewish History. London 1963.

Asch, S.,
(1880-1957; novelist and playwright).
The Guilty Ones. Atlantic Monthly 166 (1940). 713-723.

Bacher, W.,
(1850-1913; Professor at the Landesrabbinerschule, Budapest).
Die Agada der babylonischen Amoräer. Straßburg 1878.
Die Agada der Tannaiten I-II. Straßburg 1884-1890.

Baeck, L.,
(1873-1956; German Rabbi, lecturer at the Berlin Hochschule für die Wissenschaft des Judentums, and later head of the Reichsvertretung der Juden in Deutschland).
Harnacks Vorlesungen über das Wesen des Christentums. MGWJ 45 (1901). 97-120.
Die Auseinandersetzung mit dem entstehenden Christentum. LJ 5 (1929). 56-60.
Die Pharisäer: ein Kapitel jüdischer Geschichte. Berlin 1934.
Der Menschensohn. MGWJ 81 (1937). 12-24.
Das Evangelium als Urkunde der jüdischen Glaubensgeschichte. Berlin 1938.
Judaism and Christianity. Philadelphia 1958.
The Faith of Paul. JJS 3 (1952). 93-110.

Baeck, S.,
(b. 1834; Rabbi at Bömisch Leipa and later at Lissa).
Die Geschichte des jüdischen Volkes. Lissa 1878.

Baer, Y.,
(b. 1888; Professor of Mediaeval History at the Hebrew University, Jerusalem).
Some Aspects of Judaism as presented in the Synoptic Gospels. Zion 31 (1966). I-III.

Bamberger, B. J.,
(Rabbi of the Congregation Beth Emeth, Albany, N.Y.).
The Story of Judaism. New York 1957.

Baron, S. W.,
        (b. 1895; Professor of Jewish History, Literature and Institutions at
        Columbia University).
A Social and Religious History of the Jews, 1st ed. New York 1937, 2nd ed.
New York 1952.

Baum, G.,
        (R. C. priest).
The Jews and the Gospel. London 1961.

Benamozegh, E., (1822-1900; Rabbi and Professor of Theology at the Rabbinical
        School, Leghorn).
Morale juive et morale chrétienne. Paris 1867.
Israel et l'humanité. Livourne 1885.

Ben-Chorin, S.,
        Die Christusfrage an die Juden. Jerusalem 1941.

Benisch, A.,
        (1811-1878; journalist and editor of the Jewish Chronicle).
Judaism surveyed. London 1874.

Bentwich, N.,
        (b. 1883; Professor of International Relations at the Hebrew University,
        Jerusalem).
Article in Aspects of Hebrew Genius, ed. L. Simon. London 1910.

Bergmann, J.,
        Jüdische Apologetik im neutestamentlichen Zeitalter. Berlin 1908.
        Die Legenden der Juden. Berlin 1919.
        Apologetik und Apologeten. EJ 2 (1928). 1176-1194.

Bernfeld, S.,
        (1860-1940; Chief Rabbi at Belgrade, 1886-1894).
        Zur ältesten Geschichte des Christentums. JJGL 13 (1910). 89-128.

Bokser, B. Z.,
        (Rabbi at Forest Hills Jewish Centre).
        Pharisaic Judaism in Transition. New York 1935.

Brandes, G.,
        (1842-1927; Danish critic).
        Urchristentum. Berlin 1927.
        Jesus: a Myth. London 1927.

Brasch, R.,
        The Star of David. Sydney 1955.
        The Eternal Flame. Sydney 1958.
        How did it begin ? Croydon, Victoria 1965.

Brod, M.,
        (b. 1884; author and composer, later Dramaturgic Director of the
        Ha-Bimah theatre in Tel Aviv).
        Heidentum, Christentum, Judentum,
        Ein Bekenntnisbuch. I-II, München 1921-1922.

Browne, L.,
(1897-1949).
The Story of the Jews. London 1926.
How odd of God. London 1935.

Buber, M.,
(1878-1965; Professor of the Philosophy of Jewish Religion and Ethics, Frankfurt am Main, 1924-1933, and Professor of Sociology of Religion at the Hebrew University, Jerusalem, from 1938).
Two Types of Faith. London 1951.

Büchler, A.,
(1867-1939; Principal of the Jews' College, London).
Das Synedrion in Jerusalem und das grosse Beth Din in der Quaderkammer des Jerusalemischen Tempels. Wien 1902.
Studies in Jewish History. London 1956.

Carmichael, J.,
The Death of Jesus. London 1963.

Cassel, D.,
(1818-1893; German historian)
Manual of Jewish History and Literature. London 1883.

Cassel, P.,
(1821-1892; convert to Christianity and subsequently missionary with the London Society for promoting Christianity among the Jews, and Pastor at the Christuskirche, Berlin).
Apologetische Briefe I: Panthera—Stada—Onokotes: Caricaturnamen Christi. Berlin 1875.

Chajes, H. P.,
Markus-Studien. Berlin 1899.

Chwolson, D.,
(1819-1911; convert to Christianity, Professor of Oriental Languages at St. Petersburg).
Über das Datum im Evangelium Matthäi XXVI, 17. MGWJ 37 (1893). 537-555.
Das letzte Passamahl Christi und der Tag seines Todes. Leipzig 1908.
Die Blutanklage und sonstige mittelalterliche Beschuldigungen der Juden. Frankfurt a.M. 1901.
Über die Frage, ob Jesus gelebt hat. Leipzig 1910.
Beiträge zur Entwicklungsgeschichte des Judentums. Leipzig 1910.

Cohen, A.,
(1887-1957; chief minister of Birmingham Hebrew Congregation, 1913-1949, and president of the Board of Deputies of British Jews, 1949-1955).
Art. in: Judaism and the Beginnings of Christianity. London 1924. 3-47.
The Parting of the Ways: Judaism and the Rise of Christianity. London 1954.

Cohen, J.,
(1817-1899; French journalist).
Les juifs déicides, in La Vérité Israélite 2 (1860). 169-173, 193-199, 217-223, 241-249, 289-297, 313-322, 337-346, 385-394, 409-419; op.cit. 3 (1861). 6-13, 25-32, 49-58, 73-78, 97-102, 121-126, 145-151, 193-199, 217-224, 241-247, 265-270, 289-294.
Les déicides. Paris 1861.
Les pharisiens. Paris 1877.

Cohn, H. M.,
    Sein Blut komm über uns. JJGL 6 (1903). 82-90.
    Christus = Barabas. JJGL 8 (1905). 65-75.
    Christentum und Judentum. JJGL 9 (1906). 59-85.

Cohon, S. S.,
    (1888-1959; Professor of Jewish Theology at Hebrew Union College,
    Cincinnati).
    The Place of Jesus in the religious Life of his Day. JBL 48 (1929). 82-108.

Danziger, A.,
    Jewish Forerunners to Christianity. New York 1903.

Daube, D.,
    (b. 1909; Regius Professor of Civil Law, University of Oxford).
    Concerning the Reconstruction of the Aramaic Gospels. BJRL 29 (1945).
    69-105.
    Two Notes on the Passover Haggada. JTS 50 (1949). 53-57.
    The New Testament and Rabbinic Judaism. London 1956.
    Three Notes having to do with Johanan ben Zaccai. JTS 11 (1960), 53-62.

Dawidowicz, L. S.,
    The Golden Tradition: Jewish Life and Thought in eastern Europe. London
    1967.

Derenbourg, J.,
    (1811-1895; Professor of Rabbinical Hebrew at the École des Hautes
    Études).
    Essai sur l'histoire et la géographie de la Palestine. Paris 1867.
    Une stèle du temple d'Hérode. Journal Asiatique 20 (1872). 178-195.

Dessauer, J.,
    Geschichte der Israeliten. Erlangen 1846.

Dienemann, M.,
    Klausners Jesuswerke, Festschrift zum 75-jährigen Bestehen d. jüdisch-theol.
    Seminars Fränckelscher Stiftung. Breslau 1929.
    Zur Leben-Jesu-Forschung. Der Morgen 6 (1930). 373-382.

Dimont, M. I.,
    Jews, God and History. London 1964.

Dubnow, S. M.,
    (1860-1941).
    Weltgeschichte des jüdischen Volkes II. Berlin 1925.
    A short History of the Jewish People. London 1936.

Duschak, M.,
    (1815-1890; Austrian Rabbi).
    Das Mosaisch-Talmudische Strafrecht. Wien 1869.
    Die Biblisch-Talmudische Glaubenslehre. Wien 1873.
    Die Moral der Evangelien und des Talmud. Brünn 1877.

Edersheim, A.,
    (1825-1889; convert to Christianity and subsequently a missionary)
    The Life and Times of Jesus the Messiah. London 1883.
    The Temple, its Ministry and Services. London 1894.

Edgar, L. I.,
    A Jewish View of Jesus. London 1940.

Ehrlich, E. L.,
    A concise History of Israel. London 1962.

Eisler, R.,
    Das letzte Abendmahl. ZNW 24 (1925). 161-192; ZNW 25 (1926).5-37.
    Jésus d'après la version slave de Flavius Josèphe. RHR 93 (1926). 1-21.
    Flavius Josephus on Jesus called the Christ. JQR 21 (1930). 1-60.
    The Messiah Jesus and John the Baptist. London 1931.

Elbogen, I.,
    (1874-1948; teacher at the Lehranstalt für die Wissenschaft des Juden-
    tums).
    Die Religionsanschauungen der Pharisäer mit besonderer Berücksichtigung
    der Begriffe Gott und Mensch. Berlin 1904.
    Einige neuere Theorien über den Ursprung der Pharisäer und Sadduzäer.
    Jewish Studies in memory of Israel Abrahams. New York 1927. 125-148.

Enelow, H. G.,
    (1877-1934; Rabbi of Temple Emanu-El, New York).
    A Jewish View of Jesus. Selected Works III. Kingsport 1935.

Eschelbacher, J.,
    Die Vorlesungen A. Harnacks über das Wesen des Christentums. MGWJ
    46 (1902). 119-141.
    Das Judentum und das Wesen des Christentums. Berlin 1905.

Felsenthal, B.,
    (1822-1908; Rabbi in Chicago).
    Concerning Jesus, surnamed the Christ. reprinted in: Bernard Felsenthal:
    Teacher in Israel. New York 1924.

Finkel, A.,
    The Pharisees and the Teacher of Nazareth. Leiden 1964.

Finkelstein, L.,
    (b. 1895; Provost, President and Chancellor of the Jewish Theological
    Seminary, New York).
    The Pharisees, their Origin and their Philosophy. HTR 22 (1929). 185-261.
    The Pharisees: the sociological Background of their Faith I-III. 3rd ed.
    Philadelphia 1962.

Fleg, E.,
    (1874-1963; French poet and playwright).
    Jesus told by the wandering Jew. London 1934.

Fluegel, M.,
    The Messiah Ideal I-II. Baltimore 1896.

Fox, G. G.,
    The Jews, Jesus and Christ. Chicago 1953.
    Jesus, Pilate and Paul. Chicago 1955.

Frank, H.,
    Jesus: a modern Study. New York 1930.

Franz, A.,
　　Das Judentum und sein Verhältnis zu anderen Religionen. Stuttgart 1889.

Freimann, M.,
　　Wie verhielt sich das Judentum zu Jesus und dem entstehenden Christentum?
　　MGWJ 54 (1910). 697-712; MGWJ 55 (1911). 160-176, 296-316.

Friedländer, Gerald.,
　　The Jewish Sources of the Sermon on the Mount. London 1911.
　　Hellenism and Christianity. London 1912.

Friedländer, Moriz,
　　(1842-1919; Austrian theologian, and Secretary of the Vienna Israelite
　　Alliance).
　　Les Esséniens. REJ 14 (1887). 184-216.
　　Zur Entstehungsgeschichte des Christentums. Wien 1894.
　　Der vorchristliche jüdische Gnosticismus. Göttingen 1898.
　　Encore un mot sur Minim, Minout et Guilonim dans le Talmud. REJ 38
　　(1899). 194-203.
　　Geschichte der jüdischen Apologetik als Vorgeschichte des Christentums.
　　Zürich 1903.
　　Die religiösen Bewegungen innerhalb des Judentums im Zeitalter Jesu.
　　Berlin 1905.
　　Synagoge und Kirche in ihren Anfängen. Berlin 1908.

Geiger, A.,
　　(1810-1874; German Rabbi, and Teacher at the Berlin Hochschule für
　　die Wissenschaft des Judentums).
　　Sadducäer und Pharisäer. JZWL 2 (1863). 11-54.
　　Das Judentum und seine Geschichte. Breslau 1864.
　　Die neuesten Fortschritte in der Erkenntnis der Entwicklungsgeschichte des
　　Christentums. JZWL 5 (1867). 252-282.
　　Bileam und Jesus. JZWL 6 (1868). 31-37.
　　Entstehung des Christentums. JZWL 11 (1875). 8-18.

Ginzberg, A.,
　　(1856-1927; essayist, using the pseudonym Ahad Ha-am).
　　Ten Essays on Zionism and Judaism. London 1922.

Goldin, H. E.,
　　The Case of the Nazarene Reopened. New York 1948.

Goldstein, M.,
　　Jesus in the Jewish Tradition. New York 1950.

Goodman, P.,
　　(1875-1949; British journalist, editor of the Zionist Review).
　　The Synagogue and the Church. London 1908.
　　History of the Jews. London 1939.

Graetz, H. H.,
　　(1817-1891; German historian, Professor at Breslau).
　　Geschichte der Juden III. 1st ed. Leipzig 1856; 2nd ed. Leipzig 1863; 3rd ed.
　　Leipzig 1878.
　　Sinaï et Golgotha. Paris 1867.
　　Eine Localität Lod bei Jerusalem. MGWJ 27 (1878). 427-432.

Un mot sur la dogmatique du christianisme primitif. REJ 20 (1890). 11-15.
The Birth of Christianity. Open Court 13 (1899). 166-182.

Grayzel, S.,
(b. 1896; American Rabbi; Editor of the Jewish Publication Society).
A History of the Jews. Philadelphia 1966.

Greenstone, J. H., (1873-1955; Lecturer, later Principal, of Gratz College, Philadelphia).
The Messiah Idea in Jewish History. Philadelphia 1906.

Grünebaum, E.,
(1807-1893; Rabbi at Landau).
Die Sittenlehre des Judenthums. 1st ed. Mannheim 1867; 2nd ed. Straßburg 1878.

Güdemann, M.,
(1835-1918; Austrian Rabbi, Chief Rabbi in Vienna).
Religionsgeschichtliche Studien. Leipzig 1876.
Nächstenliebe. Ein Beitrag zur Erklärung des Matthäusevangeliums. Wien 1890.
Das IV. (Johannes) Evangelium und der Rabbinismus. MGWJ 37 (1893). 249-257, 297-303, 345-356.
Das Judenthum im neutestamentlichen Zeitalter in christlicher Darstellung MGWJ 47 (1903). 38-53, 120-136, 231-249.
Jüdische Apologetik. Glogau 1906.

Gutmann, J.,
Ben Setada. EJ 4 (1929). 72f.

Guttmann, M.,
(1872-1942; Lecturer at the Rabbinical Seminaries of Breslau and Budapest).
Das Judentum und seine Umwelt. Berlin 1927.
Review of J. Klausner, Jesus of Nazareth. MGWJ 75 (1931). 250-257.
Nochmals: Klausners Jesus-Werk. MGWJ 77 (1933). 18-44.

Hamburger, J.,
(1826-1911; German Rabbi, Landesrabbiner at Mecklenburg-Strelitz).
Jesus von Nazaret. Real-Encyclopädie des Judentums. Abt. III, Supplement LV. Leipzig 1897.

Hirsch, E. G.,
(1852-1923; Professor of Rabbinic Literature and Philosophy at the University of Chicago, Editor of the Jewish Encyclopaedia).
Crucifixion. JE 4 (1903). 373f.
My Religion. New York 1925.

Hirsch, Samuel,
(1815-1889; Chief Rabbi of Luxembourg, later Rabbi of the Reform Congregation, Philadelphia; father of E. G. Hirsch).
Die Religionsphilosophie der Juden. Leipzig 1842.
Les crimitières au point de vue Israélite. Archives Israélites 26 (1865). 383-390.

Hoenig, S. B.,
(of Yeshiva University, New York).
The Great Sanhedrin. New York 1953.

Hulen, A. B.,
The 'Dialogues with the Jews' as Sources for the early Jewish Argument against Christianity. JBL 51 (1932). 58-70.

Hunterberg, M.,
The crucified Jew. New York 1927.

Hyamson, M.,
(1862-1949; Rabbi in London and New York, Professor at the Jewish Theological Seminary, New York.)
Husband's Prosecution of Jesus. JQR 11 (1920). 89-97.
Review of H. G. Enelow, A Jewish View of Jesus. JQR 22 (1931). 211-217.

Isaac, J.,
Jésus et Israel. 1st ed. Paris 1948; 2nd ed. Paris 1958.
The Christian Roots of Anti-Semitism. London 1960.
The Teaching of Contempt. New York 1964.

Jacob, E.,
Christentum. EJ 5 (1930). 525-560.

Jacobs, J.,
(1854-1916; journalist and historian, editor of The American Hebrew).
As Others saw Him. London 1895.
Jesus of Nazareth in History. JE 7 (1904). 160-166.

Jelski, I.,
Die innere Einrichtung des Grossen Synedrions zu Jerusalem. Breslau 1893.

Jocz, J.,
(Professor of Systematic Theology at Wycliffe College, Toronto).
The Jewish People and Jesus Christ. London 1949.
Christians and Jews: Encounter and Mission. London 1966.

Joel, D.,
(1815-1882; German Rabbi, Professor at the Jewish Theological Seminary, Breslau).
Der Aberglaube und die Stellung des Judenthums zu demselben. Breslau 1881-2.

Joel, M.,
(1826-1890; German Rabbi, Professor at the Jewish Theological Seminary, Breslau, and Rabbi of the Breslau Congregation).
Blicke in die Religionsgeschichte zu Anfang des zweiten christlichen Jahrhunderts I-II. Breslau 1880-3.

Jonge, M. de,
Messias der kommende jüdische Mann. Berlin 1904.

Joseph, M.,
Jesus von Nazareth genannt Christus. JL 3 (1929). 237-243.

Joseph, N.S.,
Why I am not a Christian. London 1907.

Jost, I. M.,
(1793-1860; teacher at Frankfurt a.M.).
Geschichte der Israeliten. Berlin 1820.

Allgemeine Geschichte des Israelitischen Volkes. Berlin 1832.
Geschichte des Judenthums und seiner Secten. Leipzig 1857.

Juster, J.,
(1886-1914).
Les Juifs dans l'Empire Romain I-II. Paris 1914.

Kamenetzky, A. S.,
Notes sur Jésus dans les sources juives. REJ 59 (1910). 277.

Kastein, J.,
(1890-1946; pseudonym for Julius Katzenstein: author and playwright).
Eine Geschichte der Juden. Berlin 1931.

Kayserling, M.,
(1829-1905; Rabbi of the Swiss Jews, later Rabbi of the Jewish community in Budapest).
Moses Mendelssohn. JE 8 (1904). 479-485.

Klausner, J.,
(1874-1958; Professor of Modern Hebrew Literature and of Second Temple History at the Hebrew University, Jerusalem).
Jesus of Nazareth. London 1925.
Jesus von Nazareth. EJ 9 (1932). 52-78.
Nochmals: Klausners Jesus-Werk. MGWJ 77 (1933). 16-18.
From Jezus to Paul. New York 1943.

Klein, G.,
(Rabbi in Stockholm).
Zur Erläuterung der Evangelien aus Talmud und Midrasch. ZNW 5 (1904). 144-153.
Der älteste christliche Katechismus und die jüdische Propagandaliteratur. Berlin 1909.
Ist Jesus eine historische Persönlichkeit ? Tübingen 1910.

Kohler, K.,
(1843-1926; Rabbi in Detroit, Chicago and New York; President of Hebrew Union College, Editor of Jewish Encyclopaedia).
Christianity in its Relation to Judaism. JE 4 (1903). 49-59.
Jesus of Nazareth—in Theology. JE 7 (1904). 166-170.
Die Nächstenliebe im Judentum. Festschrift H. Cohen. Berlin 1912. 469-480.
Grundriss einer systematischen Theologie des Judentums auf geschichtlicher Grundlage. Leipzig 1910.
The Origins of the Synagogue and the Church. ed. H. G. Enelow. New York 1929.
Synagogue and Church in their mutual Relations. repr. in Studies Addresses and Personal Papers. New York 1931.

Krauskopf, J.,
(1858-1923; Rabbi in Kansas City and Philadelphia).
A Rabbi's Impressions of the Oberammergau Passion Play. Philadelphia 1901.

Krauss, S.,
(1866-1948; Hungarian philologist, Rabbi and Professor of Hebrew at the Jewish Seminar, Budapest; Lecturer and Principal at Vienna Theological Seminary).

Das Leben Jesu nach jüdischen Quellen. Berlin 1902.
Jesus of Nazareth—in Jewish Legend. JE 7 (1904). 170-173.
Le Nom de Jésus chez les Juifs. REJ 55 (1908). 148-151.

Kroner, T.,
Geschichte der Juden. Frankfurt a.M. 1906.

Kulischer, M.,
(1847-1919; Russian lawyer and historian).
Das Leben Jesu eine Sage. Leipzig 1876.

Lachs, S. B.,
A "Jesus Passage" in the Talmud re-examined. JQR 59 (1969). 244-247.

Landman, S. and Efron, B.,
Story without End: an informal History of the Jewish People. New York 1949.

Lapide, P. E,
The last three Popes and the Jews. London 1967.

Lauterbach, J. Z.,
(1873-1942; Professor of Talmud at Hebrew Union College, Cincinnati).
Sanhedrin. JE 11 (1905). 41-44.
The Pharisees and their Teachings. HUCA 6 (1929). 69-139.
Rabbinic Essays. Cincinnati 1951.

Learsi, R.,
Israel: a History of the Jewish People. Cleveland 1949.

Lehmann, J.,
Quelques dates importantes de la chronologie du 2e temple. REJ 37 (1898). 1-44.

Leszynsky, R.,
Die Sadduzäer. Berlin 1912.

Levison, N.,
The Jewish Background of Christianity. Edinburgh 1932.

Levy, C. H.,
Progressive Judaism and liberal Christianity. New World 8 (1899). 497-506.

Levy, Jacob,
(1819-1892; Rabbi at Breslau).
Neuhebräisches und Chaldäisches Wörterbuch über die Talmudim und Midrasch. Leipzig 1876-1889. I.236; II.272; III.499; IV.60.

Levy, J. L.,
Addresses: Series 14. Pittsburgh 1914.

Lewin, A.,
(b. 1843; German Rabbi).
Die Religionsdisputation des R. Jechiel von Paris 1240 am Hofe Ludwigs, des Heiligen, ihre Veranlassung und ihre Folgen. MGWJ 18 (1869). 97-110, 145-156, 193-210.

Lublinski, S.,
    (1868-1910; German critic and playwright).
Die Entstehung des Christentums aus der antiken Kultur. Jena 1910.

Ludwig, E.,
    (1881-1948; biographer and dramatist).
Der Menschensohn. Berlin 1928.

Magnus, K.,
    (1844-1924).
About the Jews since Bible times. London 1881. Revised ed. by C. Roth.
London 1931.
Outlines of Jewish History. 1st ed. London 1892; 2nd ed. revised by Michael
Friedländer. London 1892; freshly revised ed. London 1958.

Mann, J.,
    (1888-1940; teacher at Hebrew Union College, Cincinnati).
Jesus and the Sadducean Priests. JQR 6 (1916). 415-422.

Mantel, H.,
    (of Bar-Ilan University, Ramat Gan, Israel)
Studies in the History of the Sanhedrin. Cambridge, Mass. 1961.

Margolis, M. L.,
    (1866-1932; teacher at Hebrew Union College, and Dropsie College),
    and Marx, A., (1878-1954; Librarian of Jewish Theological Seminary,
    New York).
A History of the Jewish People. Philadelphia 1927.

Marmorstein, A.,
    (1882-1946; Rabbi in Austro-Hungary, and later Lecturer at Jews'
    College, London).
Religionsgeschichtliche Studien I-II. Skotschau 1910-2.
The Unity of God in Rabbinic Literature. HUCA 1 (1924). 467-502.
The old Rabbinic Doctrine of God. London 1927.
Les Rabbins et les Évangiles. REJ 92 (1932). 31-54.

Mattuck, I. I.,
    (1883-1954; Rabbi at the Liberal Synagogue, London).
The Trial of Jesus. London 1929.

Mayers, M.,
The History of the Jews. London 1824.

Mendelssohn, M.,
    (1729-1826).
Gesammelte Schriften III. Leipzig 1843.

Meyer, F. E.,
Einige Bemerkungen zur Bedeutung des Terminus 'Synhedrion' in den
Schriften des Neuen Testaments. NTS 14 (1968). 545-551.

Mieses, M.,
Der Ursprung des Judenhasses. Leipzig 1923.

Montefiore, C. G.,
    (1859-1939; Editor of the Jewish Quarterly Review, President of the
    Anglo-Jewish Association).

Review of M. J. Savage, Jesus and Modern Life. JQR 6 (1894). 381-395.
The Synoptic Gospels and the Jewish Consciousness. HJ 3 (1905). 649-667.
Some Elements of the religious Teaching of Jesus according to the Synoptic Gospels. London 1910.
The Synoptic Gospels. 1st ed. London 1909; 2nd ed. London 1927.
The Significance of Jesus for his own Age. HJ 10 (1912). 766-779.
Liberal Judaism and Hellenism. London 1918.
The Originality of Jesus. HJ 28 (1929). 98-111.
Rabbinic Literature and Gospel Teachings. London 1930.

Morgenstern, J., (b. 1881; Professor of Biblical and Semitic Languages at Hebrew Union College, Cincinnati).
Some significant Antecedents of Christianity. Leiden 1966.

Noah, M. M.,
(1785-1851; U. S. diplomat and playwright).
Discourse on the Restoration of the Jews. New York 1845.
The Jews, Judea and Christianity. London 1849.

Parkes, J.,
An Epistle from a High Priest of the Jews to the Chief Priest of Canterbury, on the Extension of Catholic Emancipation to the Jews. London 1821.

Perles, F.,
(1874-1933; Rabbi and University Lecturer at Königsberg).
What Jews may learn from Harnack. JQR 14 (1902). 517-543.

Perles, J., (1835-1894; Rabbi in Posen and München).
Bileam-Jesus und Pontius Pilatus. MGWJ 21 (1872). 266f.

Peynado, J. R.,
An Examination of Bishop Pearson's Exposition of the Apostles' Creed. The Occident 5 (1847). 496-499.
Letter to the Rev. A. M'Caul, D. D. The Occident 7 (1849). 25-31.

Philippson, D.,
The Reform Movement in Judaism. New York 1907.

Philippson, L.,
(1811-1889; Rabbi in Magdeburg; founder of Allgemeine Zeitung des Judenthums).
Article in Allgemeine Zeitung 35 (1865). 533ff.
Haben wirklich die Juden Jesum gekreuzigt ? 2nd ed. Leipzig 1901.

Pick, S.,
Judentum und Christentum in ihren Unterscheidungslehren. Frankfurt a.M. 1913.
Die auf Jesus gedeuteten Stellen des Alten Testaments. Frankfurt a.M. 1923.
Gottessohn (Logos). LJ 5 (1929). 70-74.
Dreieinigkeit. LJ 5 (1929). 93f.
Menschwerdung des 'Gottessohnes'. LJ 5 (1929). 107-109.
Erlösung. LJ 5 (1929). 129-131.

Polack, A. I., with Simpson, W. W.,
Jesus in the Background of History. London 1957.

Rabbi Jeshua. London 1881.

Rabbinowicz, I. M.,
    (1818-1893; doctor and Talmudic scholar).
    Le rôle de Jésus et des apôtres. Bruxelles 1866.
    Législation civile du Thalmud. Paris 1879.

Raddock, C.,
    Portrait of a People. New York 1965.

Radin, M.,
    (Professor of Law in the University of California).
    The Trial of Jesus of Nazareth. Chicago 1931.

Raphall, M. J.,
    Post-Biblical History of the Jews II. London 1856.

Reichenbach, A.,
    Die Lehre des Rabbi Jeschua von Nazareth nach den Evangelien und mit
    Aussprüchen aus dem A.T. und dem Talmud. München 1882.

Reinach, T.,
    (1860-1928; lawyer, journalist, Director of Studies at the École des
    Hautes Études, Professor of Numismatics at the Collège de France).
    Josèphe sur Jésus. REJ 35 (1897). 1-18.

Rodrigues, H.,
    Les origines du sermon de la montagne. Paris 1868.
    Le roi des juifs. Paris 1870.

Rosenberg, S. E.,
    Bridge to Brotherhood: Judaism's Dialogue with Christianity. New York
        1961.

Rosenblatt, S.,
    The Crucifixion of Jesus from the Standpoint of Pharisaic Law. JBL 75
    (1956). 315-321.

Rosenthal, F.,
    Das letzte Passamahl Jesu und der Tag seines Todes. MGWJ 38 (1894).
    97-108.

Rosenzweig, A.,
    Das Jahrhundert nach dem babylonischen Exile mit besonderer Rücksicht
    auf die religiöse Entwicklung des Judenthums. Berlin 1885.

Roth, C.,
    (1899-1970; Reader in Jewish Studies in the University of Oxford, 1939.
        1964).
    A short History of the Jewish People. 1st ed. London 1936; revised edd.
    London 1943, 1948.
    The Cleansing of the Temple and Zechariah xiv. 21. Nov T 4 (1960). 174-181.

Saalschütz, J. L.,
    (1801-1863; German Rabbi and archaeologist; Privatdocent in Hebrew
        archaeology at Königsberg University).
    Zur Versöhnung der Confessionen, oder Judenthum und Christenthum
    in ihrem Streit und Einklang. Königsberg 1844.
    Das Mosaische Recht. 2nd ed. Berlin 1853.

Sachar, A. L.,
        (b. 1899; President of Brandeis University).
    A History of the Jews. New York 1930.

Sack, I.,
    Die altjüdische Religion im Übergange vom Bibelthume zum Talmudismus.
    Berlin 1889.

Salvador, J.,
        (1796-1873).
    Histoire des institutions de Moïse et du peuple hébreu II. Paris 1828.
    Jésus-Christ et sa doctrine I-II. 1st ed. Paris 1838; 2nd ed. Paris 1864-5.
    Histoire de la domination romaine en Judée. Paris 1847.

Sandmel, S.,
        (Professor of Bible and Hellenistic Literature, Hebrew Union College).
    A Jewish Understanding of the New Testament. Cincinnati 1957.
    The Genius of Paul. New York 1958.
    'Son of Man'. Festschrift A. H. Silver. New York 1963. 355-367.
    We Jews and Jesus. London 1965.

Sarachek, J.,
    The Doctrine of the Messiah in mediaeval Jewish Literature. New York 1932.

Schechter, S.,
        (1850-1915; Lecturer in Talmud in the University of Cambridge; Presi-
        dent of Jewish Theological Seminary, New York).
    Studies in Judaism: 2nd series. Philadelphia 1908; 3rd series. Philadelphia 1924.

Schindler, S.,
    Messianic Expectations and Modern Judaism. Boston 1886.

Schlesinger, M.,
    The historical Jesus of Nazareth. New York 1876.

Schoeps, H. J.,
        (Professor of the History of Religion in the University of Erlangen).
    Aus frühchristlicher Zeit. Tübingen 1950.
    Jésus et la loi juive. RHPR 33 (1953). 1-20.
    Urgemeinde, Judenchristentum, Gnosis. Tübingen 1956.
    Israel und die Christenheit. München 1961.
    Paul. London 1961.
    The Jewish-Christian Argument. London 1963.

Schonfield, H. J.,
    The Passover Plot. London 1965.

Schreiber, E.,
    Die Prinzipien des Judenthums. Leipzig 1877.

Silver, A.H.,
        (1893-1963; American Rabbi and Zionist leader; Rabbi of The Temple,
        Cleveland, Ohio).
    A History of Messianic Speculation in Israel from the first through the
    seventeenth Centuries. New York 1927.
    Where Judaism differed. Philadelphia 1956.

Simkhovitch, V. G.,
    Towards the Understanding of Jesus. New York 1921.

Simon, O. J.,
    The Mission of Judaism. JQR 9 (1896). 177-184.
    The Mission of Judaism: a Reply. JQR 9 (1897). 403-428.

Solomon, G.,
    The Jesus of History. London 1880.
    The Heresies of the Christian Church. London 1896.

Soloweyczyk, E.,
    La Bible, le Talmud et l'Évangile. Paris 1870.
    Kol Kore (Vox Clamantis)—La Bible, le Talmud et l'Évangile: Évangile de
    Mathieu. Paris 1875.
    Évangile de Marc. Paris 1875.

Stern, L.,
    Was Jesus of Nazareth the Messiah ? London 1872.

Stern, S. M.,
    New Light on Judaeo-Christianity ? The Evidence of Abd Al-jabbar.
    Encounter 28 (1967). 53-57.
    Quotations from Apocryphal Gospels in Abd Al-jabbar. JTS 18 (1967). 53-57.

Stourdzé, H.,
    La fuite en Égypte de Josué b. Perahya et l'incident avec son prétendu
    disciple Jésus. REJ 82 (1926). 133-156.

Sulzbach, A.,
    Renan und der Judaismus. Frankfurt a.M. 1867.

Trattner, E. R.,
    As a Jew sees Jesus. New York 1931.

Troki, Isaac, (1525/33-1586/94; Karaite scholar).
    Faith strengthened. ed. M. Mocatta. London 1851.

Umen, S.,
    Pharisaism and Jesus. New York 1963.

Vogelstein, H.,
    Die Entstehung und Entwicklung des Apostolats im Judentum. MGWJ 49
    (1905). 427-449.

Weill, A.,
    Moïse et le Talmud. Paris 1864.
    Moïse, le Talmud et l'Évangile. Paris 1875.
    Le faux Jésus-Christ du Père Didon. Paris 1891.

Weill, J.,
    L'essence du Pharisaisme. REJ 65 (1913). 1-15.

Weill, M. A.,
    Le judaïsme, ses dogmes et sa mission III. Paris 1869.

Weinstock, H.,
    Jesus the Jew. New York 1902.

Weiss, L.,
    Some burning Questions: an exegetical Treatise on the Christianising of
    Judaism. Columbus 1893.

Weiss-Rosmarin, T.,
      Judaism and Christianity. New York 1943.

Wiener, M.,
      Jüdische Religion im Zeitalter der Emanzipation. Berlin 1933.

Winter, P.,
      (died 1969; Czecho-Slovak lawyer).
      μονογενὴς παρὰ πατρός ZRGG 5 (1953). 2-32.
      The Treatment of his Sources by the Third Evangelist in Luke XXI-XXIV.
         StTh 8 (1955). 138-172.
      Luke XXII, 66b-71. StTh 9 (1956). 112-115.
      Review of H. Conzelmann, Die Mitte der Zeit. ThLZ 81 (1956). 36-39.
      Review of E. Stauffer, Jerusalem und Rom. NovT 2 (1958). 318f.
      Marginal Notes on the Trial of Jesus I-II. ZHW 50 (1959). 14-33, 221-234.
      On the Trial of Jesus. Berlin 1961.
      Mc 14, 53b, 55-64 ein Gebilde des Evangelisten. ZNW 53 (1962). 260-263.
      The Marcan Account of Jesus' Trial by the Sanhedrin. JTS 14 (1963). 94-102.
      Zum Prozeß Jesu. Das Altertum 9 (1963). 157-164; reprinted with modifi-
         cations in Antijudaismus im Neuen Testament. ed. W. Eckert. München
         1967. 95-104.
      Heimholung Jesu in das jüdische Volk. Comm Viat 6 (1963). 303-307.
      A Letter from Pontius Pilate. NovT 7 (1964). 37-43.
      The Trial of Jesus and the Competence of the Sanhedrin. NTS 10 (1964).
         494-499.
      The Trial of Jesus as a Rebel against Rome. JQ 16 (1968). 31-37.

Wise, I. M.,
      (1819-1900; Rabbi in Albany, New York and Cincinnati; first President
         of the Hebrew Union College).
      The Origin of Christianity. Cincinnati 1868.
      The Martyrdom of Jesus of Nazareth. Cincinnati 1874.
      History of the Hebrews' Second Commonwealth. Cincinnati 1880.
      Three Lectures on the Origin of Christianity. Cincinnati 1883.
      A Defence of Judaism against proselytizing Christianity. Cincinnati 1889.

Wolf, A.,
      Professor Harnack's 'What is Christianity?' JQR 16 (1904). 668-689.

Zangwill, I.,
      (1864-1926; English author).
      Children of the Ghetto. London 1892.
      The Voice of Jerusalem. London 1920.

Zeitlin, S.,
      (b. 1892; Professor of Rabbinical Literature at Dropsie College, Philadel-
         phia; Co-editor of Jewish Quarterly Review).
      Studies in the Beginnings of Christianity. JQR 14 (1923). 111-139.
      The Christ Passage in Josephus. JQR 19 (1928). 231-255.
      The Slavonic Josephus and its Relation to Josippon and Hegesippus. JQR
         20 (1929). 1-50.
      Josephus on Jesus. JQR 21 (1931). 377-417.
      Jesus in the early Tannaitic Literature. Festschrift H. P. Chajes. Wien 1933.
         295-308.
      The Beginnings of Christianity and Judaism. JQR 27 (1937). 385-398.

Historical Books on Judea, the Second Commonwealth, the Pharisees and Josephus. JQR 29 (1939). 409-414.
Jewish History at the Time of Jesus. JQR 30 (1940). 409-412.
The Crucifixion of Jesus re-examined. JQR 31 (1941). 327-369; JQR 32 (1942). 175-189, 279-301.
The political Synedrion and the religious Sanhedrin. JQR 36 (1945). 109-145.
Synedrion in the Judeo-Hellenistic Literature and Sanhedrin in the Tannaitic Literature. JQR 36 (1946). 307-315.
Synedrion in Greek Literature, the Gospels and the Institution of the Sanhedrin. JQR 37 (1946). 189-198.
The Time of the Passover Meal. JQR 42 (1951). 45-50.
The Last Supper as an ordinary Meal in the Fourth Gospel. JQR 42 (1952). 251-260.
The Trial of Jesus. JQR 53 (1962). 77-88.
The Origin of the Idea of the Messiah. Festschrift A. H. Silver. New York 1963. 447-459.
Who crucified Jesus ? 4th ed. New York 1964.
The Crucifixion, a libellous Accusation against the Jews. JQR 55 (1964). 8-22.
The Dates of the Birth and the Crucifixion of Jesus. JQR 55 (1964). 1-7.
The Ecumenical Council Vatican II and the Jews. JQR 56 (1965). 93-111.

Ziegler, I.,
    Der Kampf zwischen Judentum und Christentum in den ersten drei christlichen Jahrhunderten. Berlin 1907.

Zimmels, H. J.,
    Jesus and 'Putting up a Brick'. JQR 43 (1953). 225-228.

Zipser, M.,
    The Sermon on the Mount. London 1852.

Zucker, H.,
    Studien zur jüdischen Selbstverwaltung im Altertum. Berlin 1936.

REVIEWS OF
PAUL WINTER, ON THE TRIAL OF JESUS

Beare, F. W. CJT 9 (1963), 292-296.
Benoit, P. RB 68 (1961), 593-599.
Betz, O. JR 44 (1964), 181f.
Bruns, J. E. CBQ 23 (1961), 360-363.
Burkill, T. A. NTS 8 (1962), 174f.
Davies, W. D. Commentary 33 (1962), 540f
Evans, O. E. London Quarterly and Holborn Review 187 (1962), 69f.

Finegan, J. Interpretation 16 (1962), 102-104.
Grant, F. C. JR 44 (1964), 230-237.
Grant, R. M. JBL 80 (1961), 185f.
Isaac, J. Revue Historique 85 (1961), 119-138.
Litvin, J. Gates of Zion 17 (1963), 19.
Lohse, E. Gnomon 33 (1961), 624-626.
Maier, J. Judaica 17 (1961), 249-253.
Michaelis, W. ThZ 17 (1961), 224-227.
Mikat, P. BibZ 6 (1962), 300-307.
Nineham, D.E. JTS 13 (1962), 387-392.
Oyen, H. van Christlich-jüdisches Forum 26 (1961), 1-3.
Parkes, J. JJSoc 4 (1962), 130f.
Potterie, I. de la Bib 43 (1962), 87-93.
Schalit, A. ASTI 2 (1963), 86-101.
Schweizer, E. EvTh 21 (1961), 238-240.
Soucek, J.B. CommViat 6 (1963), 197-202.
Stauffer, E. ThLZ 88 (1963), 97-102.
Zeitlin, S. JQR 53 (1962), 77-88.

NON-JEWISH BIBLIOGRAPHY

Bailey, J. A., The Traditions common to the Gospels of Luke and John, Leiden 1963.

Bammel, E., Erwägungen zur Eschatologie Jesu, TU 88 (1964), 3-32.

——, Christian Origins in Jewish Tradition, NTS 13 (1967), 317-335.

——, ed. The Trial of Jesus, Festschrift C. F. D. Moule, London 1970.

Barrett, C. K., The Gospel according to St. John, London 1958.

——, Jesus and the Gospel Tradition, London 1967.

Bartsch, H.-W., Wer verurteilte Jesus zum Tode?, NovT 7 (1964), 210-216.

Benoit, P., Les Outrages à Jésus Prophète, Neotestamentica et Patristica, Festschrift O. Cullmann, Leiden 1962, 92-110.

Betz, O., Jesu heiliger Krieg, NovT 2 (1957), 116-137.

——, What do we know about Jesus ? London 1968.

Blinzler, J., Rechtsgeschichtliches zur Hinrichtung des Zebedaïden Jakobus (Apg xii, 2), NovT 5 (1962), 191-206.

——, Johannes und die Synoptiker, Stuttgart 1965.

——, Zum Prozeß Jesu, Lebendiges Zeugnis 1 (1966), 1-21.

——, Der Prozeß Jesu, 4th ed. Regensburg 1969.

Borgen, P., Bread from Heaven, Leiden 1965.

Bornkamm, G., Jesus of Naazreth, London 1960.

——, Barth, G., and Held, H. J., Tradition and Interpretation in Matthew, London 1963.

——, art. πρεσβυτέριον, TDNT 6 (1968), 654.

Brandon, S. G. F., Jesus and the Zealots, Manchester 1967.

——, The Trial of Jesus of Nazareth, London 1968.

Bruce, F. F., The Acts of the Apostles, London 1952.

Büchsel, F., Die Blutgerichtsbarkeit des Synedrions, ZNW 30 (1931), 202-210.

——, Noch einmal: Zur Blutgerichtsbarkeit des Synedrions, ZNW 33 (1934), 84-87.

Bultmann, R., Das Evangelium nach Johannes, 11th ed. Göttingen, 1950.

——, The History of the Synoptic Tradition, Oxford 1963.

——, Theology of the New Testament I-II, London 1965.

Burkill, T. A., The Competence of the Sanhedrin, VC 10 (1956). 80-96.

——, The Trial of Jesus, VC 12 (1958), 1-18.

Bussmann, W., Synoptische Studien, Halle 1925-1931.

Cadbury, H. J., The Style and Literary Method of Luke, Cambridge, Mass. 1920.

Caird, G. B., Saint Luke, London 1963.

Catchpole, D. R., The Answer of Jesus to Caiaphas (Matt. xxvi. 64), NTS 17 (1971), 213-226.

Colpe, C., art. ὁ υἱὸς τοῦ ἀνθρώπου, TWNT 8 (1967), 403-481.

Conzelmann, H., The Theology of Saint Luke, London 1960.

——, Die Apostelgeschichte, Tübingen 1963.

——, An Outline of the Theology of the New Testament, London 1969.

Creed, J. M., The Gospel according to Saint Luke, London 1942.

Cullmann, O., The Christology of the New Testament, 2nd ed. London 1963.

Dalman, G., Die Worte Jesu, 2nd ed. Leipzig 1930.

Danby, H., The Bearing of the Rabbinical Criminal Code on the Jewish Trial Narratives in the Gospels, JTS 21 (1920), 51-76.

——, The Mishnah, Oxford 1933.

Davies, W. D., Christian Origins and Judaism, London 1962.
——, The Setting of the Sermon on the Mount, Cambridge 1964.
Derrett, J. D. M., An Oriental Lawyer looks at the Trial of Jesus and the Doctrine of Redemption, London 1966.
Dibelius, M., From Tradition to Gospel, London 1934.
——, Studies in the Acts of the Apostles, London 1956.
Dodd, C. H., Historical Tradition in the Fourth Gospel, Cambridge 1963.
Ebeling, H. J., Zur Frage nach der Kompetenz des Synedrions, ZNW 35 (1936). 290-295.
Ellis, E. E., The Gospel of Luke, London 1966.
Finegan, J., Die Überlieferung des Leidens- und Auferstehungs-Geschichte Jesu, Giessen 1934.
Flender, H., St. Luke Theologian of Redemptive History, London 1967.
Fuller, R. H., The Foundations of New Testament Christology, London 1965.
Gärtner, B., The Temple and the Community in Qumran and the New Testament, Cambridge 1965.
Goguel, M., A propos du Procès de Jésus, ZNW 31 (1932), 289-301.
Goppelt, L., The Freedom to pay the Imperial Tax, Studia Evangelica 2 (1964), 183-194.
Grundmann, W., Das Evangelium nach Markus, 3rd ed. Berlin 1965.
——, Das Evangelium nach Lukas. 2nd ed. Berlin 1961.
——, art. δόκιμος TDNT 2 (1964), 255-260.
Haenchen, E., Die Apostelgeschichte, 14th ed. Göttingen 1965.
——, Der Weg Jesu, Berlin 1966.
Hahn, F., Mission in the New Testament, London 1965.
——, Christologische Hoheitstitel, 3rd ed. Göttingen 1966.
Hare, D. R. A., The Theme of Jewish Persecution of Christians in the Gospel according to Saint Matthew, Cambridge 1967.
Hengel, M., Die Zeloten, Leiden 1961.
Herford, R. T., Christianity in Talmud and Midrash, London 1903.
Higgins, A. J. B., Jesus and the Son of Man, London 1964.
Hirsch, E., Frühgeschichte des Evangeliums, 2nd ed. Tübingen 1951.
Hoch, W., Das Glaubensgespräch zwischen J. C. Lavater und M. Mendelssohn, Judaica 3 (1947), 44-84, 89-122.
Hölscher, G., Sanhedrin und Makkoth, Tübingen 1910.
Hoffmann, R. A., Das Wort Jesu von der Zerstörung und dem Wiederaufbau des Tempels, Festschrift G. Heinrici, Leipzig 1914, 130-139.
Holzmeister, U., Zur Frage der Blutgerichtbarkeit des Synedriums, Biblica 19 (1938), 43-59, 151-174.
Hooker, M. D., Jesus and the Servant, London 1959.
——, The Son of Man in Mark, London 1967.
Hummel, R., Die Auseinandersetzung zwischen Kirche und Judentum im Matthäusevangelium, München 1963.
Hunter, A. M., Crux Criticorum—Matt. xi. 25-30—a Reappraisal. NTS 8 (1962), 241-249.
Husband, R. W., The Prosecution of Jesus, Princeton 1916.
Iersel, B. M. F. van, 'Der Sohn' in den synoptischen Jesusworten, Leiden 1961.
Jeremias, J., Zur Geschichtlichkeit des Verhörs Jesu vor dem hohen Rat, ZNW 43 (1951), 145-150.
——, ΠΡΕΣΒΥΤΕΡΙΟΝ ausserchristlich bezeugt, ZNW 48 (1957), 127-132.
——, Perikopen-Umstellungen bei Lukas? NTS 4 (1958), 115-119.
——, The Parables of Jesus, London 1963.

——, The Eucharistic Words of Jesus, London 1966.
——, art. παῖς θεοῦ TDNT 5 (1967), 677-717.
——, The Prayers of Jesus, London 1967.
Käsemann, E., Essays on New Testament Themes, London 1964.
Kilpatrick, G. D., The Trial of Jesus, London 1953.
Klostermann, E., Das Lukasevangelium, 2nd ed. Tübingen 1929.
Kramer, W., Christ Lord Son of God, London 1966.
Kümmel, W. G., Promise and Fulfilment, London 1959.
——, Introduction to the New Testament, London 1965.
Laible, H., Jesus Christus im Talmud, Berlin 1931.
Lamarche, P., Le Blasphème de Jésus devant le Sanhédrin, RSR 50 (1962), 74-85.
Leaney, A. R. C., The Gospel according to St. Luke, London 1958.
Lietzmann, H., Kleine Schriften II: Studien zum Neuen Testament, Berlin 1958.
Lindeskog, G., Die Jesusfrage im neuzeitlichen Judentum, Uppsala 1938.
——, Der Prozeß Jesu im jüdisch-christlichen Religionsgespräch. Abraham unser Vater, Festschrift O. Michel, Leiden 1963, 325-336.
Linton, O., The Trial of Jesus and the Interpretation of Psalm CX. NTS 7 (1961), 258-262.
Lohse, E., Lukas als Theologe der Heilsgeschichte, EvTh 14 (1954), 256-275.
——, Der Prozeß Jesu Christi, Ecclesia et Res Publica. Göttingen 1961, 24-39.
——, Die Frage nach dem historischen Jesus, ThLZ 87 (1962), 169f.
——, art. συνέδριον, TWNT 7 (1964), 863-869.
——, Die Geschichte des Leidens und Sterbens Jesu Christi, Gütersloh 1964.
——, art. υἱός, TWNT 8 (1967), 358-363.
Loisy, A., Les Actes des Apôtres, Paris 1920.
Marshall, I. H., The Synoptic Son of Man Sayings in recent discussion, NTS 12 (1966), 327-351.
——, The Divine Sonship of Jesus, Interpretation 21 (1967), 87-103.
McElvey, R. J., The New Temple, London 1969.
Merkel, H., Jesus und die Pharisäer, NTS 14 (1968), 194-208.
——, Markus 7, 15—das Jesuswort über die innere Verunreinigung, ZRGG 20 (1968), 340-363.
Merx, A., Die Evangelien des Markus und Lukas, Berlin 1905.
Michel, O., and Betz, O., Von Gott gezeugt. Judentum, Urchristentum, Kirche, Festschrift J. Jeremias, Berlin 1960, 3-23.
Mommsen, T., Römisches Strafrecht I, Leipzig 1899.
Moule, C. F. D., An Idiom Book of the New Testament, 2nd ed. Cambridge 1963.
——, Review of H. E. Tödt. The Son of Man in the Synoptic Tradition, Theology 69 (1966), 172-176.
——, The Phenomenon of the New Testament, London 1967.
Nineham, D. E., Saint Mark, London 1963.
Perry, A. M., The Sources of Luke's Passion Narrative, Chicago 1920.
Rankin, O. S., Jewish Religious Polemic, Edinburgh 1956.
Rehkopf, F., Die lukanische Sonderquelle, Tübingen 1959.
Rengstorf, K. H., Das Evangelium nach Lukas, 11th ed. Göttingen 1966.
Ruckstuhl, E., Die Chronologie des letzten Mahles und des Leidens Jesu, Zürich 1963.
Schlatter, A., Das Evangelium des Lukas, Stuttgart 1931.
Schmid, J., Das Evangelium nach Matthäus, 4th ed. Regensburg 1959.
Schmidt, K. L., art. κολαφίζω. TDNT 3 (1965), 818-821.
Schniewind, J., Die Parallelperikopen bei Lukas und Johannes, repr. Darmstadt 1958.
Schürer, E., Lehrbuch der Neutestamentlichen Zeitgeschichte, Leipzig 1874.

Schürmann, H., Quellenkritische Untersuchung des lukanischen Abendmahls-berichtes Lk 22, 7-38: I. Der Paschamahlsbericht, Münster 1953; II. Der Einsetzungsbericht, Münster 1955; III. Jesu Abschiedsrede, Münster 1957.

Schweizer, E., Matth. 5, 17-20—Anmerkungen zum Gesetzesverständnis des Matthäus, ThLZ 77 (1952), 479-484.

——, Der Menschensohn, ZNW 50 (1959), 185-209.

——, Lordship and Discipleship, London 1960.

——, Das Evangelium nach Markus, Göttingen 1967.

——, The Concept of the Davidic Son of God in Acts and its Old Testament Background. Studies in Luke-Acts, Festschrift P. Schubert, London 1968.

Sherwin White, A. N., Roman Society and Roman Law in the New Testament, Oxford 1963.

——, The Trial of Christ, Historicity and Chronology in the Gospels, S.P.C.K. Theological Collections 6. London 1965, 97-116.

Spitta, F., Die Apostelgeschichte, Halle 1891.

——, Die synoptische Grundschrift in ihrer Überlieferung durch das Lukas-evangelium, Leipzig 1912.

Sparks, H. F. D., St. Luke's Transpositions, NTS 3 (1957), 219-223.

Stählin, G., Die Apostelgeschichte, 11th ed. Göttingen 1966.

Stauffer, E., Jesus and his Story, London 1960.

——, Jesus und seine Bibel, Abraham unser Vater, Festschrift O. Michel, Leiden 1963, 440-449.

Strack, H. L. and Billerbeck, P., Kommentar zum neuen Testament I-IV, München 1922-1928.

Strathmann, H., Das Evangelium nach Johannes, 9th ed. Göttingen 1959.

Streeter, B. H., The Four Gospels, London 1961.

Taylor, V., Behind the Third Gospel, Oxford 1926.

Teeple, H. M., The Origin of the Son of Man Christology, JBL 84 (1965).

Tödt, H. E., The Son of Man in the Synoptic Tradition, London 1965.

Tyson, J. B., The Lukan Version of the Trial of Jesus, NovT 3 (1959), 249ff.

Unnik, W. C. van, Jesu Verhöhnung vor dem Synedrium (Mc 14,65 par.), ZNW 29 (1930), 310f.

Vielhauer, P., Aufsätze zum Neuen Testament, München 1965.

Weiss, B., Die Quellen des Lukas-Evangeliums, Berlin 1907.

——, Die Quellen der synoptischen Überlieferung, 1908.

Wellhausen, J., Das Evangelium Marci, Berlin 1903.

——, Das Evangelium Lucae, Berlin 1904.

——, Das Evangelium Johannes, Berlin 1908.

——, Kritische Analyse der Apostel geschichte, Berlin 1914.

INDEX OF PASSAGES CITED

20*

Flavius Josephus

INDEX OF AUTHORS